Inequality, Output-Inflation Trade-Off and Economic Policy Uncertainty

Eliphas Ndou · Thabo Mokoena

Inequality, Output-Inflation Trade-Off and Economic Policy Uncertainty

Evidence From South Africa

palgrave
macmillan

Eliphas Ndou
Economic Research Department
South African Reserve Bank
Pretoria, South Africa

School of Economic and Business Sciences
University of the Witwatersrand
Johannesburg, South Africa

Wits Plus, Centre for Part-Time Studies
University of the Witwatersrand
Johannesburg, South Africa

Thabo Mokoena
Department of Economic, Small Business
Development, Tourism and Environmental
Affairs
Free State Provincial Government
Bloemfontein, Free State, South Africa

ISBN 978-3-030-19802-2   ISBN 978-3-030-19803-9   (eBook)
https://doi.org/10.1007/978-3-030-19803-9

© The Editor(s) (if applicable) and The Author(s), under exclusive license to Springer Nature
Switzerland AG 2019
This work is subject to copyright. All rights are solely and exclusively licensed by the Publisher, whether
the whole or part of the material is concerned, specifically the rights of translation, reprinting, reuse
of illustrations, recitation, broadcasting, reproduction on microfilms or in any other physical way, and
transmission or information storage and retrieval, electronic adaptation, computer software, or by
similar or dissimilar methodology now known or hereafter developed.
The use of general descriptive names, registered names, trademarks, service marks, etc. in this
publication does not imply, even in the absence of a specific statement, that such names are exempt
from the relevant protective laws and regulations and therefore free for general use.
The publisher, the authors and the editors are safe to assume that the advice and information in this
book are believed to be true and accurate at the date of publication. Neither the publisher nor the
authors or the editors give a warranty, expressed or implied, with respect to the material contained
herein or for any errors or omissions that may have been made. The publisher remains neutral with
regard to jurisdictional claims in published maps and institutional affiliations.

This Palgrave Macmillan imprint is published by the registered company Springer Nature Switzerland AG
The registered company address is: Gewerbestrasse 11, 6330 Cham, Switzerland

Preface

This book shows empirical evidence in answering pertinent policy issues in South Africa and the empirical analysis includes applying the simple techniques to counterfactual analysis. The latter offers alternative scenarios. We offer motivations in each chapter, policy implications and main highlights which the readers may take out from reading the chapters. The material is suitable for policymakers, market commentators, postgraduate students, policy analysts, financial analyst, and academics. We cover areas that include income inequality, output-inflation trade-off, and economic policy uncertainty. Income inequality is a big issue and we determine if it can be due to financial and monetary policies, influence of inflation threshold, and its role as a conduit in transmitting shocks in the economy. This gap is extended to determining how its presence may exacerbate the adverse effects of these tight financial and monetary policies. The redistributive effects of monetary policy and macroprudential policies in South Africa have not been investigated, despite much discussion about this in the advanced economies following the financial crisis in 2007. We examine if the new Keynesian proposition of policy ineffectiveness is applicable in South Africa. Despite the differences which may arise amongst policymakers, it is important to determine if the income distribution matters for the effectiveness of

v

monetary policy decisions, price stability, and financial stability. The book has 34 chapters and each chapter provides the highlights of the main findings and policy implications based on robust empirical analysis. We state the motivations in each chapter, and use simple theoretical economic models. In certain estimations, we apply counterfactual analysis to offer alternative scenarios. The book is divided into the following thematic parts.

Areas Relevant to the South Africa Policy Discussions are as Follows

Income Inequality, GDP Growth and Inflation Regimes

We begin by investigating the nexus between income inequality and GDP growth in South Africa and determine whether the 4.5% consumer price inflation threshold and other channels matter in this nexus. We further determine if the inflation rate below 4.5% matters for the distributional effects of positive inflation shocks on income inequality in South Africa.

Inequality and Monetary Policy

We determine the extent to which the income inequality channel impacts the transmission of monetary policy shocks to economic activity, and, whether monetary policy shocks influence income inequality dynamics in South Africa. Given that South Africa is an open economy, we examine the roles of trade openness and financial globalisation channels in transmitting monetary policy shocks to income inequality.

The Role of the Monetary Policy Channel in Transmitting Shocks to Income Inequality

The shares of employment in the manufacturing sector has been declining while those of the services sector has been rising. The book examines the extent to which monetary policy impacts the effects of manufacturing sector and services employment shares shocks on income inequality.

Consumption Inequality

The book brings new insights into the relationship between income inequality and consumption inequality. This includes determining whether the consumption inequality channel impacts the transmission of positive income inequality shocks to credit dynamics in South Africa, and this is based on data before 2009Q1. This analysis further investigates whether price stability impacts the link between income inequality and consumption inequality.

Macroprudential Policy and Income Inequality

We examine the effects of the shocks to selected macroprudential tools on income inequality. This motivates us to determine whether positive excess capital adequacy ratio shocks and unexpected loosening of loan to value ratio have any redistributive effects via the inequality channel. We add the National Credit Act to determine its influence on the growth of income inequality. We conclude by examining the effects of an unexpected loosening in the labour market reforms on the evolution of growth of income inequality in South Africa.

Bank Concentration and Income Inequality and Other Channels

The South African banking sector has been described as oligopolistic and highly concentrated and this may impact real economic activity. The book gives insights by examining how unexpected increase in the bank concentration impacts economic growth, income inequality and employment in South Africa.

Output-Inflation Trade-Off and the Role of Inflation Regimes

This part examines if there is evidence of the trade-off in output and inflation volatilities in South Africa. In addition, we determine the extent to which the output-inflation trade-off exist in South Africa and if it is impacted by the 6% inflation threshold. The part further determines whether inflation regimes affect the transmission of nominal demand shocks to the consumer price level and whether positive nominal demand volatility shocks reduce the output-inflation trade-off.

Output Growth Persistence and Inflation

This part determines the link between the persistence of output growth and inflation regimes. We further determine if the effects of expansionary monetary policy shocks on output persistence depend on inflation regimes.

Economic Policy Uncertainty, Expansionary Monetary Policy, and Demand Policy Shocks

Economic policy uncertainty was heightened after the recession in 2009 and its impact on monetary policy transmission mechanism has not been examined in South Africa. In this context, we examine whether the economic policy uncertainty channel impacts the influence of expansionary monetary policy changes on output dynamics, bank lending rate margins and pass-through of the repo rate to bank lending rates. The analysis shows how inflation impacts the effects of expansionary monetary and fiscal policies on real GDP growth. We estimate the time-varying pass-through of the lending rate responses to the repo rate changes and loan intermediation mark-ups.

Economic Policy Uncertainty and the Lending, Credit and Corporate Cash Holding Channels

We extend the analysis of the effects of economic policy uncertainty into understanding the dynamics in the lending rates, credit dynamics, and companies' cash holdings. We examine the extent to which credit growth reacts to expansionary monetary policy shocks is impacted by heightened economic policy uncertainty. In addition, the book investigates whether companies' cash holdings impact the transmission of economic policy uncertainty shocks to capital formation. To derive policy implications, we show that an increase in the value of companies' cash holdings impacts the transmission of expansionary monetary policy shocks. The book concludes by showing the effects of an unexpected reduction in economic policy uncertainty on inflation expectations.

Policy Implications

Inequality Income Should Be Eradicated and Inflation Threshold Matters

Policymakers should eradicate the rising income inequality as it lowers GDP growth and they should implement policy initiatives that should reduce income inequality over a long horizon rather than reduce inequality transitorily. Price stability matters for the reduction in the growth of income inequality to positive inflation shocks in the inflation bands (1) below 3% and (2) when inflation is below the 4.5% threshold. Evidence shows that, although income inequality is not being depicted in the standard monetary policy transmission mechanism, there is need for it to be considered as part of the transmission mechanism. Policymakers should enhance their understanding of the ways in which monetary policy decisions, income inequality, and aggregate economy, are intertwined as this will enable an efficient design and implementation of monetary policy.

Policymakers Should Put Mechanism in Place to Mitigate the Redistributive Effects of Structural Transformation

Policies should be put in place that focus on ensuring more inclusive gains from structural transformation and policymakers should facilitate the reskilling of workers and reduce the costs of their reallocation costs when the services sector is growing at the expense of other sectors.

Price Stability Should be Considered in the Link Between Income Inequality and Consumption Inequality

Macroprudential regulators should put mechanisms in place to prevent credit extension that is not driven by fundamentals such as consumption inequalities, as this may lead to crises and unproductive uses. Evidence indicates that consumption inequality and inequalities in the consumption categories amplify the increase in credit due to positive income inequality shocks. Policymakers should enforce price stability to weaken the link between income inequality and consumption inequality. A counterfactual VAR analysis indicates that high (low) inflation amplifies (dampens) the increase in consumption inequality to positive income inequality shocks when inflation exceeds the 6% threshold. Thus, price stability matters and policymakers should pay attention to the existing structural issues in the economy and determine how these impacts on their expected policy decisions.

Redistributive Effects of Macroprudential Policies, Labour Reforms, and Banking Sector Concentration

Increased income inequality growth, following positive excess CAR shocks, and tightening standards in the National Credit Act (NCA), exacerbates the decline in the real economic activity, implying that policymakers should cast their nets wider than financial regulatory reforms and should also consider the effects of their policy changes in influencing the distributive patterns (Perugini et al. 2016). The income inequality channel is a potent transmitter of the effects of excess CAR shocks, tight NCA shocks and unexpected loosening in the loan to value ratio to real economic activity. Hence, policymakers should decisively eliminate the high levels of income inequality as these distort the transmission mechanism of macroprudential policies. Policymakers should lower entry barriers to the banking sector and introduce a sliding scale of capital adequacy ratios that increase with the size of the banks. An unexpected loosening in the labour market reforms reduces income inequality growth when complemented by increased government consumption expenditure, income tax cuts, low economic policy uncertainty and when inflation is below 6%. A weak exchange rate mitigates the reduction in the income inequality growth induced by an unexpected loosening in the labour market reforms.

Price Stability Matters for Effective Stimulatory Demand Policy Shocks to Raise Output

Evidence indicates that expansionary demand policy is less effective during high inflation and demand volatility episodes, which is consistent with predictions of the new Keynesian hypothesis. Thus, an expansionary nominal demand policy shock affecting aggregate demand will have a bigger effect on real output in the low inflation regime than in the high inflation regime. When inflation is below 6%, an expansionary monetary policy shock stimulates household consumption growth more than raising the inflation rate because prices are less flexible, or prices changes are less frequent. Evidence shows that expansionary monetary policy shocks raise output persistence more when inflation is below or equal to 6% than when it is above this threshold. Price stability matters for the size of the impact of a positive nominal demand shock (such as expansionary monetary policy shocks) on real GDP growth based on the 6% inflation threshold.

Economic Policy Uncertainty Should Be Minimised

Policymakers anticipating a certain magnitude of the impact from a stimulatory demand policy shock should consider economic policy uncertainty regimes in their policy decisions. Otherwise, policy effects may fall short of their expectations and induce more uncertainty. A low inflation and low economic policy uncertainty regime matters for amplifying the stimulatory effects of expansionary policies on GDP growth. Policymakers should consider that a large reduction in the repo rate than expected is needed to overcome the mitigating effects of elevated economic policy uncertainty in raising the bank lending rate margins even in a low inflation environment. A high economic policy uncertainty environment may require a large reduction in the policy rate by more than expected to achieve a similar impact and this may lead to extensive loosening in the credit conditions. Price stability matters as the low inflation environment propitiates the growth of companies' deposits to cushion the decline in the capital formation growth due to positive economic policy uncertainty shocks. Low economic policy uncertainty matters as evidence indicates that expansionary monetary policy shocks raise credit growth more than the counterfactual suggests in the low economic policy uncertainty regime.

Pretoria, South Africa
Bloemfontein, South Africa

Eliphas Ndou
Thabo Mokoena

Reference

Perugini, C., Holsher, J., & Collie, S. (2016). Inequality, credit and financial crises. *Cambridge Journal of Economics, 40*(1), 227–257.

Acknowledgements

We are grateful to our colleagues at the South African Reserve Bank for timely responding to data requests. We thank the anonymous reviwers of book for helpful comments. We thank Estima for Rats software support service for helping us with coding troubling shooting.

Contents

1   Introduction   1

Part I   Income Inequality, GDP Growth and Inflation Regimes

2   Income Inequality and GDP Growth Nexus in South Africa: Does the 4.5% Consumer Price Inflation Threshold and Other Channels Play a Role?   35

3   Does the Inflation Rate Below 4.5% Matter for the Distributional Effects of Positive Inflation Shocks on Income Inequality in South Africa?   51

Part II   Inequality and Monetary Policy

4   Does the Income Inequality Channel Impact the Transmission of Monetary Policy Shocks to Economic Activity?   75

xvi   Contents

5   Do Monetary Policy Shocks Influence Income
     Inequality Dynamics in South Africa?   87

6   Does Trade Openness Impact the Link Between
     Monetary Policy and Both Income Inequality
     and Consumption Inequalities?   105

7   Does Financial Globalisation Impact the Link Between
     Monetary Policy and Income Inequality?   117

Part III   The Role of the Monetary Policy Channel
            in Transmitting Shocks to Income Inequality

8   Does Monetary Policy Impact the Effects of Shares
     of Manufacturing Employment Shocks on Income
     Inequality?   135

9   Is There a Role for the Monetary Policy Channel
     in Transmitting Positive Shocks to the Services Sector
     Employment Shares to Income Inequality?   149

Part IV   Consumption Inequality and Income Inequality

10   Does the Consumption Inequality Channel Impact
     the Transmission of Positive Income Inequality Shocks
     to Credit Dynamics in South Africa? Insights Before
     2009Q1   161

11   Does Price Stability Impact the Link Between Income
     Inequality and Consumption Inequality?   175

Contents   xvii

Part V   Macroprudential Policy and Income Inequality

12 Do Positive Excess Capital Adequacy Ratio Shocks
Influence the Income Inequality Dynamics in South
Africa?   189

13 Does an Unexpected Loosening in the Loan to Value
Ratio Has Any Distributive Effects via the Inequality
Channel?   205

14 Is the Tightening in the National Credit Act a Driver
of Growth of Income Inequality?   221

15 Can an Unexpected Loosening in the Labour Market
Reforms Reduce the Growth of Income Inequality
in South Africa?   241

**Part VI   Bank Concentration, Income Inequality
and Other Channels**

16 Does the Increase in Banking Concentration Impact
Income Inequality in South Africa?   255

17 Do Positive Bank Concentration Shocks Impact
Economic Growth in South Africa?   269

18 Do Positive Bank Concentration Shocks Impact
Employment in South Africa?   281

**Part VII   Output-Inflation Trade-Off and the Role
of Inflation Regimes**

19 Is There Evidence of the Trade-Off in Output
and Inflation Volatilities in South Africa?   293

xviii   Contents

20   To What Extent Does the Output-Inflation Trade-Off
     Exist in South Africa and Is It Impacted by the Six
     Per Cent Inflation Threshold?   303

21   Do Inflation Regimes Affect the Transmission of Positive
     Nominal Demand Shocks to the Consumer Price Level?   317

22   Do Positive Nominal Volatility Shocks Reduce
     the Output-Inflation Trade-Off and Is There a Role
     for Inflation Regimes?   333

Part VIII   Output Growth Persistence and Inflation

23   Does the Persistence of Output Growth Depend
     on Inflation Regimes?   343

24   Do the Effects of Expansionary Monetary Policy
     Shocks on Output Persistence Depend on Inflation
     Regimes?   357

25   Output and Policy Ineffectiveness Proposition:
     A Perspective from Single Regression Equations   367

Part IX   Economic Policy Uncertainty, Expansionary
           Monetary Policy and Fiscal Policy Multipliers

26   Does the Economic Policy Uncertainty Channel
     Impact the Influence of Expansionary Monetary
     Policy Changes on Output Dynamics?   379

27   How Does Inflation Impact the Effects
     of Expansionary Monetary Policy and Fiscal Policies
     on Real GDP Growth?   389

Contents   xix

28 The Time-Varying Pass-Through of the Lending
Rate Responses to the Repo Rate Changes
and Loan Intermediation Mark-Ups   399

29 Do Economic Policy Uncertainty Shocks Impact
the Bank Lending Rate Margins?   415

30 Does Economic Policy Uncertainty Impact
the Pass-Through of the Repo Rate to the Bank
Lending Rates?   425

**Part X Economic Policy Uncertainty and the Lending
Rates, Credit and Corporate Cash Holding
Channels**

31 Are Credit Growth Reactions to Expansionary
Monetary Policy Shocks Weakened by Heightened
Economic Policy Uncertainty?   439

32 Do Companies' Cash Holdings Impact
the Transmission of Economic Policy Uncertainty
Shocks to Capital Formation?   453

33 Does an Increase in the Value of Companies' Cash
Holdings Impact the Transmission of Expansionary
Monetary Policy Shocks? Counterfactual Policy Analysis   471

34 Does an Unexpected Reduction in Economic Policy
Uncertainty Impact Inflation Expectations?   479

Index   493

List of Figures

Fig. 1.1	Theoretical effects of an expansionary policy shock on output and inflation	13
Fig. 1.2	Theoretical depiction of the link between inflation and output persistence	16
Fig. 1.3	The link between an expansionary policy, inflation, and economic growth	18
Fig. 1.4	A theoretical depiction of elevated macroeconomic effects on credit dynamics	20
Fig. 1.5	The link between higher uncertainty and companies' cash holdings	22
Fig. 2.1	Transmission of positive income inequality shocks to GDP growth	37
Fig. 2.2	The relationship between income inequality and GDP growth in South Africa	38
Fig. 2.3	GDP growth responses to positive income inequality shocks	40
Fig. 2.4	GDP growth responses to a positive income inequality shock	41
Fig. 2.5	Cumulative GDP growth responses to positive income inequality shocks and the role of economic policy uncertainty channel	43

xxii   **List of Figures**

Fig. 2.6	GDP growth responses to positive income inequality shocks	44
Fig. 2.7	Cumulative GDP growth responses to positive income inequality shocks	45
Fig. 2.8	Cumulative responses to a positive income inequality shock	46
Fig. 2.9	GDP growth responses to different sizes of positive income inequality shocks	47
Fig. 2.10	Actual and counterfactual cumulative GDP growth responses to positive income shocks and the role of different channels	48
Fig. 2.11	Income inequality shock scenarios and macroeconomic variable responses	49
Fig. 3.1	Depiction of the direct and indirect transmission of inflation shock to income inequality	53
Fig. 3.2	Link between income inequality and other macroeconomic variables	56
Fig. 3.3	Responses of the Gini coefficient to positive inflation shocks	57
Fig. 3.4	Responses of income inequality growth to positive inflation shocks	58
Fig. 3.5	Responses based on the additional model	59
Fig. 3.6	GDP growth and income inequality responses to negative inflation shocks based on deviations from the 4.5% threshold	60
Fig. 3.7	Responses of income inequality growth to negative inflation shocks	60
Fig. 3.8	Responses of income inequality growth to positive inflation shocks	61
Fig. 3.9	Cumulative responses of income inequality and employment growth to positive inflation shocks in various inflation bands	62
Fig. 3.10	Cumulative responses of income inequality growth and employment growth to positive inflation shocks in various inflation bands	63
Fig. 3.11	Responses of income inequality growth and GDP growth to positive inflation shocks according to inflation regimes	64

List of Figures   xxiii

Fig. 3.12	Cumulative responses of income inequality and GDP growth to positive inflation shocks according to inflation regimes	64
Fig. 3.13	Responses of income inequality level to positive inflation shocks	65
Fig. 3.14	Actual and counterfactual cumulative responses of income inequality growth to positive inflation shocks when inflation is below 4.5% and role of selected channels	67
Fig. 3.15	Cumulative income inequality growth responses to positive inflation shocks when inflation exceeds 6%	69
Fig. 3.16	Cumulative response of income inequality to policy shocks and role of inflation below the 4.5% threshold	70
Fig. 3.17	Comparison of sizes of amplifications	70
Fig. 4.1	Direct and indirect channels of monetary policy shock transmission	76
Fig. 4.2	Cumulative responses to contractionary monetary policy shocks and the role of the income inequality channel	80
Fig. 4.3	Cumulative actual and counterfactual responses to contractionary monetary policy shock and the role of the income inequality channel	81
Fig. 4.4	Cumulative responses to contractionary monetary policy shocks and the role of the income inequality channel	82
Fig. 4.5	Cumulative responses to contractionary monetary policy shocks and the role of the income inequality channel	82
Fig. 4.6	Cumulative responses to contractionary monetary policy shocks and the role of the income inequality channel	83
Fig. 5.1	Responses of income inequality growth to monetary policy shocks according to policy changes	92
Fig. 5.2	Income inequality responses to expansionary monetary policy shocks based on inflation regimes	93
Fig. 5.3	Income inequality responses to expansionary monetary policy shocks and the role of business cycles	94
Fig. 5.4	Responses to expansionary monetary policy shocks based on the exogenous VAR model	95
Fig. 5.5	Expansionary monetary policy shock scenarios and income inequality responses	96
Fig. 5.6	Responses of income inequality growth to various sizes of expansionary monetary policy shocks	97

xxiv   List of Figures

Fig. 5.7	Cumulative responses of income inequality growth to expansionary monetary policy shocks and the roles of selected channels	98
Fig. 5.8	Comparisons of amplification of various channels in income inequality growth reaction to expansionary monetary policy shocks	99
Fig. 5.9	Cumulative income inequality responses to contractionary monetary policy shocks and the role of the channels	100
Fig. 6.1	The depiction of the direct and indirect transmission channels of monetary policy shocks to income inequality	107
Fig. 6.2	Responses to positive trade openness shocks	109
Fig. 6.3	Responses to positive trade openness shocks	110
Fig. 6.4	Responses to positive trade openness shocks	111
Fig. 6.5	Responses to positive trade openness shocks	112
Fig. 6.6	Responses to contractionary monetary policy shocks and the role of trade openness	113
Fig. 6.7	Actual and counterfactual responses of income inequality growth to contractionary monetary policy shocks and the roles of the export and import channels	114
Fig. 6.8	Income inequality growth responses to expansionary monetary policy shocks and the role of the trade openness channels	115
Fig. 7.1	Transmission of monetary policy shocks and the role of the capital flow channel	119
Fig. 7.2	Income inequality growth responses to positive net capital inflow shocks	123
Fig. 7.3	Income inequality growth responses to positive net capital inflow shocks	124
Fig. 7.4	Income inequality responses to positive net capital inflow shocks	125
Fig. 7.5	Responses of income inequality growth to positive net capital inflow shocks and the role of the exchange rate channel	126
Fig. 7.6	Cumulative income inequality growth to positive net capital inflow shocks and the role of the low inflation regime channel	126
Fig. 7.7	Cumulative income inequality growth to positive net capital inflow shocks and the role of the low inflation regime channel	127

List of Figures   xxv

Fig. 7.8	Responses of income inequality growth to tight monetary policy shocks and the role of capital inflow channel	129
Fig. 7.9	Responses of income inequality growth to tight monetary policy shock and the role of capital inflow channel	129
Fig. 8.1	Sector employment shares in per cent	136
Fig. 8.2	Income inequality responses to positive manufacturing and mining sector employment shares shocks	139
Fig. 8.3	Income inequality responses	140
Fig. 8.4	Responses of income inequality to a positive manufacturing employment shares shock	141
Fig. 8.5	Responses of income inequality to shocks and the role of the monetary policy channel	143
Fig. 8.6	Responses of income inequality to shocks and the role of the monetary policy channel when inflation is below 6%	143
Fig. 8.7	Responses of income inequality and the role of the price stability channel	144
Fig. 8.8	Responses of income inequality to positive manufacturing sector employment shares shock and the role of expansionary monetary policy channel	145
Fig. 8.9	Responses of income inequality to positive manufacturing sector employment shares shock and role of contractionary monetary policy channel	146
Fig. 8.10	Responses of income inequality to positive manufacturing sector employment shares shock and the role of expansionary monetary policy	147
Fig. 9.1	A comparison of selected sectors' employment shares as percenatge of total nonagricultural employment	150
Fig. 9.2	Responses to positive services sector employment shares shock	152
Fig. 9.3	Responses to positive services sector employment shares shock	154
Fig. 9.4	Responses to a positive services sector employment shares shock	155
Fig. 9.5	Responses of income inequality to positive services sector employment shares shock and the roles of the GDP and monetary policy channels	156

xxvi   List of Figures

Fig. 9.6	Actual and counterfactual income inequality responses to positive services sector employment shares shock and the role of the low inflation regime	157
Fig. 10.1	Responses to positive income inequality shocks	165
Fig. 10.2	Positive income inequality shock scenarios and credit dynamics	165
Fig. 10.3	Credit responses to positive income inequality shocks	167
Fig. 10.4	Responses to positive income inequality shocks in the exogenous VAR model	167
Fig. 10.5	Responses to positive consumption inequality shocks	168
Fig. 10.6	Responses to positive consumption inequality shocks	170
Fig. 10.7	Responses to positive income inequality shocks and the role of the consumption inequality and consumption channels	171
Fig. 10.8	Responses to positive income inequality shocks and the role of categories of the consumption inequality channels	172
Fig. 10.9	Responses to positive income inequality shocks and the role of the consumer price inflation channels	172
Fig. 11.1	Depiction of link between income and consumption based on the lifecycle hypothesis	177
Fig. 11.2	Responses to positive income inequality shocks	179
Fig. 11.3	Consumption inequality responses to positive income inequality shocks	180
Fig. 11.4	Responses to positive income inequality shocks	181
Fig. 11.5	Responses to positive income inequality shocks and amplification by the consumer price inflation channel	182
Fig. 11.6	Responses to positive income inequality shocks and amplification by the consumer price inflation channel	183
Fig. 11.7	Responses to positive income inequality shocks and the role of inflation regimes based on the 6% threshold	184
Fig. 12.1	The relationship between excess capital adequacy ratio and income inequality	190
Fig. 12.2	Income inequality level's responses to positive excess capital adequacy ratio shocks	194
Fig. 12.3	Responses of income inequality growth to positive excess CAR shocks	195

List of Figures   xxvii

Fig. 12.4	Responses of income inequality growth to positive excess CAR shocks	195
Fig. 12.5	Responses to positive excess CAR shocks	196
Fig. 12.6	Actual and counterfactual cumulative responses of income inequality growth to positive excess CAR shock and the role of the credit growth channel	198
Fig. 12.7	Actual and counterfactual cumulative responses of income inequality growth to positive excess CAR shocks and the role of the GDP growth channel	198
Fig. 12.8	Actual and counterfactual cumulative responses of income inequality growth to positive excess CAR shocks and the role of the employment growth channel	199
Fig. 12.9	Actual and counterfactual cumulative responses of income inequality growth to positive excess CAR shocks and the role of the house price growth channel	200
Fig. 12.10	Responses to positive excess CAR shocks	202
Fig. 12.11	Credit and GDP growth responses to positive excess CAR shocks and the role of the income inequality growth channel	203
Fig. 13.1	The various relationships	207
Fig. 13.2	Income inequality responses to loose LTV shocks	210
Fig. 13.3	Responses based on VAR models	210
Fig. 13.4	The response of income inequality to a loose LTV shock	211
Fig. 13.5	Responses of income inequality growth to loose LTV shocks	212
Fig. 13.6	Responses of income inequality growth to loose LTV shock in the extended model	212
Fig. 13.7	Responses to loose LTV shocks	214
Fig. 13.8	Response to loose LTV shocks	214
Fig. 13.9	Cumulative responses of income inequality growth to loose LTV shocks and selected channels	216
Fig. 13.10	Cumulative responses of income inequality growth to loose LTV shocks and selected channels	216
Fig. 13.11	Cumulative responses of income inequality growth to loose LTV shocks and selected channels	217
Fig. 13.12	Actual and counterfactual cumulative income inequality responses to loose LTV shocks and role of GDP and credit growth	218

xxviii List of Figures

Fig. 13.13	Actual and counterfactual responses to loose LTV shocks and role of income inequality growth channel	219
Fig. 14.1	Impacts of NCA on the growth and level of income inequality	224
Fig. 14.2	Responses to NCA shock	225
Fig. 14.3	Responses to NCA shock	226
Fig. 14.4	Responses of variables using additional variables	226
Fig. 14.5	NCA shock scenarios and responses of income inequality growth	227
Fig. 14.6	Cumulative responses of income inequality growth to NCA shocks and the role of GDP growth phases	229
Fig. 14.7	Responses of income inequality growth and role of credit growth channel	231
Fig. 14.8	Role of the wage-growth channel in the income inequality growth to a tightened NCA shock	231
Fig. 14.9	Cumulative responses of the income inequality growth to the NCA shock and the role of inflation regimes	233
Fig. 14.10	Credit growth responses to the NCA shocks and the role of growth of income inequality	236
Fig. 14.11	GDP growth responses to tight NCA shocks	236
Fig. 14.12	Actual and counterfactual cumulative responses and the role of the income inequality growth channel	238
Fig. 15.1	Income inequality responses to unexpected loosening in the labour market reforms	244
Fig. 15.2	Responses of income inequality growth to unexpected loosening in labour market reforms	245
Fig. 15.3	Responses to unexpected loosening in the labour market reforms	246
Fig. 15.4	Cumulative responses to unexpected loosening in the labour market reforms and the role of GDP and inflation channels	246
Fig. 15.5	Cumulative responses to unexpected loosening in the labour market reforms and the role of employment and unemployment rate channels	247
Fig. 15.6	Cumulative responses to unexpected loosening in labour market reforms and the role of income tax and inflation channel	248
Fig. 15.7	Comparisons of size of the amplifications	249

List of Figures xxix

Fig. 15.8	Cumulative income inequality growth responses and the channels of amplification	250
Fig. 16.1	Evolution of competition in the banking sector as measured by the H-index	256
Fig. 16.2	Responses to positive bank concentration shocks	259
Fig. 16.3	Responses to positive bank concentration shocks	260
Fig. 16.4	Income inequality responses to positive bank concentration shocks	261
Fig. 16.5	Responses to positive bank concentration shocks according to banking concentration regimes	262
Fig. 16.6	Responses to positive bank concentration shocks	264
Fig. 16.7	Responses to positive bank concentration shocks	266
Fig. 17.1	Evolution of competition in the banking sector as measured by the H-index	270
Fig. 17.2	GDP responses to a positive bank concentration shock	273
Fig. 17.3	Consumption responses to a positive bank concentration shock	274
Fig. 17.4	Investment responses to a positive bank concentration shock	275
Fig. 17.5	Components of investment responses to a positive bank concentration shock	276
Fig. 17.6	GDP responses to a positive bank concentration shock and the role of different channels	278
Fig. 17.7	GDP responses to a positive bank concentration shock in the low and high concentration regimes	279
Fig. 18.1	Employment responses to a positive bank concentration shock	285
Fig. 18.2	Employment responses to a positive bank concentration shock	286
Fig. 18.3	Sector-specific employment responses to a positive bank concentration shock	287
Fig. 18.4	Employment responses to positive bank concentration shock and role of investment	288
Fig. 18.5	Manufacturing employment responses to a positive bank concentration shock	288
Fig. 19.1	The output-inflation trade-off	294
Fig. 19.2	Shifts in the South African output-inflation trade-offs	297
Fig. 19.3	The trade-off between output growth volatility and inflation volatility	299

xxx   List of Figures

Fig. 19.4	Scatterplot between output growth volatility and inflation volatility	300
Fig. 19.5	Trade-off between output growth volatility and inflation volatility for various volatility scenarios	300
Fig. 20.1	Theoretical effects of an expansionary policy shock on output and inflation	304
Fig. 20.2	Responses to positive nominal demand shock	308
Fig. 20.3	Responses to positive nominal demand shock	309
Fig. 20.4	Responses to positive nominal demand shocks	310
Fig. 20.5	Responses to positive nominal demand shocks	311
Fig. 20.6	Inflation responses and fluctuations to a positive nominal demand shock	314
Fig. 20.7	Cumulative responses to a nominal demand shock and the role of trend inflation	315
Fig. 21.1	Theoretical depiction of the price level response to a positive nominal demand shock	319
Fig. 21.2	Inflation responses and fluctuations to a positive nominal demand shock in the 1990Q1–2017Q1 period	325
Fig. 21.3	Inflation responses and fluctuations to a positive nominal demand shock during the inflation-targeting period	326
Fig. 21.4	Real GDP growth responses to a positive nominal demand shock and the role of inflation regimes during the inflation-targeting period	327
Fig. 21.5	Accumulated real actual and counterfactual real GDP growth responses to a positive nominal demand shock and the role of inflation in 2000Q1–2017Q1	328
Fig. 21.6	Accumulated real actual and counterfactual real GDP growth responses to a positive nominal demand shock and the role of inflation in 1990Q1–2017Q1	329
Fig. 21.7	Comparisons of real GDP growth amplifications by inflation regimes	329
Fig. 22.1	Output-inflation trade-off parameter response to positive inflation volatility shocks	337
Fig. 22.2	Positive nominal demand volatility shock and output-inflation trade-off parameter responses	338
Fig. 22.3	Positive nominal demand volatility shock and output-inflation trade-off parameter responses and amplifications by inflation volatility	339

Fig. 22.4	Comparison of amplification by inflation volatilities according to inflation regimes	339
Fig. 23.1	Theoretical depiction of the link between inflation and output persistence	345
Fig. 23.2	Frequency of price changes in quarters based on Kiley (2000) approach	348
Fig. 23.3	Output persistence, regimes, and inflation	350
Fig. 23.4	The relationship between output persistence and the consumer inflation rate	351
Fig. 23.5	Impacts of inflation on output persistence according to inflation regimes	352
Fig. 23.6	Relationship between inflation versus output persistence and price flexibility	353
Fig. 23.7	Responses to positive inflation shocks	353
Fig. 23.8	Responses of household consumption growth to an expansionary monetary policy shock and the amplification by the price flexibility measure	354
Fig. 24.1	Output persistence responses and fluctuations due to an expansionary monetary policy shock	360
Fig. 24.2	Output persistence responses to expansionary monetary policy shocks and the role of inflation regimes	361
Fig. 24.3	Output persistence responses to expansionary monetary policy shocks and the role of the economic policy uncertainty channels	363
Fig. 24.4	Responses of household consumption growth to expansionary monetary policy shocks and amplification effects by output persistence	364
Fig. 24.5	Responses of household consumption growth to a positive wage growth shock and amplification by output persistence	365
Fig. 25.1	Impacts of nominal GDP on real GDP	371
Fig. 25.2	Transition graphs	375
Fig. 26.1	The depiction of the transmission of elevated uncertainty shocks	381
Fig. 26.2	GDP growth responses to economic policy uncertainty shocks	383
Fig. 26.3	Accumulated GDP growth responses to an expansionary monetary policy shock and the role of economic policy uncertainty regimes	384

xxxii   List of Figures

Fig. 26.4	Accumulated responses to expansionary monetary policy shock in the low inflation regime	386
Fig. 27.1	The link between expansionary policy, inflation, and economic growth	390
Fig. 27.2	GDP growth responses to expansionary policies	392
Fig. 27.3	Responses and the proportion of fluctuations due to expansionary policies	392
Fig. 27.4	Accumulated effects of inflation on monetary and fiscal policy multipliers	394
Fig. 27.5	GDP growth responses and the role of the low inflation regime	394
Fig. 27.6	Responses of expansionary monetary policy multiplier effects on positive inflation shock	395
Fig. 27.7	Inflation effects on the impact of expansionary fiscal policy on GDP	396
Fig. 27.8	GDP growth responses to monetary policy shocks in the low inflation regime	397
Fig. 28.1	Weighted lending rate and repo rate	403
Fig. 28.2	The size of the interest rate pass-through and loan intermediation mark-ups	404
Fig. 28.3	The size of pass-through and mark-ups during the tightening and loosening phases	405
Fig. 28.4	The size of interest pass-through and loan intermediation mark-ups during the policy rate tightening and loosening periods	406
Fig. 28.5	Time-varying interest rate pass-through, loan intermediation mark-up and the repo rate	407
Fig. 28.6	The relationship between lending rate spread and time-varying pass-through	409
Fig. 28.7	The relationship between credit growth and the time-varying interest rate pass-through	410
Fig. 29.1	Bank lending rate margins responses to economic policy uncertainty shocks according to uncertainty regimes	418
Fig. 29.2	Bank lending rate margins responses to negative and positive economic policy uncertainty shocks	419
Fig. 29.3	Accumulated bank lending rate margins responses to positive uncertainty shocks	420

List of Figures   xxxiii

Fig. 29.4	Accumulated real GDP growth responses to negative uncertainty shocks and the role of bank lending rate margins	421
Fig. 30.1	Estimated time varying pass-through of the repo rate to lending rate	426
Fig. 30.2	Lending rate responses to negative and positive economic policy uncertainty shocks	429
Fig. 30.3	Positive economic policy uncertainty shock scenarios and lending rate responses	429
Fig. 30.4	Negative economic policy uncertainty shock scenarios and the lending rate responses	430
Fig. 30.5	Accumulated lending rate responses to positive repo rate shocks and the role of the economic policy uncertainty changes	431
Fig. 30.6	Accumulated lending rate responses to positive repo rate shocks and the role of the economic policy uncertainty changes	432
Fig. 30.7	Accumulated lending rate responses to positive the repo rate shocks and the role of economic policy uncertainty changes	433
Fig. 30.8	Accumulated lending rate responses to positive repo rate shocks and the role of the economic policy uncertainty changes	433
Fig. 30.9	Accumulated lending rate responses to repo rate loosening shock	434
Fig. 31.1	Theoretical depictions of elevated macroeconomic effects on credit dynamics	441
Fig. 31.2	Responses of credit growth and lending rate spread dynamics to uncertainty shocks	444
Fig. 31.3	Responses of credit growth and credit condition index to uncertainty shocks	445
Fig. 31.4	Credit growth responses to expansionary monetary policy responses	446
Fig. 31.5	Credit growth responses to expansionary monetary policy responses and role of uncertainty	448
Fig. 31.6	Credit growth responses to expansionary monetary policy responses and the role of the economic policy uncertainty channels	449

xxxiv   List of Figures

Fig. 31.7	Credit growth responses to an expansionary monetary policy shock	450
Fig. 32.1	Link between higher uncertainty and companies' cash holding	455
Fig. 32.2	Relationship between economic policy uncertainty and companies' deposits	457
Fig. 32.3	Cross correlations	458
Fig. 32.4	Impacts of negative and positive economic policy uncertainty on growth of companies' deposits and role of inflation regimes	459
Fig. 32.5	Responses of growth of companies' deposit to negative and positive economic policy uncertainty shocks	460
Fig. 32.6	Growth of companies' deposits to different economic policy uncertainty shock scenarios	461
Fig. 32.7	Growth of companies' deposits responses to economic policy uncertainty shocks	462
Fig. 32.8	Growth of companies' deposits and credit responses to economic policy uncertainty shocks	462
Fig. 32.9	Response of capital formation growth to positive economic policy uncertainty shocks	463
Fig. 32.10	Responses to negative uncertainty shocks and role of inflation regimes	464
Fig. 32.11	Accumulated capital formation growth responses to positive uncertainty shocks and the role of inflation regimes	466
Fig. 32.12	Accumulated capital formation growth responses to negative uncertainty shocks and the role of inflation regimes	467
Fig. 32.13	Capital formation responses to expansionary monetary policy shock and role of economic policy uncertainty	468
Fig. 33.1	Accumulated credit growth responses to expansionary monetary policy shocks according to uncertainty regimes	474
Fig. 33.2	Accumulated responses to expansionary monetary policy shocks according to inflation regimes	475
Fig. 33.3	Accumulated responses to negative economic policy uncertainty shocks	476
Fig. 34.1	A depiction of the transmission of the unexpected reduction in the economic policy uncertainty	481

List of Figures xxxv

Fig. 34.2	Responses to unexpected reduction in economic policy uncertainty	483
Fig. 34.3	Evidence from the expanded model	484
Fig. 34.4	Depictions of the unexpected reduction in the economic policy uncertainty shock scenarios	485
Fig. 34.5	Responses to various shocks of unexpected reduction in economic policy uncertainty	485
Fig. 34.6	Responses to unexpected reduction in economic policy uncertainty	487
Fig. 34.7	Economic policy uncertainty shock scenarios and inflation expectations	487
Fig. 34.8	Responses to unexpected economic policy uncertainty shock and the role of the exchange rate channel	488
Fig. 34.9	Responses to unexpected economic policy uncertainty shock and the role of CPI inflation	489
Fig. 34.10	Responses to unexpected economic policy uncertainty shock and the role of the GDP channel	490

List of Tables

Table 19.1	Average volatilities, trade-off and economic growth	296
Table 20.1	Impact of inflation regimes	313
Table 20.2	Estimated coefficients	313
Table 21.1	Unrestricted cointegration rank test (Trace)	322
Table 21.2	Unrestricted cointegration rank test (Maximum Eigenvalue)	322
Table 21.3	Estimates of long run coefficient or pass-through according to inflation regimes in given periods	323
Table 21.4	Speed of price adjustment	324
Table 23.1	Magnitudes of output persistence measures according to inflation regimes and model specifications	348
Table 23.2	Evidence from logistic smooth transition autoregression	349
Table 25.1	Impacts of nominal GDP growth on Real GDP growth based on Eqs. (25.6)–(25.9)	373
Table 25.2	Impacts of nominal GDP growth on real GDP growth	374
Table 28.1	Cointegration tests	411
Table 28.2	Cointegration and asymmetry tests based on MTAR	412

1

Introduction

The South African economy has been growing at a slow pace since the onset of financial crisis in 2007. The economy experienced recessions in the 2009Q1–2009Q3 and 2018Q1–2018Q2 periods. The weak and volatile economic growth does not lead to high job creation. In addition, the subdued growth will not contribute in reducing high unemployment, high income inequality, and may exacerbates other socio-economic imbalances. Given this context the South African policymakers have pointed out in several occasions the need for structural reforms to grow the economy. Below we state the recent developments, which are core for the discussions in the book:

- World Bank (2018) report indicated that South Africa has the highest income inequality in the world.
- After the recession in 2009, economic policy uncertainty increased significantly.
- There is increased companies cash holdings in the form of bank deposits post the recession in 2009.
- There is weak gross fixed capital formation contributions to overall GDP growth.

© The Author(s) 2019
E. Ndou and T. Mokoena, *Inequality, Output-Inflation
Trade-Off and Economic Policy Uncertainty*,
https://doi.org/10.1007/978-3-030-19803-9_1

- Monetary policymakers strongly emphasised the importance of the 4.5% midpoint of the inflation target band.
- South African Reserve Bank has adopted the financial stability mandate and has a macroprudential toolkit.
- Credit growth continues to be very sluggish compared to rates observed before the recession in 2009.
- The South African Reserve Bank (SARB) granted banking licences to new banking entrants, which may induce competition in many ways.
- The central bank points out that the problem of economic growth is structural in nature.

There are views from the public which suggests that monetary policy could be used to deal with growth and employment issues in the country. To the contrary, there are also views which suggest that attaining price stability supports growth and employment. What is missing in these discussions is the lack of empirical evidence from both sides in the discourse. This includes the lack of the availability of empirical evidence on (1) whether in South Africa induces redistributive effects or not, (2) when does the principle of policy ineffectiveness of demand management policy apply, (3) how does inequality impacts the monetary and macroprudential policy transmission mechanism. The policy engagements on these issues is missing despite much discussion about this in the advanced economies. This is despite monetary policymakers having indicated their desire to keep inflation below the 4.5% level. This desire has been communicated in several occasions and that keeping inflation low would protect the purchasing power of the poor. Surprisingly the influence of attaining 4.5% has not been articulated with regards to the distributional effects of financial policies. In contributing to the discussion, we examine if the new Keynesian proposition of policy ineffectiveness is applicable in stimulating demand or if there are no redistributive effects. Despite the differences which may arise among policymakers, it is important to determine if the income distribution matters for the effectiveness of monetary policy transmission mechanism, price stability, and financial stability.

We consider the macroeconomic effects of the preceding developments in writing this book. Each chapter provides the highlights of

1 Introduction   3

the main findings and policy implications based on robust empirical analysis. The analysis in each chapter states the motivations, uses simple theoretical economic models, in certain empirical models we apply counterfactual analysis to offer alternative policy scenarios.

We state the main policy lessons based on the analysis, in the last section of this introduction.[1] The book is separated into the following thematic parts, which are explored in detail in the different sections.

- Income inequality, GDP growth, and inflation regimes.
- Income equality and monetary policy.
- The role of the monetary policy channel in transmitting shocks to income inequality.
- Consumption inequality, income inequality, and credit dynamics.
- Bank concentration and income inequality.
- Macroprudential policy and income inequality.
- Output-inflation trade-off and the role of inflation regimes.
- Output growth persistence and inflation.
- Economic policy uncertainty, expansionary monetary, and fiscal policy multipliers.
- Economic policy uncertainty, lending rates, credit dynamics, and companies' cash holdings.

---

[1]The book delves in these issues and shows that policymakers did not indicate the possible existence of the policy ineffectiveness theory nor did they indicate whether policy ineffectiveness could be dependent on whether inflation is above or below the current threshold of six per cent. It is possible that monetary policy may be a conduit in transmitting shocks to income inequality and be a driver of income inequality. The effectiveness of monetary policy may become distorted by income inequality. These are examined in detail in the book from various angles. The policy ineffectiveness theory suggests that demand management policies are ineffective. In this setting, new classical economics suggests that policy interventions should not exist because inflation is costlier than unemployment. In addition, the short-run Philips curve is very steep, and the economy is self-correcting, and this works smoothly and quickly. In contrast, the new Keynesian theory suggests that policy interventions are needed, because unemployment is costlier than inflation. In this case, the Philips curve is flat. However, the self-correcting mechanism is rather slow and unreliable. Does the theory of policy ineffectiveness hold in South Africa and is this constrained by inflation regimes?

1.1 The Book Fills the Following Policy Research Gaps Stated Below

1.1.1 Policymakers Should Make It Clear That Income Inequality Is a Source of Adverse Macroeconomic Effects and Price Stability Is Crucial in Dampening the Adverse Effects

Income inequality has implications for economic growth and macroeconomic stability. At least two theories predict that the impact of income inequality shocks on GDP growth is ambiguous. The *adverse income inequality effects theory* suggests that income inequality may slow down GDP growth by dampening investment (Grigoli and Robles 2017).[2] Stiglitz (2015) suggests that the influence of wealth groups on regulatory processes can lead to financial imbalances, which can slow down GDP growth. By contrast, *favorable income inequality effects theory* suggests that inequality provides incentives for innovation and productivity improvements and this will raise GDP growth. Alternatively, income inequality may foster investment to the extent that rich people have a higher propensity to save (Kaldor 1957). The inconclusiveness in the relationship between income inequality and GDP growth requires empirical analysis. Evidence indicates that rising income inequality significantly lowers GDP growth and that price stability matters. This is because maintaining inflation below the 4.5% threshold minimises the adverse effects of positive income inequality shocks on GDP growth. The adverse effects of income inequality shocks on GDP growth are exacerbated by elevated economic policy uncertainty, depressed employment growth, weakened investment, especially residential and non-residential investment. Certainty in economic policy is needed to avert exacerbating the adverse effects of positive income inequality shocks on GDP growth. Second, policymakers should implement policy initiatives that reduce income inequality for a long time rather than transitorily. Such reduction in

---

[2]Some channels through which inequality leads to adverse economic reaction include increased leveraging and financial cycle, which precipitate financial crises (Rajan 2011).

1 Introduction 5

income inequality may stimulate GDP growth directly and the increase will be further amplified by rising investment.

The Level at Which Inflation Reduces Income Inequality Matters

We further examine the link between inflation and income inequality amidst the SARB's preference to have consumer price inflation below the 4.5% threshold. We argue that the socio-economic benefits of the 4.5% inflation threshold have not been empirically quantified in South Africa. This includes linking the distributional effects of positive inflation shocks on income inequality above and below the 4.5% consumer price inflation threshold. Lopez (2003) suggests that price stabilisation is beneficial for reducing income inequality through the preservation of the real value of fiscal transfers.[3] Evidence reveals that income inequality growth declines due to positive inflation shocks when inflation is (1) below 3% and (2) when it is below the 4.5% threshold level. In addition, employment growth rises significantly and reaches the bigger peak values when inflation is (1) below 3% and (2) when it is below 4.5%. Despite employment growth rising significantly when inflation is within the 3–6% band or when it is below the 6% threshold, income inequality growth rises. This evidence reveals that there is a threshold level within the existing inflation target band in which the unexpected positive inflation impulses lead to rising GDP growth while reducing income inequality growth. We show that the amplification effects by the inflation regime below the 4.5% threshold in lowering income inequality is bigger due to personal income tax cut shocks, followed by positive government consumption shocks. This implies that the expansionary fiscal policy tools can be used to lower income inequality and the reduction is enlarged by inflation when it is below the 4.5% threshold.

---

[3]However, other justifications have been pointed out in the literature. Theory suggests that inflation has direct effects on income inequality through various channels, including changes in real valuation of financial and nonfinancial assets (Bulir 2001). Whereas Romer and Romer (1999) put forward that high inflation can create expectations of future macroeconomic instability and lead to distortionary economic policies which may impact on inequality.

6   E. Ndou and T. Mokoena

Therefore price stability matters even in the discussion of income inequality.

1.1.2 We Show That Income Inequality Rises Due to Contractionary Monetary Policy Shocks as Well That Income Inequality as a Transmission Channel Worsens the Impacts of These Shocks on Real Economic Activity

This book investigates the influence of monetary policy shocks on income distribution, and also examines the extent to which the income inequality channel impacts the transmission of monetary policy shocks to real economic activity. The book determines whether the income inequality channel accentuates or dampens the transmission of monetary policy shocks to real economic activity. The findings from this assessment may help in facilitating the design of effective monetary policy transmission mechanism. This is because the attainment of price stability is also a *public good*. Hence, if income inequality impedes or exacerbates the transmission of monetary policy shocks, then the implementation of structural reforms needs to be intensified to eliminate income inequality and its adverse effects.

Income Inequality Matters as a Transmission Channel of Monetary Policy Shocks to Real Economic Activity

Evidence reveals that the income inequality channel accentuates the decline in real economic activity, following contractionary monetary policy shocks. Income inequality dampens the increases in the marginal propensity to consume, employment growth, GDP growth, and disposable income growth, due to expansionary monetary policy shocks. From a policy perspective, Monnin (2017) argues that income inequality matters in understanding and gauging the reaction of the economy to monetary policy impulses and decision makers should take this dimension into account when designing and calibrating policies. This should be considered despite income inequality not being depicted in the standard monetary policy transmission mechanism; but recent evidence indicates that it should be part of the transmission channels.

The Distributional Effects of Monetary Policy Shocks Matter

The debates regarding the interaction between monetary policy and the dispersion of income distribution increased after the United States of America (US) Fed, Bank of England and European Central Bank embarked on stimulus activities following the recent financial crisis. Hence, central bankers, such as Carney (2016), argue that all monetary policy actions having distributional effects matter. This is echoed by Voinea and Monnin (2017) who advise that taking income inequality concerns seriously would strengthen central banks' independence and improve their policy decisions. In addition, central bankers in the US have examined the link between monetary policy and income inequality. Do monetary policy shocks influence income inequality dynamics in South Africa?[4] The objective is to determine whether the effects, from a South African perspective, differ from those observed in other countries. We find that income inequality declines due to the expansionary monetary policy shocks and the declines are significantly bigger when inflation is below 4.5%, when it is within 4.5–6% and when it is below 3%. A counterfactual analysis reveals that actual income inequality growth declines more in the presence of the employment growth, the economic growth, and the household disposable income growth channels, than when these channels are shut off. This indicates that increases in employment growth, disposable income growth and GDP growth, following an expansionary monetary policy shock, amplify the reductions in income inequality growth. Conclusions from recent studies suggest that having a solid grasp of the ways that monetary policy decisions, income inequality, and aggregate economy are intertwined,

---

[4]The findings in this empirical undertaking should not be viewed as advocating for monetary policy to be used to solve income inequality problems in South Africa.

is important for an efficient design and implementation of monetary policy.

1.1.3 The Determination of the Link Between the Rising Income Inequality and Consumption Inequality Is Important

The link between income inequality and consumption inequality has not been given much attention by policymakers in South Africa, including the role of monetary policy in this relationship. This is an opportunity to advocate for the role of price stability to start featuring prominently in policy discussions, particularly pertaining to the relationship between income inequality and consumption inequality. We also determine whether there is a link between credit dynamics, consumption inequality and income inequality. This is because recent studies suggest that both income inequality and consumption inequality may be the triggers of credit dynamics. Therefore, inequality as a structural issue in South Africa should be an important aspect in the discussions of credit dynamics, rather than its role being underestimated. It is important for policymakers to disentangle the influence of both income and consumption inequalities in driving credit dynamics. The book fills the policy gaps by showing the direct link between the growth in income inequality (as measured by the Gini coefficient) and consumption inequality. The influence of monetary policy is missing in the literature linking the growth of income inequality and consumption inequality. Hence, the book shows that it is important to focus on the link between income inequality and consumption inequality and how this is affected by the inflation channel. The book fills policy gaps by determining how the price stability channel influences the transmission of positive income inequality shocks to consumption inequality. In this context, an inflation threshold of six per cent is used. Unlike prior research, the analysis further examines whether the price stability channel impacts the transmission of positive income inequality shocks to various categories of consumption inequality.

1.1.4 Macroprudential Policy Impacts Income Inequality and Policy Effects Are Transmitted via the Income Inequality Channel to Impact Real Economic Activity

Literature indicates that policymakers tend to overlook the potential costs of macroprudential tools and this includes their influence on income inequality dynamics. This is affirmed by the warnings of Johansson and Wang (2014) and Demirgüç-Kunt and Levine (2009) that it is a disadvantage for policymakers to overlook the relationship between financial policy and inequality. They argue that overlooking this relationship may lead to undesirable consequences in the allocation of financial resources to certain sectors in the economy. The misallocation will impact the efficiency in the financial sector, which may limit economic opportunities. How could the misallocation and efficiency be linked to income inequality? This is because, from a social perspective, the lowering of efficiency limits economic opportunities for the poor due to repressive financial policies. These policies have been found to increase the level of income inequality. This salient aspect via the distributive channel, including income inequality, has been under-researched, more so in South Africa. We examine the link between income inequality and two macroprudential policy tools.

Holding Excess Capital Adequacy Ratio Above the Minimum Required Has Redistributive Effects and These Matter

Do positive excess CAR shocks drive income inequality dynamics in South Africa? In addition, does the income inequality growth channel impact the transmission of positive excess CAR shocks to real economic activity? Evidence indicates that positive excess CAR shocks significantly raise income inequality growth. This indicates that there are huge output losses and redistributive effects linked to rising income inequality induced by excess capital adequacy ratio above the minimum requirements. The rising income inequality growth channel amplifies the effects of positive excess CAR shocks to credit growth and other real economic activity variables. The adverse amplification effects have not received attention in policy discussions.

Changes in the Loan to Value Ratios Have Redistributive Effects

The second macroprudential dimension has to do with the effects of loan to value (LTV) ratios. The loosening of LTVs has distributional consequences beyond issues of financial stability. The book examines the impacts of unexpected loosening in the LTV ratio on income inequality. We ask: To what extent does an unexpected loosening in LTV ratio impact income inequality dynamics? In addition, to what extent does the income inequality channel accentuate or dampen the transmission of loose LTV shocks to real economic activity? Evidence indicates that a loose LTV shock reduces income inequality growth significantly. In addition, an unexpected increase in income inequality leads to a tightening in LTV ratio. In addition, evidence indicates that the declining income inequality growth amplifies the increase in house price inflation, credit growth and increases both the residential and non-residential investment growth. This shows that the income inequality channel is a potent transmitter of loose LTV shocks to the real economic activity. Policymakers should decisively eliminate the high levels of income inequality as these distort the transmission mechanism of macroprudential policies.

Changes in the Lending Standards via the National Credit Act Matter for Income Inequality

As far as the effects of raising credit standards through the National Credit Act (NCA) are concerned, evidence reveals that the NCA raises income inequality. This book further determines the extent to which growth in income inequality has impacted the transmission of the NCA shocks to credit growth, residential investment growth, and GDP growth using counterfactual approaches. The book reveals that the tightening in the NCA standards lowers both the actual responses of the credit growth, residential investment growth, and GDP growth more than the counterfactual suggests. This evidence shows that the income inequality channel is a potent conduit in the transmission of the NCA shocks to real economic activity. Given the above undesirable outcome, we recommend that policymakers should consider income inequality, credit and business cycles in order to attenuate the adverse effects of the tightening of the NCA credit standards.

1.1.5 Increases in the Banking Sector Concentration Levels, Raise Income Inequality, Slows Down Economic Growth and Employment, Suggesting That the Banking Sector Concentration Levels Should Not Be Given Low Priority in Policy Discussions.

Following the granting of new banking licences by SARB to new banking sector entrants in 2018, the book examines if there is a relationship between income inequality and bank concentration levels. We examine the extent to which positive bank concentration shocks impact income inequality in South Africa. In addition, the book shows the extent to which employment, credit, unemployment, and GDP, transmit the positive bank concentration shocks to income inequality as measured by the Gini coefficient. The book fills research gaps regarding the studies focusing on the link between bank concentration and income inequality in South Africa. We fill the gap by examining the extent to which the banking system's concentration impacts income inequality. The gaps include determining the strength of the link between bank concentration and labour market performance as one of the channels through which it may operate to impact income inequality. In addition, the link between bank concentration and GDP is examined as a separate transmission channel. In assessing the transmission of the positive bank concentration shocks to income inequality, the book further utilises counterfactual analysis to determine the influence of the following channels: credit, GDP, employment, and unemployment.

Evidence reveals that income inequality rises significantly to positive bank concentration shocks. In addition, income inequality fluctuates, following a positive bank concentration shock. The counterfactual analysis reveals that the increase in income inequality to positive bank concentration shocks is amplified by the declining credit and GDP, as well as rising unemployment. Therefore, it is desirable that bank concentration should be reduced and competition increased to lower income inequality via the indicated channels.

1.1.6 Policymakers Should Consider the Influence of Inflation Regimes When Discussing the Output-Inflation Trade-Off and the Policy Ineffectiveness Proposition of a Demand Management Policy Shock on Output

There are policy gaps regarding how the interaction between the output-inflation trade-off is constrained by inflation regimes and the quantification of the extent to which the new Keynesian economics hypothesis holds in South Africa. This hypothesis implies that demand policy is less effective in countries with high trend inflation and where prices are less rigid. This book assesses the four dimensions. First, we determine the extent to which the output-inflation trade-off exists in South Africa from the new Keynesian perspective and ascertain if it is impacted by the 6% inflation threshold. Second, we determine the extent to which the positive nominal volatility shocks reduce the output-inflation trade-off and if this is dependent on inflation regimes. Third, we determine if inflation regimes affect the transmission of positive nominal demand shocks to the consumer price level. Fourth, we assess the extent to which the elevated nominal volatilities make expansionary policy to be ineffective in achieving maximum real output and low inflation. This is linked to theory, suggesting that positive nominal demand shocks will have bigger real effects in the region where prices are less responsive, because quantities will adjust more than prices. In some instances, the relevance of inflation regimes is assessed based on three regimes defined as (1) a high regime when inflation exceeds 6%, (2) a low regime when inflation is below 6%, and (3) when it is below the 4.5% inflation threshold. The latter follows the monetary authorities' preference to have consumer price inflation and inflation expectations around 4.5%. There are two forms of trade-offs that are examined in this section.

The Depiction of Trade-Off

The policy ineffectiveness propositions have been posited by new Keynesian and new Classical theories regarding the effects of nominal demand shocks. As shown in Fig. 1.1, the effectiveness of an expansionary policy shock depends on the slope of the aggregate supply curve (S). A positive nominal demand shock (such as an expansionary policy which increased government spending ΔG or monetary stimulus ΔR) will shift the aggregate demand (D) curve from D1 to D2 resulting in three possible output outcomes. The outcomes indicate a trade-off between output and inflation outcomes. In this case, the outcomes are dependent on the slope of the supply curve.

If the supply curve is S1, then output does not change and prices react fully, suggesting that an expansionary policy shock is fully passed through to prices. Based on supply curve S3, the expansionary policy is fully passed onto output without any effect on prices. Using the supply

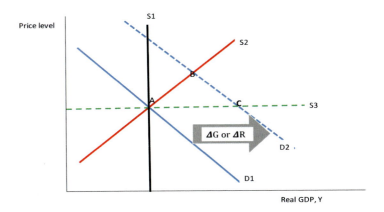

Fig. 1.1 Theoretical effects of an expansionary policy shock on output and inflation (*Source* Authors' drawing)

curve S2 shows that both real output and prices respond to an expansionary policy shock. Theoretically, there is an output-inflation trade-off induced by an expansionary policy shock. Is this supported by data analysis? And does price stability impact the trade-off?[5] The determination of the size of the output-inflation trade-off can either refute or ascertain the prevalence of the policy ineffectiveness proposition. This book, in determining the policy ineffectiveness hypothesis, tests the new Keynesian theory on nominal rigidities by investigating whether trend inflation has an impact on the magnitudes of demand policy on real GDP. Does trend inflation impact the transmission of positive nominal demand shocks on impacting the output-inflation trade-off? In fact, Ball et al. (1988) point out the importance of menu costs in the new Keynesian theory to show that the real effects of a nominal demand shock depend on how often adjustments are made to prices.[6] The faster (slower) the speed of adjustment of prices, the smaller (larger) the real effects of such nominal demand shocks, this implies a steeper (flatter) Philips curve. In addition, they postulated that a demand policy would be less effective in countries with high trend inflation because prices are less rigid, which leads agents to alter prices rather than change quantities.

Evidence Indicates the Prevalence of New Keynesian Hypothesis in South Africa

Evidence in the book confirms the prevalence of new Keynesian hypothesis which implies that demand policy is less effective in a high inflation environment and when there are elevated demand volatility situations. In addition, the book shows there is more price rigidity in the low inflation regime than in the high inflation regime, following

---

[5]During a period of high inflation, prices are less rigid.

[6]The new classical economics suggests that policy intervention should not exist because inflation is costlier than unemployment; the short-run Philips curve is very steep; and the economy is self-correcting and it works smoothly and quickly. In contrast, the new Keynesian theory suggests that policy interventions, because unemployment is costlier than inflation, the Philips curve is flat, and that the self-correcting mechanism is rather slow and unreliable.

a positive nominal demand shock. This suggests that expansionary demand policy shocks will have bigger real effects in the low inflation regime, since the prices exhibit rigidities relative to much flexibility inherent in the high inflation regime. Thus, an expansionary demand policy shock will be more effective in raising real output much higher in the low inflation regime than in the high inflation regime. Therefore, the minimisation of volatility in implementing the demand policy shock is important. Hence, price stability should be enforced to minimise inflation volatility.

1.1.7 The Book Shows It Is Important for Policymakers to Show the Extent to Which Inflation Persistence and Inflation Regimes Constrain the Size of Output Persistence

Ball et al. (1988) and Kiley (2000), among others, indicate that output fluctuations around the trend are less persistent in high inflation economies. However, these authors do not determine the inflation threshold that induces nonlinearity. Hence, the book shows that the effects depend on an inflation threshold. Figure 1.2 depicts the link between output persistence and inflation regimes and the related amplification dynamics. Figure 1.2 does not show the ideal inflation threshold leading to differential effects. The depiction in Fig. 1.2 indicates inflation regimes have different implications for price flexibility or output persistence, and the amplification effects of shocks to real economic activity. The persistence of real output growth movements is entirely determined by the degree of price stickiness. The propagation of shocks to real economic activity depends on output persistence. The book quantifies the importance of the link between output growth persistence and inflation regimes. This includes examining whether the output-inflation trade-off is impacted by the role of price flexibility and we determine the average frequency of price changes in the spirit of Kiley (2000). Showing where output persistence is higher is important for an expansionary monetary policy shock to (1) potentially raise the persistence effects directly, (2) or indirectly enable the effective enlargement of the propagation effects.

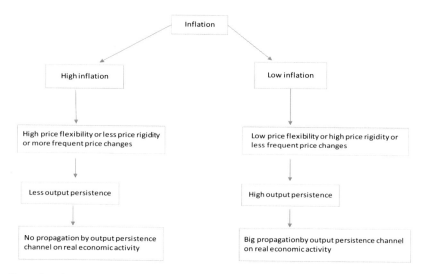

Fig. 1.2 Theoretical depiction of the link between inflation and output persistence (*Source* Authors' drawing)

In addition, the analysis shows the extent to which inflation below 6% determines how price flexibility impacts the transmission of expansionary monetary policy shocks to household consumption growth. This book shows policymakers the inflation regimes in which output persistence effects are bigger. Because this helps policymakers, when embarking on policy initiatives, to stimulate economic growth to facilitate further the propagation of the impacts of real shocks to real economic activity by strengthening the output persistence channel. Evidence reveals that the sizes of output persistence measures are smaller when inflation is above the 6% threshold relative to when inflation is less or equal to 6%. In addition, the average frequency of price changes is relatively shorter in the high inflation regime than in the low regime. This indicates that price flexibility depends on the inflation regimes.

In policy terms, evidence implies that a larger expansionary monetary policy shock than expected will raise output persistence significantly and the amplification effects will be enlarged in the low inflation regime. Thus, price stability matters for the size of the impact of a positive nominal demand shock (such as expansionary monetary policy shocks) on real GDP growth based on the inflation threshold. Therefore, there is high likelihood that an expansionary monetary policy shock in the low inflation regime will uplift real GDP growth more than in the high inflation regime, *ceteris paribus*.

1.1.8 The Book Determines Whether the Economic Policy Uncertainty Channels and Inflation Regimes Impact the Effects of Expansionary Monetary and Fiscal Policies on Output Growth

Is it important to revisit the subject of policy multiplier effects on economic growth with emphasis on the role of inflation regimes? Koelln et al. (1996) examined the extent to which fiscal and monetary policy multipliers decrease with rising trend inflation.[7] Ball et al. (1988) tested whether fiscal and monetary policy multipliers were smaller in countries with high inflation rates. These studies conclude that trend inflation impacts fiscal and monetary policy multiplier effects on economic growth. The problem with generalising the inflation effects is like the "*sand*" and "*grease*" arguments of inflation. This book shows that inflation effects cannot be generalised but should be contextualised to separate the size of policy multipliers when inflation is above or below the six per cent inflation threshold. Having determined the prevalence of policy ineffectiveness proposition in South Africa, the book determines whether the economic policy uncertainty channel impacts the influence of expansionary monetary policy changes on output dynamics. We also determine if the inflation level and persistence reduce the multiplier effects of expansionary monetary and fiscal policies on GDP growth. In Fig. 1.3, an expansionary policy shock can have either a direct or indirect impact on economic growth. Indirectly, the transmission or pass-through of the expansionary policy effects may be impacted

---

[7]Their work differed from that of Ball et al. (1988) by allowing for differential effects of monetary policy and government spending. They test the new Keynesian proposition that sticky prices increase the effects of government spending and monetary policy on gross national product. They found little evidence of the new Keynesian sticky price model.

Fig. 1.3 The link between an expansionary policy, inflation, and economic growth (*Source* Authors' drawing)

by the prevailing inflation regimes which impact the pricing behaviour and inflation persistence before affecting economic growth. Hence, this analysis considers the role of inflation regimes.

Evidence indicates that the size of increases in the output growth responses to expansionary monetary and fiscal policy shocks are much bigger in the low inflation regime than in the high regime. In general, a rising trend inflation, elevated economic policy uncertainty, and higher inflation persistence, will lower the size of multiplier effects of expansionary monetary and fiscal policy effects on output. In contrast, inflation stickiness in the low inflation regime (i.e. below 6%) propagates or magnifies the size of policy multiplier effects on economic growth. This implies that any attempts to use the expansionary policies when inflation exceeds 6% will not lead to the realisation of the expected maximum multiplier effects.

1.1.9 The Book Further Offers Insights into the Extent to Which Economic Policy Uncertainty Impacts the Lending Rates and Credit Growth

The linkage between economic policy uncertainty and credit market indicators (that is, the lending rate margins and credit growth) has not been quantified or discussed in detail in policy discussions. This encompasses determining the extent to which economic policy uncertainty shocks impact the lending rate margins and the pass-through of the repo rate changes to the bank lending rates. The policy gaps are filled by examining the role of the economic policy uncertainty channel on credit dynamics from the four perspectives. These are as follows:

1 Introduction 19

- Determining the direct effects of uncertainty shocks on credit growth dynamics;
- Determining the role of economic policy uncertainty regimes in impacting the reaction of credit growth to an expansionary monetary policy shock;
- Determining the amplification effects of economic policy uncertainty in transmitting expansionary monetary policy shocks to credit growth;
- Showing that the economic policy uncertainty regimes affect the ability of the credit conditions index to transmit expansionary monetary policy shocks to credit growth.

Figure 1.4 shows a theoretical depiction of the transmission mechanism of uncertainty shocks to credit dynamics, via two main channels, but this is not exhaustive of all the channels. The first channel alludes that elevated macroeconomic uncertainty impacts the strategies of financial institutions' lending decisions, screening of customers, and decisions on how best to allocate credit (Chi and Li 2017). Thus, heightened macroeconomic uncertainties make it difficult for lending institutions to allocate credit. In addition, due to asymmetries in the information, banks may allocate scarce credit loans to those borrowers with poor prospects for future gains. As a result, increased information asymmetries can directly increase credit risks, and raise the cost of debt and ration credit extension. In the second channel, the elevated uncertainty shocks lead to increases in financial frictions, leading to high risk premia and decreases in credit growth.

Evidence reported in the literature points to prolonged negative responses of output to positive policy uncertainty shocks (Ndou et al. 2018). This is consistent with the "wait and see" hypothesis. It follows logically that the depressing effects of uncertainty shocks on output growth should have implications for credit dynamics, and the latter's reactions to expansionary monetary policy shocks.

Indeed, the results show that elevated levels of economic policy uncertainty prevent the lending rate margins from falling as expected due to the expansionary monetary policy shock. Evidence indicates that

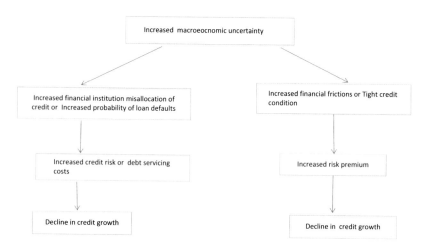

Fig. 1.4 A theoretical depiction of elevated macroeconomic effects on credit dynamics (*Source* Authors' drawing and Ndou et al. [2018])

positive (negative) economic policy uncertainty shocks lower (raise) credit extension and tighten (loosen) credit conditions.

There are three policy implications. First, a large reduction in the repo rate than expected may overcome the mitigating effects of elevated economic policy uncertainty in raising the lending rate margins despite a low inflation environment. Second, this implies that credit growth will remain very subdued due to high economic policy uncertainty, which tightens credit conditions. This counters the stimulatory effects of expansionary monetary policy shocks. Third, a large reduction in the policy rate than expected may be required to achieve a similar impact when uncertainty is elevated, and this may lead to extensive loosening in the credit conditions.

1.1.10 The Book Shows That Economic Policy Uncertainty Impacts the Dynamics of Companies' Cash Holdings and Capital Formation

The book quantifies the extent of influence exerted by the economic policy uncertainty channels on companies' cash holdings. This has not been determined in South Africa. The influence is separated into (1) showing whether the increased value of companies' cash holdings impacts the transmission of expansionary monetary policy shocks; and (2) showing that the increased value of companies' cash holdings impacts the transmission of economic policy uncertainty shocks to capital formation.

Theoretically, there are three motives for holding cash. These are the transactions, the precautionary and the speculative motives. The transaction motive refers to cash held for daily business activities. The precautionary motive implies accumulating cash to meet unanticipated contingencies that may arise. The speculative motive argues for accumulating cash to be used for profit-making opportunities that may arise. Figure 1.5, depicts the transmission mechanism of elevated uncertainty on how it affects the value of cash holding through financial constraints, agency conflicts and the real option channel. The effect of the last channel is further attributed to the increased value of the option to *"wait and see" strategy*. The less severe agency conflicts, severe financially constraints, and the real option channel predicts increased cash holdings after elevated uncertainty. Despite showing all these channels in Fig. 1.5, the analysis focuses on the relevance of the real option channel in South Africa.

Bloom (2009) show that uncertainty reduces corporate investment by increasing the value of the option to *"wait and see"*. This causes firms to wait for additional information before taking actions.[8] Im et al. (2017), found that in North America increased firm-level uncertainty affects the value of cash holdings, indicating the influence of real option effects and the financial constraints channels. So, is there a real option channel in South Africa? This book contributes to studies that assess the effects of uncertainty on corporate cash holdings. These studies on the uncertainty effects focused on firm-level uncertainty or aggregate uncertainty as a driver of corporate cash holdings. The book does not focus on the effects of policy uncertainty by decomposing them into idiosyncratic and permanent shocks. However, the analysis shows the differential

---

[8]Bernanke (1983).

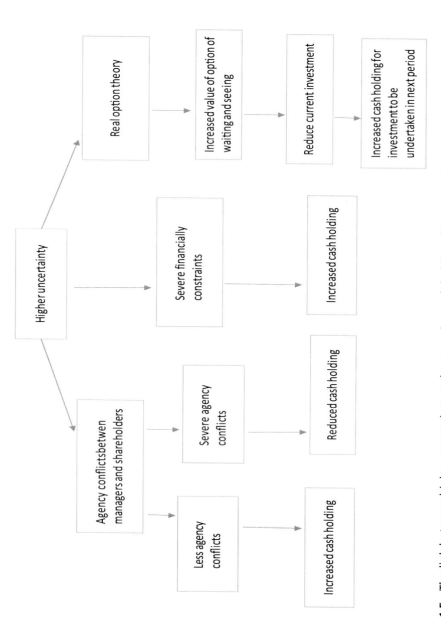

Fig. 1.5 The link between higher uncertainty and companies' cash holdings (*Source* Authors' drawing)

effects of transitory, unchanged negative and positive uncertainty shocks on growth of companies' deposits. In addition, Baum et al. (2002) examined the link between uncertainty and the value of cash holdings and tested the three channels depicted in Fig. 1.5.

This study includes the role of price stability based on the 6% inflation threshold to show the influence of low and high inflation regimes. The analysis further shows the effects of shock scenarios, distinguishing between the transitory and the unchanged negative and positive economic policy uncertainty shocks. The book further applies the counterfactual approach to analyse policy issues to determine several policy relevant matters.

In policy terms, the slowdown in credit growth could be linked to a weakened role of deposits in credit creation in the high economic policy uncertainty regime. The policy implication is that the multiplier mechanism in the credit creation based on deposits is weakened in the high economic policy uncertainty periods and this weakens the stimulatory effects of expansionary monetary policy shocks. A positive economic policy uncertainty shock retards growth of capital formation, an outcome consistent with the predictions of the real option theory. However, a negative economic policy uncertainty shock raises capital formation only when inflation is below or equal to 6% and lowers it above this threshold. In policy terms, this implies price stability matters as low inflation environment makes the growth of companies' deposits to cushion the decline in the capital formation growth due to positive economic policy uncertainty shocks.

1.1.11 We Determine Whether an Unexpected Reduction in Economic Policy Uncertainty Impacts Inflation Expectation Dynamics

The book determines whether an unexpected reduction in economic policy uncertainty impacts inflation expectation dynamics. Theory and evidence suggest that well-anchored inflation expectations should not react to temporary news or shocks to economic variables. Evidence indicates that an unexpected reduction in economic policy uncertainty lowers all the inflation expectations. This suggests that an unexpected reduction in economic policy uncertainty has direct impact on inflation expectations and may lead to the anchoring of inflation expectations. Evidence shows that the actual inflation expectations decline more than the counterfactual response. This suggests that an exchange rate appreciation and reduction in the consumer price inflation, following an unexpected reduction in economic policy uncertainty, leads to further reductions in the inflation expectations.

1.2 The Main Policy Lessons Based on Evidence in the Book

Policymakers should eradicate the rising income inequality as it lowers GDP growth and they should implement policy initiatives that should reduce income inequality over a long horizon rather than reduce inequality transitorily. Such a reduction in income inequality may stimulate GDP growth. In addition, evidence indicates by maintaining inflation below the 4.5% threshold minimises the adverse effects of positive income inequality shocks on GDP growth. Moreover, evidence from the counterfactual analysis indicates that positive income inequality shocks are transmitted via other channels to reduce GDP growth.

Price stability matters for the reduction in the growth of income inequality to positive inflation shocks in the inflation bands (1) below 3% and (2) when it is below 4.5% threshold level. In addition, employment growth rises significantly and reaches the bigger peak values when inflation is (1) below 3% and (2) below 4.5%. Despite, employment growth rising significantly when inflation is within the 3–6% band or below the 6% threshold, income inequality growth rises.

Evidence shows even though income inequality is not being depicted in the standard monetary policy transmission mechanism, there is need for it to be considered as part of the transmission mechanism. This is because the income inequality channel accentuates the decline in real economic activity, following contractionary monetary policy shocks. In addition, income inequality dampens the increases in marginal propensity to consume, employment growth, GDP growth and disposable income growth due to the expansionary monetary policy shocks. That's income inequality matters in the understanding and gauging of the reaction of the economy to monetary policy impulses and decision makers should take this dimension into account when designing and calibrating policies (Monnin 2017).

Policymakers should enhance the understanding of the ways in which monetary policy decisions, income inequality, and aggregate economy, are intertwined as this will enable an efficient design and implementation of monetary policy. Evidence confirms the prevalence of the distributive effects of monetary policy changes. We find that magnitudes of decline in income inequality due to expansionary monetary policy shocks are significantly bigger (1) when inflation is below 4.5%, (2) when it is within the 4.5–6% target band and below 3%.

Policies should be put in place that focus on ensuring more inclusive gains from structural transformation and policymakers should facilitate the reskilling of workers and reduce the costs of their reallocation costs when the services sector is growing at the expense of other sectors. Evidence reveals that unexpected increase in the services sector employment shares leads to significant increase in income inequality but the counterfactual analysis reveals increases are dampened by when inflation is below the 4.5 or 6% threshold.

The Financial globalisation and trade openness channels have opposing influences in transmitting the monetary policy shocks to income inequality. Financial globalisation impacts the link between monetary policy and income inequality as the net capital inflow channel dampens the increase in income inequality, following a tight monetary policy shock. Trade openness channel dampens the rising income inequality due to a contractionary monetary policy shock. From a policy perspective, this calls for an optimal monetary response to consider the income inequality reaction in the calibration of monetary policy effects on the optimal net capital inflows to have a desirable effect.

Policymakers should lower the entry barriers to the banking sector and introduce a sliding scale of capital adequacy ratios that increase with the size of the banks. Evidence indicates that increases in the banking sector concentration raises income inequality while lowering economic growth and employment rate in South Africa. The increase in income inequality to positive bank concentration shocks is amplified by the declining credit and GDP, as well as rising unemployment.

Macroprudential regulators should put mechanisms in place to prevent credit extension that is not driven by fundamentals such as consumption inequalities as this may lead to crises and unproductive uses. Evidence indicates that consumption inequality and inequalities in the consumption categories amplify the increase in credit due to the positive income inequality shocks.

Policymakers should enforce price stability to weaken the link between the income inequality and consumption inequality. A counterfactual VAR analysis indicates that high (low) inflation amplifies (dampens) the increase in consumption inequality to positive income inequality shocks when inflation exceeds the 6% threshold. Price stability matters and policymakers should pay attention to existing structural issues in the economy on how these impact the expected policy decision.

Increased income inequality growth, following the positive excess CAR shocks,[9] **and tightening standards in National Credit Acts (NCA), exacerbates the decline in the real economic activity which, implies that policymakers should cast their nets wider than financial regulatory reforms and consider the effects of their policy changes in influencing the distributive patterns (Perugini et al.** 2016). Because evidence from counterfactual analysis indicates that the actual decline in credit and GDP growth due to unexpected increase in excess capital adequacy ratio (CAR) above minimum required exceeds those of the counterfactual responses. Evidence reveals that the tightening in NCA raises income inequality and the rise in growth of income inequality due tightening NCA exacerbates the reduction in credit growth, residential investment growth and GDP growth.

The income inequality channel is a potent transmitter of the effects of loosening in the LTV ratio to the real economic activity,

---

[9]Excess capital adequacy ratio above minimum required.

1 Introduction   27

hence policymakers should decisively eliminate the high levels of income inequality as these distort the transmission mechanism of macroprudential policies. Evidence from counterfactual VAR approach analysis shows the declining income inequality amplifies the increase in the house price growth, residential investment growth, and credit growth due to LTV shocks.

An unexpected loosening in the labour market reforms reduces income inequality growth when complemented by increased government consumption expenditure, income tax cuts, low economic policy uncertainty and inflation below 6%. A weak exchange rate mitigates the reduction in the income inequality growth induced by an unexpected loosening in the labour market reforms.

Evidence indicates that expansionary demand policy is less effective during high inflation and demand volatilities episodes, which is consistent with predictions of the new Keynesian hypothesis. Therefore, policymakers should minimise the volatility of inflation when implementing demand policies and ensure that price stability is enforced to minimise inflation volatility.

Thus, an expansionary nominal demand policy shock affecting aggregate demand will have a bigger effect on real output in the low inflation regime than in the high inflation regime. Evidence reveals that real output rises much higher in the low inflation regime than in the high inflation regime to a positive nominal demand policy shock.

When inflation is below 6%, an expansionary monetary policy shock stimulates household consumption growth more than raising the inflation rate because prices are less flexible or prices changes are less frequent. Evidence shows that the average frequency of price changes is relatively shorter in the high inflation regime than in the low regime. The increased (reduced) price flexibility in the high (low) inflation regime weakens (increases) the responses of household consumption growth to an expansionary monetary policy shock.

Evidence shows that expansionary monetary policy shocks raise output persistence more when inflation is below or equal to 6% than when it is above this threshold. In addition, the low economic policy uncertainty magnifies the output persistence response to expansionary monetary policy shocks. By contrast, high economic policy uncertainty lowers the output persistence response to an expansionary monetary policy shock.

Price stability matters for the size of the impact of a positive nominal demand shock (such as expansionary monetary policy shocks) on real GDP growth based on the six per cent inflation threshold. Therefore, there is high likelihood that expansionary monetary policy shocks in the low inflation regime will raise real GDP growth more than in the high inflation regime, *ceteris paribus*.

Policymakers anticipating a certain magnitude of the impact from a stimulatory demand policy shock should consider economic policy uncertainty regimes in their policy decisions. Otherwise policy effects may fall short of their expectations and induce more uncertainty. Evidence shows that low economic policy uncertainty amplifies the increase in economic growth to an unexpected cut in the repo rate. By contrast, the actual economic growth responses rise less than the counterfactual responses in the high economic policy uncertainty regime.

A low inflation and low economic policy uncertainty regime matter for increasing the stimulatory effects of expansionary policies on GDP growth. This is because magnitudes of the multiplier effects of expansionary monetary and fiscal policies on output are bigger in the low inflation environment and low economic policy uncertainty regime than in the high inflation regime. The high trend inflation and elevated economic policy uncertainty dampen the multiplier effects of expansionary policies.

Policymakers should consider that a large reduction in the repo rate than expected is needed to overcome the mitigating effects of elevated economic policy uncertainty in raising the bank lending rate margins even in a low inflation environment. Evidence indicates that elevation in economic policy uncertainty raises the bank lending rate margins. By contrast, the subsiding economic policy uncertainty lowers the bank lending rate margins.

A high economic policy uncertainty environment may require a large reduction in the policy rate by more than expected to achieve a similar impact and this may lead to extensive loosening in the credit conditions. The findings show that elevated economic policy uncertainty directly weakens the transmission of the effects of expansionary monetary policy shocks onto credit growth. This implies that credit growth will remain very subdued due to high economic policy uncertainty, which tightens the credit conditions environment. Thus, economic policy uncertainty regimes matter for the efficacy of the credit conditions channel in transmitting expansionary monetary policy shocks to credit growth.

Price stability matters as the low inflation environment makes the growth of companies' deposits to cushion the decline in the capital formation growth due to positive economic policy uncertainty shocks. Evidence shows that rising (declining) economic policy uncertainty raises (reduces) growth of companies' deposits. The increase in the growth of companies' deposits accentuates the decline in the capital formation, following a positive economic policy uncertainty shock. The decline is large when inflation exceeds the six per cent threshold than below this limit.

Low economic policy uncertainty matters as evidence indicates that expansionary monetary policy shocks raise credit growth more than the counterfactual suggests in the low economic policy uncertainty regime. This suggests that, in the low economic policy uncertainty environment, the slowdown in companies' deposits growth due to an expansionary monetary policy shock amplifies increases in the credit growth. By contrast, expansionary monetary policy shock raises credit growth less than the counterfactual in the high uncertainty regime. This is due to an increase in the growth of companies' deposits in the high uncertainty regime, which dampens credit growth.

An unexpected reduction in the economic policy uncertainty lowers inflation expectations. This suggests that an unexpected reduction in economic policy uncertainty has a direct impact on the inflation expectations and may lead to anchoring of inflation expectations.

References

Ball, L., Makiw, G., & Romer, D. (1988). The new Keynesian economics and output-inflation trade-off. *Brooking Papers on Economic Activity, 1,* 1–65.

Baum, C., Caglayan, M., & Ozkan, N. (2002). *The impact of macroeconomic uncertainty on bank lending behavior* (Computing in Economics and Finance, No. 94). Liverpool: University of Liverpool Management School.

Bernanke, B. (1983). Irreversibility, uncertainty and cyclical investment. *The Quarterly Journal of Economics, 98*(1), 85–106.

Bloom, N. (2009). The impact of uncertainty shocks. *Econometrica, Econometric Society, 77*(3), 623–685.

Bulir, A. (2001). Income inequality: Does inflation matter? *IMF Staff Papers, 48*(11), 1–5. Palgrave Macmillan.

Carney, M. (2016, June 30). *Uncertainty, the economy and policy.* Speech by Mr Mark Carney, Governor of the Bank of England and Chairman of the Financial Stability Board, at the Bank of England, London.

Chi, Q., & Li, W. (2017). Economic policy uncertainty, credit risks and banks' lending decisions: Evidence from Chinese commercial banks. *China Journal of Accounting Research, 10*(1), 33–50.

Demirgüç-Kunt, A., & Levine, R. (2009). Finance and inequality: Theory and evidence. *Annual Review of Financial Economics, 1,* 287–318.

Grigoli, F., & Robles, A. (2017). *Inequality overhang* (IMF Working Paper, 17/76). Washington, DC: International Monetary Fund.

Im, H.J., Park, H., & Zhao, G. (2017). Uncertainty and the value of cash holding. *Economic Letters,* Issue 55, 43–48.

Johansson, A., & Wang, X. (2014). Financial sector policies and income inequality. *China Economic Review, 31,* 367–378.

Kaldor, N. (1957). A model of economic growth. *The Economic Journal, 67*(268), 591–624.

Kiley, M. (2000). Endogenous price stickiness and business cycle persistence. *Journal of Money, Credit, and Banking, 32*(1), 28–53. Wiley Periodicals, Inc.

Koelln, K., Rush, M., & Waldo, D. (1996). Do government multipliers decrease with inflation? *Journal of Monetary Policy, 38*(3), 495–505.

Lopez, H. (2003). *Macroeconomics and inequality* (The World Bank [PRMPR]). Washington, DC: World Bank.

Monnin, P. (2017). *Monetary policy, macroprudential regulation and inequality.* Available at SSRN: https://ssrn.com/abstract=2970459 or http://dx.doi.org/10.2139/ssrn.2970459.

Ndou, E., Gumata, N., & Ncube, M. (2018). *Exchange rate shocks and global economic uncertainities: Transmission channels into South Africa.* Palgrave Macmillan.

Perugini, C., Holsher, J., & Collie, S. (2016). Inequality, credit and financial crises. *Cambridge Journal of Economics, 40*(1), 227–257.

Rajan, R. (2011). *Fault lines: How hidden fractures still threaten the world economy.* Princeton: Princeton University Press.

Romer, C.D., & Romer, D. (1999). Monetary policy and well-being of the poor. *Economic Review, Federal Reserve Bank of Kansas City* (first quarter), 21–49.

Stiglitz, J. (2015). *The price of inequality: How today's divided society endangers our future.* New York: W. W. Norton.

Voinea, L., & Monnin, P. (2017). *Inequality should matter for central banks.*

World Bank. (2018, March). *Overcoming poverty and inequality in South Africa: An assessment of drivers, constraints and opportunities.*

Part I
Income Inequality, GDP Growth and Inflation Regimes

2

Income Inequality and GDP Growth Nexus in South Africa: Does the 4.5% Consumer Price Inflation Threshold and Other Channels Play a Role?

Main Highlights

- Evidence indicates that positive income inequality shocks significantly lower GDP growth. In addition, evidence indicates there are benefits to keeping inflation below the 4.5% threshold compared to above this limit. This is because maintaining inflation below the 4.5% threshold minimises the adverse effects of positive income inequality shocks on GDP growth.
- Moreover, evidence from the counterfactual analysis indicates positive income inequality shocks are transmitted via other channels to reduce GDP growth.
- The adverse effects of income inequality shocks on GDP growth are exacerbated by elevated economic policy uncertainty, depressed employment, weakening investment, especially residential and non-residential investment. These findings imply certainty in economic policy is needed to avert exacerbating the adverse effects of positive income inequality shocks on GDP growth.

© The Author(s) 2019
E. Ndou and T. Mokoena, *Inequality, Output-Inflation Trade-Off and Economic Policy Uncertainty*,
https://doi.org/10.1007/978-3-030-19803-9_2

- Second, policymakers should implement policy initiatives that should reduce income inequality for a long time rather than transitorily. Such reduction in income inequality may stimulate GDP growth directly and the increase will be further amplified by rising investment.

2.1 Introduction

The forecast of the South African GDP growth in 2018 indicate a sluggish economic recovery. In addition, the World Bank (2018) suggests that South Africa should deal with income inequality issues to spur GDP growth. This optimistic advice is given despite the existence of two theories predicting that the impact of income inequality shocks on GDP growth is ambiguous. The *adverse income inequality effects theory* suggests that income inequality may slow down GDP growth by dampening investment (Grigoli et al. 2016).[1] Stiglitz (2012) suggests that the influence of wealth groups on regulatory processes can lead to financial imbalances, which can slow down GDP growth. By contrast, *favorable income inequality effects theory* suggest inequality provides incentives for innovation and huge productivity (Lazear and Rosen 1981) and this will raise GDP growth. Alternatively, income inequality may foster investment to the extent, that rich people have a higher propensity to save (Kaldor 1957). The inconclusiveness in the relationship between income inequality and GDP growth requires empirical analysis. To what extent does an unexpected increase in income inequality exert adverse effects on GDP growth?

As displayed in Fig. 2.1, positive income inequality shocks can have direct and indirect effects on GDP growth, irrespective of theoretical

---

[1]Some channels through which inequality leads to adverse economic reaction include increased leveraging and financial cycle, which precipitate financial crises.

2 Income Inequality and GDP Growth Nexus in South Africa ...

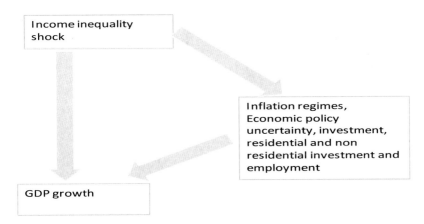

Fig. 2.1 Transmission of positive income inequality shocks to GDP growth (*Source* Authors' drawing)

predictions. The indirect transmission suggests that inflation regimes, economic policy uncertainty, investment including its components and employment channels, can impact the transmission of income inequality shocks to GDP growth. Such depiction of the influence of indirect channels has not featured in the literature linking income inequality and GDP growth.

This chapter fills policy research gaps in the following ways based on the inclusion of indirect transmission channels. First, the chapter determines whether the inflation threshold of 4.5% impacts the transmission of income inequality shocks to GDP growth. Second, the chapter examines whether the economic policy uncertainty channel impacts the transmission of positive income inequality shocks onto GDP growth. Third, the chapter shows the extent to which investment and its components (that is, residential and nonresidential) transmit positive income inequality shocks to GDP growth. Fourth, the interaction amongst income inequality growth, GDP growth and consumer price inflation below the 4.5% threshold has not been investigated in South Africa. The results presented in the analysis are robust to different techniques and model specifications. Approaches used in this chapter include

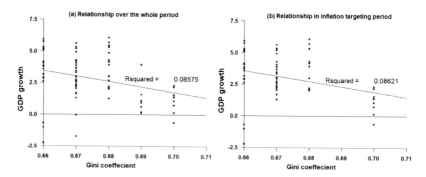

Fig. 2.2 The relationship between income inequality and GDP growth in South Africa (*Source* Authors' calculations)

vector autoregression (VAR) models, which allows examining simultaneously the effects in both directions. Similarly, Atems and Jones (2015) employed a bivariate VAR model and assumed that changes in income inequality affect growth with a one year delay.

2.2 The Impact of Income Inequality on GDP Growth

This section uses quarterly (Q) data spanning 1993Q1–2016Q3. All growth rates used in this chapter are expressed as year-on-year rates. The income inequality is captured by the Gini coefficient used in Gumata and Ndou (2017) and other data are sourced from the South African Reserve Bank. Figure 2.2 shows a negative relationship between income inequality and GDP growth. The negative finding is robust to using both the full sample and the sample from the inflation-targeting period.

What is the impact of a positive income inequality shock on GDP growth? The effects are determined via several approaches beginning with Eqs. (2.1–2.3). The models vary depending on the number of explanatory variables. The variables include credit growth, repo rate, employment growth, CPI inflation and 2007 financial crisis dummy variable.

2 Income Inequality and GDP Growth Nexus in South Africa ... 39

$$
\text{GDP\_growth}_t = \text{constant} + \sum_{i=1}^{4} \text{GDP\_growth}_{t-i}
$$

$$
+ \sum_{i=0}^{2} \text{Credit\_growth}_{t-i} + \text{crisis\_dummy}
$$

$$
+ \sum_{i=0}^{2} \text{Gini\_growth}_{t-i} + \sum_{i=0}^{2} \text{CPI\_inflation}_{t-i}
$$

$$
+ \sum_{i=0}^{2} \text{Repo\_rate}_{t-i} + \varepsilon_t \tag{2.1}
$$

$$
\text{GDP\_growth}_t = \text{constant} + \sum_{i=1}^{2} \text{GDP\_growth}_{t-i}
$$

$$
+ \sum_{i=0}^{2} \text{Gini\_growth}_{t-i} + \sum_{i-0}^{2} \text{Credit\_growth}_{t-i}
$$

$$
+ \text{crisis\_dummy} + \sum_{i=0}^{2} \text{Employment\_growth}_{t-i}
$$

$$
+ \sum_{i=0}^{2} \text{CPI\_inflation}_{t-i} + \varepsilon_t \tag{2.2}
$$

$$
\text{GDP\_growth}_t = \text{constant} + \sum_{i=1}^{4} \text{GDP\_growth}_{t-i}
$$

$$
+ \sum_{i=0}^{2} \text{Gini\_growth}_{t-i} + \sum_{i=0}^{2} \text{Credit\_growth}_{t-i}
$$

$$
+ \text{crisis\_dummy} + \varepsilon_t \tag{2.3}
$$

Figure 2.3 shows the responses of GDP growth to positive income inequality shocks. GDP growth declines significantly to positive income inequality shocks. The decline is robust to different model specifications. The decline lasts at most eight quarters. And the peak decline is

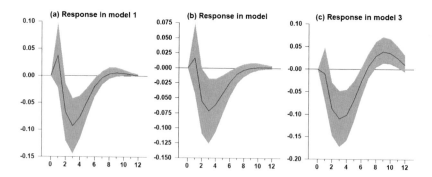

Fig. 2.3 GDP growth responses to positive income inequality shocks (*Note* The grey shaded bands denote the 16th and 84th percentile confidence bands. *Source* Authors' calculations)

nearly 0.10 percentage points which occurs in the third quarter after the shock.

We further test the robustness of the evidence that positive income inequality lowers GDP growth. Three models are estimated and are specified as follows: Model A is a bivariate VAR model which includes GDP growth and income inequality growth as endogenous variables. In this model, exogenous variables include consumer price inflation, employment growth, and a crisis dummy for the financial crisis that began in 2007 to the end of the sample and zero otherwise. Model B is a bivariate VAR model which includes income inequality growth and GDP growth as endogenous variables. The exogenous variables include consumer price inflation, employment growth and a crisis dummy. The third model is an exogenous VAR (Exo_VAR) model. This model uses credit growth and GDP growth as endogenous variables. Employment growth and income inequality growth are exogenous variables. All models are estimated using two lags and 10,000 Monte Carlo draws.

Figure 2.4 shows the responses of GDP growth to positive income inequality shocks. The positive income inequality shocks reduce GDP growth significantly, but the duration of the effects differs over horizons. The decline in GDP growth is bigger in Models A and B than in the exogenous VAR model.

2 Income Inequality and GDP Growth Nexus in South Africa ...

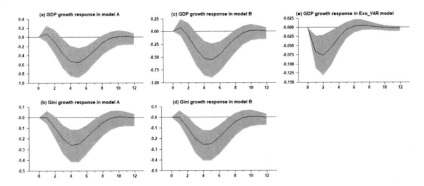

Fig. 2.4 GDP growth responses to a positive income inequality shock (*Note* The grey band denotes the 16th and 84th percentile confidence bands. *Source* Authors' calculations)

Figure 2.4 further shows the reverse causality. That is, do positive GDP growth shocks impact income inequality? In Fig. 2.4b, d income inequality growth declines significantly for nearly two years to a positive GDP growth shock. In policy terms, this evidence shows that improvements in GDP growth could lower income inequality significantly.

2.3 Does the Economic Policy Uncertainty Channel Influence the Response of GDP Growth to Income Inequality Shocks?

Economic policy uncertainty (EPU) has been pointed out several times in 2017 as a driver of sluggish GDP growth in South Africa. Consequently, this section examines the role of growth of economic policy uncertainty in transmitting positive income inequality shocks to GDP growth. The economic policy uncertainty variable used in this chapter is based on Hlatshwayo and Saxegaard (2016). Two approaches are applied. The first approach (LIN_Model) is based on the Eqs. (2.4) and (2.5) which includes growth of the economic policy uncertainty

(EPU_growth), while the coefficient of this variable is set to zero in the second model. The differences in the responses of GDP growth between the two models measures the size of the influence of growth of the economic policy uncertainty channel. All models are estimated using 10,000 bootstrap draws.

$$
\begin{aligned}
\text{GDP\_growth}_t = {} & \text{constant} + \sum_{i=1}^{2} \text{GDP\_growth}_{t-i} + \sum_{i=0}^{2} \text{Gini\_growth}_{t-i} \\
& + \sum_{i=0}^{2} \text{EPU\_growth}_{t-i} + \text{crisis\_dummy} \\
& + \sum_{i=0}^{2} \text{CPI\_inflation}_{t-i} + \varepsilon_t
\end{aligned}
\tag{2.4}
$$

$$
\begin{aligned}
\text{GDP\_growth}_t = {} & \text{constant} + \sum_{i=1}^{2} \text{GDP\_growth}_{t-i} \\
& + \sum_{i=0}^{2} \text{Gini\_growth}_{t-i} + \text{crisis\_dummy} \\
& + \sum_{i=0}^{2} \text{CPI\_inflation}_{t-i} + \varepsilon_t
\end{aligned}
\tag{2.5}
$$

The second approach estimates VAR models in which growth of economic policy uncertainty is endogenous in one model while it is exogenous in the other model. The differences in the responses of GDP growth from the two models indicate the role of economic policy uncertainty. These two approaches determine the robustness of the results.

In Fig. 2.5, the decline in GDP growth to positive income inequality shocks is robust to different model specifications. The size of GDP growth decline is larger in the presence of growth of the economic policy uncertainty channel. Evidence indicates that the presence of elevated

2 Income Inequality and GDP Growth Nexus in South Africa … 43

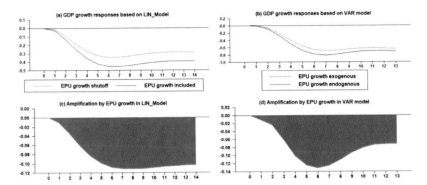

Fig. 2.5 Cumulative GDP growth responses to positive income inequality shocks and the role of economic policy uncertainty channel (*Source* Authors' calculations)

economic policy uncertainty worsens the decline in GDP growth to positive income inequality shocks. This suggests that certainty in economic policy is needed to avert the adverse effects of positive income inequality shocks on GDP growth.

2.4 Does the Consumer Price Inflation Channel Matter for Transmitting Income Inequality Shocks to GDP Growth?

This section further examines the extent to which consumer price inflation influences the transmission of positive income inequality shocks to GDP growth. However, the focus is on the influence of the inflation threshold of 4.5%. That is, is this inflation threshold desirable from a structural perspective when dealing with GDP growth problems related to income inequality? The purpose is to disentangle the role of the inflation threshold of 4.5% using Eq. (2.6). The CPI inflation band dummy is equal to values of inflation in the indicated inflation band and zero otherwise. Three inflation bands used in the analysis are: below 4.5%, above 4.5% and 4.5–6%. The dummy for each of the variables are included separately in Eq. (2.6)

$$\text{GDP\_growth}_t = \text{constant} + \sum_{i=1}^{2} \text{GDP\_growth}_{t-i}$$

$$+ \sum_{i=0}^{2} \text{Gini\_growth}_{t-i} + \sum_{i=0}^{2} \text{Credit\_growth}_{t-i}$$

$$+ \text{crisis\_dummy} + \sum_{i=0}^{2} \text{CPI\_inflation\_band}_{t-i} + \varepsilon_t \quad (2.6)$$

Figure 2.6a reveals that a positive income inequality shock leads to a prolonged decline in GDP growth when the shock happens when inflation exceeds the 4.5% threshold than when it is below this threshold. In addition, Fig. 2.6b shows that a positive income inequality shock depresses GDP growth significantly for long periods when the shock occurs when inflation is within the 4.5–6% band than below this band. This evidence supports the notion that by maintaining inflation below 4.5% will help reduce the severity of positive income inequality shocks on GDP growth.

We perform a counterfactual analysis to determine the role of the inflation regime below the 4.5% threshold in transmitting the positive income inequality shocks to GDP growth. This is done by estimating

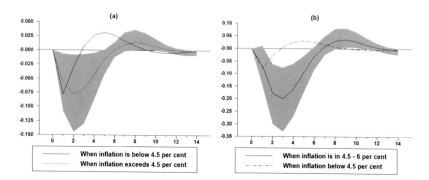

Fig. 2.6 GDP growth responses to positive income inequality shocks (*Note* The grey shaded bands denote the 16th and 84th percentile confidence bands. *Source* Authors' calculations)

2 Income Inequality and GDP Growth Nexus in South Africa ...

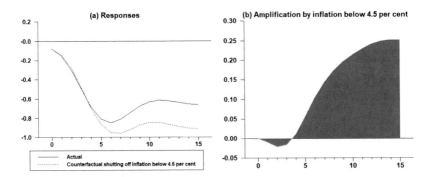

Fig. 2.7 Cumulative GDP growth responses to positive income inequality shocks (*Source* Authors' calculations)

a counterfactual VAR model. The model includes income inequality growth, GDP growth and an inflation dummy variable. The credit growth and employment growth are included as exogenous variables. The inflation dummy is equal to the values of consumer price inflation below or equal to 4.5% and zero otherwise. The inflation channel based on the inflation below 4.5% is shut off to calculate the counterfactual impulse responses. The model is estimated using two lags and 10,000 Monte Carlo draws. The responses of GDP growth are shown in Fig. 2.7. The actual cumulative GDP growth decline is lower than the counterfactual suggests. This shows that inflation below 4.5% mitigates the decline in GDP growth to positive income inequality shocks. This shows that monetary policy makers may justify keeping inflation below 4.5% if the objective includes mitigating the effects of positive income inequality in impacting GDP growth.

This section tests the robustness of the preceding result using a counterfactual VAR model based on whether inflation below the 4.5% threshold is endogenous or exogenous in the models. The influence of inflation is based on the difference in the GDP growth responses to positive income inequality shocks when inflation is endogenous and being exogenous in the other model. The exogenous VAR model includes income inequality growth and GDP growth as endogenous variables. Whereas credit growth, a dummy for the consumer price

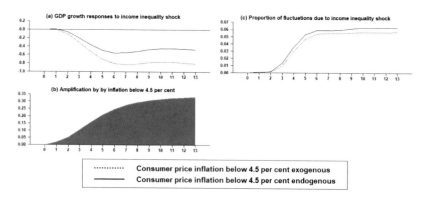

Fig. 2.8 Cumulative responses to a positive income inequality shock (*Source* Authors' calculations)

inflation below 4.5% threshold and employment growth are exogenous. However, the endogenous VAR model includes income inequality growth, GDP growth and a dummy for the consumer price inflation below the 4.5% threshold as endogenous variables. All models are estimated using two lags and 10,000 Monte Carlo draws.

The gap between the responses of GDP growth in the endogenous model and exogenous models shown in Fig. 2.8, measures the size of the amplification by the inflation channel below 4.5%. GDP growth declines more when the inflation variable is exogenous than when it is endogenous in Fig. 2.8a. This suggests that the inflation regime below 4.5% threshold mitigates the adverse effects of income inequality on GDP growth. The negative amplifications due to the inflation channel are shown in Fig. 2.8b. The results are robust to the inclusion of the dummy for financial crisis beginning in 2007.

We further determine whether the positive income inequality shocks impact GDP growth in an asymmetrical manner. The asymmetry is based on the size of positive income inequality growth shocks. The shocks are measured as standard deviations (s.d). Figure 2.9 shows that large positive income inequality shocks lead to big declines in GDP growth than small sized positive income inequality shocks.

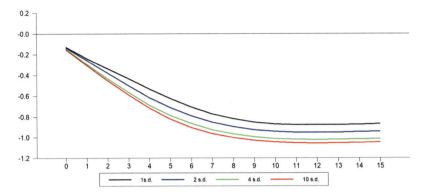

Fig. 2.9 GDP growth responses to different sizes of positive income inequality shocks (*Source* Authors' calculations)

2.5 Which Channels Transmit Positive Income Inequality Shocks to GDP Growth?

The preceding evidence reveals the direct effects of positive income inequality shocks on GDP growth. It is important to determine the relevance of the indirect channels through which positive income inequality shocks are transmitted to GDP growth. The determination of the relevance of indirect channels is done using counterfactual VAR models. The models include income inequality growth, GDP growth, and a selected economic indicator channel. The economic indicators include annual growth in the following variables: fixed capital formation (investment), nonresidential fixed capital formation (nonresidential investment), residential fixed capital formation (residential investment) and employment. These channels are included separately in the models. The counterfactual GDP growth is the response based on shutting off the indicated channel. The models are estimated using two lags and 10,000 Monte Carlo draws. In Fig. 2.10, the actual GDP growth impulse responses decline more than the counterfactual suggests. This indicates that the presence of these channels exacerbates the decline in GDP growth to positive income inequality shock. Thus, income inequality directly and indirectly via other channels retards GDP growth.

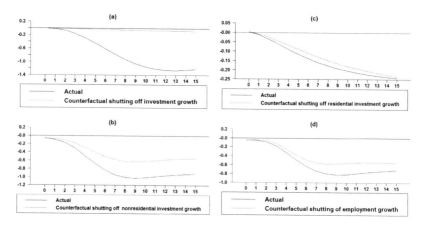

Fig. 2.10 Actual and counterfactual cumulative GDP growth responses to positive income shocks and the role of different channels (*Source* Authors' calculations)

2.6 What Should Policymakers Do?

This section shows the direct effects of the unexpected reduction in income inequality growth on the evolution of GDP growth and residential and nonresidential investment growth. The results are based on the preceding VAR model specification, with the investment components included separately in the model. We use three scenarios as shown in Fig. 2.11. The depiction includes transitory reduction, persistent and continued reduction. GDP growth rises less to a transitory shock than to a shock that reduces income inequality over a prolonged period. This evidence implies that policymakers should embark on policy initiatives that have long-lasting impacts on the reduction of the income inequality. Both the residential and nonresidential investment channels rise following an unexpected reduction in income inequality shock as shown in Fig. 2.11c, d. Policymakers should consider that such reductions may stimulate GDP growth directly and indirectly via other channels.

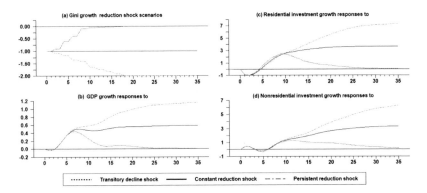

Fig. 2.11 Income inequality shock scenarios and macroeconomic variable responses (*Source* Authors' calculations)

2.7 Conclusion and Policy Implications

This chapter revisited the link between income inequality and GDP growth, given that theoretical models predict ambiguous effects. In addition, this chapter determined whether the inflation threshold of 4.5% above and below it impacted the transmission of positive income inequality shocks to GDP growth. Furthermore, this chapter used counterfactual approaches to examine whether economic policy uncertainty, employment, investment and the residential and nonresidential investment channels transmitted positive income inequality shocks to GDP growth. Evidence indicates that a positive income inequality shock significantly lowers GDP growth. In addition, evidence indicates it is beneficial to keep inflation below the 4.5% threshold compared to above this limit. This is because maintaining inflation below 4.5% minimises the adverse effects of positive income inequality shocks on GDP growth. Moreover, evidence from the counterfactual analysis indicates that positive income inequality shocks are transmitted via other channels to reduce GDP growth. The adverse effects of income inequality shocks on GDP growth are exacerbated by elevated economic policy uncertainty, depressed employment, and weakening in investment (nonresidential investment and residential activities). First, these findings imply certainty in economic policy is needed to avert exacerbating the adverse effects of positive income inequality shocks on GDP growth. Second, policymakers should implement policy initiatives that should reduce income inequality for a long time rather than transitorily. Such a reduction in income inequality may stimulate GDP growth directly and the increase will be further amplified by rising investment, residential and nonresidential investment channels.

References

Atems, B., & Jones, J. (2015). Income inequality and GDP growth: A panel VAR approach. *Empirical Economics, 48*(4), 1541–1561.

Banerjee, A. V., & Duo, E. (2003). Inequality and growth: What can the data say? *Journal of GDP Growth, 8*(3), 267–299.

Barro, R. J. (2000). Inequality and growth in a panel of countries. *Journal of GDP Growth, 5*(1), 5–32.

Grigoli, F., Paredes, E., & Di Bella, G. (2016). *Inequality and growth: A heterogenous approach* (IMF Working Paper, WP/16/244).

Gumata, N., & Ndou, E. (2017). *Labour market and fiscal policy adjustments to shocks: The role and implications for price and financial stability in South Africa.* Cham, Switzerland: Palgrave Macmillan.

Hlatshwayo, S., & Saxegaard, M. (2016). *The consequences of policy uncertainty: Disconnects and dilutions in the South African real effective exchange rate-export relationship* (IMF Working Paper, 1, WP/16/113).

Kaldor, N. (1957). A model of GDP growth. *The Economic Journal, 67*(268), 591–624.

Lazear, E., & Rosen, S. (1981). Rank-order tournaments as optimum labor contracts. *Journal of Political Economy, 89*(5), 841–864.

Okun, A. M. (2015). *Equality and efficiency: The big tradeoff.* Washington, DC: Brookings Institution Press.

Ostry, J. D., & Berg, A. (2011). *Inequality and unsustainable growth: Two sides of the same coin?* (International monetary fund SDN/11/08).

Ostry, J. D., Berg, A., & Tsangarides, C. J. (2014). *Redistribution, inequality, and growth.* (International monetary fund SDN/14/02).

Stiglitz, J. E. (2012). *The price of inequality: How today's divided society endangers our future.* New York and London: W. W. Norton.

World Bank. (2018, March). *Overcoming poverty and inequality in South Africa: An assessment of drivers, constraints and opportunities.*

3

Does the Inflation Rate Below 4.5% Matter for the Distributional Effects of Positive Inflation Shocks on Income Inequality in South Africa?

Main Highlights

- Evidence reveals that income inequality growth declines to positive inflation shocks only when inflation is (1) below 3% and (2) when it is below 4.5% threshold level. In addition, employment growth rises significantly and reaches the bigger peak values when inflation is (1) below 3% and (2) below 4.5%. Despite, employment growth rising significantly when inflation is within the 3–6% band or below the 6% threshold, the income inequality growth rises. In addition, evidence reveals that there is a threshold level within the existing inflation target band in which unexpected positive inflation impulses lead to rising GDP growth while reducing income inequality growth.
- This chapter concludes by examining the relevance of the inflation regime below the 4.5% threshold in transmitting expansionary fiscal and monetary policy shocks to income inequality growth. The fiscal policy shocks include increased government consumption, income tax cut.

© The Author(s) 2019
E. Ndou and T. Mokoena, *Inequality, Output-Inflation Trade-Off and Economic Policy Uncertainty*,
https://doi.org/10.1007/978-3-030-19803-9_3

- The amplification effects by the inflation regime below 4.5% threshold is bigger to personal income tax cut shocks, followed by government consumption shocks. This implies expansionary fiscal policy tools can be used to lower income inequality and the reduction is amplified by inflation when it is below 4.5% threshold.

3.1 Introduction

Chapter 2 investigated the income inequality and GDP growth nexus in South Africa and whether the 4.5% consumer price inflation threshold and other channels play a role. Evidence from the counterfactual analysis indicates there are benefits to keeping inflation below the 4.5% threshold compared to above this limit. This is because maintaining inflation below the 4.5% threshold minimises the adverse effects of positive income inequality shocks on GDP growth. This chapter examines the link between inflation and income inequality, amidst the SARB's preference to have consumer price inflation below the 4.5% threshold. It is important to remind economic agents that any useful economic threshold to be taken seriously, should lead to differential reactions of certain economic indicators to shocks above and below the threshold.[1] The failure of any threshold to influence the differential reactions weakens its adoption as the limit value. Based on this aspect of threshold, this chapter argues that the socio-economic benefits of the 4.5% inflation threshold have not been empirically quantified in South Africa. This includes linking the distributional effects of positive inflation shocks on the income inequality above and below the 4.5% consumer price inflation threshold. This chapter adds the influence of the 4.5% inflation threshold in endorsing that price stability is needed to reduce inequality and poverty as in Menna and Tirelli (2017). This reduction is purported to happen when the inflation portfolio composition of the poorer household is skewed towards a larger share of

---

[1] The problem with such threshold is that empirical research advocates for an endogenously determined threshold within a specific economic model.

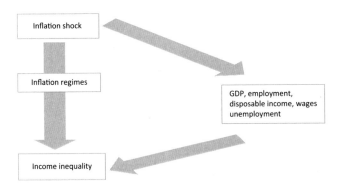

Fig. 3.1 Depiction of the direct and indirect transmission of inflation shock to income inequality (*Source* Authors' drawing)

money holdings. In addition, Bulir (2001) suggests that price stabilisation is beneficial for reducing income inequality through preserving the real value of fiscal transfers.[2]

In linking price stability (*based on the 4.5% consumer price inflation threshold*) and income inequality, this chapter asks the following: Does the 4.5% inflation threshold make income inequality to react differently to the positive inflation shocks above and below this limit? How do the effects of inflationary pressures arising below this threshold compare to those arising within the existing 3–6% band, in influencing income inequality dynamics in South Africa? In addition, does the inflation below the 4.5% threshold transmit expansionary fiscal and monetary policy shocks to income inequality growth? In this regard, the aspects of fiscal policy shocks examined include the increased government consumption, and reduction in personal income tax.

As depicted in Fig. 3.1, the direct influence of positive inflation shocks on income inequality may depend on existing inflation regimes. Whereas, the indirect channels suggest that inflationary shocks are

---

[2]However, other justifications have been pointed out in the literature. Theory suggests that inflation has direct effects on income inequality through various channels, which includes changes in real valuation of financial and nonfinancial assets (Bulir 2001). Whereas Romer and Romer (1999) put forward that high inflation can create expectations of future macroeconomic instability and lead to distortionary economic policies which impact on inequality.

transmitted to income inequality via other channels such as GDP growth, employment growth, wage growth, disposable income growth, and unemployment rate channel. Consequently, this chapter applies a counterfactual analysis to show the size of the amplifications linked to the role of indirect channels in determining the size of the redistributive effects of positive inflation shocks on income inequality. That is, would the income inequality growth react differently in the presence or absence of the indirect channels depicted in Fig. 3.1? Would income inequality react to the positive inflation shock which arises when inflation is below the 4.5% threshold?

Why is it important to revisit the relationship between inflation and income inequality? First, recent studies in other economies suggest that higher inflation rate is accompanied by greater income inequality. However, the strength of the linkage between inflation and income inequality in South Africa is still unknown. Second, the preference by monetary policymakers of the inflation rate to be below 4.5% threshold has not been accompanied by an empirical quantification from the redistributive perspective, which includes income inequality. This is important because the country is portrayed as the most unequal in the world. Third, in the absence of empirical support, it remains unknown if the 4.5% inflation threshold is the most optimal level that can lead to differential effects of inflation shocks on income inequality. This study will reveal if Bulir (2001)'s argument of a U-shaped relationship between inflation and income inequality is applicable below and above the 4.5% threshold. This chapter examines whether the inflation rate below the 4.5% threshold impacts income inequality differently in comparison to other inflation bands and this is discussed in the following sections.[3]

This chapter differs from Bulir (2001) who tests the nonlinear effects of inflation on income inequality through representing inflation with a set of inflation dummies. First, this chapter tests if the South African monetary policymakers' preference for inflation to be below the 4.5% threshold leads to any differential effects of positive inflation shocks on

---

[3]This suggests reducing inflation in high inflation regime may decrease inequality. However, reducing inflation in low inflation regime might come at cost of higher inequality. Albanesi (2007) shows that higher inflation raises income inequality.

the income inequality dynamics above and below this limiting value. Second, the chapter fills policy research gaps as there are no studies from the South African perspective other than Ndou and Gumata (2017) who properly quantify the benefits of inflation below the 4.5% threshold in comparison to other inflation bands. This is despite the policymakers' preference to making 4.5% threshold a de facto target. In addition, there are no studies that have quantified the costs or benefits of keeping inflation at or below 4.5% from the redistributive point of view.[4] Third, this chapter fills policy research gaps by assessing the macroeconomic effects of inflation below 4.5% threshold level in comparison to other inflation bands from the redistributive perspective via the income inequality channel. Furthermore, the chapter fills policy gaps by showing how the redistributive effects of positive inflation shocks are amplified by certain channels. The focus is on the positive inflation shocks when inflation is below 4.5% threshold. Furthermore, the chapter shows the channels that amplify income inequality reaction to inflation shocks when inflation exceeds 6% threshold.

3.2 The Link Between Income Inequality and Other Macroeconomic Variables

The relationships between income inequality and other macroeconomic variables based on scatterplots are shown in Fig. 3.2. Income inequality is captured by the Gini coefficient (*referred to as Gini in the graphs*) and is obtained from Gumata and Ndou (2017). The growth rates used in analysis are at annual rates. The relationship is based on quarterly (Q) data spanning 1993Q1–2016Q3. The scatterplots indicate the direct linkages. The negative relationships in Fig. 3.2a–c show that improvements in GDP growth, employment growth and disposable income growth lower income inequality. In contrast, the positive relationship

---

[4]In addition, Ndou and Gumata (2017) showed that inflation tend to lead to high economic growth when inflation is below 4.5% and government spending amplifies GDP and credit growth. In addition, the trade-off between inflation and output volatility is bigger below the 4.5% inflation rate.

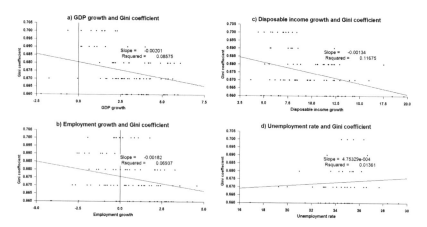

Fig. 3.2 Link between income inequality and other macroeconomic variables (*Source* Authors' calculations)

in Fig. 3.2d suggests that increased unemployment rate raises income inequality.

It is possible that the effects of positive inflation shocks on these variables may be indirectly passed through onto income inequality. Indeed, the later, sections will apply the counterfactual analysis to capture the role of indirect channels depicted in Fig. 3.1. The counterfactual analysis will show the size of the amplifications linked to the influence of the indirect channels in determining the redistributive effects of positive inflation shocks on income inequality.

3.3 Does Inflation Impact the Level and Growth of Income Inequality?

Before examining the nonlinear effects of positive inflation shocks on income inequality, this chapter begins by estimating the relationship between income inequality and consumer price inflation using VAR models. The relationship is determined by estimating bivariate VAR model using quarterly (Q) data from 1993Q1 to 2016Q3. The VAR models are estimated using two lags and 10,000 Monte Carlo draws. The first VAR model (Model 1) includes consumer price

3 Does the Inflation Rate Below 4.5% Matter …   57

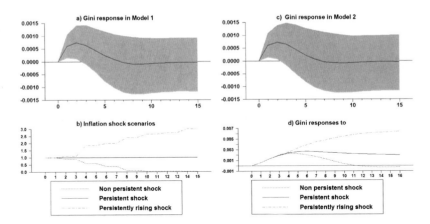

Fig. 3.3 Responses of the Gini coefficient to positive inflation shocks (*Note* The grey shaded band denotes the 16th and 84th percentile confidence bands. *Source* Authors' calculations)

inflation (*referred to as inflation*) and income inequality level.[5] The second VAR model (Model 2) uses the reverse ordering.

In Fig. 3.3, income inequality levels rise significantly for nearly a year to positive inflation shocks. The increase in income inequality to positive inflation shocks is robust to the ordering of variables in the models. In addition, the income inequality levels rise significantly to the persistent positive inflation shocks than to non-persistent impulses.

We further investigate the effects of positive inflation shocks on income inequality growth using VAR models. The bivariate VAR model includes annual consumer price inflation and income inequality growth. The exogenous variables include GDP growth and a dummy for financial crisis that began in 2007 to end of sample and zero otherwise. The model is estimated using two lags and 10,000 Monte Carlo draws. In Fig. 3.4a, income inequality growth rises significantly for eight quarters to an unexpected 1% increase in the inflation rate. At the peak, the income inequality growth rises by 0.2 percentage points. This evidence

---

[5]The use of income inequality in levels is due to test of integration indicating inflation is I(0) and I(1).

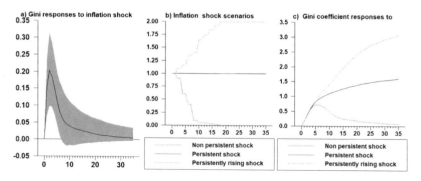

Fig. 3.4 Responses of income inequality growth to positive inflation shocks (*Note* The grey shaded band denotes the 16th and 84th percentile confidence bands. *Source* Authors' calculations)

indicates that rising inflation has distributional effects through increasing the growth of income inequality.

In addition, Fig. 3.4b shows the scenarios of positive inflation shocks. The three scenarios depict (1) persistently rising, (2) persistent, and (3) non-persistent positive inflation shocks. Evidence suggests that the reaction of income inequality growth depends on the persistence of the positive inflation shocks. Income inequality growth rises for long periods to persistently increasing inflation in Fig. 3.4c. In contrast, income inequality rises transitorily to less persistent positive inflationary shocks. This evidence indicates that rising inflation in general raises income inequality growth.

How robust is the increase in income inequality to positive inflation shocks to the addition of other variables? In this instance, GDP growth is added in the models to test the robustness of the results. The results based on the preceding positive inflation shock scenarios are shown in Fig. 3.5. In Fig. 3.5b, positive inflation shocks reduce GDP growth. However, the decline is bigger to a persistently rising positive inflation shock than to a non-persistent shock.

In addition, positive inflation shocks have adverse effects on GDP growth while raising income inequality. Moreover, the income inequality growth rises more to persistent positive inflation shock than to non-persistent shock. The rising income inequality growth following positive inflation shocks is robust to the inclusion of GDP growth of the model.

3 Does the Inflation Rate Below 4.5% Matter ... 59

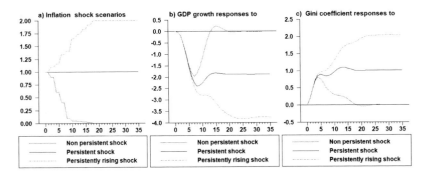

Fig. 3.5 Responses based on the additional model (*Source* Authors' calculations)

3.3.1 How Would Inflation Shocks to Negative Deviations from 4.5% Inflation Rate Impact Income Inequality Growth?

Is it appropriate to generalise the effects of positive inflation shock on increasing income inequality without the use of inflation thresholds? This chapter determines the effects of unexpected reduction in the inflation rate from the 4.5% threshold using three inflation shock scenarios. These are non-persistent, persistent and persistently declining inflation shock. The scenarios of negative inflation shocks are shown in Fig. 3.6a. Impulse responses in Fig. 3.6b, c indicates that the unexpected decline from the 4.5% inflation threshold raises economic growth, while reducing income inequality growth. The increase in GDP growth is much higher when inflation declines much more from the 4.5% threshold level compared to a transitory decline. In addition, the income inequality growth is reduced much more to bigger declines in the inflation rate from the 4.5% compared to that induced by the short-lived deviations from this inflation point. This evidence indicates that inflation shocks have big distributional effects via the income inequality channel, and these effects are minimised when inflation is reduced much more below the 4.5% threshold level.

The analysis further applies the modified version of the Killian and Vigfussion (2011) bivariate VAR asymmetric approach. This will determine whether there are asymmetric effects of shocks to inflation based

60 E. Ndou and T. Mokoena

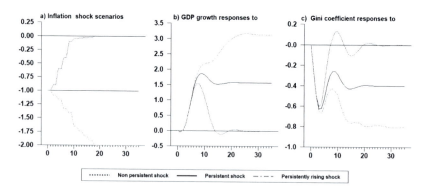

Fig. 3.6 GDP growth and income inequality responses to negative inflation shocks based on deviations from the 4.5% threshold (*Source* Authors' calculations)

on deviations from the 4.5% inflation threshold level. The shocks are measured by standard deviations (s.d.). The results are shown in Figs. 3.7 and 3.8. The income inequality growth declines more to large reductions in inflation from the 4.5% threshold than small sized shocks. This finding implies that the size of negative inflation shocks matter for the reduction in the income inequality growth.

In addition, Fig. 3.8 shows the reactions of income inequality growth to a positive shock to the deviations of inflation from the 4.5% target.

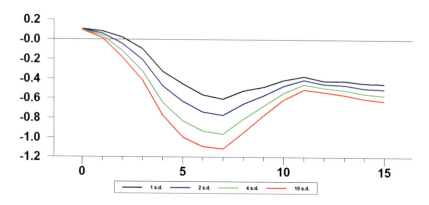

Fig. 3.7 Responses of income inequality growth to negative inflation shocks (*Source* Authors' calculations)

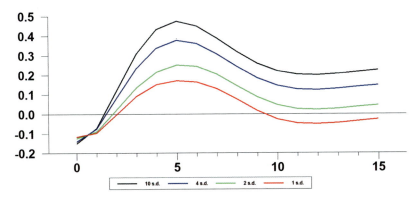

Fig. 3.8 Responses of income inequality growth to positive inflation shocks (*Source* Authors' calculations)

The bigger positive shocks to inflation deviations from 4.5% lead to larger increases in the income inequality growth. Thus, the increase in the income inequality growth gets bigger with the increase in the size of the inflation shocks to those positive deviations of inflation above 4.5% level.

3.3.2 How Beneficial Is Inflation Being Equal or Below the 4.5% Level to Employment Growth and Income Inequality Growth Relationship in Comparison to Other Bands?

This section examines the nonlinear effects of inflation bands on the income inequality growth and employment growth using VAR models. The objective is to distinguish whether positive inflation shocks that arise in the indicated inflation bands matter. The estimated VAR model includes an inflation dummy, income inequality growth and employment growth. The results discussed in this section are robust to different orderings. The inflation dummy equals to the value of the inflation in the indicated band and zero otherwise. The inflation bands are: below 3%, below 4.5%, above 4.5%, 3–6%, below 6% and above 6%. The inflation dummies are included separately in the model. The models are

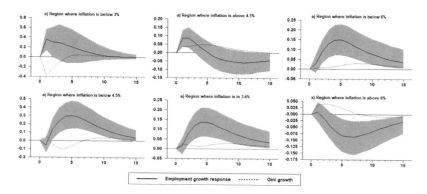

Fig. 3.9 Cumulative responses of income inequality and employment growth to positive inflation shocks in various inflation bands (*Note* The grey shaded band denotes the 16th and 84th percentile confidence bands. *Source* Authors' calculations)

estimated using two lags and 10,000 Monte Carlo draws. Figure 3.9 shows the responses according to inflation bands. The responses of employment growth and income inequality growth to the positive inflation shocks in each band are shown in Fig. 3.9.

It is evident in Fig. 3.9 that income inequality growth declines only when inflation is (1) below 3% and (2) when it is below 4.5% threshold levels respectively. In addition, employment growth rises very much and reaches higher peak values when inflation is (1) below 3% and (2) below 4.5%. Despite, employment growth rising significantly when inflation is in the 3–6% band or below 6% threshold, the income inequality growth rises. This evidence shows that inflation bands matter for the positive inflation shocks to impact the link between income inequality growth and the employment growth dynamics. These findings reveal that there is a threshold level within the existing inflation-target band in which unexpected inflation impulses lead to diverging reactions between employment growth and income inequality growth.

In Fig. 3.9f, employment growth declines while income inequality growth rises to positive inflation shocks which arise when inflation is above the 6% threshold level.

Which inflation band has bigger effects on lowering the income inequality growth while having large stimulatory effects in employment growth? Figure 3.10 shows a comparison of the cumulative responses of income inequality growth and employment growth to positive inflation

3 Does the Inflation Rate Below 4.5% Matter ...

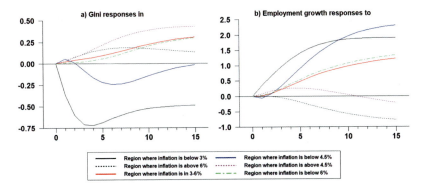

Fig. 3.10 Cumulative responses of income inequality growth and employment growth to positive inflation shocks in various inflation bands (*Source* Authors' calculations)

shocks in the various bands. The peak decline in income inequality growth is realised when inflation is below 3% followed by when inflation is below 4.5%. In addition, the peak employment growth is achieved when inflation is below 3% and below 4.5%. Employment growth rises very little when inflation is in the 3–6% band and below 6%. In addition, employment growth declines more when inflation exceeds 6% than just above 4.5%. This evidence reveals that positive inflation shocks that arise when inflation is below 4.5% threshold have stimulatory effects on employment growth while reducing income inequality growth.

3.3.3 How Beneficial Is When Inflation Is Equal to or Below 4.5% to Economic Growth and Income Inequality in Comparison to Other Bands?

Employment growth is replaced with GDP growth in the preceding VAR model. The objective is to show the reactions of GDP growth and income inequality growth to positive inflation shocks in various inflation bands. The impulse responses are shown in Fig. 3.11. The responses show that positive shocks to inflation when it exceeds 6% have adverse effects on GDP growth while raising income inequality growth.

How robust are the preceding findings to the simultaneous inclusion of economic growth and employment growth in the same model?

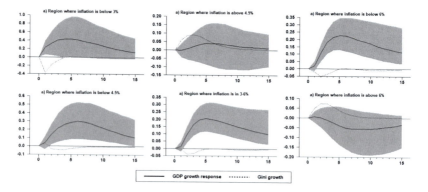

Fig. 3.11 Responses of income inequality growth and GDP growth to positive inflation shocks according to inflation regimes (*Note* The grey shaded band denotes the 16th and 84th percentile confidence bands. *Source* Authors' calculations)

The cumulative impulse responses to positive inflation shocks in the various inflation bands are shown in Fig. 3.12. Income inequality growth declines significantly when inflation is below 3% followed by when inflation is below 4.5%. In addition, the cumulative GDP growth increases are much higher when inflation is below 3% and below 4.5%. Furthermore, employment growth rises much higher when inflation is below 4.5%. These findings are robust to the inclusion of wages growth in the model.

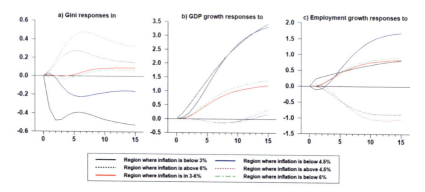

Fig. 3.12 Cumulative responses of income inequality and GDP growth to positive inflation shocks according to inflation regimes (*Source* Authors' calculations)

3.3.4 Do the Inflation Bands Impact the Level of Income Inequality?

This section determines the nonlinear effects of positive inflation shocks on income inequality levels using inflation bands. The inflation bands are: below 3%, less than 4.5%, 3–6%, below 6%, above 4.5%, and above 6%. The inflation bands are captured using the dummy variables. The inflation dummy equals to the value of inflation in the indicated band and zero otherwise. This will reveal the influence of the inflation bands in impacting the income inequality levels based on bivariate VAR models. The impulse responses are shown in Fig. 3.13. All the positive inflationary shocks arising when inflation is below the 6% threshold reduce the level of income inequality. However, the different magnitudes of the decline indicate the nonlinearity of positive inflation shocks on the level of income inequality. The level of income inequality declines much more when inflation is below 3% compared to when inflation is below 4.5%. It is evident that income inequality level declines not very much when inflation is in the 3–6% band as well as below 6%. In contrast, income inequality rises very much when inflation exceeds 4.5 and above 6%.

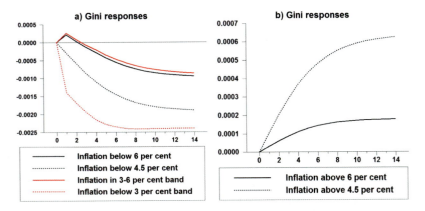

Fig. 3.13 Responses of income inequality level to positive inflation shocks (*Source* Authors' calculations)

3.3.5 Channels of Transmission of Positive Inflation Shocks When Inflation Is Below 4.5% Level

The chapter concludes the investigation by performing a counterfactual analysis to determine the channels (*Channels*) that may transmit the positive inflation shocks when inflation is below the 4.5% threshold level to income inequality. CPI_inflation_below4.5 is dummy which equals to values of inflation below or equal to 4.5% and zero otherwise. The channels examined include determining the role of disposable income growth, employment growth, unemployment rate and GDP growth. This is determined by applying a shutting-off approach using Eqs. (3.1) and (3.2). These models are estimated using 10,000 bootstraps draws.

$$\text{Gini\_growth}_t = \text{constant} + \sum_{i=1}^{4} \text{Gini\_growth}_{t-i}$$

$$+ \sum_{i=0}^{4} \text{Channel}_{t-i} + \text{crisis\_dummy}$$

$$+ \sum_{i=0}^{2} \text{CPI\_inflation\_below } 4.5_{t-i} + \varepsilon_t \quad (3.1)$$

$$\text{Gini\_growth}_t = \text{constant}$$

$$+ \sum_{i=1}^{4} \text{Gini\_growth}_{t-i} + \text{crisis\_dummy}$$

$$+ \sum_{i=0}^{2} \text{CPI\_inflation\_below } 4.5_{t-i} + \varepsilon_t \quad (3.2)$$

Equation (3.2) shuts off each channel in transmitting the effects of positive inflation shocks to income inequality growth. The gap between the actual response of income inequality growth and the counterfactual response measures the influence of the indicated channel. In Fig. 3.14a, income inequality growth declines more in the presence of disposable

3 Does the Inflation Rate Below 4.5% Matter ...

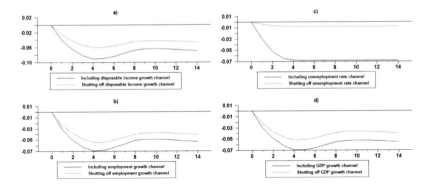

Fig. 3.14 Actual and counterfactual cumulative responses of income inequality growth to positive inflation shocks when inflation is below 4.5% and role of selected channels (*Source* Authors' calculations)

income channel than when this channel is shut off in the model. In addition, in Fig. 3.14b income inequality growth declines more in the presence of the high employment growth than when this channel is shut off in the model. This evidence suggests that inflation being below the 4.5% threshold level enables the reduction in income inequality growth and this is facilitated by increasing employment growth and disposable income growth. Figure 3.14c reveals that income inequality growth declines more in the presence of low unemployment rate than when this channel is shut off in the model. Figure 3.14d reveals that income inequality growth declines more in the presence of the high GDP growth than when this channel is shut off in the model.

This analysis further shows the influence of different channels in passing through positive inflationary shocks in the region where inflation exceeds 6% to income inequality growth. The analysis distinguishes between the roles of *negative GDP growth episodes* from those when *GDP growth is positive*. Two GDP growth dummy variables are constructed to separate the role of economic growth expansionary phases from the contractionary phases. The negative GDP growth dummy is equal to the negative GDP growth rates and zero otherwise. The positive GDP growth dummy is equal to the positive GDP growth rates and zero otherwise. This section separates the roles of economic growth expansionary and contractionary phases in the transmission of positive inflation shocks to income inequality growth. In addition, the results also show the role of wage growth and the unemployment rate channels. The analysis applies the counterfactual approach to determine the role of the business cycle, wages growth and unemployment rate channels in transmitting positive inflation shocks to income inequality growth using models (3.3) and (3.4). CPI_inflation_above6 is dummy which equals values of inflation above 6% and zero otherwise. The equations are estimated using 10,000 bootstraps draws.

$$\text{Gini\_growth}_t = \text{constant} + \sum_{i=1}^{4} \text{Gini\_growth}_{t-i}$$

$$+ \sum_{i=0}^{4} \text{Channel}_{t-i} + \text{crisis\_dummy}$$

$$+ \sum_{i=0}^{2} \text{CPI\_inflation\_above } 6_{t-i} + \varepsilon_t \qquad (3.3)$$

$$\text{Gini\_growth}_t = \text{constant}$$

$$+ \sum_{i=1}^{4} \text{Gini\_growth}_{t-i} + \text{crisis\_dummy}$$

$$+ \sum_{i=0}^{2} \text{CPI\_inflation\_above } 6_{t-i} + \varepsilon_t \qquad (3.4)$$

In Fig. 3.15, income inequality growth rises more than the counterfactual to positive inflation shocks when inflation exceeds the 6% level. The big amplification in income inequality growth is due to the negative GDP growth followed by wage growth channel. The unemployment rate channel has the least amplifying effects on the income inequality growth reaction to the positive inflation shocks when inflation exceeds 6%.

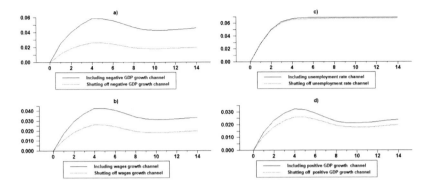

Fig. 3.15 Cumulative income inequality growth responses to positive inflation shocks when inflation exceeds 6% (*Source* Authors' calculations)

3.3.6 Policy Implications Based on the Role of Inflation Below the 4.5% Threshold

This analysis concludes by examining the role of the consumer price inflation below 4.5% threshold in transmitting expansionary policy shocks to income inequality. The VAR model is estimated with two lags and 10,000 Monte Carlo draws. This includes examining the effects of following policy shocks namely: (1) expansionary government consumption spending shock, (2) income tax cut shock, and (3) expansionary monetary policy shock. This is determined by estimating counterfactual VAR models which includes a policy variable, income inequality growth, and inflation dummy. The policy variables include growth of government consumption spending, growth of income tax and changes in the repo rate. The inflation dummy is equal to the value of inflation when it is below 4.5% and zero otherwise. The models include GDP growth, employment growth, exchange rate changes and dummy for financial crisis beginning in 2007 as exogenous variables. The inflation dummy variable is shut off in the model to determine the counterfactual responses. Figure 3.16 shows the cumulative actual and counterfactual responses. In all instances, the actual responses decline more than the counterfactual. This suggests that inflation below 4.5% threshold enables the reduction in income inequality growth. Therefore,

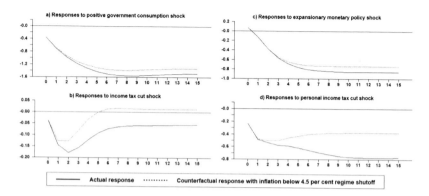

Fig. 3.16 Cumulative response of income inequality to policy shocks and role of inflation below the 4.5% threshold (*Source* Authors' calculations)

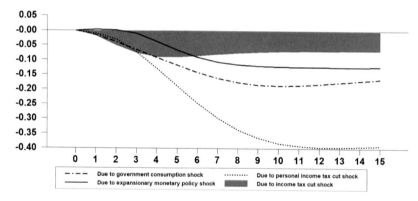

Fig. 3.17 Comparison of sizes of amplifications (*Source* Authors' calculations)

it is important to keep inflation below the 4.5% threshold to amplify the potency of expansionary policies in reducing growth of income inequality.

The magnitudes of amplifications by inflation below 4.5% threshold from the preceding graph are shown in Fig. 3.17. The amplifications by the inflation channel are bigger to personal income tax cut shocks followed by government consumption spending shocks. Among the shocks the income tax cut shock has the least effect amplified by inflation below 4.5 threshold.

3.4 Conclusion

Does the 4.5% inflation threshold exert differential effects of positive inflation shocks on income inequality above and below it? How do the effects of inflationary shocks arising below this threshold compare to those arising within the existing target band in driving income inequality in South Africa? Evidence reveals that income inequality growth declines to positive inflation shocks only when inflation is (1) below 3% and (2) when it is below the 4.5% threshold level. In addition, employment growth rises very much and reaches peak values when inflation is (1) below 3% and (2) below 4.5%. Despite employment growth rising significantly when inflation is within the 3–6% band or below 6% threshold, income inequality growth rises. In addition, evidence reveals that there is a threshold level within the existing inflation target band in which unexpected positive inflation impulses lead to rising GDP growth while reducing income inequality growth. This chapter concludes by examining the relevance of the inflation regime below the 4.5% threshold in transmitting expansionary fiscal and monetary policy shocks to income inequality growth. The fiscal policy shocks include increased government consumption, personnel income tax cut and income tax reduction. The amplification by the inflation regime below the 4.5% threshold is bigger to personal income tax cut shocks followed by government consumption shocks. This implies expansionary fiscal policy tools can be used to lower income inequality; and the reduction is amplified by inflation when it is below 4.5% threshold.

References

Albanesi, S. (2007). Inflation and income inequality. *Journal of Monetary Economics, 54*(4), 1088–1114.

Bulir, A. (2001). Income inequality: Does inflation matter? *IMF Staff Chapter, 48*(1), 139–159.

Gumata, N., & Ndou, E. (2017). *Labour market and fiscal policy adjustments to shocks: The role and implications for price and financial stability in South Africa.* Cham: Palgrave Macmillan.

Killian, L., & Vigfussion, R.J. (2011). Are the responses of the US economy asymmetric in energy price increases and decreases. *Quantitative Economics, 2*(3), 417–453.

Menna, L., & Tirelli, P. (2017). Optimal inflation to reduce inequality. *Review of Economic Dynamics, 24,* 79–94.

Romer, C.D., & Romer, D. (1999). Monetary policy and the well-being of the poor. *Economic Review, Federal Reserve Bank of Kansas City* (first quarter), 21–49.

Part II
Inequality and Monetary Policy

4

Does the Income Inequality Channel Impact the Transmission of Monetary Policy Shocks to Economic Activity?

Main Highlights

- This chapter examines the extent to which income inequality in South Africa impacts the transmission of monetary policy shocks to the aggregate economy using counterfactual approaches.
- Evidence reveals that the income inequality channel accentuates the decline in real economic activity following contractionary monetary policy shocks.
- In addition, income inequality dampens the increases in marginal propensity to consume, employment growth, GDP growth and disposable income growth due to the expansionary monetary policy shocks.
- From a policy perspective, Monnin (2017) argues that income inequality matters in understanding and gauging the reaction of the economy to monetary policy impulses and decision makers should take this dimension into account when designing and calibrating policies. This dimension should be considered despite income inequality not being depicted in the standard monetary policy transmission mechanism, but recent evidence indicates it should be part of the transmission channels.

© The Author(s) 2019

E. Ndou and T. Mokoena, *Inequality, Output-Inflation Trade-Off and Economic Policy Uncertainty*,
https://doi.org/10.1007/978-3-030-19803-9_4

75

4.1 Introduction

South Africa has been reported to exhibit high income disparities and is ranked amongst the most unequal societies in the world. Recent empirical findings indicate that income distribution may influence the transmission of monetary policy shocks, which has wider implications on economic activity. Hence, the discussions regarding the link between monetary policy and income inequality dynamics is inevitable. This study assesses whether income inequality is a conduit that transmits monetary policy shocks to real economic activity. As depicted in Fig. 4.1, monetary policy shocks may impact the real economic activity either directly or indirectly. In the two-stage transmission mechanism, the monetary policy shocks will first impact income inequality, thereafter, impact real economic activity. This chapter shows that it is important to quantify the sizes of the indirect effects of monetary policy shocks passed onto the real economic activity via the income inequality channel.

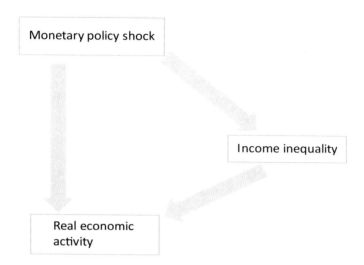

Fig. 4.1 Direct and indirect channels of monetary policy shock transmission (*Source* Authors' drawing)

4 Does the income inequality channel impact ... 77

This chapter does not investigate the influence of monetary policy shocks on income distribution, but examines the extent to which the income inequality channel impacts the transmission of monetary policy shocks to real economic activity. So, what would have happened to the reaction of certain economic indicators when the income inequality channel is shut off in transmitting the monetary policy shocks? Does the income inequality channel accentuate or dampen the transmission of monetary policy shocks to real economic activity? The findings from this assessment may help in facilitating the design of effective monetary policy transmission mechanism. This is because the attainment of price stability is also a *public good*. Hence, if income inequality impedes or exacerbates the transmission of monetary policy shocks, then the implementation of structural reforms needs to be intensified to eliminate income inequality and its adverse effects.

Why is determining whether income inequality impacts monetary policy transmission mechanism important from the South African perspective? First, empirical evidence from other studies indicates that income inequality may impede the transmission of monetary policy shocks to real economic activity. In addition, other studies indicate that via the limited asset participation, which is most likely due to income inequality, this may alter the transmission of monetary policy shocks to aggregate demand in new the Keynesian model. This suggests that monetary policy conduct must be adapted to reflect this. In addition, Bilbie (2008) suggests that the size of the excluded group matters in determining the magnitude and the direction of the impact of monetary policy shocks on the economy.[1] Furthermore, Voinea and Monnin (2017) point out that taking income inequality concerns seriously can strengthen the central banks' independence and improve their policy decisions. Moreover, Monnin (2017) suggests that central banks

---

[1]It is indicated in Areosa and Areosa (2016) that the combination of heterogeneous labour productivity among households and limited financial market participation is linked to inflation and inequality.

wishing to stimulate aggregate demand should try to reach the people who will react most strongly to changes in income distribution, including disposable income. Studies such as Guerello (2016) reveal that consumption elasticity due to monetary policy shocks depends on income distribution.[2] Hence, the income inequality channel may not be ignored in the transmission of monetary policy changes.

Theory suggests that households' responses to monetary policy changes depend on different conditions. These conditions include the differing marginal propensities to consume of different income groups, differing households' access to banks, or financial markets. These characteristics may influence the monetary policy transmission mechanism. This may be limited for low income households to both the direct and indirect impacts following changes in interest rates. The impact of monetary policy changes depends on each household's income, indebtedness profile, and disposable income. Thus, income distribution can induce different impacts on the economy for the same monetary policy shock.

This chapter does not refute the benefits linked to the enforcement of price stability mandate by a central bank, in supporting the purchasing power of a currency. This may presupposes that preserving the purchasing power reduces income inequality. This presumption seems to ignore the existence of the U-shaped influence of inflation on income inequality found in Bulir (2001). The nonlinear relationship suggests that there is an optimal inflation rate around which both low and high inflation may raise income inequality. Despite the non-recognition of the U-shaped or nonlinearity, policymakers have not indicated the extent to which the income inequality channel influences the transmission of monetary policy decisions. The prevalence of this income inequality channel is still unknown in South Africa. This chapter fills policy research gaps by examining the extent to which income distribution in South Africa influences the transmission of monetary policy shocks using counterfactual models. Second, the chapter fills policy research gaps by assessing whether the income inequality channel accentuates

---

[2]Voinea and Monnin (2017) find that the transmission of monetary policy is more efficient for middle income households.

or dampens the transmission of monetary policy shocks to real economic activity. Third, this chapter fills policy research gaps by showing monetary policymakers, that it is, important to understand and quantify the extent to which policy decisions and income distribution are intertwined. Recent literature argues that this may help policymakers to better and efficiently design and even implement effective monetary policy decisions.[3]

4.2 Does the Income Inequality Channel Impact the Transmission of Monetary Policy Shocks to Real Economic Activity?

The analysis begins by examining the extent to which income inequality impacts the responses of GDP growth, household consumption growth, employment growth, marginal propensity to consume and unemployment.[4] The analysis uses quarterly (Q) data spanning 1993Q1 to 2016Q3. This analysis performs counterfactual VAR analysis to determine whether the income inequality channel accentuates or dampens contractionary monetary policy shocks to various economic activities. The counterfactual VAR model includes the policy rate, a selected economic indicator, and income inequality growth. The income inequality is captured by the Gini coefficient used in Gumata and Ndou (2017) and other data are sourced from the South African Reserve Bank. The models are estimated using two lags and 10,000 Monte Carlo draws. All growth rates denote year-on-year changes. The counterfactual impulse responses shut off the income inequality growth channel in transmitting the effects of contractionary monetary policy shocks to real economic activity. The gap between the actual response of the economic indicator and its counterfactual is a measure of the influence of the income inequality channel in transmitting contractionary monetary policy shocks.

---

[3]This requires estimating the magnitude of the inequality transmission channel through which monetary policy influences the economy.

[4]This is calculated as 5 year rolling impact of household disposable income on household consumption.

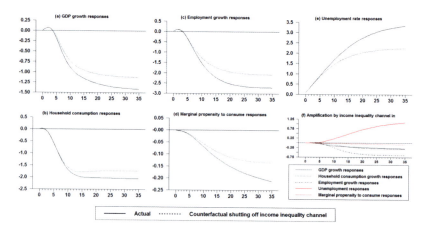

Fig. 4.2 Cumulative responses to contractionary monetary policy shocks and the role of the income inequality channel (*Source* Authors' calculations)

In Fig. 4.2 contractionary monetary policy shocks reduce GDP growth, household consumption growth, employment growth and marginal propensity to consume. However, the unemployment rate rises following a contractionary monetary policy shock. The actual GDP growth, household consumption growth, employment growth and marginal propensity to consume decline more than the counterfactual suggests. This evidence shows that the rise in income inequality, following a contractionary monetary policy shock, accentuates the decline in real economic activity.

The actual unemployment rate rises more than the counterfactual suggests following a contractionary monetary policy shock. This shows that rising income inequality, following a contractionary monetary policy shock, accentuates the increase in the unemployment rate. This finding indicates that the impacts of contractionary monetary policy shocks get amplified by the high income inequality. Hence, policymakers should be cognisant that their expected impacts may be worsened by the unintended consequences via the redistributive channel due to the adverse influence of increased income inequality. Such outcomes probably may require decision makers to thoroughly consider the adjustment of the size of policy rate adjustments.

4 Does the income inequality channel impact ...

$$\text{Macro}_t = \text{constant} + \sum_{i=1}^{4} \text{Macro}_{t-i} + \sum_{i=0}^{4} \text{Cpi\_inflation}_{t-i}$$
$$+ \sum_{i=0}^{1} \text{Repo rate}_{t-i} + \varepsilon_t \tag{4.1}$$

$$\text{Macro}_t = \text{constant} + \sum_{i=1}^{4} \text{Macro}_{t-i} + \sum_{i=0}^{4} \text{Cpi\_inflation}_{t-i}$$
$$+ \sum_{i=0}^{4} \text{Gini}_{t-i} + \sum_{t=0}^{1} \text{Repo rate}_{t-i} + \varepsilon_t \tag{4.2}$$

The robustness of the preceding finding is tested using Eqs. (4.1) and (4.2). The *Macro* in both equations refers to the household consumption growth, GDP growth, employment growth and unemployment rate variables. These variables are included separately in the model. The gap between the actual and counterfactual responses captures the size of the amplifications due to the income inequality channel. The impulse responses are shown in Fig. 4.3.

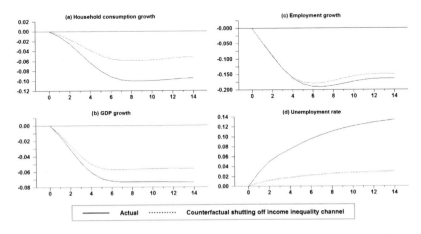

Fig. 4.3 Cumulative actual and counterfactual responses to contractionary monetary policy shock and the role of the income inequality channel (*Source* Authors' calculations)

4.2.1 Does the Transmission of the Expansionary Monetary Policy Shocks Get Impacted by the Income Inequality Channel?

The analysis further examines the extent to which the income inequality channel impacts the transmission of the expansionary monetary policy shocks to employment growth, disposable income growth, GDP growth and household consumption growth. Figure 4.4 shows the cumulative actual and counterfactual responses. In all these cases, the counterfactual exceeds the actual responses.

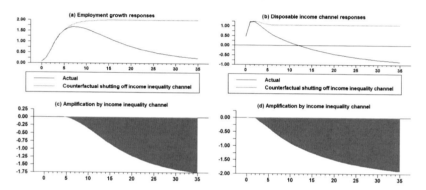

Fig. 4.4 Cumulative responses to contractionary monetary policy shocks and the role of the income inequality channel (*Source* Authors' calculations)

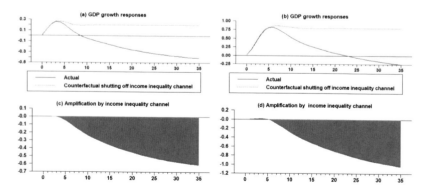

Fig. 4.5 Cumulative responses to contractionary monetary policy shocks and the role of the income inequality channel (*Source* Authors' calculations)

This suggests that the income inequality channel dampens the increase in employment growth, GDP growth and household disposable income growth. This may be reflective of the role of earnings and wages inequalities in explaining the dampening effects. Figure 4.5 shows the cumulative responses to expansionary monetary policy shocks and the role of the income inequality channel. GDP growth rises less than counterfactual suggests. This indicates that income inequality dampens the rising GDP growth.

4.2.2 Does the Income Inequality Channel Transmit Monetary Policy Shocks Asymmetrically to Marginal Propensity to Consume?

This chapter further examines the responses of the marginal propensity to consume (MPC) to contractionary and expansionary monetary policy shocks. The contractionary monetary policy dummy is equal to the value of positive repo rate changes and zero otherwise. In contrast, the expansionary monetary policy dummy is equal to the value of negative repo rate changes and zero otherwise. These policy dummies replace the policy rate in the preceding counterfactual VAR model but are included in the model separately. In Fig. 4.6, the contractionary monetary policy shocks reduce the marginal propensity to consume. However, the actual marginal propensity to consume (MPC) declines more than the

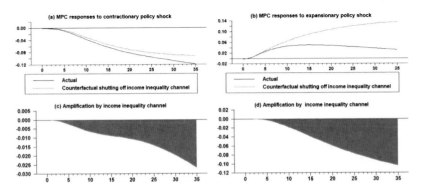

Fig. 4.6 Cumulative responses to contractionary monetary policy shocks and the role of the income inequality channel (*Source* Authors' calculations)

counterfactual suggests. Thus, the increase in income inequality, following the contractionary monetary policy shock, worsens the decline in the marginal propensity to consume. In contrast, the expansionary monetary policy shocks raise both the actual and counterfactual marginal propensities to consume. But the counterfactual reactions exceed the actual responses. This evidence shows that the influence of the income inequality channel cannot be ignored in the discussions of the monetary policy transmission mechanism. This is despite, income inequality not being depicted in the standard transmission mechanism.

4.3 Conclusion and Policy Implications

This chapter examined the extent to which income inequality in South Africa impacted the transmission of monetary policy shocks to the aggregate economy using counterfactual approaches. That is, does the income inequality channel accentuate or dampen the transmission of monetary policy shocks to real economic activity? This assessment is important in facilitating the design of effective monetary policy reactions in which the attainment of price stability is a *public good* (Voinea and Monnin 2017). Evidence reveals that the income inequality channel accentuates the decline in real economic activity following the contractionary monetary policy shocks. In addition, income inequality dampens the increases in marginal propensity to consume, employment growth, GDP growth and disposable income growth due to expansionary monetary policy shocks. Monnin (2017) argues that income inequality matters in understanding and gauging the reaction of the economy to monetary policy impulses and decision makers should take this dimension into account when designing and calibrating policies. This should be considered despite income inequality not being depicted in the standard monetary policy transmission mechanism, but recent evidence indicates it should be part of the transmission channels. For instance, Voinea and Monnin (2017) suggest that the banking-sector statistics, when published, should include the distribution of deposits and credits by income groups. This is because a policy that benefits only a few without displaying undeniable aggregate welfare improvement should be considered with caution by decision makers.

References

Areosa, W. D., & Areosa, M. B. M. (2016). Inequality channel of monetary transmission. *Journal of Macroeconomics, 48*, 214–230.

Auclert, A. (2016). *Monetary policy and redistribution channel.* https://web.stanford.edu/~aauclert/mp_redistribution.pdf.

Auclert, A., & Rognlie, M. (2016). http://web.stanford.edu/~aauclert/inequads.pdf.

Bilbie, F. O. (2008). Limited asset markets participation, monetary policy and inverted aggregate demand logic. *Journal of economic theory, 31*(2), 463–496.

Bivens, J. (2011). *Gauging the impact of the fed on inequality during the recession.* https://www.frbsf.org/economic-research/files/el2011-21.pdf.

Bulir, A. (2001). Income inequality: Does inflation matter? *IMF Staff Papers, 48*(11), 1–5. Palgrave Macmillan.

Coibion, O. (2012). Are the effects of monetary policy shocks big or small? *American Economic Journal of Macroeconomics, 4*(2), 1–32.

Coibion, O., Gorodnichenko, Y., Kueng, L., & Silvia, J. (2017). *Innocent bystanders? Monetary policy and inequality in the US.* https://www.nber.org/papers/w18170.

Doepke, M., Scheneider, M., & Selezneva, V. (2015). *Distribution effects of monetary policy* (Working Paper).

Furceri, D., & Loungani, P. (2018). The distributional effects of capital account liberalization. *Journal of Development Economics, 130*, 127–144.

Guerello, C. (2016). *Conventional and unconventional monetary policy vs. households income distribution: An empirical analysis for the euro area* (mimeo).

Gumata, N., & Ndou, E. (2017). *Labour market and fiscal policy adjustments to shocks: The role and implications for price and financial stability in South Africa.* Cham, Switzerland: Palgrave Macmillan.

Koedijk, K., Loungani, P., & Monnin, P. (2018). Monetary policy, macroprudential regulation and inequality: An introduction to the special section. *Journal of international money and finance, 85*, 163–167.

Monnin, P. (2017). *Monetary policy, macroprudential regulation and inequality* (ECP, Discussion Note 2017/2).

Mumtaz, H., & Theophilopoulou, A. (2017). The impact of monetary policy on inequality in the UK. An empirical analysis. *European Economic Review, 98,* 410–423.

O'farrell, R., Rawdanowicz, L., & Inaba, K. (2016). *Monetary policy and inequality* (OECD Economics Department Working Paper No. 1281). Paris: OECD Publishing.

Voinea, L., & Monnin, P. (2017). *Inequality should matter for central banks.*

Zdzienicka, A., Chen, S., Diaz Kalan, F., Laseen, S., & Svirydzenk, K. (2015). *Effects of monetary and macroprudential policies on financial conditions: Evidence from the United States* (IMF Working Paper 15/288).

5

Do Monetary Policy Shocks Influence Income Inequality Dynamics in South Africa?

Main Highlights

- Evidence indicates that expansionary monetary policy shocks reduces income inequality significantly for nearly a year. This confirms the prevalence of the distributive effects of monetary policy changes.
- We find that income inequality declines due to expansionary monetary policy shocks and the declines are significantly bigger when inflation is below 4.5% and when it is within 4.5–6% and below 3%.
- A counterfactual analysis reveals that actual income inequality growth declines more in the presence of employment growth, economic growth, and household disposable income growth channels, than when these channels are shut off. This indicates that increases in employment growth, disposable income growth and GDP growth, following an expansionary monetary policy shock, amplify the reductions in income inequality growth.
- This evidence implies that policymakers should create more jobs and raise economic growth for these channels to amplify the effects of expansionary monetary policy shocks in reduce income inequality growth.

© The Author(s) 2019
E. Ndou and T. Mokoena, *Inequality, Output-Inflation Trade-Off and Economic Policy Uncertainty*,
https://doi.org/10.1007/978-3-030-19803-9_5

87

- Conclusions from recent studies suggest that having a solid grasp of the ways that monetary policy decisions, income inequality, and aggregate economy, are intertwined is important for an efficient design and implementation of monetary policy.

5.1 Introduction

Chapter 4 examined the extent to which income inequality in South Africa impacts the transmission of monetary policy shocks to the aggregate economy using counterfactual approaches. Evidence reveals that the income inequality channel accentuates the decline in real economic activity following contractionary monetary policy shocks. From a policy perspective, Monnin (2017) argues that income inequality matters in understanding and gauging the reaction of the economy to monetary policy impulses, and decision makers should take this dimension into account when designing and calibrating policies. This should be considered despite income inequality not being depicted in the standard monetary policy transmission mechanism, but recent evidence indicates it should be part of the transmission channels.

Chapter 4 examined the indirect role of income inequality in transmitting shocks to real economic activity. This chapter examines the direct effects of monetary policy shocks on income inequality. This is due to debates regarding the interaction between monetary policy and the increasing dispersion of income distribution after the United States of America (US) Fed, Bank of England and European Central Bank embarked on stimulus activities following the recent financial crisis. Hence, the opinions from central bankers, such as, Carney (2016) arguing that all monetary policy actions have distributional effects matter. This is echoed by Voinea and Monnin (2017) who advises that taking income inequality concerns seriously would strengthen central banks' independence and improve their policy decisions. In addition, central bankers in the US have examined the link between monetary policy and income inequality. In view of other central bankers' concerns about income inequality, this chapter asks: Do monetary policy shocks influence income inequality dynamics in South Africa? In addition, to what extent do wages inflation, consumer price inflation, employment growth, economic growth, and household disposable income growth, transmit expansionary monetary policy shocks to growth of income inequality? The findings in this empirical undertaking should not be viewed as advocating for monetary policy to be used to solve income inequality problems in South Africa. Rather, the objective is to determine if the effects from a South African perspective differ from those observed in other countries.

Theory does not refute the link between monetary policy actions and income inequality. However, theories indicate that the directional response of income inequality to monetary policy decisions may be different, reflecting the structure of income distribution. For instance, the income composition hypothesis suggests that monetary policy changes have a bigger impact on the low income households who get a large share of income from labour.[1] In addition, the labour income heterogeneity theory suggests that an increase in labour market income activity due to expansionary monetary policy will benefit low income households more and probably reduce income inequality. Furthermore, the capital income heterogeneity theory postulates that expansionary monetary policy has different effects on the returns of different assets for the households who do not hold the same asset portfolios. An empirical undertaking is needed to ascertain the link in South Africa.

Why has literature taken so long to look at the link between monetary policy and income inequality and determining which economic channels amplify the effects in South Africa? First, this may be explained by the inference from Voinea and Monnin's (2017) suggestion that the impacts of monetary policy might be negligible or even offsetting each other. However, without an empirical undertaking it will be inadequate to use this suggestion as an a priori to rule out at least some unintended distributive consequences of the monetary policy actions. Secondly, recent studies reveal that all kinds of economic policy actions, including monetary policy, have some distributional impact. Third, the

---

[1] These would benefit more from monetary policy action that boosts labour returns more than returns on capital.

price stability objective does not exempt central bankers from assessing the impacts of their actions on the distribution of income. This should be more pertinent if monetary policy shocks have intended outcomes.

The influence of monetary policy changes on income inequality dynamics is important for the following reasons. First, studies such as Furceri and Loungani (2018) reveal that the distribution of income and changes in this distribution may affect the transmission mechanism of monetary policy. Second, studies suggest that central banks, primarily concerned with aggregate effects of their policies, may benefit much more from understanding the impacts of their policies on income inequality. This is because attaining balanced economic growth, which encompasses the distribution of the benefits and costs of price stability, is also a *public good* (Voinea and Monnin 2017).

To a large extent recent evidence does not refute that monetary policy has distributional effects in other economies. In fact, evidence points to the potency of both expansionary and contractionary monetary policy shocks on income inequality. For instance, Guerello (2016) finds that expansionary monetary policy leads to a decrease in income inequality. Mumtaz and Theophilopolou (2017) found that expansionary monetary policy reduces income inequality significantly.[2] Huber and Stephens (2014) find that a 100-basis-point reduction in the policy rate reduces the Gini coefficient by 0.4%. In addition, Bivens (2015) shows that expansionary monetary policy could reduce income inequality if the economy is close to full employment. Furthermore, Furceri and Loungani (2018) found the decrease in income inequality after an unexpected monetary policy expansion is greater in countries with a higher share of labour income, indicative of the labour income heterogeneity channel or the income composition channel that affects income inequality. Moreover, Coibion et al. (2017) find that monetary policy tightening in the US increases income inequality for high-earning households and lowers labour income for low-earning households.[3]

---

[2]See also Coibion et al. (2017).

[3]O'Farrell et al. (2016) found a 1 percentage point decrease in the policy rate decreases the Gini coefficient by up to 0.02% after 3 years. In addition, Guerello (2016) finds similar results for the Euro area. See also Colciago et al. (2018) for comparison.

This chapter fills policy research gaps in the link between monetary policy actions and income inequality. First, the chapter fills policy research gaps by showing the counterfactual effects and whether the persistence of shocks matters. Second, this chapter differs from Furceri and Loungani (2018) as we do not point only to asymmetric effects of positive and negative monetary policy shocks, but, we determine the extent of the impact of the size of asymmetric expansionary monetary policy shocks on income inequality. The chapter further fills policy research gaps by comparing the sizes of the amplifications by different channels due to expansionary monetary policy shocks on income inequality growth. Empirical evidence shows that the impact of expansionary monetary policy shocks depends on the business cycle phases and the inflation regimes. The effects are bigger especially when the consumer price inflation is below the 4.5% threshold. The empirical findings are robust to different model specifications.

5.2 Do Monetary Policy Shocks Have an Impact Income Inequality in South Africa?

The analysis begins by examining the responses of the growth of income inequality (Gini_g_{t-i}) to positive and negative monetary policy shocks. This is based on Eq. (5.1). The negative and positive repurchase rate changes are captured by Repo_change and these are included separately in the model. The repo rate change variable (Repo_change) is replaced by two dummy variables, which are included in the model interchangeably. The negative changes dummy is equal to negative values of the repo rate changes and zero otherwise. The positive changes dummy equal to positive values of the repo rate changes and zero otherwise. The other variables include the following: employment growth (Employment_g_{t-i}), consumer price inflation (CPI_inflation), and GDP growth (GDP_g_{t-i}). All the growth rates are annual rates. The model is estimated using 10 000 bootstrap draws. The consumer price inflation is referred to as inflation. The section uses quarterly (Q) data spanning 1993Q1–2016Q3. The income inequality is captured by the Gini coefficient used in Gumata and Ndou (2017) and other data are sourced from the South African Reserve Bank.

$$\text{Gini\_g}_t = \text{constant} + \sum_{i=1}^{4} \text{Gini\_g}_{t-i} + \sum_{i=0}^{4} \text{Employment\_g}_{t-i}$$
$$+ \sum_{i=0}^{4} \text{GDP\_g}_{t-i} + \sum_{i=0}^{4} \text{CPI\_inflation}_{t-i}$$
$$+ \sum_{i=0}^{2} \text{Repo\_change}_{t-i} + \text{crisis\_dummy} \qquad (5.1)$$

Figure 5.1 shows the responses of income inequality growth to monetary policy shocks. All shocks denote one per cent change in the repo rate. An expansionary monetary policy shock lowers income inequality growth and the peak decline of nearly 0.3 percentage points occurs in the second quarter. The significant reduction in income inequality lasts for four quarters. In contrast, the contractionary monetary policy shock raises income inequality significantly for nearly four quarters. The peak increase in income inequality is nearly 0.2 percentage points. Thus, both expansionary and contractionary monetary policy shocks have a significant impact on the income inequality dynamics.

The analysis further examines the responses of the level of income inequality to expansionary monetary policy shocks and whether the responses are influenced by high and low inflation regimes. To avoid

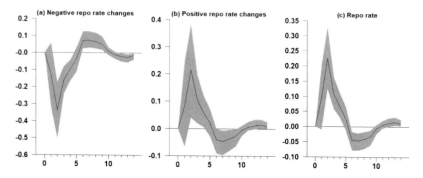

Fig. 5.1 Responses of income inequality growth to monetary policy shocks according to policy changes (*Note* The grey shaded bands denotes the 16th and 84th percentile confidence bands. *Source* Authors' calculations)

5 Do Monetary Policy Shocks Influence Income ...

overgeneralising the role of inflation and to enable proper policy advice we consider the 4.5% inflation threshold, this is midpoint of target band. This section separates inflation into various bands. The bands include the following: inflation below 3%; inflation below 4.5%, and inflation between 4.5 and 6%. Three policy rate dummy variables are constructed to capture the changes in the policy rate constrained by where inflation may be at the time in each band. The first policy rate dummy equals to the values of negative changes in the repo rate when inflation is below or equal to 3% and zero otherwise. The second policy rate dummy is equal to the negative changes in the repo rate when inflation is below or equal to 4.5% and zero otherwise. The third policy rate dummy is equal to negative changes in the repo rate when inflation is in 4.5–6% band and zero otherwise. The Repo_change in Eq. (5.1) is replaced with the policy rate dummies and these are included in the model separately.

The responses of the income inequality to monetary policy changes based on the inflation regimes are shown in Fig. 5.2. Income inequality declines to expansionary monetary policy and the declines are significantly bigger when inflation is below 4.5% and when it is within 4.5–6% than just below 3%.

We further assess the influence of GDP growth regimes on impacting the role of expansionary monetary policy shocks on the level of income inequality. Three economic growth aspects examined include:

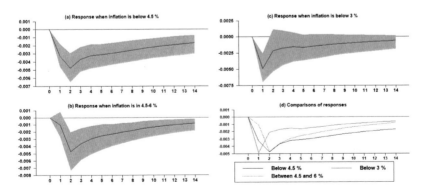

Fig. 5.2 Income inequality responses to expansionary monetary policy shocks based on inflation regimes (*Note* The grey shaded bands denotes the 16th and 84th percentile confidence bands. *Source* Authors' calculations)

(1) no growth or contractionary phases; (2) expansionary phases; and (3) without considering economic growth phases. This is determined by estimating Eq. (5.2).

$$\text{Gini}\_g_t = \text{constant} + \sum_{i=1}^{4}\text{Gini}\_g_{t-i} + \sum_{i=0}^{4}\text{Employment}\_g_{t-i}$$

$$+ \sum_{i=0}^{4}\text{GDP}\_g_{t-i} + \sum_{i=0}^{4}\text{CPI\_inflation}_{t-i}$$

$$+ \sum_{i=0}^{2}\text{Policyrate\_dummy}_{t-i} + \text{crisis\_dummy} \qquad (5.2)$$

Three policy rate dummy $\left(\text{Policyrate\_dummy}_{t-i}\right)$ variables are created. The first policy rate dummy equals values of negative repo rate changes when economic growth is either zero or negative and zero otherwise. The second policy rate dummy equals to the values of negative repo rate changes when economic growth exceeds zero per cent and zero otherwise. The third policy rate dummy equals to the negative values of repo rate changes without considering economic growth phases. Evidence in Fig. 5.3 indicates that expansionary monetary policy shocks lower income inequality irrespective of economic growth phases. However,

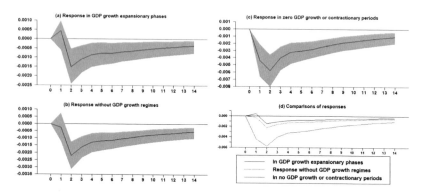

Fig. 5.3 Income inequality responses to expansionary monetary policy shocks and the role of business cycles (*Note* The grey shaded bands denotes the 16th and 84th percentile confidence bands. *Source* Authors' calculations)

an expansionary monetary policy shock has a bigger impact during the periods of no economic growth and in contractionary phases than in expansionary phases.

So far evidence indicates that monetary policy actions have distributive effects. This evidence is robust to using the growth and the level of income inequality in the model. In addition, evidence is robust to considering the influence of inflation regimes and business cycles on impacting the policy rate's influence on income inequality dynamics.

5.2.1 How Robust Are the Findings to Different Techniques?

How robust are these findings to allowing for the feedback effects of income inequality in interacting with other variables to an exogenous monetary policy shock? It is in the latter context that the analysis further examines the effects of monetary policy shocks using an exogenous VAR model. The model uses GDP growth, employment growth, and household disposable income growth, as endogenous variables. The exogenous variables include the exchange rate changes, inflation, financial crisis dummy, and either negative or positive repo rate changes. The repo rate changes are included in the model separately. The results, based on the model using variables expressed in growth rates, are shown in Fig. 5.4a, c.

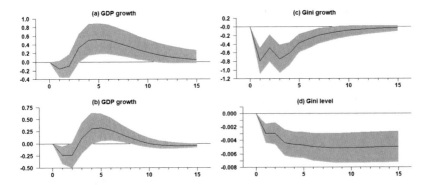

Fig. 5.4 Responses to expansionary monetary policy shocks based on the exogenous VAR model (*Note* The grey shaded bands denotes the 16th and 84th percentile confidence bands. *Source* Authors' calculations)

In Fig. 5.4 the income inequality growth declines due to an expansionary monetary policy shock. The income inequality growth is replaced with the level of income inequality in the exogenous VAR model. The results in Fig. 5.4b, d are from a model with Gini coefficient in levels, GDP in level and household disposable income in levels. Similarly, the level of income inequality declines due to the expansionary monetary policy shocks. In addition, GDP rises due to expansionary monetary policy shocks, albeit with different lags. The declining income inequality responses to expansionary monetary policy shocks are robust to the inclusion of employment growth and household disposable income growth as endogenous variables in the model. Overall, evidence is robust to the inclusion of additional channels in the transmission of monetary policy shocks to changes in income equality. The next sections will show the extent to which these channels transmit the monetary policy shocks to changes in income inequality.

5.2.2 Does the Persistence of the Expansionary Monetary Policy Shocks Matter?

To answer this question requires us to show the different scenarios of expansionary monetary policy shocks on both the level and growth of income inequality. The scenarios include short-lived, persistent, and aggressive monetary policy loosening shocks. These are just scenarios and not a justification for mechanical implementation of monetary

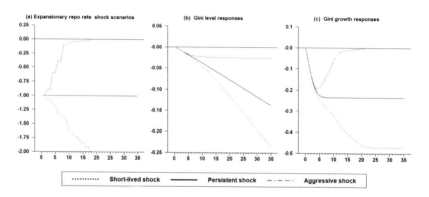

Fig. 5.5 Expansionary monetary policy shock scenarios and income inequality responses (*Source* Authors' calculations)

policy. In Figs. 5.5b and c, the aggressive loosening in the policy rate leads to a large reduction in the income inequality growth compared to a short-lived loosening shock. These findings show that the persistence of the expansionary monetary policy shocks matter for the evolution of both the level and growth of income inequality.

Is there evidence of asymmetric effects of the expansionary monetary policy shocks on both the level and growth of income inequality? The modified version of the Killian and Vigfussion (2011) bivariate VAR asymmetric approach is applied to test the prevalence of asymmetric effects of expansionary policy rate shocks. The model consists of the repo rate changes and growth of income inequality. The size of the shock is measured in standard deviations (s.d.). In Fig. 5.6, income inequality declines much more due to the large reductions in the policy rate than to small-sized reductions. This shows that the size of the expansionary monetary policy shocks matter for the reduction in income inequality. Hence, monetary policymakers may have a role in influencing the socio-economic wellbeing of the society.

Robustness tests reveal that the level of income inequality declines more to large expansionary monetary policy shocks than to small-sized shocks. This suggests there is an asymmetric effect based on the size of the expansionary monetary shock.

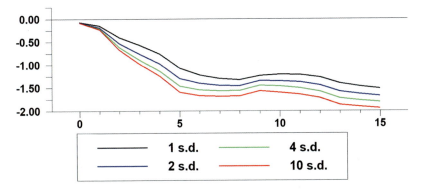

Fig. 5.6 Responses of income inequality growth to various sizes of expansionary monetary policy shocks (*Note* s.d. refers to standard deviation shock. *Source* Authors' calculations)

5.2.3 The Channels That Transmit the Monetary Policy Shocks to Income Inequality Based on Counterfactual Analysis

The section further performs counterfactual analysis to determine the roles of certain channels in transmitting expansionary monetary policy shocks to changes in income inequality. This is based on the counterfactual VAR model which includes negative repo rate changes, income inequality growth, and a specific transmission channel. The channels are captured by GDP growth, wage growth, household disposable income growth, and employment growth. These channels are included separately into the model. The models are estimated using two lags and 10,000 Monte Carlo draws. The exogenous variables include the exchange rate changes and the 2007 financial crisis dummy. These channels are shut off in the model to determine the counterfactual responses. This section estimates counterfactuals by shutting off the responses of income inequality growth channel to expansionary monetary policy shocks.

Figure 5.7 shows the responses of income inequality growth to expansionary monetary policy shocks. Like the preceding findings,

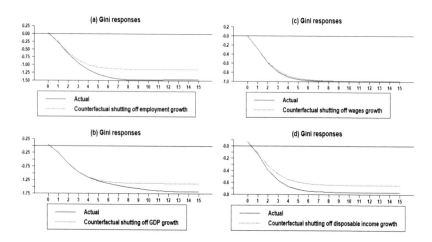

Fig. 5.7 Cumulative responses of income inequality growth to expansionary monetary policy shocks and the roles of selected channels (*Source* Authors' calculations)

5 Do Monetary Policy Shocks Influence Income ...

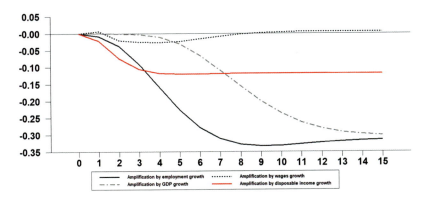

Fig. 5.8 Comparisons of amplification of various channels in income inequality growth reaction to expansionary monetary policy shocks (*Source* Authors' calculations)

income inequality growth declines due to expansionary monetary policy shocks. However, the actual income inequality growth declines more than the counterfactuals suggest. This evidence shows that improvements in employment growth, GDP growth, wage growth, and disposable income growth, following expansionary monetary policy shocks, amplify the reduction in the growth of income inequality.

Figure 5.8 shows the different sizes of amplifications from various channels during the reductions of income inequality growth. The employment channel is the biggest amplifier of the decline in the income inequality growth following the expansionary monetary policy shock. In comparison, economic growth has less amplifying ability than employment growth. The disposable income and wage growth have small amplifying effects on income inequality following expansionary monetary policy shocks. This evidence shows that increasing job creation and economic growth could be the needed amplifying channels in transmitting expansionary monetary policy shocks to the reduction in income inequality growth.

The analysis further shows the roles of GDP growth, wage growth and disposable income growth in transmitting the contractionary

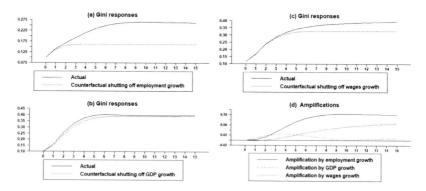

Fig. 5.9 Cumulative income inequality responses to contractionary monetary policy shocks and the role of the channels (*Source* Authors' calculations)

monetary policy shocks to income inequality growth. This is based on counterfactual VAR models, which include positive repo rate changes dummy, income inequality growth, and selected transmission channel. The positive repo rate changes dummy is equal to the positive values of the repo rate changes and zero otherwise. The channels are captured by GDP growth, wage growth, and employment growth. These channels are included separately in the model. The models are estimated using two lags. The exogenous variables include the exchange rate changes and crisis dummy. These channels are shut off in the model to determine the counterfactual responses. Figure 5.9 shows the responses of income inequality growth to contractionary monetary policy shocks. The actual income inequality growth rises more than the counterfactual reaction to the contractionary monetary policy shock. This suggests that the weakened employment growth, depressed wage inflation and the decline in economic growth amplify the increase in income inequality following contractionary monetary policy shock. The comparisons of amplifications indicate that employment growth is a big amplifier of the increase in income inequality growth than economic growth and wages inflation to contractionary monetary policy shocks.

5.3 Conclusion

Do monetary policy shocks influence income inequality dynamics in South Africa? Evidence indicates that expansionary monetary policy shock reduces income inequality significantly for nearly a year. This confirms the prevalence of the distributive effects of monetary policy changes. The analysis avoids over generalising the role of consumer price inflation by separating consumer price inflation into various bands and then using the dummy variable approach to capture their effects. The bands include: consumer price inflation below 3%, below 4.5% and within the 4.5–6%. The declines in income inequality due to the expansionary monetary policy shocks are significantly bigger (1) when inflation is below 4.5%, (2) when it is within 4.5–6% and (3) below 3%. The evidence indicates that expansionary monetary policy shocks reduce income inequality growth and this is robust to the inclusion of the influence of both high and low inflation regimes and business cycles. Second, to what extent do the employment growth, economic growth, and household disposable income growth channels transmit expansionary monetary policy shocks to growth of income inequality? Counterfactual analysis reveals that actual income inequality growth declines more in the presence of these channels than when they are shut off. This indicates that increases in employment growth, disposable income growth, and GDP growth, following an expansionary monetary policy shock, amplify the reductions in income inequality growth. First, this evidence implies policymakers should create more jobs and raise economic growth for these channels to amplify the effects of expansionary monetary policy shocks to reduce income inequality growth. Second, it may be important to heed Voinea and Monnin's (2017) advice that the impacts of monetary policy shocks might seem negligible or thought to be offsetting each other. However, it cannot be a priori ruled out that there are at least some unintended distributive consequences. Third, conclusions from recent studies suggest that having a solid grasp of the ways that monetary policy decisions, income inequality, and aggregate economy are intertwined, is important for an efficient design and implementation of monetary policy.

References

Bivens, J. (2015). *Gauging the impact of the fed on inequality during the recession* (Brooking Institution Working Paper).

Carney, M. (2016). *Mark Carney's right, not everyone benefits from free trade and globalisation—The semi-rich don't.* https://www.forbes.com/sites/timworstall/2016/12/05/mark-carneys-right-not-everyone-benefits-from-free-trade-and-globalisation-the-semi-rich-dont/#6efc0efd6433.

Coibion, O. (2012). Are the effects of monetary policy shocks big or small. *American Economic Journal of Macroeconomics, 4*(2), 1–32.

Coibion, O., Gorodnichenko, Y., Kueng, L., & Silvia, J. (2017). Innocent bystanders? Monetary policy and inequality in the US. *Journal of Monetary Economics, 88,* 70–89.

Colciago, A., Samarina, A., & de Haan, J. (2018). *Central bank policies and income and wealth inequality: A Survey* (De Nederlandsche Bank Working Paper No. 594).

Furceri, D., & Loungani, P. (2018). The distributional effects of capital account liberalization. *Journal of Development Economics, 130,* 127–144.

Guerello, C. (2016). *Conventional and unconventional monetary policy vs. Households income distribution: An empirical analysis for the euro area (mimeo).*

Gumata, N., & Ndou, E. (2017). *Labour market and fiscal policy adjustments to shocks: The role and implications for price and financial stability in South Africa.* Cham, Switzerland: Palgrave Macmillan.

Huber, E., & Stephens, J. D. (2014, April 1). Income inequality and redistribution in post-industrial democracies: Demographic, economic and political determinants. *Socio-Economic Review, 12*(2), 245–267.

Killian, L., & Vigfussion, R. (2011). Are the responses of the U.S. economy asymmetric in energy price increases and decreases? *Quantitative Economics, 2,* 419–453.

Koedijk, K., Loungani, P., & Monnin, P. (2017). Monetary policy, macroprudential regulation and inequality: An introduction to the special section. *Journal of International Money and Finance, 85,* 163–167.

Monnin, P. (2017). *Monetary policy, Macroprudential regulation and inequality* (ECP, Discussion Note 2017/2).

Mumtaz, H., & Theophilopolou, A. (2017). The impact of monetary policy on inequality in the UK. An empirical analysis. *Eurpoean Economic Review, 98*, 410–423.

O'Farrell, R., Rawdanowicz, L., and Inaba, K. (2016). *Monetary policy and inequality* (OECD Economics Department Working Papers, No. 1281). OECD publishing Paris.

Voinea, L., & Monnin, P. (2017, February 16). *Inequality should matter for central banks* (CEP).

Zdzienicka, A., Chen, S., Diaz Kalan, F., Laseen, S., & Svirydzenk, K. (2015). *Effects of monetary and macroprudential policies on financial conditions: Evidence from the United States* (IMF Working Paper 15/288).

6

Does Trade Openness Impact the Link Between Monetary Policy and Both Income Inequality and Consumption Inequalities?

Main Highlights

- Evidence reveals that positive trade openness shocks reduce both the income and consumption inequalities.
- Evidence from the counterfactual VAR models which shut off the trade openness channel in transmitting contractionary monetary policy shocks to income inequality, reveals that the counterfactual income inequality growth rises more than the actual reaction. This suggests that trade openness channel dampens the rising income inequality due to the contractionary monetary policy shocks.
- The trade openness channel mitigates the increase in income inequality by nearly half of the peak increase, following a contractionary monetary policy shock.

© The Author(s) 2019
E. Ndou and T. Mokoena, *Inequality, Output-Inflation Trade-Off and Economic Policy Uncertainty,*
https://doi.org/10.1007/978-3-030-19803-9_6

105

6.1 Introduction

The World Economic Outlook (WEO 2007) Chapter 4 reveals that trade liberalisation or openness is associated with a reduction in income inequality. In addition, the same report indicates that increased financial openness is associated with high income inequality. Amidst these pronouncements, could the trade openness channel impact the relationship between income inequality and contractionary monetary policy shocks in South Africa?

It is the objective of this chapter to continue the discussion of monetary policy effects on income inequality and this includes the role of the trade openness channel. This differentiates this analysis from other studies which did not include the role of the trade openness channel. The role of trade openness in transmitting monetary policy shocks to growth of income inequality in South Africa has not featured in policy discussions. This is despite the widely accepted view that monetary policy shocks impact the exchange rate and consumer price inflation which has influence on income inequality. Nevertheless, macroeconomic theory suggests these are determinants of exports and imports dynamics.

This chapter is neither reviewing the applicability of trade models nor determining which models may be applicable to the South African situation. Nonetheless, the chapter includes the theoretical predictions of trade openness effects on income inequality outcomes. For instance, theoretical models such as the Heckschler-Ohlin-Samuelson suggest that globalisation reduces inequality between countries due to developments in trade and economic geography (Dutt and Mukhopadhyay 2009). The link between trade liberalisation and income inequality could be explained by the Stopler-Samuelson theorem. The theorem is hinged on assumptions which include (1) two countries with two-factors and (2) the role of tariffs which impact the payments to skilled and unskilled workers. The theorem suggests that lowering tariffs in a developing country which has abundance of low-skilled labour, would lead to wage increases of these workers. By contrast, a reduction of tariffs should put downward pressure on the compensation of high-skilled workers. Alternatively, the tariff reduction on imports, leads to declines in the price of importable high skill intensive products. This may lead

6 Does Trade Openness Impact the Link Between Monetary Policy ...

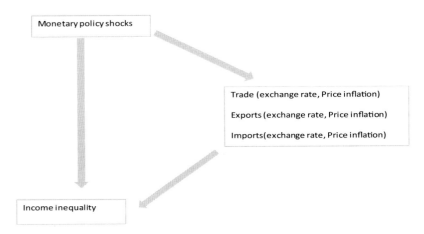

Fig. 6.1 The depiction of the direct and indirect transmission channels of monetary policy shocks to income inequality (*Source* Authors' drawing)

to a decline in the compensation of scarce but high-skilled workers. By contrast, the price of exportable low skill intensive goods for which the country has relatively abundant factor increases, which raises the compensation of low-skilled workers.

Figure 6.1 shows the direct and indirect transmission channels of monetary policy shocks to income inequality. The second stage of the indirect transmission happens when trade openness, impacts income inequality via both the import and export channels. This may be due to the wage adjustment channel. Beyond the wage adjustment channels, it is accepted that monetary policy impacts both the exchange rate and consumer price inflation. In addition, theory indicates that the exchange rate and consumer price inflation influences export and import dynamics. For instance, a contractionary monetary policy shock that appreciates the exchange rate will reduce export volumes while raising import volumes. By contrast, an expansionary monetary policy shock which depreciates the exchange rate, would raise the competitiveness of exports while making imports expensive.

The determination of the role of the trade openness channel in the passthrough of monetary policy shocks to income inequality is a missing gap in policy research discussion. This gap exists despite Fig. 6.1 showing that monetary policy shocks directly influence trade openness variables. Hence, this chapter extends the analysis in the WEO (2007) which links trade openness and income inequality by including the influence of monetary policy shocks. This chapter further applies a counterfactual approach to show the size of the influence of the trade openness channel in propagating or mitigating the passthrough of monetary policy shocks to income inequality.

Evidence in this analysis reveals that the unexpected increase in trade openness reduces income inequality significantly. This occurs via both the export and import channels. The counterfactual approach shows that trade openness dampens the rise in income inequality following contractionary monetary policy shocks. This may be due to the exchange rate appreciation which lowers both import price and consumer price inflation following contractionary monetary policy shocks.

6.2 The Impact of Trade Openness on Income Inequality

The chapter begins the analysis by examining the effects of unexpected increase in trade openness on the income inequality dynamics. This examination is extended to determine the link between trade openness and consumption inequality. The consumption inequality is measured by the two-quarters moving variance of log household consumption. Income inequality is measured by the Gini coefficient. The analysis uses quarterly (Q) data spanning 1993Q1 to 2016Q4. The de facto trade openness is based on the sum of exports and imports as percentage of GDP. It should be noted that the analysis is not testing the competing influences of different measures of trade openness. But the focus is on using the measure of trade openness, that is directly influenced by monetary policy shocks because its components react to monetary policy changes.

The direct effects of unexpected increase in trade openness are determined by estimating a bivariate VAR model. The model includes growth of trade openness and growth of income inequality. Growth of

6 Does Trade Openness Impact the Link Between Monetary Policy ...

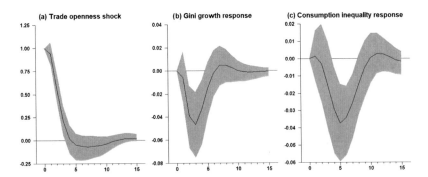

Fig. 6.2 Responses to positive trade openness shocks (*Note* The shocks are 1% positive trade openness shock. The grey shaded bands denotes the 16th and 84th percentile confidence bands. Gini denotes the Gini coefficient. *Source* Authors' calculations)

trade openness is measured by the growth of the sum of the exports and imports as a percentage of GDP. All growth rates refer to year-on-year changes in the variables. The models are estimated using two lags and 10,000 Monte Carlo draws. GDP growth is used as an exogenous variable.

In Fig. 6.2, the positive trade openness shock is highly transitory and lasts four quarters. The growth of income inequality declines significantly for nearly five quarters. The peak decline occurs in the third quarter. The income inequality measure is substituted with the consumption inequality measure. This tests the robustness of the results. Figure 6.2c shows the response of consumption inequality to a positive trade openness shock. Consumption inequality declines significantly for nearly seven quarters. This, evidence confirms that positive trade openness shock reduces both the income inequality and consumption inequality.

In addition, the analysis shows the responses of growth of income inequality using two additional model specifications. The first model is an exogenous VAR (Endo_VAR) model. The trade openness indicator is exogenous while growth of income inequality (Gini_growth) and GDP growth are endogenous. The model is estimated with two lags and 10,000 Monte Carlo draws. In addition, Eq. (6.1) depicts the single equation model (LIN_model). This model is used to determine the impact of trade openness on the growth of income inequality. The model is estimated with 10,000 bootstraps draws.

$$\text{Gini\_growth}_t = \text{constant} + \sum_{i=1}^{2} \text{Gini\_growth}_{t-i}$$
$$+ \sum_{i=0}^{4} \text{Trade\_openness\_growth}_{t-i}$$
$$+ \text{crisis\_dummy} + \varepsilon_t \quad (6.1)$$

The responses of growth of income inequality based on the additional models are shown in Fig. 6.3. The growth of income inequality declines significantly for less than three quarters in the exogenous VAR model. However, the growth of income inequality declines for nearly a year in the LIN_model. Therefore evidence indicates that income inequality declines to positive trade openness shocks and the finding is robust to the technique used to estimate it.

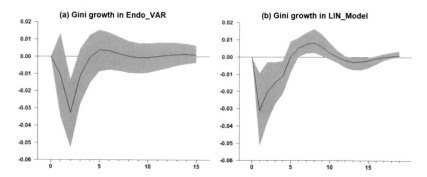

Fig. 6.3 Responses to positive trade openness shocks (*Note* The shocks are 1% positive trade openness shock. The grey shaded bands denotes the 16th and 84th percentile confidence bands. *Source* Authors' calculations)

6 Does Trade Openness Impact the Link Between Monetary Policy … 111

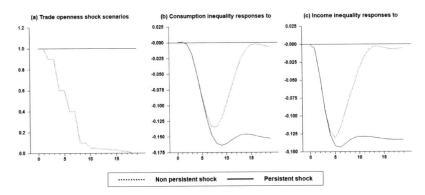

Fig. 6.4 Responses to positive trade openness shocks (*Source* Authors' calculations)

Does the persistence of positive trade openness shock matter? Consequently, the analysis distinguishes between persistent and non-persistent positive trade openness shock scenarios, on impacting both the income and consumption inequalities. The effects are determined by estimating bivariate VAR models using two lags and 10,000 Monte Carlo draws.

Figure 6.4a, shows the two trade openness shock scenarios. The growth of income inequality declines more to a persistent positive trade openness shock than to non-persistent shock in Fig. 6.4b. In addition, a persistent positive trade openness shock leads to persistent reduction in the growth of income inequality in Fig. 6.4c than in the case of the non-persistent shock. This evidence shows that the persistence of trade openness shocks matters for both the income and consumption inequalities.

Does it matter which component of trade openness shock is used in the analysis? The analysis assesses the effects of export and import growth shocks on income inequality. These components are included in the model separately. This is determined by replacing the trade openness indicator in the bivariate VAR models with annual growth of (1) imports and (2) exports. Figure 6.5 shows responses of the growth of income inequality and consumption inequality to positive export

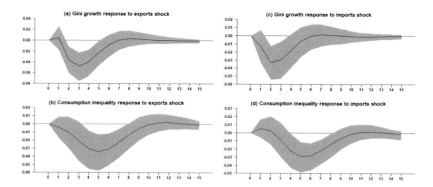

Fig. 6.5 Responses to positive trade openness shocks (*Note* The shocks are 1% positive trade openness shock. The grey shaded bands denotes the 16th and 84th percentile confidence bands. *Source* Authors' calculations)

and import shocks. Both shocks lower significantly the growth of income inequality and consumption inequality, over different horizons. However, the inequalities retreat back to the pre-shock levels. The impact of positive trade openness shock on reducing the income inequality is consistent with that reported in WEO (2007).[1]

6.2.1 Impact of Trade Openness on the Effects of Contractionary Monetary Policy Shocks on Income Inequality

The preceding section revealed that an unexpected increase in trade openness reduces income inequality. This section examines the role of trade openness as a conduit of transmitting monetary policy shocks to income inequality.

The main objective of this section is to evaluate the extent to which the trade openness channel impacts the transmission of monetary policy shocks to growth of income inequality. Thus, the chapter asks: to what extent is the indirect transmission channel via the trade openness

---

[1] The WEO (2007) revealed that trade openness lowered income inequality and the results were robust to the use of exports growth shocks.

6 Does Trade Openness Impact the Link Between Monetary Policy … 113

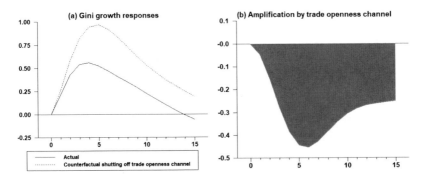

Fig. 6.6 Responses to contractionary monetary policy shocks and the role of trade openness (*Note* The shocks are one positive standard deviation repo rate shock. *Source* Authors' calculations)

relevant to understanding the link between monetary policy and income inequality? To disentangle this effect, requires the application of counterfactual VAR approach. Consequently, the chapter applies a counterfactual VAR analysis to determine the role of trade openness in transmitting contractionary monetary policy shocks to growth of income inequality.

The VAR model includes the repo rate, growth of income inequality, and a growth of the indicator of trade openness. The model is estimated using two lags and 10,000 Monte Carlo draws. The counterfactual impulse response shuts off the trade openness channel. In Fig. 6.6, the contractionary monetary policy shock raises the growth of income inequality. However, the counterfactual growth of income inequality rises more than the actual reaction. This suggests that the trade openness channel dampens the rising income inequality due to contractionary monetary policy shocks. The sizes of the amplifications are shown in Fig. 6.6b. Thus, nearly half of the increase in the growth of income inequality is due to the mitigating effects of the trade openness channel.

Therefore, evidence reveals that despite income inequality rising due to contractionary monetary policy shocks, the trade openness channel dampens the actual growth of income inequality by nearly half of the size of the peak increase. This section separates the effects of trade openness by showing the effects between those due to the export and

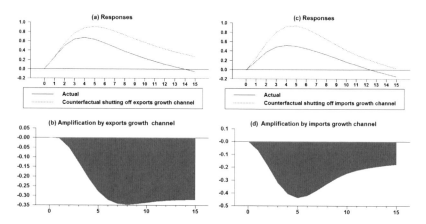

Fig. 6.7 Actual and counterfactual responses of income inequality growth to contractionary monetary policy shocks and the roles of the export and import channels (*Note* The shocks are one positive standard deviation repo rate shock. *Source* Authors' calculations)

import channels. The export and import growth channels are included separately in the model. The export and import channels are shut off in the model. Figure 6.7 shows that the counterfactual growth of income inequality exceeds the actual response irrespective of whether the model includes export or import growth channels. This shows that both the export and import channels dampen the growth of income inequality following the contractionary monetary policy shocks.

Would the effects differ when analysing the effects of expansionary monetary policy shocks? The analysis further examines the role of the growth of exports and imports channels in transmitting expansionary monetary policy shocks to income inequality growth. This will determine if these channels also mitigate the passthrough of monetary policy shocks to income inequality. In Fig. 6.8, the expansionary monetary policy shocks lower the growth of income inequality irrespective of whether the import or export channels are operative or shut-off in the models. Irrespective of the channel included in the model, the counterfactual response declines more than the actual reaction. This suggests that the export, import and trade openness channels mitigate the decline in the growth of income inequality.

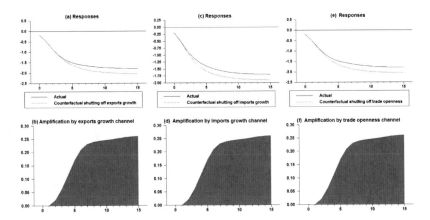

Fig. 6.8 Income inequality growth responses to expansionary monetary policy shocks and the role of the trade openness channels (*Note* The shocks are one positive standard deviation repo rate shock. *Source* Authors' calculations)

6.3 Conclusion

Does trade openness impact the link between monetary policy and both income inequality and consumption inequality? Evidence reveals that positive trade openness shock reduces both the income and consumption inequalities. Second evidence reveals that contractionary monetary policy shock leads to increased growth of income inequality. Counterfactual VAR models are estimated to determine the role of trade openness in transmitting contractionary monetary policy shocks to growth of income inequality. The counterfactual is determined by shutting off the trade openness variables in transmitting contractionary monetary policy shocks to income inequality. The counterfactual growth of income inequality rises more than the actual reaction to contractionary monetary policy shocks. This suggests that trade openness channel dampens the rising income inequality due to contractionary monetary policy shock. The trade openness channel mitigates the increase in income inequality by nearly half of the peak increase following contractionary monetary policy shock.

References

Dutt, A. K., & Mukhopadhyay, K. (2009). International institutions, globalisation and inequality among nations. *Progress in Development, 9*(4).

World Economic Outlook, October 2007: Globalization and Inequality. https://books.google.co.za/books?isbn=1451923856.

7

Does Financial Globalisation Impact the Link Between Monetary Policy and Income Inequality?

Main Highlights

- The chapter applies a counterfactual analysis to show the role of net capital inflow channel in transmitting tight monetary policy shocks to growth of income inequality. We find that counterfactual growth of income inequality rises less than the actual responses.
- This evidence suggests that net capital inflow channels dampen the increase in income inequality, following a tight monetary policy shock. This may be indicative of the dominance of exchange rate appreciation and accompanying reduction in consumer price inflation in lowering income inequality, rather than the reduction in economic growth, following tight monetary policy shocks.
- From policy perspective, this evidence calls for an optimal monetary response to consider the income inequality reaction in the calibration of the monetary policy effects on the optimal net capital inflows to have a desirable effect from a social perspective.

© The Author(s) 2019
E. Ndou and T. Mokoena, *Inequality, Output-Inflation Trade-Off and Economic Policy Uncertainty*,
https://doi.org/10.1007/978-3-030-19803-9_7

117

7.1 Introduction

The preceding chapter showed the impact of monetary policy shocks on income inequality and how its affected by trade openness. This chapter continues to assess how the link between income inequality and monetary policy shocks is impacted by the capital inflows channels. This is motivated by the weakening of the rand against the United States (US) dollar, which is attributed to US Fed raising interest rates, imposition of tariffs by large economies and the weak South African economic growth. The synchronised policy rate adjustments should mitigate the distortionary capital flow movements, *ceteris paribus*. The consideration of the effects of the synchronised interest rate adjustments on income inequality is absent in the discussion of synchronised policy rate movements, despite South Africa being reported as having the highest income inequality in the world. This chapter advances the view that policymakers considering synchronised policy rate movements to avert the adverse effects of disruptive capital flows, should consider the influence of capital flows' on income inequality dynamics. Does the net capital inflow channel impact the ability of monetary policy shocks to influence income inequality in South Africa?

The role of net capital inflow channel in transmitting monetary policy shocks to growth of income inequality in South Africa has not been considered in the monetary policymaking decisions, and it remains elusive. This is happening despite, monetary policymakers' concerns about the adverse inflationary effects due to the large currency depreciation associated with heightened capital outflows propelled by the expected and actual US Fed policy rate tightening. In addition, the World Bank (2018) report and Fitch rating (2018) indicate the issue of inequality cannot be ignored in a country like South Africa which has high income inequality.

This chapter argues there is a need to determine the influence of financial globalisation on impacting the link between monetary policy and income inequality. It may be reasonable and timeously to ask: Are the distortionary effects of elevated capital outflows justifiable from a social perspective if these flows impact the manner in which tight monetary policy shocks relate to income inequality?

7 Does Financial Globalisation Impact the Link ...

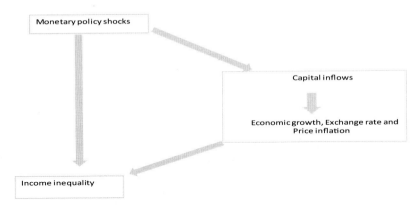

Fig. 7.1 Transmission of monetary policy shocks and the role of the capital flow channel (*Source* Authors' drawing)

This chapter is neutral in the debates advocating that increases in net capital inflows are good for dampening inflation pressures by appreciating the exchange rate. However, other plausible economic reasons suggest that net capital inflows may increase demand for skilled workers, thereby widening income inequality. An increase in the demand for skilled personnel widens the inequality between the skilled and unskilled workers' income. Hence, it is important to show the role of net capital flows in linking monetary policy and income inequality in South Africa.

A theoretical motivation for this analysis is illustrated in Fig. 7.1. The depiction, shows the direct and indirect channels in transmitting monetary policy shocks to income inequality. The direct channel shows that monetary policy impacts income inequality. The potency of the direct channel cannot be disputed, given the magnitudes of evidence in recent literature. The indirect channel shows that the monetary policy shocks, are being transmitted via the net capital inflows channel in the first stage. In the second stage, the net capital inflows by impacting the exchange rate and consumer price inflation, influences income inequality dynamics. Despite, literature examining the direct effects of monetary policy on income inequality, the indirect effects of capital inflows in transmitting monetary policy shocks onto income inequality have yet to be assessed. This chapter fills policy gaps by showing that net capital inflows channel, is a conduit that transmits monetary policy shocks to income inequality.

Theory predicts that tight monetary policy shocks should attract net capital inflows or even deter the outflows, *ceteris paribus*. And an increase in net capital inflows should appreciate the exchange rate and lower consumer inflation pressures. The overall impact of net capital inflows on economic growth is debatable. Some studies indicate stimulatory effects of capital inflows on economic growth. By contrast, there are studies which point out that capital inflows crowd out investment.

This chapter fills policy research gaps in several ways. First, this chapter examines the extent to which the capital inflow channel influences the impact of monetary policy shocks on driving income inequality dynamics in South Africa. A discussion pointing to the potency of the transmission of monetary policy shocks to income inequality via the capital flow channel is missing in South Africa. Second, the chapter fills policy research gaps by showing the direct link between net capital flows and income inequality and shows further, the linkage is influenced by the exchange rate channel. Third, the chapter fills an important policy research gap in South Africa by showing the influence of net capital flows on the transmission of monetary policy shocks to income inequality.

7.2 Recent Literature Evidence

Evidence in this book indicates that tight monetary policy shocks raise income inequality in South Africa. This recent evidence does not refute the notion that monetary policy has distributional effects via the income inequality channel as reported in other economies. In fact, evidence points to the potency of both expansionary and contractionary monetary policy shocks on income inequality. For instance, Guerello (2016) found that expansionary monetary policy leads to a decrease in income inequality. Mumtaz and Theophilopolou (2017) found that expansionary monetary policy reduces income inequality economically and significantly.[1] Huber and Stephens (2014) found that a 100 basis

---

[1]See also Coibion et al. (2017)

point reductions in policy rate reduces the Gini coefficient by 0.4%. In addition, Bivens (2015) shows that expansionary monetary policy could reduce income inequality if the economy is close to full employment. Furthermore, Furceri et al. (2016) found that the decrease in income inequality after an unexpected monetary policy expansion is greater in countries with a higher share of labour income, indicative of the existence of labour income heterogeneity channel or income composition channel that affects income inequality. Moreover, Coibion et al. (2017) found that monetary policy tightening in the United States increases income inequality for high earning households and lowers the labour income of low earning households.[2]

Evidence in the literature also points to the potency of the second part in Fig. 7.1 in which the indirect transmission of monetary policy shocks to income inequality happens via the net capital inflows channel. This evidence is presented in Chapter 4 of the *World Economic Outlook* (2007). The WEO (2007) reports that increased financial liberalisation is associated with increased income inequality. The report explicitly indicates that the disequalising effect of increased financial openness, through foreign direct investment, works by increasing the premium on higher skills rather than limiting opportunities for economic advancement. The report further argues that FDI is often directed to high-skill sectors in host countries. Increase in FDI from advanced economies to developing economies could increase demand for skilled labour in both countries, thereby increasing inequality. However, empirical evidence on these channels is mixed, with negative effects in the short run or even inconclusive findings. The other literature suggests that capital account liberalisation may increase access to financial resources for the poor, whereas others have suggested that by increasing the likelihood of financial crises, greater financial openness may disproportionately hurt the poor. The WEO (2007) report shows that the inward FDI exacerbates the income inequality in developing economies, while outward FDI leads to negative effects on inequality in developed economies.

---

[2]O'Farrell et al. (2016), found a percentage lower policy rate increase net Gini coefficient by up to 0.02% after 3 years. In addition, Guerello (2016) finds that similar results for the Euro area.

7.3 What Are the Effects of Positive Net Capital Inflow Shocks on Income Inequality in South Africa?

The chapter begins by estimating various models to determine the effects of positive net capital flow shocks on income inequality. The income inequality is measured by the Gini coefficient. The models are given by Eqs. (7.1) and (7.2). The Gini_growth denotes the annual growth of Gini coefficient. The equations are estimated with 10,000 bootstraps draws.

$$
\begin{aligned}
\text{Gini\_growth}_t = {} & \text{constant} + \sum_{i=1}^{4} \text{Gini\_growth}_{t-i} \\
& + \sum_{i=0}^{2} \text{Net\_Capital\_inflow}_{t-i} + \sum_{i=1}^{2} \text{GDP\_growth}_{t-i} \\
& + \sum_{i=1}^{2} \text{Wages\_growth}_{t-i} + \sum_{i=0}^{2} \text{CPI\_inflation}_{t-i} \\
& + \text{crisis\_dummy} + \epsilon_t
\end{aligned}
\tag{7.1}
$$

$$
\begin{aligned}
\text{Gini\_growth}_t = {} & \text{constant} + \sum_{i=1}^{4} \text{Gini\_growth}_{t-i} \\
& + \sum_{i=0}^{2} \text{Net\_Capital\_inflow}_{t-i} \\
& + \text{crisis\_dummy} + \epsilon_t
\end{aligned}
\tag{7.2}
$$

In Fig. 7.2, the positive net capital inflow shock raises income inequality, and this is followed by a reduction after one year. This evidence reveals that the effects of positive net capital inflow shocks on growth of income inequality dynamics are mixed.

Are the preceding effects robust to using different model specifications? In answering this question, this analysis utilises different model specifications to determine the robustness of the effects of positive capital inflow shocks on

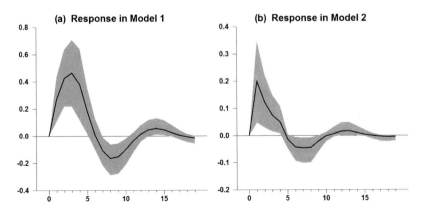

Fig. 7.2 Income inequality growth responses to positive net capital inflow shocks (*Note* The grey shaded band denotes the 16th and 84th percentile confidence bands. *Source* Authors calculation)

driving growth of income inequality. As a precursor to the main purpose of this study, several VAR models are estimated and a number of variables in the models ranges from two to six variables. The models are estimated using quarterly (Q) data spanning 1993Q1 to 2016Q3. The models are estimated using two lags and include a constant and other dummy variables. The first VAR model (*Model 1*) includes net capital flows as a per cent of GDP and growth of income inequality. The results are tested to determine their robustness to the reverse ordering effects. The robustness test is done through estimating four VAR models to determine the effects of positive net capital inflow shock on the growth of income inequality. *Model 3* is an Exogenous VAR model in which growth of income inequality, GDP growth, CPI inflation, and wages inflation are endogenous while net capital inflow as percent of GDP and crisis dummy are exogenous. *Model 4* consists of the net capital inflows as a per cent of GDP and growth of income inequality as endogenous whereas the repo rate, a crisis dummy, and GDP growth are exogenous. *Model 5* consists of net capital inflows, as percent of GDP growth of income inequality, CPI inflation and exchange rate changes as endogenous, while the crisis dummy is exogenous. *Model 6* consists of net capital inflow, as percent of GDP growth of income inequality, wage growth, employment growth, and GDP growth as endogenous variables whereas the repo rate and a crisis dummy are exogenous. All models are estimated using two lags and 10,000 Monte Carlo draws.

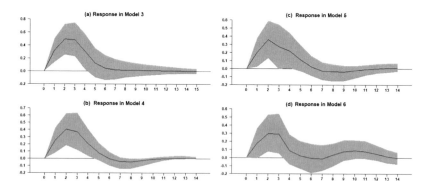

Fig. 7.3 Income inequality growth responses to positive net capital inflow shocks (*Note* The grey shaded band denotes the 16th and 84th percentile confidence bands. *Source* Authors calculation)

The responses of the growth of income inequality to positive net capital flow shocks are shown in Fig. 7.3 and these are presented according to different models. In all instances, positive net capital inflow shocks raise income inequality. This indicates the robustness of the findings to the different model specifications.

The analysis further shows the effects of positive net capital inflow shocks on the level of income inequality. The effects are determined by estimating bivariate VAR models. The models are estimated using 10,000 Monte Carlo draws. The net capital inflow shock is divided into portfolio and foreign direct inflows as a per cent of GDP. In the other model, income inequality is replaced with consumption inequality. In Fig. 7.4, the income inequality rises to positive net capital inflow, portfolio inflow, and direct inflow shocks. In addition, the net capital inflow shock raises consumption inequality. The increase in income inequality to positive net capital inflow shocks is robust to various categories of capital inflows.

7.3.1 Channels Which Transmit Positive Net Capital Inflow Shocks to Income Inequality

Economic theory predicts that increases in net capital inflows should appreciate the exchange rate. So, how potent are the exchange rate and consumer price inflation channels in transmitting positive net capital

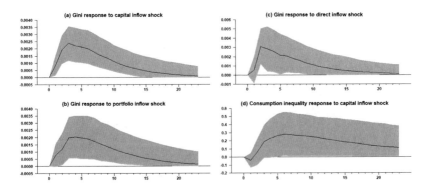

Fig. 7.4 Income inequality responses to positive net capital inflow shocks (*Note* The grey shaded band denotes the 16th and 84th percentile confidence bands. *Source* Authors calculation)

inflow shocks to growth of income inequality? It is important to examine if the exchange rate channel influences the transmission of positive net capital inflow shocks to income inequality through a counterfactual VAR approach. The models include a category of capital inflows, growth of income inequality and growth of the exchange rate. The models are estimated with two lags and 10,000 Monte Carlo draws. The counterfactual impulse responses shut off the exchange rate channel in transmitting positive net capital inflow shocks to growth of income inequality. The responses are shown in Fig. 7.5. In all instances the counterfactual responses of growth of income inequality rise more than the actual reactions. This suggests that the appreciating exchange rate, following a positive net capital inflow shock, dampens the increase in growth of income inequality.

7.3.2 The Role of the Inflation Channel

The study further examines the role of the inflation channel in transmitting net capital inflow shocks to growth of income inequality using the counterfactual VAR approach. The models are estimated using 10,000 Monte Carlo draws. The exchange rate variable is replaced with consumer price inflation in the preceding model. The counterfactual impulse responses shut off the consumer price inflation channel in transmitting the positive net capital inflow shocks to growth of income

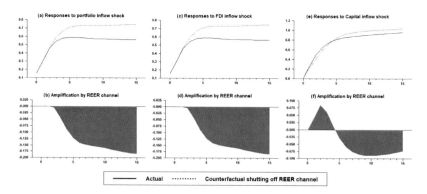

Fig. 7.5 Responses of income inequality growth to positive net capital inflow shocks and the role of the exchange rate channel (*Source* Authors' calculations)

inequality. The analysis separates the effects of inflation when it is above the 6% threshold from those below this threshold using a dummy variable approach. The first dummy (high inflation regime) equals to the values of inflation above 6% and zero otherwise. The second dummy (low inflation regime) equals to the values of inflation below or equal to 6% and zero otherwise. These dummy indicators are included in the model separately. The responses of income inequality are shown in Fig. 7.6. In all instances, the counterfactual responses of growth of income inequality rise more than the actual responses. This suggests that the decline

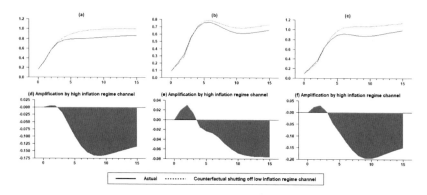

Fig. 7.6 Cumulative income inequality growth to positive net capital inflow shocks and the role of the low inflation regime channel (*Source* Authors' calculations)

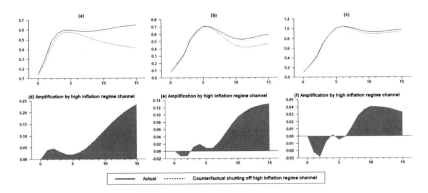

Fig. 7.7 Cumulative income inequality growth to positive net capital inflow shocks and the role of the low inflation regime channel (*Source* Authors' calculations)

in the inflation rate in the low inflation regime, following a positive net capital inflow shock, dampens the increase in growth of income inequality.

The responses showing the influence of high inflation regime are shown in Fig. 7.7. In all instances the counterfactual responses of the growth of income inequality rise more than the actual responses. This suggests that the high inflation regime, following a positive net capital inflow shock, amplifies the increase in the growth of income inequality. This evidence reveals that the role of consumer price inflation depends on whether inflation exceeds 6% or not. Nonetheless, this evidence indicates that income inequality would be much lower when inflation is below the 6% inflation threshold.

7.4 Does the Net Capital Inflow Channel Impact the Transmission of Monetary Policy Shocks to Growth of Income Inequality?

Indeed, the preceding evidence reveals that positive net capital inflow shocks raise income inequality. But when the source of capital flows shock is not indicated in the model, it may bias the effects, if these are dependent on the shock. Hence, this section examines the extent to which net capital inflows, driven by a tight monetary policy shock, influence the reaction of income inequality dynamics. It should be noted that a tight monetary policy shock and the increase in net capital inflows should appreciate the exchange rate, which should reduce inflationary pressures. The weakening inflationary pressures should, in turn, dampen the increase in income inequality, following tight monetary policy shocks, as depicted in Fig. 7.1.

The role of net capital inflow channel in transmitting tight monetary policy shocks to the growth of income inequality is determined by estimating a counterfactual VAR model. The counterfactual responses shut off the net capital inflow channel in transmitting monetary policy shocks to growth of income inequality. The seventh VAR model (*Model 7*) includes the repo rate, growth of income inequality and net capital inflows as a per cent of GDP. The eighth VAR model (*Model 8*) includes the repo rate, growth of income inequality, wage inflation, and net capital inflows as a per cent of GDP. In both models the consumer price inflation and GDP growth are included as exogenous variables. The models are estimated using two lags and 10,000 Monte Carlo Draws. The net capital inflow channel in both models is shut off to calculate the counterfactual response of the growth of income inequality.

In both Figs. 7.8 and 7.9 the counterfactual responses rise less than the actual responses. This suggests that the net capital inflow channels dampen the increase in income inequality, following tight monetary policy shocks. This may be indicative of the dominance of exchange rate appreciation and the accompanying reduction in consumer price inflation rather than the reduction in economic growth following tight monetary policy shocks. The counterfactual responses shut off the net capital inflow channel in transmitting monetary policy shocks to growth of income inequality. How robust are the findings to additional variables? The ninth VAR model (*Model 9*) includes the repo rate, growth of income inequality, wage inflation, consumer price inflation, and net capital inflow as per cent of GDP. The tenth VAR model (*Model 10*) includes the repo rate, growth of income inequality, wage inflation, consumer price inflation, exchange rate growth, and net capital inflow

7 Does Financial Globalisation Impact the Link ... 129

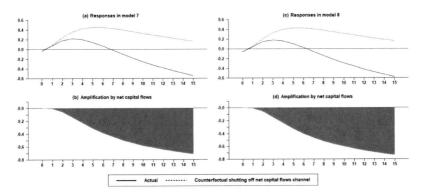

Fig. 7.8 Responses of income inequality growth to tight monetary policy shocks and the role of capital inflow channel (*Source* Authors' calculations)

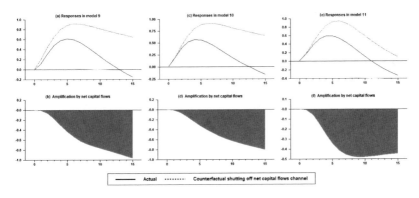

Fig. 7.9 Responses of income inequality growth to tight monetary policy shock and the role of capital inflow channel (*Source* Authors' calculations)

as per cent of GDP. The eleventh VAR model (*Model 11*) includes the repo rate, growth of income inequality, consumer price inflation, exchange rate growth, and net capital inflow as a per cent of GDP. The GDP growth and crisis dummy are included as exogenous variables in all models. The models are estimated using two lags and 10,000 Monte Carlo Draws. The net capital inflow channel in both models is shut off to calculate the counterfactual response of growth of income inequality. Evidence indicates that net capital inflows channels dampen the increase in income inequality to tight monetary policy shocks.

7.5 Conclusion

The chapter applies a counterfactual analysis to show the role of net capital inflow channel in transmitting tight monetary policy shocks to growth of income inequality. The net capital inflow channel is shutoff in transmitting tight monetary policy shocks to growth of income inequality to get a counterfactual reaction. The counterfactual growth of income inequality rises less than the actual responses. This suggests that the net capital inflow channel dampen the increase in income inequality following a tight monetary policy shock. This may be indicative of the dominance of exchange rate appreciation and accompanying reduction in consumer price inflation rather than the reduction in economic growth following tight monetary policy shocks. This evidence calls for the optimal monetary response that considers income inequality in the calibration of monetary policy for net capital inflows to have a desirable effect from a social perspective.

References

Bivens, J. (2015). *Gauging the impact of the fed on inequality during the recession* (Working Chapter). Brookings Institution.

Coibion, O. (2012). Are the effects of monetary policy shocks big or small? *American Economic Journal of Macroeconomics, 4*(2), 1–32.

Coibion, O., Gorodnichenko, Y., Kueng, L., & Silvia, J. (2017). Innocent bystanders? Monetary policy and inequality in the US. *Journal of Monetary Economics, 88*, 70–89.

Furceri, D., & Loungani, P. (2018). The distributional effects of capital account liberalization. *Journal of Development Economics, 130*, 127–144.

Guerello, C. (2016). *Conventional and unconventional monetary policy vs. Households income distribution: An empirical analysis for the euro area* (mimeo).

Killian, L., & Vigfussion, R. J. (2011). Are the responses of the U.S. economy asymmetric in energy price increases and decreases? *Quantitative Economics, 2*, 419–453.

Koedijk, K., Loungani, P., & Monnin, P. (2018). Monetary policy, macroprudential regulation and inequality: An introduction to the special section. *Journal of international money and finance, 85*: 163–167.

Monnin, P. (2017). *Monetary policy, macroprudential regulation and inequality* (ECP, Discussion Note 2017/2).

Mumtaz, H., & Theophilopoulou, A. (2017). The impact of monetary policy on inequality in the UK. An empirical analysis. *European Economic Review, 98*, 410–423.

O'Farrell, R., Rawdanowicz, L., & Inaba, K. (2016). Monetary policy and inequality (OECD Economics Department Working Chapters No. 1281). Paris: OECD Publishing.

Voinea, L., & Monnin, P. (2017, February). *Inequality should matter for central banks* (CEP 16).

World Economic Outlook. (2007). International Monetary Fund, Chapter 3.

Zdzienicka, A., Chen, S., Diaz Kalan, F., Laseen, S., & Svirydzenk, K. (2015). *Effects of monetary and macroprudential policies on financial conditions: Evidence from the United States* (IMF Working Chapter 15/288).

Part III

The Role of the Monetary Policy Channel in Transmitting Shocks to Income Inequality

8

Does Monetary Policy Impact the Effects of Shares of Manufacturing Employment Shocks on Income Inequality?

Main Highlights

- Evidence reveals that an unexpected increase in the manufacturing, tradeable, and mining sector employment shares, leads to significant reduction in income inequality.
- The reduction in income inequality, due to shocks from these sectors' employment shares, is amplified by low inflationary environment (that is, the consumer price inflation below or equal to 6%).
- In addition, the reduction in income inequality is further amplified by the low repo rate level when consumer price inflation is below the 6% threshold.
- This evidence reveals that inflation regimes matter for expansionary monetary policy to influence the reduction in income inequality due to improved manufacturing sector employment shares.

© The Author(s) 2019
E. Ndou and T. Mokoena, *Inequality, Output-Inflation Trade-Off and Economic Policy Uncertainty,*
https://doi.org/10.1007/978-3-030-19803-9_8

8.1 Introduction

Figure 8.1 shows that employment shares of the tradeable sector (that is, combined shares of manufacturing and mining sectors employment) in South Africa have been declining in the last two decades. The downward trend could reflect a shift from the tradeable sector towards the services sector. According to IMF's World Economic Outlook published in April 2018, WEO (2018), the declining trend may not be a policy concern if the shift in the employment from the manufacturing sector to the services sector is not hindering the economy-wide productivity growth.[1] In addition, the WEO (2018) found that the declining share of manufacturing sector employment raises income inequality.

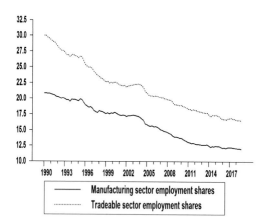

Fig. 8.1 Sector employment shares in per cent (*Note* These employment shares are expressed as per cent of the total non-agricultural employment. *Source* Authors' calculations and South African Reserve Bank)

This chapter argues that the role of monetary policy cannot be left out of the analysis because it influences the costs of financing and consumer price inflation dynamics. In addition, recent studies indicate

---

[1]In addition, the report suggests that there are prospects for developing economies to gain ground towards advanced economy income levels. In addition, the WEO (2018) noted the displacement of workers from the manufacturing sector to services sector in the advanced economies coincided

8 Does Monetary Policy Impact the Effects of Shares ... 137

that monetary policy is a big driver of income inequality dynamics. Hence, this chapter examines whether the monetary policy channel is a transmitter of the positive shocks to employment shares onto income inequality. The chapter further examines whether the effects depend on monetary policy stance. In addition, the analysis distinguishes the role of inflation when it is above and below the 6% inflation threshold. In contrast, to the WEO (2018) objective, this chapter examines whether positive shocks to manufacturing sector employment shares can significantly lower income inequality and whether this effect is influenced by the monetary policy channel.

To ascertain if there are differential effects in the tradeable sector, the analysis compares the income inequality responses to positive shocks to manufacturing employment shares to those of the mining sector employment shares.

Why is this study important? It is important to examine whether policymakers' efforts aimed at increasing the employment shares of the manufacturing sector may contribute to dealing with the currently large income inequalities in South Africa. First, this follows the Industrial Development Corporation (IDC) and Department of Trade and Industry (DTI) implementing programmes to revive the manufacturing sector via the Black Industrialist Programme. The revival of this sector may have implications for the income inequality dynamics. Second, the WEO (2018) highlights that, where shares of manufacturing employment have declined more, this may have exposed the situation to the inequality enhancing trends, leading to a rise in labour income inequality within all the sectors. Third, it is possible that changes in the manufacturing sector employment shares could reflect trends in incomes and demand, and this has implications for the economy facing weak economic growth.[2]

---

with a rise in income inequality and the increase was driven by larger disparities in earnings across all sectors. Topalova (2005) suggests that the benefits of liberalisation must be realised at substantial social costs, unless additional policies are devised to redistribute some gains from the winners to the losers.

[2]Policymakers should heed that demand for manufactures increases faster than demand for food and services in the earlier stages of development; however, the reverse happens at the later stages of a country's development. However, the decline in the relative price of manufactures could dampen the relative shift away from their consumption as income grows (WEO 2018).

Evidence in this chapter reveals that an unexpected increase in the manufacturing, tradeable, and mining sector employment shares leads to a significant reduction in income inequality. The decline from these sectors' employment shares is amplified by the consumer price inflation when it is below or equal to 6%. The effects are also amplified by the low repo rate level when consumer price inflation is below the 6% threshold. However, the effects of these shocks are mitigated by the elevated repo rate levels. The influence of expansionary monetary policy stance differs, depending on whether consumer price inflation is above or below the 6% threshold. The expansionary monetary policy channel accentuates the decline in income inequality when consumer price inflation is below 6%. The expansionary monetary policy channel mitigates the decline in income inequality when the consumer price inflation exceeds the 6% threshold. This implies that when manufacturing jobs are disappearing, policymakers need to facilitate the reskilling of former manufacturing workers and reduce the costs of their reallocations, while strengthening safety nets to alleviate the adverse effects of joblessness and job transitions for the workers and their communities (WEO 2018).

8.2 The Effects of Employment Shares on Income Inequality

This section begins the empirical examination of the role of the manufacturing sector employment shares in driving income inequality dynamics. The effects are examined by estimating VAR models. The models are estimated using two lags and 10,000 Monte Carlo draws. The results test whether the ordering of the variables matters. The models are estimated using quarterly (Q) data spanning 1993Q1 to 2016Q4. The income inequality is measured by the Gini coefficient obtained from Gumata and Ndou (2017). The first VAR includes manufacturing employment as a share of total non-agricultural employment (manufacturing employment shares) and income inequality. The second VAR model (Model 2) includes income inequality and manufacturing employment shares. The third VAR model (Model 3) includes mining employment share of total non-agricultural employment (mining employment share) and income

8 Does Monetary Policy Impact the Effects of Shares ...

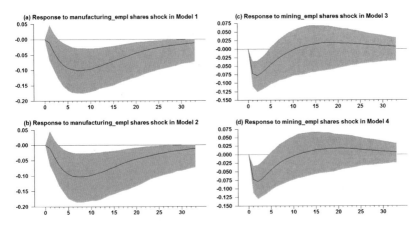

Fig. 8.2 Income inequality responses to positive manufacturing and mining sector employment shares shocks (*Note* The shocks are a one positive standard deviation in magnitude _empl implies employment. The grey shaded bands denote the 16th and 84th percentile confidence bands. *Source* Authors' calculations)

inequality. The fourth VAR model (Model 4) includes income inequality and the mining employment shares.

The responses of income inequality to positive manufacturing and mining sector employment shares shocks are shown in Fig. 8.2. Income inequality declines significantly for prolonged periods in Models 1 and 2. This suggests that the unexpected increase in the share of the manufacturing sector employment in the total non-agricultural employment may significantly reduce income inequality. The reduction is independent of whether the manufacturing employment share is placed before or after income inequality. In addition, the analysis presents the results based on the link between mining sector employment shares and income inequality. The positive mining employment shock lowers income inequality significantly for less than a year. The impact of the positive mining employment shares shock on income inequality is independent of the ordering of the variables in the model.

The analysis further separates the effects of mining sector employment shares between gold mining and non-gold mining shares. The mining sector employment shares in the preceding model is replaced with these components, which are included in the model individual. In addition, the analysis compares the income inequality responses to positive mining

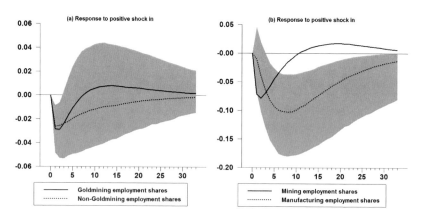

Fig. 8.3 Income inequality responses (*Note* The shocks are a one positive standard deviation in magnitude. The grey shaded bands denote the 16th and 84th percentile confidence bands. *Source* Authors' calculations)

and manufacturing sector employment shares shock. Do the effects of the positive mining employment shares shock depend on whether it is gold or non-gold mining component? In Fig. 8.3a, there is no significant statistically differential decline in the response of income inequality to the positive gold mining and non-gold mining employment shares shocks. In Fig. 8.3b, income inequality declines more due to the positive manufacturing employment shares shock than to a mining employment shares shock of the same magnitude. The difference in the decline is statistically significant.

8.2.1 How Robust Are the Results to the Different Model Specifications?

The analysis further tests the robustness of the preceding results using different specifications and techniques. Equations (8.1) and (8.2) are estimated using 10,000 bootstraps draws. The shocks refer to a positive one per cent increase in the share of manufacturing employment (Manufacturing_emplyshare) shock. NEER denotes the nominal effective exchange rate. The crisis-dummy is equal to one from the beginning of 2007Q3 to end of the sample and zero otherwise. The period include low and volatile economic growth as well as the heightened economic policy uncertainty.

8 Does Monetary Policy Impact the Effects of Shares ...

$$\text{Gini}_t = \text{constant} + \sum_{i=1}^{2} \text{Gini}_{t-i}$$
$$+ \sum_{i=0}^{1} \text{Manufacturing\_emplyshare}_{t-i}$$
$$+ \text{crisis\_dummy} + \varepsilon_t \qquad (8.1)$$

$$\text{Gini}_t = \text{constant} + \sum_{i=1}^{2} \text{Gini}_{t-i}$$
$$+ \sum_{i=0}^{1} \text{Manufacturing\_emplyshare}_{t-i}$$
$$+ \text{crisis\_dummy} + \varepsilon_t \qquad (8.2)$$

The responses of income inequality to positive manufacturing sector employment shares shock based on these estimated equations, are shown in Fig. 8.4. Income inequality declines significantly to a positive shock in the share of manufacturing employment. The decline in

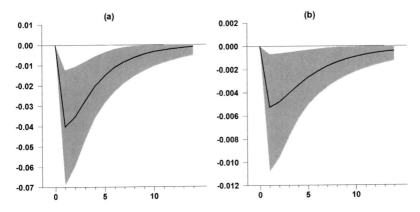

Fig. 8.4 Responses of income inequality to a positive manufacturing employment shares shock (*Note* The grey shaded bands denote the 16th and 84th percentile confidence bands. *Source* Authors' calculations)

income inequality is robust to different model specifications. Therefore, the increase in this sector's employment shares is important for the reduction of income inequality.

8.3 Is There a Role for the Monetary Policy Channel?

The role of monetary policy is assessed via two channels. The channels are (1) the repo rate and (2) consumer price inflation. The latter is measured by the 6% inflation threshold (the upper end of the inflation target band). The influence of these channels is determined by estimating counterfactual VAR models. The baseline counterfactual VAR model includes sectoral employment shares, income inequality, and monetary policy indicator. The sectoral shocks include the manufacturing, mining, and the tradeable sector employment shares.[3] These sectoral employment shares are included in the model separately. The models are estimated using two lags and 10,000 Monte Carlo draws. The role of the monetary policy channel is determined by shutting off the monetary policy channel in transmitting the positive manufacturing employment shares shock to income inequality.

The first analysis determines if the policy rate channel matters in the transmission of employment shares shock to income inequality. The actual and counterfactual income inequality responses are shown in Fig. 8.5. The counterfactual reaction declines more than the actual income inequality responses. This suggests that elevated repo rate levels mitigate the decline in income inequality following positive shocks to manufacturing, tradeable and mining sector employment shares.

Second, the chapter examines whether the level of the repo rate in the low inflation regime (that is, when inflation is below the 6% threshold) influences the transmission of positive shocks from the employment shares to income inequality. This is done by using a policy rate dummy

---

[3]The tradeable sector refers to the sum of the manufacturing and mining sector employment shares as a per cent of total non-agricultural employment.

8 Does Monetary Policy Impact the Effects of Shares ...

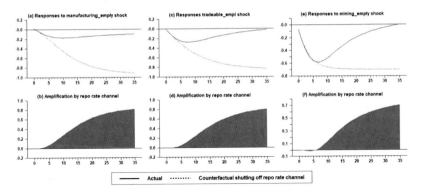

Fig. 8.5 Responses of income inequality to shocks and the role of the monetary policy channel (*Note* The shocks are one positive standard deviation in magnitude and _empl denotes employment shares. *Source* Authors' calculations)

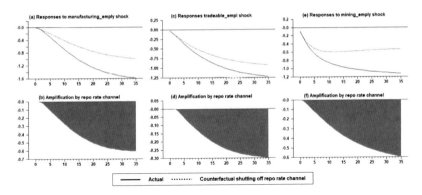

Fig. 8.6 Responses of income inequality to shocks and the role of the monetary policy channel when inflation is below 6% (*Note* The shocks are one positive standard deviation in magnitude and _empl denotes employment shares. *Source* Authors' calculations)

which equals the value of the repo rate when inflation is below 6% and zero otherwise. The repo rate in the baseline counterfactual VAR model is replaced with the policy rate dummy. The results are shown in Fig. 8.6. In all instances, the actual income inequality declines more than the counterfactual. This suggests that the lower repo rate levels in the low inflation regime amplify the decline in income inequality to positive shocks in the manufacturing, tradeable, and mining sector employment shares.

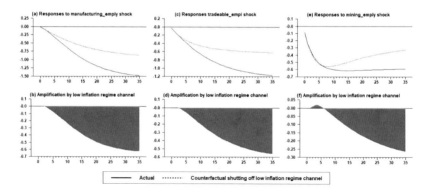

Fig. 8.7 Responses of income inequality and the role of the price stability channel (*Note* The shocks are one positive standard deviation in magnitude and _empl denotes employment shares. *Source* Authors' calculations)

Third, the analysis examines the influence of inflation below the 6% threshold in the transmission of positive shocks to manufacturing, tradeable and mining sector employment shares. This is examined by replacing the policy rate variable in the baseline counterfactual VAR model with the inflation dummy. The inflation dummy equals to value of consumer price inflation below or equal to 6% and zero otherwise. The responses of income inequality to three sector shocks are shown in Fig. 8.7. In all instances, the actual income inequality declines more than the counterfactual. This suggests that a low inflation regime increases the decline in income inequality due to positive shocks in the manufacturing, tradeable, and mining sector employment shares.

8.3.1 Do Expansionary Monetary and Contractionary Monetary Policy Channels Impact the Transmission of Positive Shocks to Manufacturing Sector Employment Shares onto Income Inequality Differently?

The preceding counterfactual VAR analysis did not examine the extent to which the effects of an expansionary monetary policy channel impact the transmission of positive shocks from manufacturing sector

8 Does Monetary Policy Impact the Effects of Shares ...

employment shares to income inequality. The baseline counterfactual VAR model includes manufacturing sector employment shares, income inequality, and monetary policy indicator. The analysis uses two dummies to distinguish the expansionary policy from the contractionary policy stance. The expansionary monetary policy dummy equals to the values of negative repo rate changes and zero otherwise. The contractionary monetary policy dummy equals to the values of positive repo rate changes and zero otherwise. These two monetary policy stance dummies are included separately in the counterfactual VAR model. These two monetary policy channels are shut off in the model to calculate the counterfactual income inequality responses due to a positive shock to manufacturing employment shares. Figure 8.8a shows that actual income inequality declines more than the counterfactual. The latter happens when the expansionary monetary policy channel is shut off. This suggests that expansionary monetary policy channel amplifies the reduction in income inequality following a positive shock to manufacturing employment shares. The sizes of negative amplifications are shown in Fig. 8.8b.

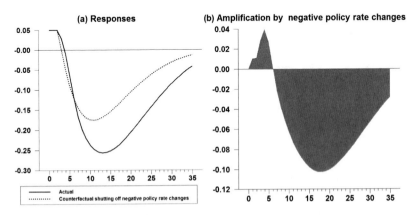

Fig. 8.8 Responses of income inequality to positive manufacturing sector employment shares shock and the role of expansionary monetary policy channel (*Note* The shocks are one positive standard deviation in magnitude. *Source* Authors' calculations)

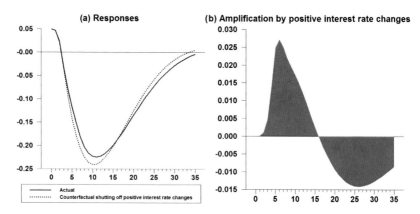

Fig. 8.9 Responses of income inequality to positive manufacturing sector employment shares shock and role of contractionary monetary policy channel (*Note* The shocks are one positive standard deviation in magnitude. *Source* Authors' calculations)

The income inequality responses, when considering the role of contractionary monetary policy channels, are shown in Fig. 8.9a. The counterfactual income inequality declines more than the actual. This suggests that contractionary monetary policy mitigates the reduction in income inequality following a positive shock to manufacturing sector employment shares.

8.3.2 Do the Effects of Expansionary Monetary Policy Depend on Whether Inflation Is Below or Above the 6% Threshold?

The analysis further examines the extent to which the effects of expansionary monetary policy channel are impacted by whether inflation is above or below the 6% inflation threshold. In this respect, two expansionary monetary policy dummies are created. The first dummy equals to values of negative repo rate changes when consumer price inflation is below the 6% threshold and zero otherwise. The second dummy is

8 Does Monetary Policy Impact the Effects of Shares ...

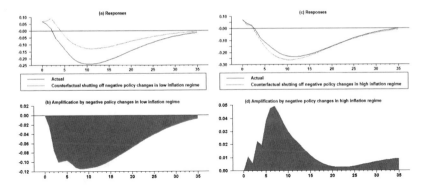

Fig. 8.10 Responses of income inequality to positive manufacturing sector employment shares shock and the role of expansionary monetary policy (*Note* The shocks are one positive standard deviation in magnitude. *Source* Authors' calculations)

equal to values of negative repo rate changes when consumer price inflation is above the 6% threshold and zero otherwise. The analysis refers to inflation below 6% as a low inflation regime. The analysis also refers to inflation above 6% as high inflation regime. These two expansionary monetary policy dummies are included separately in the preceding counterfactual VAR model. These are shut off in the model to calculate the counterfactual income inequality responses to positive shocks to manufacturing sector employment shares.

Figure 8.10a shows that actual income inequality declines more than the counterfactual. The sizes of negative amplifications are shown in Fig. 8.10b. By contrast, Fig. 8.10c reveals that the counterfactual income inequality declines more than the actual. This reveals that an expansionary monetary policy channel in the high inflation regime (when inflation exceeds 6%) dampens the reduction in income inequality, following positive shocks to manufacturing sector employment shares. This evidence reveals that inflation regimes matter for an expansionary monetary policy shock to influence the reduction in income inequality due to improved manufacturing employment shares.

8.4 Conclusions

This chapter investigated the extent to which the monetary policy channel impacts the transmission of positive shocks to manufacturing sector employment shares to income inequality. In addition, the chapter shows the role of monetary policy and price stability channels in transmitting shocks to tradeable and mining sector employment shares to income inequality. Evidence reveals that unexpected increase in the manufacturing, tradeable and mining sector employment shares leads to significant reduction in the income inequality. The decline from these sectors employment shares is amplified by the consumer price inflation that is below or equal to 6%. The effects are also amplified by the repo rate channel when consumer price inflation is below the 6% threshold. However, the effects of these shocks are mitigated by elevated repo rate levels. Moreover, analysis focusing on the influence of the manufacturing sector on income inequality only reveals that its effects are amplified by expansionary monetary policy. The influence of expansionary monetary policy differs depending on whether consumer price inflation is above or below the 6% threshold. The expansionary monetary policy accentuates the decline in income inequality when consumer price inflation is below 6%. Whereas it mitigates it when consumer price inflation exceeds the 6% threshold.

References

Gumata, N., & Ndou, E. (2017). *Labour market and fiscal policy adjustments to shocks: The role and implications for price and financial stability in South Africa*. Cham, Switzerland: Palgrave Macmillan.

Topalova, P. (2005). *Trade liberalisation, poverty and inequality: Evidence from Indian districts* (NBER Working Chapter No. 11614).

World Economic Outlook. (2018). Manufacturing jobs: Implications for productivity and inequality (Chap. 3). https://www.imf.org/en/Publications/WEO/Issues/2018/03/20/world-economic-outlook-april-2018.

9

Is There a Role for the Monetary Policy Channel in Transmitting Positive Shocks to the Services Sector Employment Shares to Income Inequality?

Main Highlights

- Evidence reveals that an unexpected increase in the services sector employment shares leads to a significant increase in income inequality.
- In addition, the counterfactual analysis reveals that when the inflation is below the 4.5 or 6% threshold, it dampens the increase in income inequality from positive shocks to the services sector employment shares.
- Moreover, the counterfactual analysis reveals that high GDP growth, the elevated repo rate levels, and exchange rate depreciation channels amplify the impact of positive shocks to the services sector employment shares onto income inequality.

9.1 Introduction

The employment shares of the services sector have been rising as depicted in Fig. 9.1. The rising services sector employment shares may be a contributor to rising inequality due to significant demand for

© The Author(s) 2019
E. Ndou and T. Mokoena, *Inequality, Output-Inflation Trade-Off and Economic Policy Uncertainty,*
https://doi.org/10.1007/978-3-030-19803-9_9

149

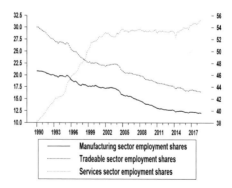

Fig. 9.1 A comparison of selected sectors' employment shares as percenatge of total nonagricultural employment (*Source* Authors' calculations and South African Reserve Bank)

high-skilled workers. In this context, the employment shares for the sectors are expressed as per cent of the total non-agricultural employment. In addition, the WEO (2018) noted the increased displacement of workers from the manufacturing sector to the services sector in advanced economies. This displacement coincided with a rise in income inequality and the increase was driven by larger disparities in earnings across all sectors. It is important for this chapter, to examine whether the increasing employment share of the services sector is contributing to rising income inequality in South Africa. This chapter examines whether the monetary policy channel impacts the transmission of positive shocks to the services sector employment shares to income inequality. In addition, the chapter compares the influence of the monetary policy channel to that emanating from other channels.

In an ideal situation, the rising trend of the services sector employment shares need not hinder the economy-wide productivity growth.[1] In addition, employment in some of the tradable service industries, which includes financial intermediaries, tend to be skill intensive, whereas the skill intensity of other service industries is linked to

---

[1] In addition, the report suggests that there are prospects for developing economies to gain ground towards advanced economy income levels.

9 Is There a Role for the Monetary Policy Channel ... 151

relatively high labour productivity growth (WEO 2018). Moreover, productivity levels in the services sector tend to converge to the global frontier (that is, to the productivity level in the most productive countries), just as in manufacturing. The rise in the employment shares of those services sectors therefore can boost the growth of aggregate productivity, and aid the convergence of income per worker across countries (WEO 2018). Topalova (2005) suggests that the benefits of liberalisation can be realised at substantial social costs unless additional policies are devised to redistribute some gains from the winners to the losers.

Unlike the WEO (2018), this chapter assesses whether the unexpected increase in the share of the services sector employment raises income inequality. We ask: Do positive shocks to the services sector employment shares lower income inequality? In addition, is the impact of the services sector employment shares on income inequality influenced by the monetary policy, consumer price inflation, and the exchange rate channels? The analysis further distinguishes between the roles of inflation when it is above and below the 6% inflation threshold. This chapter fills policy gaps by examining the role of the monetary policy channel which was not included in WEO (2018). In addition, the analysis examines the role of price stability. This study examines the role of the consumer price inflation channel below and above 6% threshold in transmitting the shocks in services sector employment shares to income inequality.

9.2 The Results

The analysis begins by estimating a bivariate VAR model with the services sector employment shares and income inequality. The services sector employment is expressed as a percentage of total non-agricultural employment. Income inequality is measured by the Gini coefficient. The Gini coefficient is obtained from Gumata and Ndou (2017). The other data is obtained from the South African Reserve Bank. The analysis uses quarterly data spanning 1993Q1 to 2016Q4.

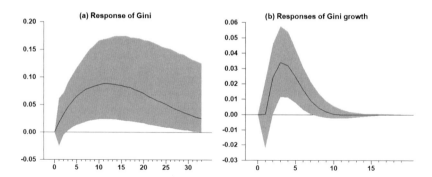

Fig. 9.2 Responses to positive services sector employment shares shock (*Note* The grey shaded bands denote the 16th and 84th percentile bands. Gini refers to Gini coefficient. *Source* Authors' calculations)

The models are estimated using two lags and 10,000 Monte Carlo draws. The exogenous variables include disposable income, GDP level, and the nominal effective exchange rate (NEER) and these variables are log transformed. A second model using the same variables is estimated but uses growth rates rather than levels. The results, based on both models using levels and growth rates, are shown in Fig. 9.2. The responses in Fig. 9.2a are to a positive shock to the service sector employment shares. The results reveal that an unexpected increase in the services sector employment shares raises the level of income inequality in Fig. 9.2a. The results in Fig. 9.2b are based on the bivariate VAR model with growth of the services sector employment shares and growth of income inequality. In addition, the positive shocks to the growth of the services sector employment share raises the growth of income inequality significantly for nearly three quarters.

How robust is the effect of the services sector employment shares on the growth of income inequality? The section further estimates different models for robustness checks in answering the preceding question. The first two models are given by Eqs. (9.1) and (9.2). The analysis further tests the robustness of the preceding results using different specifications and techniques. Equations (9.1) and (9.2) are estimated using 10,000 boostrap draws and serv_emplyshare_growth refers to service sector employment shares. The shocks refer to a positive one per cent increase in

9 Is There a Role for the Monetary Policy Channel ...   153

the share of services employment. Crisis_dummy equals to one beginning in 2007Q3 to end of sample and zero otherwise. This includes period of heightened economic policy uncertainty, low and volatile economic growth. Positive_repo_rate_changes dummy is equal to positive of values of changes in the repo rate and zero otherwise. CPI_inflation_above_six_percent dummy equals to values of inflation above 6% and zero otherwise.

$$
\begin{aligned}
\text{Gini\_growth}_t = \text{constant} &+ \sum_{i=1}^{2} \text{Gini\_growth}_{t-i} \\
&+ \sum_{i=0}^{4} \text{Serv\_emplyshare\_growth}_{t-i} \\
&+ \sum_{i=0}^{4} \text{GDP\_growth}_{t-i} + \sum_{i=0}^{4} \text{Positive\_repo\_rate\_changes}_{t-i} \\
&+ \sum_{i=0}^{4} \text{CPI\_inflation\_above\_six\_percent}_{t-i} \\
&+ \text{crisis\_dummy} + \varepsilon_t
\end{aligned} \tag{9.1}
$$

$$
\begin{aligned}
\text{Gini\_growth}_t = \text{constant} &+ \sum_{i=1}^{2} \text{Gini\_growth}_{t-i} \\
&+ \sum_{i=0}^{2} \text{Serv\_emplyshare\_growth}_{t-i} \\
&+ \text{crisis\_dummy} + \varepsilon_t
\end{aligned} \tag{9.2}
$$

The responses based on these estimated equations are shown in Fig. 9.3. In addition, GDP growth, the positive repo rate changes dummy, and inflation above 6% dummy, are shut off in the Eq. (9.1) to calculate the counterfactual income inequality responses from positive shocks to the service sector employment shares. These coefficients are set to zero, leading to Eq. (9.2). The income inequality increases significantly from a positive one per cent increase in the share of the services sector employment. The increase in income inequality is robust to different model specifications. In addition, Fig. 9.3c shows the combined roles of GDP growth, positive

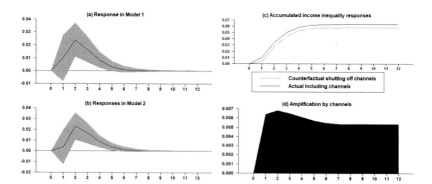

Fig. 9.3 Responses to positive services sector employment shares shock (*Note* The grey shaded bands denote the 16th and 84th percentile bands. *Source* Authors' calculations)

repo rate changes, and high inflation regime, that is, inflation rate above the 6% threshold. The actual growth of income inequality rises more than the counterfactual reaction, which suggests that high GDP growth, tight monetary policy stance, and high inflation above 6%, amplify the increase in income inequality due to positive shocks to the services sector employment shares. The sizes of amplification are shown in Fig. 9.3d.

9.2.1 Amplifications

This section examines the role of various channels in transmitting positive shocks from the services sector employment shares to income inequality. This is based on estimating Eq. (9.3). Various scenarios are tested using different counterfactual scenarios which shut off selected channels. The counterfactuals (1) shuts off GDP, NEER and the repo rate, (2) shuts off NEER, (3) shuts off the repo rate, and (4) shuts off GDP, respectively. The NEER is inverted so an increase denotes a depreciation. This counterfactual calculations are consistent with setting the estimated coefficients of these variables in Eq. (9.3) to zero. The analysis shuts off the indicated channels to determine their roles in transmitting positive shocks from the services sector employment shares to income inequality. The actual and counterfactual reactions are then compared to calculate the size of the amplification by the GDP channel.

9 Is There a Role for the Monetary Policy Channel ...

$$\text{Gini}_t = \text{constant} + \sum_{i=1}^{2} \text{Gini}_{t-i} + \sum_{i=0}^{4} \text{Service\_sector\_employment\_shares}_{t-i}$$

$$+ \sum_{i=0}^{4} \text{GDP}_{t-i} + \sum_{i=0}^{4} \text{Repo\_rate}_{t-i}$$

$$+ \sum_{i=0}^{4} \text{NEER}_{t-i} + \text{crisis\_dummy} + \varepsilon_t \qquad (9.3)$$

The amplifications, based on the model estimated in levels, are shown in Fig. 9.4a, b. Income inequality rises much higher when GDP, NEER and the repo rate channels, can operate in the model than when they are shut off. In addition, Fig. 9.4b shows amplifications when the model is estimated in levels and when the NEER channel is shut off. Income inequality rises much higher when the NEER channel can operate in the model than when it is shut off. This evidence reveals that positive shocks to services sector employment shares raises income inequality and the effects are amplified by high GDP, high interest rate levels, and a weaker exchange rate.

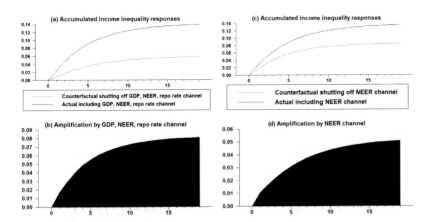

Fig. 9.4 Responses to a positive services sector employment shares shock (*Source* Authors' calculations)

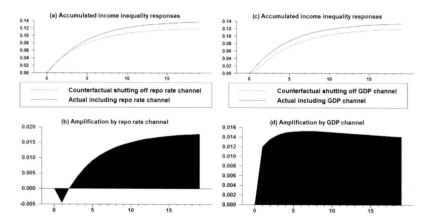

Fig. 9.5 Responses of income inequality to positive services sector employment shares shock and the roles of the GDP and monetary policy channels (*Source* Authors' calculations)

The preceding analysis shuts off the combined effects of GDP, NEER and the repo rate simultaneously in the model. However, we show in this section the separate effects due to the GDP and the repo rate channels. The analysis shuts off the GDP channel to determine its role in transmitting positive shocks from the service sector employment shares to income inequality. The gap between the actual and counterfactual reactions measures the size of the amplifications by the GDP and the repo rate channels.

Figure 9.5 shows the responses of income inequality to positive shocks to services sector employment shares shock and the role of GDP and monetary policy channel. These channels amplify increase in income inequality.

9.2.2 The Role of Price Stability Based on the 6% Inflation Threshold

The analysis includes the role of the price stability channel. The role of monetary policy is assessed via the influence of the 4.5 and 6% inflation thresholds. This is determined via the counterfactual VAR approach. The model includes the services sector employment shares, income inequality, and the inflation dummy. The inflation dummy is equal to

9 Is There a Role for the Monetary Policy Channel ...

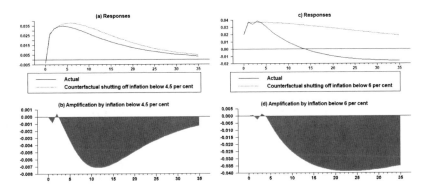

Fig. 9.6 Actual and counterfactual income inequality responses to positive services sector employment shares shock and the role of the low inflation regime (*Source* Authors' calculations)

the value of the inflation below the threshold and zero otherwise. The inflation dummies are included separately in the model. The model is estimated using two lags and 10,000 Monte Carlo draws. The role of price stability channel is determined by shutting off the indicated inflation regime channel in transmitting positive shocks to services sector employment shares to income inequality. Figure 9.6 shows that actual income inequality rises less than the counterfactual. This shows that both inflation regimes below the 4.5 and 6% thresholds have a dampening effect on income inequality. This suggests that price stability matters for the transmission of the unexpected increase in services sector employment shares to income inequality.

9.3 Conclusion

This chapter has investigated the extent to which the monetary policy channel impacts the transmission of positive shocks to the service sector employment shares to income inequality. The monetary policy channel is captured by the repo rate and inflation channels. In addition, the section showed the role of the repo rate, consumer price inflation, GDP, and the exchange rate channels, in transmitting positive shock to the services sector employment shares to income inequality.

This was done by estimating various counterfactual VAR models. The counterfactual VAR models shuts off the role of the consumer price inflation, GDP, repo rate, and the exchange rate channels in transmitting positive shocks to the services sector employment shares to income inequality. Evidence reveals that unexpected increase in the services sector employment shares leads to significant increase in the income inequality. In addition, the counterfactual VAR reveals that the inflation regime below 4.5 or 6% threshold dampens the increase in income inequality from positive shocks to the services sector employment shares. In addition, the counterfactual reveals high GDP, repo rate and exchange rate channels are amplifiers of positive shocks to the services sector employment shares onto income inequality. According to WEO (2018), this evidence implies that policies should focus on ensuring more inclusive gains from structural transformation rather than on supporting manufacturing employment. This implies that, when manufacturing jobs are disappearing, policymakers need to facilitate the reskilling of former manufacturing workers and reduce the costs of their reallocations, while strengthening safety nets to alleviate the adverse effects of joblessness and job transitions for the workers and their communities (WEO 2018).

References

Topalova, P. (2005). *Trade liberalisation, poverty and inequality: Evidence from Indian districts* (NBER Working Section No. 11614).

WEO. (2018). Chapter 3: Manufacturing jobs: Implications for productivity and inequality. *World Economic Outlook.* https://www.imf.org/en/Publications/WEO/Issues/2018/03/20/world-economic-outlook-april-2018.

Part IV

Consumption Inequality and Income Inequality

10

Does the Consumption Inequality Channel Impact the Transmission of Positive Income Inequality Shocks to Credit Dynamics in South Africa? Insights Before 2009Q1

Main Highlights

- Evidence indicates that credit increases significantly due to positive income inequality shocks. Thus, evidence confirms the link between income inequality and credit dynamics.
- The study further determines the role of the consumption inequality and consumption growth channels using counterfactual VAR models in transmitting positive income inequality shocks to credit extension. The actual credit rises more than the counterfactual responses. This suggests that consumption, consumption inequality, and inequalities in consumption categories amplify the increase in credit due to positive income inequality shocks.
- This evidence confirms that income inequality drives credit dynamics and the strength of this link requires policymakers to pay attention to existing structural issues in the economy. This implies that macroprudential regulators should put mechanisms in place which should prevent credit extension that is not driven by fundamentals as this may lead to crises and unproductive uses.

© The Author(s) 2019
E. Ndou and T. Mokoena, *Inequality, Output-Inflation Trade-Off and Economic Policy Uncertainty*,
https://doi.org/10.1007/978-3-030-19803-9_10

161

10.1 Introduction

Credit changes can be induced either by supply or demand factors. However, recent studies suggest both income and consumption inequalities may be the triggers of credit changes. Given that, income inequality is a big structural issue in South Africa, it should be an important aspect in the discussions of credit dynamics, rather than its role being underestimated. It is important for policymakers to disentangle the influence of both income and consumption inequalities in driving credit dynamics.

Indeed, the roles of both income and consumption inequalities dynamics have been pointed out in recent studies as potential drivers of credit dynamics. For instance, Perugini et al. (2013) found that an increase in income inequality leads to an increase in the supply of credit from those at the top of the distribution to meet the demand from those at the bottom of the distribution.[1] This chapter examines whether household consumption inequality (consumption inequality) channel impacts the transmission of positive income inequality shocks to credit dynamics in South Africa before 2009Q1. This chapter further determines the role of the consumption inequality and household consumption growth channels in transmitting positive income inequality shocks to credit. The analysis estimates various counterfactual VAR models. This includes determining whether household consumption, consumption inequality, and inequalities in the household consumption categories amplify the increase in credit, following positive income inequality shocks.

Why is it important to investigate the link between credit and income inequality? First, credit growth rose at a faster pace prior to the recession of 2009. In addition, growth in unsecured lending gathered momentum after this period. Second, credit growth has remained at lower levels post 2010. This coincided with periods of changes in banking regulation. Third, the recent slowdown in credit coincided with increases in the lending spreads, which possibly hinted at changes in how banks implement their profitability undertakings. In this instance,

---

[1]Perugini et al. (2013) argues that higher income inequality favors the rich and credit availability, because the rich have a higher propensity to save.

10 Does the Consumption Inequality Channel Impact ... 163

the reduced growth in credit could reflect changes in banks' profit motives, such that profits may be driven more by raising the price of credit, while restricting the volumes of credit. Amidst these changes, the roles of the income inequality and consumption inequality channels have not featured in the policy discussions.

Some researchers attest that increased income inequality leads to increased credit growth as funds seek profitable investment. Milanovic (2009) argues that rising inequality in the United States led to vast accumulations of wealth at the top of the income distribution. The accumulations led to a glut of funds seeking profitable investment. According to Milanovic (2009), the prevalence of higher income inequality causes those at a lower level of the income distribution to borrow more to maintain consumption expenditure as their incomes fall.[2] Indeed, evidence in recent studies indicates the existence of a significant link between income inequality and credit dynamics. For instance, simulations in Kumhof et al. (2012), based on calibrating a model to the UK data, indicate that increased inequality endogenously leads to credit expansion and increased leverage. However, other studies indicate the prevalence of "consumption cascades". For instance, evidence in Bertrand and Morse (2013) indicates that, an unexpected increase in the consumption expenditure of rich households raises the consumption expenditure of non-rich households.

The chapter examines the extent to which consumption inequality transmits positive income inequality shocks to credit. Why is it important to include consumption inequality channel in determining credit dynamics? First, Frank et al. (2010)'s theoretical model of consumer behavior is hinged on the concept of relativity of consumption in its foundations. They hypothesize that rising inequality leads to cascading expenditure increases. This arises when increased expenditure by some people makes other economic agents just below them on the income scale to spend more as well. Second, Kumhof and Ranciere's model argue that households at the bottom of the income distribution borrow to maintain consumption after a credit shock impacts the distribution

---

[2]This finding is consistent with previous US based studies on the relationship between income inequality and household.

of permanent income.[3] Third, Duesenberry (1947), hypothesize that a household's consumption expenditure in a given period is a function of some previously attained maximum level of consumption expenditure, and of the consumption expenditure of reference households. Thus, this theory explicitly allows for a relationship between the redistribution of income and aggregate consumption behavior.

This chapter fills policy research gaps by examining the extent to which positive income inequality shocks explain credit dynamics in South Africa. In addition, the analysis examines if the relationship is amplified by the consumption inequality and consumption growth channels and whether the results depend on consumption categories.[4]

10.2 Do the Changes in Income Inequality Drive Credit Dynamics?

The analysis starts by examining the direct link between income inequality as measured by the Gini coefficient and credit expressed in levels (hereafter *referred to as credit*). GDP is expressed in levels. The analysis is performed using quarterly (Q) data spanning 1993Q1 to 2008Q4. The Gini coefficient is obtained from Gumata and Ndou (2017) and other data is obtained from the South African Reserve Bank. We estimated several models to test whether a significant relationship between income inequality and credit exists. The first model (Model 1) is a bivariate VAR model. The model includes income inequality and the credit. In addition, a trivariate VAR model (Model 2) is estimated. This includes income inequality, credit, and GDP. In both models, income inequality, credit, and GDP are log transformed and multiplied by 100, so that impulses can be interpreted as percentage deviations from the trend. In both models, the exogenous variables include a crisis dummy.

---

[3]Recent empirical evidence in the United States strongly suggests that the observed rise in measured income inequality in recent decades has been predominantly driven by increased dispersion in permanent income, with increased variability of transitory income playing a much smaller role.

[4]It is not the purpose of this chapter to examine the preceding aspects and whether consumption inequality rises either much more slowly within groups.

10 Does the Consumption Inequality Channel Impact ...

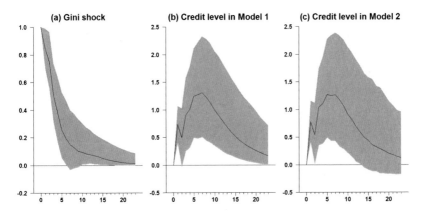

Fig. 10.1 Responses to positive income inequality shocks (*Note* The grey shaded bands denote the 16th and 84th percentile confidence bands. *Source* Authors' calculations)

The dummy equals to one from 2007Q3 to end of sample and zero otherwise.

In Fig. 10.1, credit rises significantly due to positive income inequality shocks, however, the increases last for less than 16 quarters in the extended model. Credit rises by about 1.5 per cent at the peak impact, which occurs at around eight quarters. Thus, evidence confirms the link between income inequality and credit dynamics.

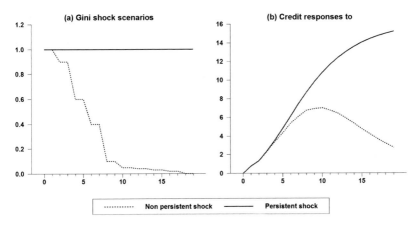

Fig. 10.2 Positive income inequality shock scenarios and credit dynamics (*Note* Gini refers to Gini coefficient. *Source* Authors' calculations)

This preliminary evidence indicates the existence of a statistically significant relationship between income inequality and credit dynamics. In addition, the analysis in Fig. 10.2, shows the effects of two income inequality shock scenarios. One scenario depicts a constant increase in income inequality, whereas the second scenario depicts a non-persistent increase in income inequality. Credit rises more to persistent income inequality shock in Fig. 10.2 than to a non-persistent income inequality shock.

10.2.1 How Robust Is the Preceding Evidence to a Different Technique?

The chapter further examines the robustness of the reaction of credit to positive income inequality shocks using Eqs. (10.1) and (10.2). Gini refers to Gini coefficient.

$$
\text{Credit\_level}_t = \text{constant} + \sum_{i=0}^{2} \text{Gini}_{t-i} + \sum_{i=1}^{4} \text{Credit\_level}_{t-i}
$$

$$
+ \sum_{i=0}^{4} \text{GDP\_level}_{t-i} + \text{crisis\_dummy} + \varepsilon_t \qquad (10.1)
$$

$$
\text{Credit\_level}_t = \text{constant} + \sum_{i=0}^{2} \text{Gini}_{t-i} + \sum_{i=1}^{4} \text{Credit\_level}_{t-i}
$$

$$
+ \text{crisis\_dummy} + \varepsilon_t \qquad (10.2)
$$

These models are estimated using 10,000 bootstrap draws. Irrespective of the model estimated, credit rises significantly at least over two years in Fig. 10.3. This evidence further confirms that income inequality drives credit dynamics and the strength of this link requires policymakers to pay attention to existing structural issues in the economy.

The section further estimates an exogenous VAR model to test the robustness of the preceding evidence. The exogenous VAR includes the income inequality as an exogenous variable in the model, whereas both credit and GDP, are endogenous variables. The exogenous VAR model

10 Does the Consumption Inequality Channel Impact ...

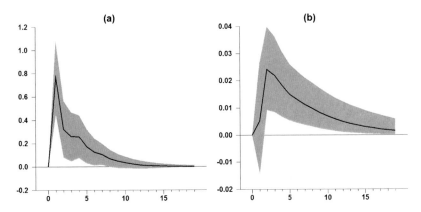

Fig. 10.3 Credit responses to positive income inequality shocks (*Note* The grey shaded bands denote the 16th and 84th percentile confidence bands. *Source* Authors' calculations)

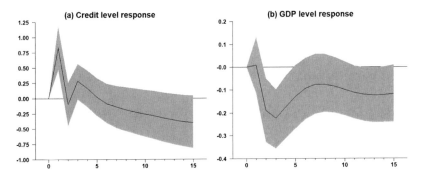

Fig. 10.4 Responses to positive income inequality shocks in the exogenous VAR model (*Source* Authors' calculations)

is estimated with two lags and 10,000 Monte Carlo draws. The model includes a recession dummy and a financial crisis dummy as exogenous variables. In Fig. 10.4, credit rises significantly to positive income inequality for two quarters. However, GDP declines significantly for six quarters. This evidence suggests that positive income inequality shocks raise credit levels and the finding is robust to different model specifications and techniques.

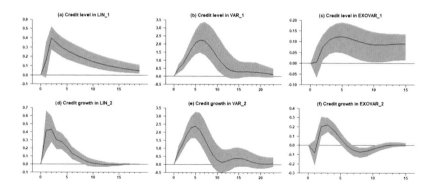

Fig. 10.5 Responses to positive consumption inequality shocks (*Note* The grey shaded bands denote the 16th and 84th percentile confidence bands. *Source* Authors' calculations)

10.2.2 Is the Consumption Inequality Channel an Amplifier of Positive Income Inequality Shocks on Credit Dynamics?

Prior to examining the role of the consumption inequality channel in transmitting positive income shocks to credit, the analysis first shows the effects of consumption inequality shocks on (1) the credit level and (2) credit growth. Consumption inequality is measured by the variance of the household consumption spending. The effects of consumption inequality are estimated using Eqs. (10.3) and (10.4) respectively. The reaction of credit from the two equations are denoted by LIN_1 and LIN_2 in Fig. 10.5. The models are estimated using 10,000 bootstraps draws.

$$\text{Credit\_level}_t = \text{constant} + \sum_{i=0}^{4} \text{Consumption\_inequality}_{t-i}$$
$$+ \sum_{i=1}^{4} \text{Credit\_level}_{t-i}$$
$$+ \sum_{i=0}^{4} \text{GDP\_level}_{t-i} + \text{crisis\_dummy} + \varepsilon_t \quad (10.3)$$

10 Does the Consumption Inequality Channel Impact ... 169

$$\text{Credit\_growth}_t = \text{constant} + \sum_{i=0}^{4} \text{Consumption\_inequality}_{t-i}$$

$$+ \sum_{i=1}^{4} \text{Credit\_growth}_{t-i}$$

$$+ \sum_{i=0}^{4} \text{GDP\_growth}_{t-i} + \text{crisis\_dummy} + \varepsilon_t \qquad (10.4)$$

In addition, several models are estimated to ascertain the robustness of the findings. The VAR model 1 (VAR_1) consists of the credit level and consumption inequality as endogenous variables while GDP is exogenous. VAR model 2 (VAR_2) consists of credit growth and consumption inequality as endogenous variables, whereas GDP growth is exogenous. The exogenous VAR model 1 (EXOVAR_1) consists of the credit and GDP as endogenous variables, while consumption inequality is exogenous. The exogenous VAR model 2 (EXOVAR_2) consists of credit growth and GDP growth as endogenous variables, while consumption inequality is exogenous. The models include dummies which capture structural changes in the economy. These models are estimated using two lags and 10,000 Monte Carlo draws.

All impulse responses in Fig. 10.5 indicate that both credit growth and the credit level rise significantly to positive consumption inequality shocks. This evidence confirms that unexpected increase in consumption inequality drives the credit dynamics in South Africa. In addition, the analysis determines whether the persistence of positive consumption inequality shocks matter for credit dynamics.

Figure 10.6 shows the two positive consumption inequality shock scenarios and the results are based on the estimated bivariate VAR models. In Fig. 10.6b, c, credit rises more to persistent shocks than to non-persistent shocks. This evidence reveals that the persistence of positive consumption inequality shocks matter for both the credit growth and credit level dynamics.

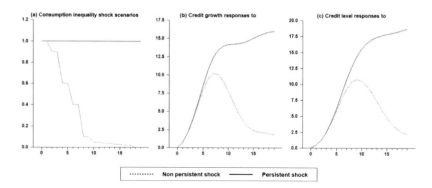

Fig. 10.6 Responses to positive consumption inequality shocks (*Source* Authors' calculations)

10.2.3 Do Consumption Inequality and Inflation Channels Transmit Positive Income Inequality Shocks to the Credit Dynamics?

The preceding evidence reveals that an unexpected increase in consumption inequality drives credit dynamics. Hence, it is important to empirically determine whether the link between income inequality and credit is reinforced or mitigated by the prevalence of the consumption inequality channel. The analysis further examines the relevance of the consumption channel in transmitting positive income inequality shocks to credit.

This study further determines the role of the consumption inequality and consumption growth channels using counterfactual VAR models. The models include income inequality, credit, and either consumption inequality or consumption as endogenous variables. The exogenous variables include GDP and other structural dummies. The models are estimated using two lags and 10,000 Monte Carlo Draws. The consumption inequality and consumption channels are shut off in the model to estimate the counterfactual responses to positive income inequality shocks. The channels are included separately in the model. The impulse responses are shown in Fig. 10.7. The actual credit rises more than the counterfactual responses. This suggests that consumption inequality and consumption magnify the increase in credit, following positive income inequality shocks.

10 Does the Consumption Inequality Channel Impact ...

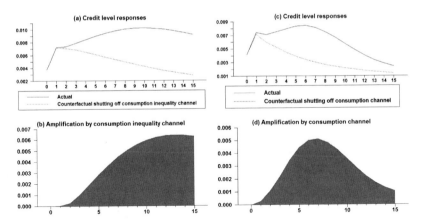

Fig. 10.7 Responses to positive income inequality shocks and the role of the consumption inequality and consumption channels (*Source* Authors' calculations)

Do the effects of positive income inequality on credit depend on whether it is aggregated consumption or consumption inequality or inequality in disaggregated consumption? This section separates the effects of consumption inequality according to consumption categories. The consumption categories include durable goods and non-durable goods consumption. The non-durable goods are combined with services consumption. The impulse responses are shown in Fig. 10.8. Evidence shows that these categories amplify the effects of positive income inequality on credit.

The section further shows the role of the inflation channel but distinguishes the effects between the low inflation and high inflation regimes. The threshold is based on the six per cent inflation. Two inflation dummy variables are created. The first dummy equals to the values of inflation when it exceeds the six per cent threshold and zero otherwise. The second dummy equals to the value of inflation when it is below six per cent threshold and zero otherwise. These dummy variables are included separately in the model. The impulse responses are shown in Fig. 10.9. Evidence shows that inflation plays different roles. When inflation is below the six per cent threshold, it dampens the increase in credit due to positive income inequality shocks. By contrast, when inflation is above the six per cent threshold, it amplifies the increases in credit to positive income inequality shocks.

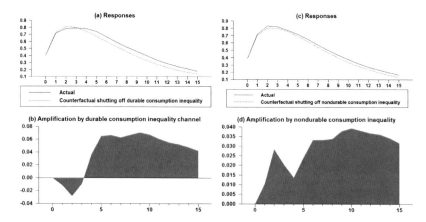

Fig. 10.8 Responses to positive income inequality shocks and the role of categories of the consumption inequality channels (*Source* Authors' calculations)

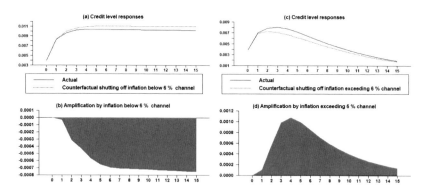

Fig. 10.9 Responses to positive income inequality shocks and the role of the consumer price inflation channels (*Source* Authors' calculations)

10.3 Conclusions

This chapter examined the extent to which the consumption inequality channel impacted the transmission of positive income inequality shocks to credit dynamics in South Africa before 2009Q1. Evidence reveals that credit increases significantly to positive income inequality shocks. However, the increases last for around 16 quarters. Thus, evidence confirms the link between income inequality and credit dynamics. The study further determined the role of the consumption inequality and consumption growth channels by estimating counterfactual VAR models. The consumption inequality and consumption channels are shut off in the models to estimate the counterfactual credit responses to positive income inequality shocks. The actual credit rises more than the counterfactual responses. This suggests that consumption and inequalities in the consumption categories amplify the increase in credit following positive income inequality shocks.

References

Bertrand, M., & Morse, A. (2013). *Trickle-down consumption* (NBER working chapter series, No. 18883).

Duesenbery, J. S. (1947). *Income, savings and the theory of consumer behaviour.*

Frank, R. H., Levine, A. S., & Oege, D. (2010, September 13). Expenditure cascades. *SSRN.* Available from http://ssrn.com/abstract=1690612.

Kumhof, M., & Rancière, R. (2010). *Inequality, leverage and crises* (IMF working chapters 10/268).

Kumhof, M., Lebarz, C., Ranciére, R., Richter, A. W., & Throckmorton, N. A. (2012). *Income inequality and current account imbalances* (IMF working chapters 12/08).

Milanovich, B. (2009). Two views on the cause of the global crisis—Part I. *Yale Global Online.* Available from http://yaleglobal.yale.edu/content/two-views-global-crisis. Accessed 7 November 2013.

Milanovich, B. (2010). *The haves and the have-nots: A brief and idiosyncratic history of global inequality.* New York: Basic Books.

Perugini, C., Hölscher, J., & Collie, S. (2013). *Inequality, credit expansion and financial crises* (PRA paper 51336).

11

Does Price Stability Impact the Link Between Income Inequality and Consumption Inequality?

Main Highlights

- Evidence reveals that consumption inequality rises significantly to positive income inequality shocks.
- A counterfactual VAR analysis indicates that high inflation amplifies the increase in consumption inequality to positive income inequality shocks when inflation exceeds the 6% threshold. In addition, evidence reveals that low inflation dampens the increase in consumption inequality when inflation is below the 6% threshold.
- This evidence reveals that price stability matters. Therefore, policymakers should enforce price stability to weaken the link between the income inequality and consumption inequality.

11.1 Introduction

Chapter 10 examined the extent to which the consumption inequality channel impacted the transmission of positive income inequality shocks to credit dynamics in South Africa as to get the insights before 2009Q1. Evidence

© The Author(s) 2019
E. Ndou and T. Mokoena, *Inequality, Output-Inflation Trade-Off and Economic Policy Uncertainty,*
https://doi.org/10.1007/978-3-030-19803-9_11

175

reveals that consumption growth, consumption inequality, and inequalities in consumption categories amplify the increase in credit due to the positive income inequality shocks. This evidence confirms that income inequality drives credit dynamics and the strength of this link requires policymakers to pay attention to existing structural issues in the economy. This chapter extends the analysis by introducing the role of monetary policy in the link between income inequality and consumption inequality as an issue requiring attention by policymakers in South Africa. There is a need to advocate for the role of price stability to start featuring prominently in the policy discussions, particularly those pertaining to the relationship between income inequality and consumption inequality. It should be noted that, this chapter is neither reviewing the applicability of the permanent income hypothesis nor the life-cycle hypothesis. However, this chapter offers the basis to begin the discussion on this matter. The questions investigated are as follows: To what extent is there a link between income inequality and consumption inequality? And how is the link between the income inequality and consumption inequality influenced by the 6% inflation threshold? In addition, the chapter shows the effects according to the categories of consumption expenditure.

Several studies have debated which is the better measure of inequality between income and consumption. For instance, Meyer and Sullivan (2013) articulated a strong case for using consumption rather than income in the measurement of inequality. These authors argue that this is due to income inequality's shortcomings regarding the measurement of disparities in consumption that result from differences in the accumulation of assets or access to credit. In addition, Hasset and Mathur (2012) also examined the role of consumption inequality. The most recent literature indicates that consumption is generally smoother and less volatile than income. This is because income is subject to various shocks such as unemployment, promotions, illnesses, and divorces. Whereas people try to maintain a stable level of consumption throughout the life cycle (Sarlo 2016). We do not discuss which is a better measure of inequality. The chapter examines the link between income inequality and consumption inequality and how their relationship is impacted by price stability.

Attanasio et al. (2012) documented that income inequality in the United States increased dramatically in the last three decades. However, they argue that no consensus has been reached regarding whether the increase in income inequality was matched by an equally large increase in consumption inequality. Their evidence indicates that consumption inequality within the United States between 1980 and 2010 increased by nearly the same amount as income inequality.

Economic theory suggests there is a link between consumption insurance and income shocks. These theories include complete market hypothesis, which assumes that consumption is fully insured against idiosyncratic shocks to both transitory and permanent income shocks. The permanent income hypothesis suggests that personal saving is the only source to smooth income shocks. In addition, the life-cycle hypothesis depicted in Fig. 11.1 links consumption and income. The life-cycle hypothesis suggests that consumption will exceed income in the early stages of life cycle. This is due to economic agents borrowing, which exceeds their consumption. This may include consumption of durables related to own households. In a certain life cycle state, the income is assumed to be higher than spending needs. This is a period in which economic agents save because income tends to exceed consumption. The retirement stage involves dissaving. In this stage, economic agents use monies accumulated in earlier period to finance their post-retirement needs, hence consumption exceeds income.

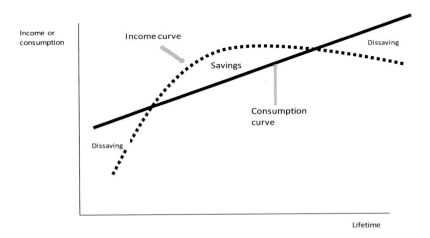

Fig. 11.1 Depiction of link between income and consumption based on the life-cycle hypothesis (*Source* Authors' drawing)

This chapter fills policy gaps by showing the direct link between the growth of income inequality and consumption inequality. Income inequality is measured by the Gini coefficient. The influence of monetary policy captured via the inflation channel is missing in the literature linking the growth of income inequality and consumption inequality. Hence, this analysis shows it is important to focus on the link between growth of income inequality and consumption inequality, and how this is affected by the inflation channel. This chapter fills policy research gaps by determining how price stability influences the transmission of positive income inequality shocks to consumption inequality. In this context, an inflation threshold of 6% is used. Unlike prior research, the analysis further examines if the price stability channel impacts the transmission of positive income inequality shocks to various categories of consumption inequality.

This chapter examines a fundamental question given the structural problem of income inequality besieging the South African economy. Does price stability impact the link between income inequality and consumption inequality? Evidence reveals that consumption inequality rises significantly to positive income inequality shocks. In addition, evidence shows that consumer price inflation that is below the 6% threshold dampens the increases in durable goods, non-durable, and services consumption inequalities than when the inflation channel is not shut off in the model. The dampening impact by consumer price inflation implies that price stability matters and should be maintained to reduce the income inequality from raising consumption inequality.

11.2 Is There a Significant Link Between Income Inequality and Consumption Inequality?

The section starts by examining the direct link between the growth of income inequality as measured by the Gini coefficient and consumption inequality as measured by two-quarter moving variance of the log household consumption. The section uses quarterly (Q) data spanning 1993Q1 to 2016Q4. The analysis begins by estimating a bivariate VAR model. The model includes growth of income inequality and

11 Does Price Stability Impact the Link Between Income Inequality ...

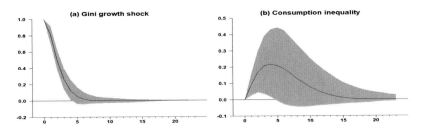

Fig. 11.2 Responses to positive income inequality shocks (*Note* A shock denotes an unexpected one positive percentage point in the growth of income inequality. The grey shaded bands denote the 16th and 84th percentile confidence bands. *Source* Authors' calculations)

consumption inequality. The results are robust to using four-quarter moving variance. The model is estimated using two lags and 10,000 Monte Carlo draws as selected by AIC. All models estimated controlled for the structural changes using dummy variables. The crisis dummy equals to one beginning in 2007Q3 to end of sample and zero otherwise. The Gini coefficient is obtained from Gumata and Ndou (2017) and other data is obtained from the South African Reserve Bank.

The effects of positive income inequality shock on consumption inequality are shown in Fig. 11.2. Consumption inequality rises significantly to positive income inequality shock. The peak increase in consumption inequality is reached in the fourth quarter. In addition, income inequality shock lasts for only five quarters. Thus, evidence confirms that positive income inequality shock is a driver of consumption inequality dynamics.

So, how robust is the preceding finding that consumption inequality rises, following a positive income inequality shock to the application of different techniques? To answer this question, this section further estimates two models. These models have important implications for the interaction between the growth of income inequality and consumption inequality. The first model is an exogenous VAR (Exogenous_VAR), which includes GDP growth and consumption inequality as endogenous variables. In this model, growth of income inequality is an exogenous variable. The second model (LIN_model) is given by Eq. (11.1). The model is estimated using 10,000 bootstraps draws.

$$\text{Consumption\_inequality}_t = \text{constant}$$
$$+ \sum_{i=1}^{4} \text{Consumption\_inequality}_{t-i}$$
$$+ \sum_{i=0}^{4} \text{Gini\_growth}_{t-i}$$
$$+ \sum_{i=0}^{4} \text{GDP\_growth}_{t-i}$$
$$+ \text{crisis\_dummy} + \varepsilon_t \qquad (11.1)$$

Evidence in Fig. 11.3, shows that irrespective of the model assumptions, consumption inequality rises to positive income inequality shocks. The rise in consumption inequality is robust to the different model specifications and assumptions.

The study further shows the two scenarios of positive income inequality shocks and the reactions of consumption inequality. The shocks denote scenarios of the constant income inequality changes and a weakening income inequality. The two shock scenarios are shown in

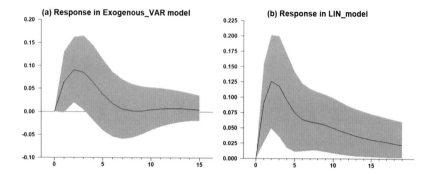

Fig. 11.3 Consumption inequality responses to positive income inequality shocks (*Note* A shock denotes an unexpected one positive percentage point in the growth of income inequality. The grey shaded bands denote the 16th and 84th percentile confidence bands. *Source* Authors' calculations)

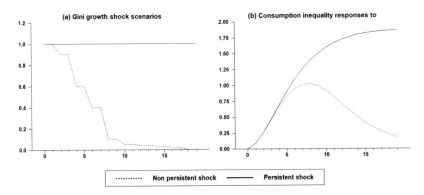

Fig. 11.4 Responses to positive income inequality shocks (*Source* Authors' calculations)

Fig. 11.4a. Consumption inequality responses to both shock scenarios are shown in Fig. 11.4b. The consumption inequality rises much higher to persistent income inequality shock than to a non-persistent shock.

11.2.1 Does Price Stability Impact the Transmission of Positive Income Inequality Shocks to Consumption Inequality?

This section further assesses the role of the inflation channel in transmitting positive income inequality shocks to consumption inequality. The potency of the inflation channel is examined by estimating a counterfactual VAR model. The model includes growth of income inequality, consumption inequality and consumer price inflation. The model is estimated using two lags and 10,000 Monte Carlo draws. The counterfactual consumption inequality response is determined by shutting off the consumer price inflation channel in transmitting positive income inequality shocks to consumption inequality.

Figure 11.5 shows the responses of consumption inequality and the size of amplifications due to the consumer price inflation channel. The actual consumption inequality response exceeds the counterfactual response. This suggests that elevated consumer price inflation amplifies the increase in consumption inequality due to positive income

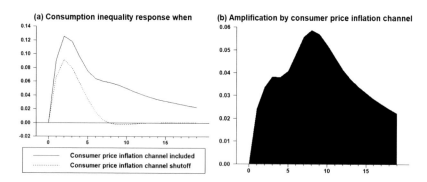

Fig. 11.5 Responses to positive income inequality shocks and amplification by the consumer price inflation channel (*Note* A shock denotes an unexpected one positive standard deviation in growth of income inequality)

inequality shock. This evidence reveals that price stability matters. Therefore, policymakers should enforce price stability to weaken the link between the income inequality and consumption inequality.

We further ask an important question: Would the results differ when using consumption categories? To investigate this, the analysis examines the role of consumer price inflation in transmitting positive income inequality shocks to the different consumption categories. The categories include durable, non-durable, and services consumption inequalities. The preceding model is used but consumption inequality is replaced with inequalities in consumption categories. In addition, the consumer price inflation channel is shut off to calculate the counterfactual consumption responses.

The responses of various consumption inequality categories are shown in Fig. 11.6. In all cases, the actual increase in inequality among all consumption categories exceeds those of their counterfactual reactions. This reveals that elevated consumer price inflation channel amplifies the increase in consumption inequality to positive income inequality shocks. This implies that the role of the elevated inflation channel in amplifying consumption inequality increase due to positive income inequality is not limited to aggregate households' consumption inequality but further applies to its categories.

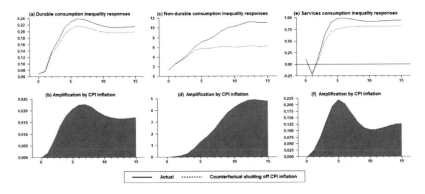

Fig. 11.6 Responses to positive income inequality shocks and amplification by the consumer price inflation channel (*Note* A shock denotes an unexpected one positive standard deviation in growth of income inequality)

11.2.2 Does the 6% Inflation Threshold Matter for the Link Between Income Inequality and Consumption Inequality?

The analysis further decomposes the consumer price inflation channel into high and low inflation regimes based on whether inflation exceeds the 6% threshold or not. The analysis replaces consumer price inflation in the preceding model with two inflation dummies. The first inflation dummy (high inflation regime) equals to the values of consumer price inflation above the 6% threshold and zero otherwise. The second inflation dummy (low inflation regime) equals to the values of consumer price inflation equal to or below the 6% threshold and zero otherwise. These inflation dummies are included separately in the model to capture the role of the inflation channel and to determine if its influence varies with whether inflation exceeds 6% or not.

In Fig. 11.7a, the actual consumption inequality exceeds the counterfactual in the high inflation regime (inflation over the 6% threshold) than when this regime is shut off in the model. This evidence indicates that high inflation amplifies the increase in consumption inequality when inflation exceeds the 6% threshold. The sizes of the amplification

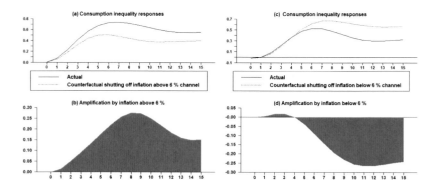

Fig. 11.7 Responses to positive income inequality shocks and the role of inflation regimes based on the 6% threshold (*Note* A shock denotes an unexpected one positive standard deviation in growth of income inequality)

in the consumption inequality in the high inflation regime are shown in Fig. 11.7b.

In contrast, Fig. 11.7c reveals that counterfactual consumption inequality exceeds the actual reaction when inflation is below the 6% threshold is included in the model than when it is shut off in the model. This evidence indicates that low inflation dampens the increase in consumption inequality when inflation is below the 6% threshold. The sizes of amplification in consumption inequality in the low inflation regime are shown in Fig. 11.7d. This evidence shows that inflation plays a role in the relationship between income inequality and consumption inequality. Therefore, policymakers should be aware that this link is impacted by inflation when it is above and below the 6% threshold.

11.3 Conclusion

This chapter started with a fundamental question: Does price stability impact the link between income inequality and consumption inequality? We find that consumption inequality rises significantly to a positive income inequality shock. The peak increase in consumption inequality is reached in the fourth quarter. In addition, the income inequality shock lasts only five quarters. Thus, evidence confirms that positive income inequality is a driver of consumption inequality dynamics. The chapter further assesses the role of the inflation channel in transmitting positive income inequality shocks to consumption inequality. The potency of the inflation channel is examined by estimating a counterfactual VAR model which shuts off the consumer price inflation channel in transmitting positive income inequality shocks to consumption inequality. In all cases, the actual increases in inequalities in all consumption categories exceed those of their counterfactual reactions. This implies that the role of an elevated inflation channel in amplifying consumption inequality increases due to positive income inequality is not limited to aggregate households' consumption inequality but further applies to the categories. Evidence indicates that high inflation amplifies the increase in consumption inequality when inflation exceeds the 6% inflation threshold. By contrast, evidence indicates that low inflation dampens the increase in consumption inequality when inflation is below the 6% threshold.

References

Aguiar, M., & Bils, M. (2011). *Has consumption inequality mirrored income inequality* (NBER working section number 16807).

Attanasio, O., Hurst, E., & Pistaferri, L. (2012). *The evolution of income, consumption and leisure inequality in the US, 1980–2010* (NBER working section No. 17982).

Hasset, K., & Mathur, A. (2012). *A new measure of consumption inequality.* American Enterprise Institute.

Krueger, D., & Perri, F. (2005). *Does income inequality lead to consumption inequality? Evidence and theory* (CFS Working Chapter, No. 2005/15). Goethe University, Center for Financial Studies (CFS).

Meyer, B., & Sullivan, J. (2013). Consumption and income inequality and the great recession. *American Economic Review, Sections and Proceedings, 103*(3), 178–183.

Sarlo, C. (2016). *Consumption inequality in Canada? Is the gap growing?* Fraser Institute.

Part V

Macroprudential Policy and Income Inequality

12

Do Positive Excess Capital Adequacy Ratio Shocks Influence the Income Inequality Dynamics in South Africa?

Main Highlights

- Evidence reveals that positive excess CAR shocks raises income inequality growth.
- Evidence from counterfactual analysis indicates that the actual declines in credit and GDP growth due to positive excess CAR shock exceeds those of the counterfactual responses. This suggests that increased income inequality growth following the positive excess CAR shocks exacerbates the decline in the real economic activity.
- From policy perspective, Perugini et al. (2016) suggests that policy-makers should cast their nets wider than financial regulatory reforms and consider the effects of their policy changes on influencing the distributive patterns, which include income inequality.

© The Author(s) 2019
E. Ndou and T. Mokoena, *Inequality, Output-Inflation Trade-Off and Economic Policy Uncertainty*,
https://doi.org/10.1007/978-3-030-19803-9_12

12.1 Introduction

Literature that determines the effectiveness of macroprudential tools has paid little attention on the related output costs, which includes income inequality and wealth distribution. This is not surprising since these tools are intended to have targeted effects on certain sectors in the economy. The aim of these tools is to mitigate the systematic risks in specific sectors. Gumata and Ndou (2017) showed the tightening in macroprudential policies could complement tight monetary policy by lowering consumer price inflation and inflation expectations. This chapter focuses on the link between excess capital adequacy ratio and income inequality. The excess capital adequacy ratio (excess CAR) refers to capital adequacy ratio above the minimum required. The subsequent chapters will look at the effects of loosening loan to value ratio and National Credit Act. It should be noted that the latter is not a tool of the Macroprudential toolkit at the South Africa Reserve Bank.

In Fig. 12.1a, the excess CAR is positively related to income inequality. The income inequality is captured by the Gini coefficient used in Gumata and Ndou (2017) and other data is sourced from the South African Reserve Bank. In addition, the excess CAR exhibits a negative relationship with GDP growth and employment growth in Fig. 12.1b, c. All growth rate used in this analysis are expressed as

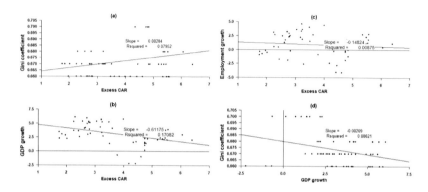

Fig. 12.1 The relationship between excess capital adequacy ratio and income inequality (*Source* Authors' calculation)

12 Do Positive Excess Capital Adequacy Ratio Shocks Influence … 191

annual rates. An increase in GDP growth is needed to lower income inequality in Fig. 12.1d. Motivated by these basic relationships, this chapter investigates the following questions: Do positive excess CAR shocks drive income inequality dynamics in South Africa? In addition, does the income inequality growth channel impacts the transmission of positive excess CAR shocks to real economic activity?

Indeed, literature indicates policymakers tend to overlook the potential costs of macroprudential tools. This is affirmed by Johansson and Wang (2014) and Demirguc-Kunt and Levine (2009) warnings that it is a disadvantage for policymakers to overlook the relationship between financial policy and inequality. They argue that overlooking this relationship may lead to undesirable consequences in the allocation of financial resources to certain sectors in the economy. The misallocation will impact the efficiency in the financial sector which may limit economic opportunities.

How could the misallocation and efficiency be linked to income inequality? This is because from a social perspective, the lowering of efficiency limits economic opportunities for the poor due to repressive financial policies. These policies have been found to increase the level of income inequality. This salient aspect via the distributive channel which includes income inequality has been under researched, more so in South Africa. This is despite, the Stiglitz (2015) postulation that the lowering of collateral requirements or policy interventions, which includes the reduction in banks' capital adequacy requirements, does not raise the overall efficiency in the economy. In contrary, these actions lead to an increase in income inequality. There are also lessons from the Gabraith's (2012) finding that increases in inequality in US are mainly driven by financial and macroeconomic policy choices. Carpantier et al. (2017) showed that amongst households with active mortgages with high loan to value ratios at the time of the acquisition are related to high contributions to wealth inequality today.

This chapter differs from the literature that assesses the effects of capital requirements as it focuses on the effects of excess capital adequacy ratio above the minimum required on the income inequality dynamics. This chapter contributes to literature on distributive effects of macroprudential policies by looking at the channels that transmit positive excess CAR shock to the level and growth of income inequality. This differs from the Carpantier et al. (2017) argument that costs of income inequality are captured in output losses which indicates why it has been overlooked as a potential collateral damage of macroprudential policies.

This chapter fills policy research gaps by showing that income inequality is not irrelevant to decisions pertaining to financial stability. In addition, the chapter fills policy research gaps by estimating counterfactual VAR models to capture the relevance of transmission channels. In addition, the chapter fills policy research gaps through showing the role of credit growth, GDP growth, house price growth and employment growth channels in transmitting positive excess CAR shocks to income inequality. The potency of these channels in determining the redistributive effects of positive excess CAR shocks to the income inequality has not been examined. Hence, Perugini et al.'s (2016) advice is that policymakers should cast the net wider than financial regulatory reforms and consider the effects of their policy changes on influencing the distributive patterns. This chapter investigates the extent to which macroprudential policy effectiveness and income inequality are related, irrespective of whether it is intended or unintended policymakers' outcome.

Evidence indicates that positive excess CAR shock significantly raise income inequality growth. The result is robust to different model specifications. This indicates that there are huge output losses and redistributive effects linked to rising income inequality induced by excess capital adequacy ratio above the minimum requirements. A counterfactual analysis was performed to determine if income inequality transmits positive excess CAR shocks to real economic activity. The counterfactual response is calculated by shutting off the income inequality channel from transmitting positive excess CAR shocks to GDP and credit growth in the model. Evidence indicates that both declines in actual economic growth and credit growth exceeds the counterfactual responses. Evidence from the counterfactual analysis confirms that increased income inequality following the positive excess CAR shocks exacerbates the decline in real economic activity. Therefore, the income inequality growth channel is a transmitter of positive excess CAR shocks to credit growth and other real economic activity.

12.2 Does an Unexpected Increase in the Excess Capital Adequacy Ratio Impact the Level of Income Inequality?

The analysis begins by examining the extent to which positive excess CAR shocks impacts on the (1) level of income inequality and (2) growth of income inequality (*after here referred to as income inequality growth*). The effects are determined through estimating various models. The models use quarterly (Q) data starting in 2000Q1 and ending in 2016Q3. The income inequality is captured by the Gini coefficient used in Gumata and Ndou (2017) and other data is sourced from the South African Reserve Bank. Four models are estimated with the income inequality variable in levels form and this is replaced with growth of income inequality in the latter models. The first VAR model (Model 1) includes excess CAR, income inequality, and credit as endogenous variables while GDP and employment are exogenous. The second VAR model (model 2) includes excess CAR, income inequality, and GDP as endogenous while credit and employment are exogenous. The third model is given by Eq. (12.1) estimated using 10,000 bootstrap draws. The *crisis dummy* equals to one from the beginning of financial crisis in 2007 and other periods of economic volatilities and zero otherwise.

$$\text{Gini}_t = \text{constant} + \sum_{i=1}^{4} \text{Gini}_{t-i} + \sum_{i=0}^{2} \text{Excess\_CAR}_{t-i}$$

$$+ \sum_{i=0}^{4} \text{Credit}_{t-i} + \text{Crisis\_dummy} \qquad (12.1)$$

The fourth model is an exogenous VAR which includes income inequality, GDP and credit as endogenous variables. In this model, GDP and employment and excess CAR are exogenous. All VAR models are estimated using one lag and 10,000 Monte Carlo Draws. In all instances, the positive excess CAR shock denotes a one per cent increase in excess

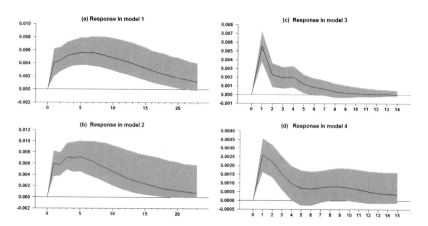

Fig. 12.2 Income inequality level's responses to positive excess capital adequacy ratio shocks (*Note* The grey shaded area denotes the 16th and 84th percentile confidence bands. *Source* Authors' calculations)

CAR unless otherwise stated. In Fig. 12.2, the income inequality variable rises significantly to positive excess CAR shocks in all models. This shows that positive excess CAR shocks raise the level of income inequality.

Would the influence of positive excess CAR shocks on income inequality differ when using income inequality growth? Figure 12.3 shows the responses to positive excess CAR shock and two shock scenarios based on bivariate VAR model. The model includes excess CAR and income inequality growth. The model is estimated using two lags and 10,000 Monte Carlo draws. In Fig. 12.3a, the excess CAR shock is persistent and does not die quickly. The income inequality growth rises significantly over all horizons in Fig. 12.3b. The peak income inequality growth of nearly 0.8 percentage points is achieved within two quarters of the positive excess CAR shock. In addition, in Fig. 12.3d, the income inequality growth rises very much to a persistent positive excess CAR shock than to a non-persistent shock.

The robustness of the preceding results is done through expanding the bivariate VAR model which includes the credit growth and GDP growth.

12 Do Positive Excess Capital Adequacy Ratio Shocks Influence ... 195

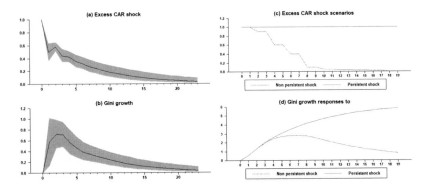

Fig. 12.3 Responses of income inequality growth to positive excess CAR shocks (*Note* The grey shaded area denotes the 16th and 84th percentile confidence bands. *Source* Authors' calculations)

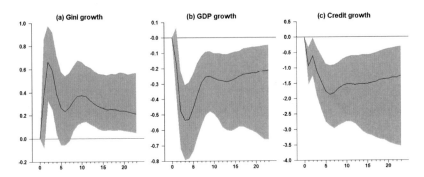

Fig. 12.4 Responses of income inequality growth to positive excess CAR shocks (*Note* The grey shaded area denotes the 16th and 84th percentile confidence bands. *Source* Authors' calculations)

This enables testing whether the additional variables respond as per theoretical expectations and responses are shown in Fig. 12.4. The income inequality growth rises significantly over all horizons in Fig. 12.4a. In addition, GDP growth and credit growth decline significantly over all horizons in Fig. 12.4b, c. At the peak decline, GDP growth declines by 0.5 percentage points around the fourth quarter. The credit growth declines by nearly 2 percentage points in the sixth quarter at its peak. These variables' reactions are consistent with theoretical expectations of unexpected increase in the excess CAR. The potency of these channels in transmitting positive excess CAR shocks to income inequality growth is examined in the latter sections.

The analysis further tests the robustness of this evidence using two VAR models. In the first VAR model (Endo_VAR), excess CAR is endogenous, together with income inequality growth, GDP growth and credit growth. In the second VAR model (Exo_VAR) the excess CAR is an exogenous variable while the income inequality growth, GDP growth, credit growth are endogenous variables. The models are estimated with one lag and 10,000 Monte Carlo draws.

The responses of income inequality growth are shown in Fig. 12.5. The income inequality growth rises significantly over all horizons in the endogenous VAR model in Fig. 12.5a. However, the inequality growth rises transitorily when excess CAR is exogenous in Fig. 12.5d. Overall, evidence indicates that positive excess CAR shock raises the income inequality growth. Both GDP growth and credit growth decline in Fig. 12.5b, e, c, and f, irrespective of whether excess CAR is exogenous or endogenous. But, the declines are not persistent in the exogenous VAR model compared to those in the endogenous model. This shows that positive excess CAR shock lowers both the GDP and credit growth rates, albeit the reactions tend to vary over the horizons.

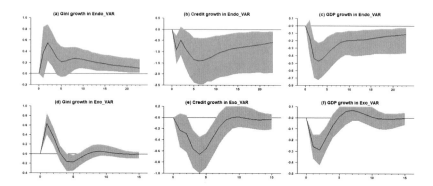

Fig. 12.5 Responses to positive excess CAR shocks (*Note* The grey shaded area denotes the 16th and 84th percentile confidence bands. *Source* Authors' calculations)

12.2.1 Channels Which Transmit the Positive Excess CAR Shocks to Income Inequality Growth

This section performs counterfactual analysis to determine the channels that may transmit the positive excess CAR shocks to income inequality growth (Gini_g). This is determined using the shutting off approach using various models. The counterfactual model is given by Eq. (12.3). The actual responses are based on Eq. (12.2). The channels (channel$_{t-i}$) examined include credit growth, GDP growth, employment growth and house price growth. The channels are included individual in the model. The counterfactual impulse response shuts off each channel in transmitting the effects of positive excess CAR shocks to income inequality growth. The gap between the actual responses of income inequality growth and counterfactual measure the size of influence for these channels in transmitting positive excess CAR shocks.

$$\text{Gini\_}g_t = \text{constant} + \sum_{i=1}^{4} \text{Gini\_}g_{t-i}$$

$$+ \sum_{i=0}^{2} \text{Excess\_CAR}_{t-i} + \sum_{i=0}^{4} \text{Channel}_{t-i}$$

$$+ \text{crisis\_dummy} + \varepsilon_t \qquad (12.2)$$

$$\text{Gini\_}g_t = \text{constant} + \sum_{i=1}^{4} \text{Gini\_}g_{t-i} + \sum_{i=0}^{2} \text{Excess\_CAR}_{t-i}$$

$$+ \text{crisis\_dummy} + \varepsilon_t \qquad (12.3)$$

The Credit Channel

The first channel examined is the relevance of credit channel in the transmission of positive excess CAR shocks to income inequality growth. In Fig. 12.6, income inequality growth rises more when including credit growth channel than when this channel is shutoff in the model. This suggests that the declining credit growth amplifies the rise in income inequality growth following positive excess CAR shocks.

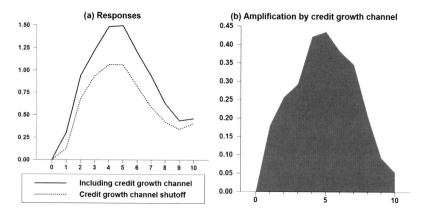

Fig. 12.6 Actual and counterfactual cumulative responses of income inequality growth to positive excess CAR shock and the role of the credit growth channel (*Source* Authors' calculation)

The Economic Growth Channel

The second channel examined is the economic growth channel. Figure 12.7 shows the role of GDP growth channel in transmitting positive excess CAR shocks to income inequality growth. The income inequality growth rises more than the counterfactual suggests. This suggests

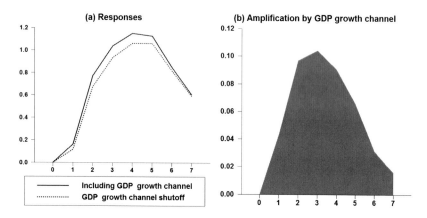

Fig. 12.7 Actual and counterfactual cumulative responses of income inequality growth to positive excess CAR shocks and the role of the GDP growth channel (*Source* Authors' calculation)

12 Do Positive Excess Capital Adequacy Ratio Shocks Influence ...

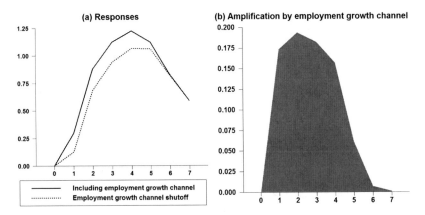

Fig. 12.8 Actual and counterfactual cumulative responses of income inequality growth to positive excess CAR shocks and the role of the employment growth channel (*Source* Authors' calculation)

that a contraction in GDP growth following a positive excess CAR shock amplifies the rise in income inequality growth. This shows that policymakers in tightening the excess CAR should consider the state of the GDP growth.

The Employment Channel

The analysis further looks at the role of employment channel in transmitting positive excess CAR shocks to income inequality growth. Figure 12.8 shows the role of employment growth channel in transmitting positive excess CAR shock to income inequality growth. The income inequality growth rises more than the counterfactual suggests. This suggests that the contraction of employment growth following a positive excess CAR shock amplifies the rise in income inequality growth.

The House Price Growth Channel

The last channel examined is the role of house price growth in transmitting positive excess CAR shocks to income inequality growth.

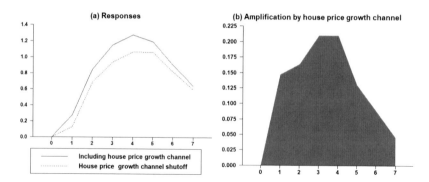

Fig. 12.9 Actual and counterfactual cumulative responses of income inequality growth to positive excess CAR shocks and the role of the house price growth channel (*Source* Authors' calculation)

Figure 12.9 shows the role of the house price growth channel in transmitting positive excess CAR shock to income inequality growth. The income inequality growth rises more than the counterfactual suggests. This suggests that the contraction of house price growth following a positive excess CAR shock amplifies the rise in income inequality growth.

12.2.2 Does the Income Inequality Growth Channel Impacts the Transmission of Positive Excess CAR Shocks to Real Economic Activity?

The preceding analysis has shown that positive excess CAR shocks raise income inequality growth, and this is accentuated by certain channels included in the model. Hence, this chapter examines the extent to which income inequality growth impacts the transmission of positive excess CAR shocks to credit growth and GDP growth. This section present the results from various models determining the robustness of the role of income inequality growth channel on impacting how the positive excess CAR shocks affect credit growth. The various models for determining the positive excess CAR shocks effects on credit growth and GDP growth are given by Eqs. (12.4)–(12.7). These equations are used to determine the actual and counterfactual responses of credit growth (credit_g_{t-i}) and GDP growth (GDP_g_{t-i}) to positive excess CAR shocks. Income inequality channel is captured by (inequality_g).

$$
\text{Credit\_}g_t = \text{constant} + \sum_{i=1}^{2} \text{Credit\_}g_{t-i}
$$

$$
+ \sum_{i=0}^{2} \text{Excess\_CAR}_{t-i}
$$

$$
+ \sum_{i=0}^{4} \text{Inequality\_}g_{t-i} + \varepsilon_t \qquad (12.4)
$$

$$
\text{Credit\_}g_t = \text{constant} + \sum_{i=1}^{2} \text{Credit\_}g_{t-i}
$$

$$
+ \sum_{i=0}^{4} \text{Excess\_CAR}_{t-i} + \varepsilon_t \qquad (12.5)
$$

$$
\text{GDP\_}g_t = \text{constant} + \sum_{i=1}^{2} \text{GDP\_}g_{t-i}
$$

$$
+ \sum_{i=1}^{2} \text{Excess\_CAR}_{t-i} + \sum_{i=1}^{2} \text{Inequality\_}g_{t-i}
$$

$$
+ \sum_{i=1}^{2} \text{Credit\_}g_{t-i} + \varepsilon_t \qquad (12.6)
$$

$$
\text{GDP\_}g_t = \text{constant} + \sum_{i=1}^{2} \text{GDP\_}g_{t-i}
$$

$$
+ \sum_{i=0}^{2} \text{Excess\_CAR}_{t-i}
$$

$$
+ \sum_{i=0}^{2} \text{Credit\_}g_{t-i} + \varepsilon_t \qquad (12.7)
$$

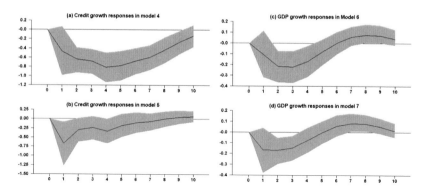

Fig. 12.10 Responses to positive excess CAR shocks (*Note* The grey shaded area denotes the 16th and 84th percentile confidence bands. *Source* Authors' calculations)

In Fig. 12.10, credit growth declines significantly for nearly 8 quarters in Eq. (12.4), which is longer than 4 quarters in Eq. (12.5). This shows that the inclusion of income inequality growth makes credit growth to remain depressed over long periods. In addition, the peak decline is larger in the presence of the income inequality growth channel, than when it is shut off in the model. This evidence reveals that income inequality growth plays an important role in transmitting positive excessive CAR shocks to credit growth. In addition, the chapter shows the responses of GDP growth to the positive excess CAR shocks in Fig. 12.10c, d. GDP growth declines significantly to positive excess CAR shocks. The contraction is longer in the presence of the income inequality growth channel than when this channel is shut off in the model. This finding is robust to the inclusion of consumer price inflation in both models.

The main objective of this section is to show the role of the income inequality growth channel in transmitting positive excess CAR shocks. This is determined by the gap between the responses when income inequality channel is included in the model than when it is excluded. Figure 12.11 shows the actual and the counterfactual responses of both

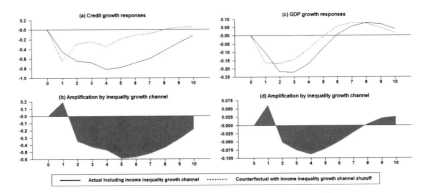

Fig. 12.11 Credit and GDP growth responses to positive excess CAR shocks and the role of the income inequality growth channel (*Source* Authors' calculations)

credit and GDP growth to positive excess CAR shocks. The size of amplifications suggests that the income inequality growth worsens the decline in the credit growth and GDP growth. This evidence confirms that increased income inequality following the positive excess CAR exacerbates the decline in real economic activity.

12.3 Conclusion

Do the positive excess capital adequacy ratio (excess CAR) shocks drive income inequality dynamics in South Africa? Evidence reveals that positive excess CAR shocks raise income inequality growth. In addition, the chapter investigated whether the income inequality growth channel impacts the transmission of positive excess CAR shocks to real economic activity using a counterfactual approach. Evidence indicates that the actual decline in both credit and GDP growth exceeds that of the counterfactual responses. This suggests that increased income inequality growth following the positive excess CAR shocks exacerbates the decline in real economic activity. Perugini et al. (2016) suggests that policymakers should cast their nets wider than financial regulatory reforms and consider the effects of their policy changes in influencing the distributive patterns, including income inequality. Thus, policymakers should consider the adverse effects of income inequality when financial institutions hold more excess of capital adequacy reserves above the minimum required.

References

Ampudia, M., van Vlokhoven, H., & Zochowski, D. (2014). *Financial fragility of the Euro area households* (Working chapter series 1737). European Central Bank.

Carpantier, F. F., Olivera, J., & van Kerm, P. (2017, forthcoming). Macroprudential policy and household wealth inequality. *Journal of International Money and Finance, 6,* 87–105.

Demirguc-Kunt, A., & Levine, R. (2009). Finance and inequality: Theory and evidence. *Annual Review of Financial Economics, 1,* 287–318.

Gabraith, J. K. (2012). *Inequality and instability: A study of the world economy just before the great crisis.* New York: Oxford University Press.

Gumata, N., & Ndou, E. (2017). *Labour market and fiscal policy adjustments to shocks: The role and implications for price and financial stability in South Africa.* Cham, Switzerland: Palgrave Macmillan.

Johansson, A. C., & Wand, X. (2014). Financial sector policies and income inequalities. *China Economic Review, 31,* 367–378.

Perugini, C., Holscher, J., & Collie, S. (2016). Inequality, credit and financial crises. *Cambridge Journal of Economics, 40*(1), 227–257.

Stiglitz, J. E. (2015). *New theoretical perspectives on the distribution of income and wealth amongst individuals: Part IV—Land and credit* (NBER working chapters 21192).

13

Does an Unexpected Loosening in the Loan to Value Ratio Has Any Distributive Effects via the Inequality Channel?

Main Highlights

- Evidence indicates that an unexpected loosening in the loan to value (LTV) ratio reduces income inequality growth significantly.
- Evidence from counterfactual VAR approach analysis shows declining income inequality amplify the increase in house price growth, residential investment growth and credit growth due to LTV shocks.
- Since income inequality channel is a potent transmitter of loose LTV shocks to the real economic activity, hence policymakers should decisively eliminate the high levels of income inequality as these distort the transmission mechanism of macroprudential policies.

© The Author(s) 2019
E. Ndou and T. Mokoena, *Inequality, Output-Inflation Trade-Off and Economic Policy Uncertainty*,
https://doi.org/10.1007/978-3-030-19803-9_13

13.1 Introduction

The effects of positive excess capital adequacy ratio shocks on the income inequality dynamics in South Africa have been assessed in Chapter 12. Evidence reveals that a positive excess CAR shock raises income inequality growth and counterfactual analysis indicates that the actual decline in credit and GDP growth due to this shock exceeds those of the counterfactual responses. This suggests that increased income inequality growth following the positive excess CAR shocks exacerbates the decline in the real economic activity. This suggests that policymakers should cast their nets wider than the financial regulatory reforms and consider the effects of their policy changes on influencing the distributive patterns, which include income inequality (Perugini et al. 2015). This chapter examines the impacts of the unexpected loosening in the loan to value ratio on income inequality. This is due to implications derived from the latest empirical research which shows that Central Bankers who ignore the impact of income inequality on the financial stability may be missing the key determinant of financial fragility. So, to what extent does a loose loan to value ratio (*hereafter referred to as LTV*) shock impact income inequality dynamics? In addition, we determine the extent to which the income inequality channel accentuates or dampens the transmission of loose LTV shocks to real economic activity.

Theory is unequivocal that macroprudential policies can impact income and wealth distribution. According to Frost and van Stralen (2017) macroprudential policies have direct distributive effects. For instance, a high LTV or debt to income ratio may restrict a household with limited financial wealth to purchase a house. Alternatively, well implemented macroprudential tools could smooth credit markets and asset price developments over the financial cycle. This may reduce the redistribution of wealth due to the changes in credit delinquencies and asset valuation changes. These outcomes have implications for income and wealth distributions.

The scatterplot in Fig. 13.1a reveals a negative relationship between LTV and income inequality. The negative relationship implies that

13 Does an Unexpected Loosening in the Loan to Value Ratio ...

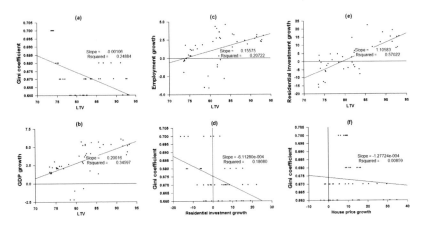

Fig. 13.1 The various relationships (*Source* Authors' calculations)

a loosening in LTV lowers income inequality. LTV and Gini coefficient are obtained from Gumata and Ndou (2017) and other data are obtained from the South African Reserve Bank. The LTV is in percentage form. In addition, there is a positive relationship between LTV and employment growth, GDP growth, and residential investment growth. The increases in both growth rates of residential investment and house prices are associated with a decline in income inequality. All growth rates denote year-on-year changes.

Why is it important to look at the link between LTV and income inequality dynamics from the South African perspective? First, this is because the current research linking macroprudential regulation and income inequality in South Africa is scarce. This happens even though recent literature indicates the availability of good theoretical explanations linking macroprudential policies and both income inequality and wealth distribution. Second, the extent to which income inequality impacts the transmission of LTV shocks to real economic activity is unknown. Third, policy advice based on evidence in advanced economies suggests that incorporating the link between central bank actions and income inequality can help shape optimal macroprudential regulation outcomes. Fourth, central banks have been perceived to downplay the distributional effects of their policies (which include macroprudential regulations), because their policies purportedly have negligible effects on income inequality and wealth redistribution.[1] This is in contrast with recent empirical evidence which shows that neither monetary policy nor macroprudential regulations are neutral in terms of income redistribution. For instance, Frost and van Straden (2017) find a positive association between macroprudential policies and both market and net income inequality. In addition, their evidence indicates that LTV limits have positive association with net income inequality.

In addition, Punzi and Rabitsch (2015) reveal that households' wealth structure matters when designing countercyclical macroprudential measures. For instance, macroprudential policies should tighten to curb excessive lending only for households that react the most after a house price shock. This policy action can improve individual and social welfare more than the macroprudential policy that targets all households uniformly.[2] Furthermore, Frost and van Stralen (2017), find that countries with countercyclical buffers, concentration limits or limits of growth in direct credits tend to experience higher income inequality. Carpantier et al. (2017) show that caps on LTV ratio can decrease wealth inequality, depending on the underlying structure of the economy.[3]

This chapter fills policy research gaps by examining the extent to which an unexpected loosening in LTV has distributive effects via the income inequality channel. Second, the chapter fills policy research gaps by determining the relevance of the income inequality channel on impacting the transmission of unexpected loosening in LTV ratio to real economic activity.

---

[1]Whether monetary policy and macroprudential regulation increase or decrease income inequality significantly it is an empirical question. This is echoed by the recent editorial in the Journal of money and finance (2017) which focuses on the theme of *monetary policy, macroprudential regulation and inequality: AN introduction to special edition.* The editorial indicates that the distributional effects of central bank actions which includes macroprudential regulations.

[2]In addition, studies also show that macroprudential policies in fostering price stability may impact inequality.

[3]The size of LTV ratios on housing prices on credit costs and inter-generational transfers.

13.2 Is There a Relationship Between LTV Ratio and Income Inequality in South Africa?

The analysis begins by examining the link between unexpected loosening in LTV and (1) the level of income inequality and (2) growth of income inequality. The income inequality is measured by the Gini coefficient obtained from Gumata and Ndou (2017). The chapter uses quarterly (Q) data starting in 2004Q4–2015Q2. The analysis estimates Eqs. (13.1)–(13.3), which relates the level of the income inequality to LTV. The models are estimated with 10,000 bootstrap draws. The additional models are estimated as robustness tests. This includes using the GDP and credit (measured by total loans and advances). The latter captures the role of credit dynamics. All growth rates used in the chapter are year-on-year rates. All LTV shocks denote a one per cent unexpected increase in LTV ratio.

$$\text{Gini}_t = \text{constant} + \sum_{i=1}^{4} \text{Gini}_{t-i} + \sum_{i=0}^{1} \text{LTV}_{t-i} + \varepsilon_t \quad (13.1)$$

$$\text{Gini}_t = \text{constant} + \sum_{i=1}^{4} \text{Gini}_{t-i} + \sum_{i=0}^{4} \text{GDP}_{t-i}$$
$$+ \sum_{i=0}^{1} \text{LTV}_{t-i} + \varepsilon_t \quad (13.2)$$

$$\text{Gini}_t = \text{constant} + \sum_{i=1}^{4} \text{Gini}_{t-i} + \sum_{i=0}^{4} \text{Credit}_{t-i}$$
$$+ \sum_{i=0}^{1} \text{LTV}_{t-i} + \varepsilon_t \quad (13.3)$$

The impulse responses of income inequality are shown in Fig. 13.2. The loose LTV shock leads to a decline in income inequality. And the

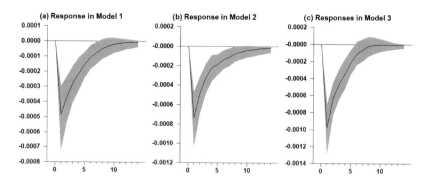

Fig. 13.2 Income inequality responses to loose LTV shocks (*Note* The grey shaded area denote the 16th and 84th percentile confidence bands. *Source* Authors' calculations)

negative impact of loose LTV shock on income inequality is robust to the various model specifications.

This chapter further estimates bivariate VAR models using one lag and 10,000 Monte Carlo draws to test the robustness of the negative impact of the loosening LTV shock. The first VAR model (Model 1) includes LTV and income inequality. The second VAR model (Model 2) includes income inequality and LTV. Figure 13.3, shows the trajectories of the loosening LTV shock and the responses of income inequality to this shock.

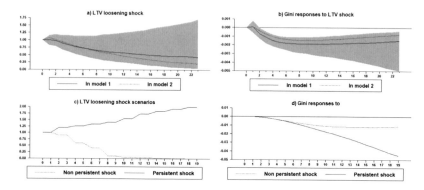

Fig. 13.3 Responses based on VAR models (*Note* The grey shaded area denote the 16th and 84th percentile confidence bands. *Source* Authors' calculations)

13 Does an Unexpected Loosening in the Loan to Value Ratio ...

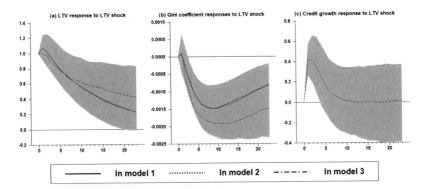

Fig. 13.4 The response of income inequality to a loose LTV shock (*Note* The grey shaded area denote the 16th and 84th percentile confidence bands. *Source* Authors' calculations)

In Fig. 13.4, the loose LTV shock tends to be persistent. Income inequality declines significantly to a loose LTV shock. Income inequality tends to remain significantly depressed over long periods. This is irrespective of whether the model includes GDP and credit or not. In addition, the chapter further shows the effects of the persistent and non-persistent LTV shocks. Income inequality declines more to a persistently loosening LTV shock than to a non-persistent shock.

A third VAR model is estimated. The model includes LTV ratio, income inequality and credit. The impulses responses are shown in Fig. 13.4. The income inequality declines significantly in all the models. The declines are not significantly different as they are bounded within the same confidence band. This indicates the findings are robust to model ordering and the addition of the credit variable.

13.2.1 How Robust Is the Negative Effect of Loose LTV Shock on Income Inequality Growth?

This chapter further tests the robustness of the negative relationship between loose LTV shock and income inequality growth. The robustness test is based on two bivariate VAR models estimated using one lag and 10,000 Monte Carlo draws. The first VAR model (Model 1) includes LTV and income inequality growth. The second VAR model (Model 2) uses the reverse ordering. The loose LTV shock reduces income inequality growth significantly and this is robust to the model specifications. In addition, the unexpected increase in income inequality leads to significant tightening in the LTV ratio. This shows the prevalence of the feedback effects (Fig. 13.5).

How robust is the preceding conclusion to the addition of credit growth in the model? Figure 13.6 shows that income inequality growth

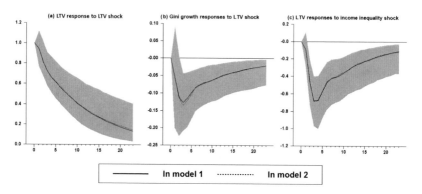

Fig. 13.5 Responses of income inequality growth to loose LTV shocks (*Note* The grey shaded area denote the 16th and 84th percentile confidence bands. *Source* Authors' calculations)

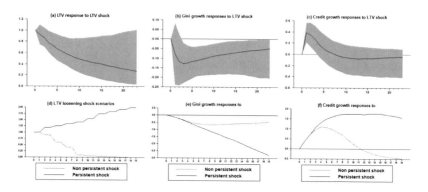

Fig. 13.6 Responses of income inequality growth to loose LTV shock in the extended model (*Note* The grey shaded area denote the 16th and 84th percentile confidence bands. *Source* Authors' calculations)

declines significantly to a loose LTV shock. In addition, credit growth rises significantly for a year. This finding indicates that the decline in income inequality growth is robust to the inclusion of credit growth in the model. In addition, Fig. 13.6 shows the responses to two scenarios of loose LTV shocks. The persistent loosening LTV shock leads to prolonged decline in income inequality growth than a non-persistent shock. Furthermore, the persistent loose LTV shock leads to a prolonged increase in credit growth than a non-persistent loosening shock. This evidence shows the decline in income inequality growth is robust to the inclusion of credit growth and to the persistence of loose LTV shock.

13.2.2 Channels That Transmit Loose LTV Shocks

The analysis further examines the channels transmitting loose LTV shocks to income inequality growth. These channels include the residential investment growth, non-residential investment growth, house price growth, GDP growth and employment growth. The estimated counterfactual VAR model includes LTV, income inequality growth and a macroeconomic variable. The counterfactual responses include shutting off the role of the indicated macroeconomic variable channel in transmitting LTV shocks to income inequality growth. The channels are included separately in the model. These include credit growth, residential investment growth, non-residential investment growth, house price growth, GDP growth and employment growth. The models are estimated using one lag and 10,000 Monte Carlo draws.

In Fig. 13.7, a loose LTV shock raises residential investment significantly over 15 quarters. The peak increase of one percentage point is achieved in the fifth quarter. In addition, house price growth rises significantly over all horizons. This evidence shows that a loose LTV shock significantly impacts the residential investment activities. Figure 13.7 further shows that residential investment and house price rise significantly to a persistent loosening LTV shock than to a transitory shock. This shows that the persistence of the loose LTV shocks matter for residential investment and house price dynamics.

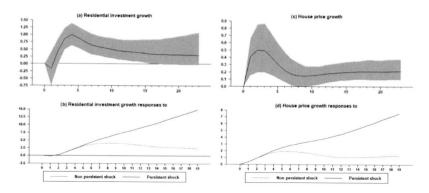

Fig. 13.7 Responses to loose LTV shocks (*Note* The grey shaded area denote the 16th and 84th percentile confidence bands. *Source* Authors' calculations)

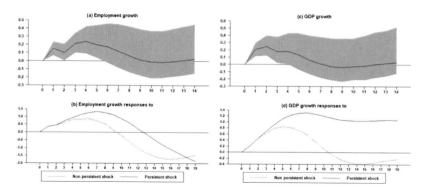

Fig. 13.8 Response to loose LTV shocks (*Note* The grey shaded area denote the 16th and 84th percentile confidence bands. *Source* Authors' calculations)

In addition, Fig. 13.8 shows the responses of employment growth and GDP growth to a loose LTV shock. The employment growth rises significantly for nearly 6 quarters. GDP growth also rises significantly for nearly five quarters. Both variables increase by nearly 0.3 percentage points at the peak increases. The increase in employment growth could be linked to the residential investment activity which may raise demand for more labour probably for construction purposes. The increased residential investment activity would raise GDP growth.

13.2.3 How Important Are the Selected Channels in Transmitting Loose LTV Shocks to Income Inequality Growth?

To answer this question, the analysis performs a counterfactual analysis to determine the potency of the various channels that may be transmitting loose LTV shocks to income inequality growth. This is determined by estimating a counterfactual model which shuts off specific channels in transmitting the effects of loose LTV shock to income inequality growth (Gini_g). The effects are determined by estimating Eqs. (13.4) and (13.5).

$$\text{Gini}\_g_t = \text{constant} + \sum_{i=1}^{4} \text{Gini}\_g_{t-i} + \sum_{i=0}^{2} \text{LTV}_{t-i}$$

$$+ \sum_{i=0}^{2} \text{Channel}_{t-i} + \text{Crisis\_dummy} + \varepsilon_t \quad (13.4)$$

The counterfactual is calculated by setting the coefficients of the indicated channel to zero in Eq. (13.4), leading to Eq. (13.5).

$$\text{Gini}\_g_t = \text{constant} + \sum_{i=1}^{4} \text{Gini}\_g_{t-i}$$

$$+ \sum_{i=0}^{2} \text{LTV}_{t-i} + \text{Crisis\_dummy} + \varepsilon_t \quad (13.5)$$

The gap between the actual responses of income inequality growth and the counterfactual reaction measures the size of influence of the indicated channel. The channels examined include residential investment growth, house prices growth, GDP growth, credit growth, non-residential investment growth and employment growth.

In Fig. 13.9, the actual income inequality growth declines more than the counterfactual responses. This suggests that increased residential

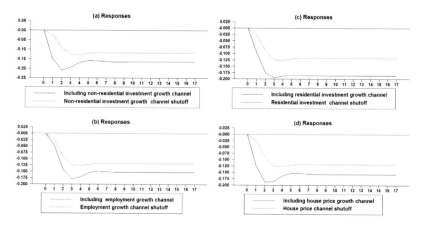

Fig. 13.9 Cumulative responses of income inequality growth to loose LTV shocks and selected channels

investment, non-residential investment, employment and house price channels due to loose LTV shock amplify the declines in income inequality growth than the counterfactual suggests. In Fig. 13.10, income inequality growth declines more than the counterfactual suggests. This shows that the role of the GDP growth, the unemployment, the investment growth and the credit growth channels accentuate the decline

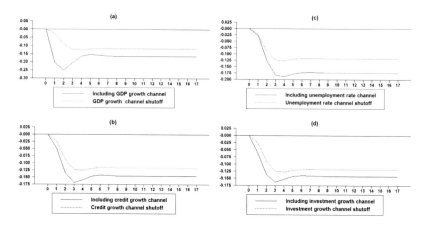

Fig. 13.10 Cumulative responses of income inequality growth to loose LTV shocks and selected channels (*Source* Authors' calculations)

in income inequality growth, following the loose LTV shocks. This evidence suggests that an improvement in GDP growth, lower unemployment, increased investment and increased credit growth accentuates the decline in income inequality growth, following a loose LTV shock.

The analysis further examines the role of the non-residential investment growth and employment growth channels in transmitting loose LTV shocks to income inequality growth. In Fig. 13.11, the actual decline in the growth of income inequality exceeds that of the counterfactual. This suggests that non-residential investment and employment growth channels propagate the decline in the growth of income inequality.

In Fig. 13.12, the income inequality measure declines more in the presence of the transmission channels than when these channels are shut off in the model. The analysis further examines the role of GDP growth and credit growth in transmitting shocks to the income inequality measure using the preceding approach. Income inequality declines more than the counterfactual suggests. This shows that improved GDP growth and credit growth, following a loose LTV shock, leads to more declines in income inequality.

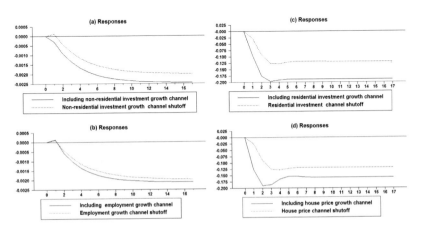

Fig. 13.11 Cumulative responses of income inequality growth to loose LTV shocks and selected channels (*Source* Authors' calculations)

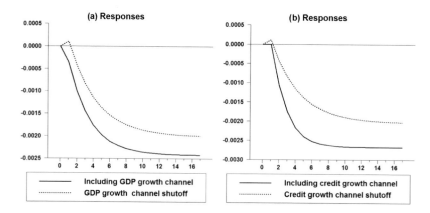

Fig. 13.12 Actual and counterfactual cumulative income inequality responses to loose LTV shocks and role of GDP and credit growth (*Source* Authors' calculations)

13.2.4 Does the Income Inequality Channel Impact the Transmission of Loose LTV Shocks to Real Economic Activity?

The chapter concludes the analysis by examining the extent to which income inequality growth as a channel transmits loose LTV shocks to three macroeconomic variables (Macro_ind). These variables include house price growth, credit growth and residential investment. The variables are included separately in Eqs. (13.6) and (13.7). Equation (13.6) is used to estimate the actual impulse responses of macroeconomic indicator variable to loose LTV shock. The estimated coefficients of growth of income inequality in Eq. (13.7) are set to zero to enable the calculation of the counterfactual impulse responses. The gaps between the actual and counterfactual responses captures the role of income inequality growth channel.

$$\text{Macro\_ind}_t = \text{constant} + \sum_{i=1}^{2} \text{Macro\_ind}_{t-i} + \sum_{i=0}^{2} \text{LTV}_{t-i}$$

$$+ \sum_{i=0}^{2} \text{Income\_growth}_{t-i} + \varepsilon_t \quad (13.6)$$

$$\text{Macro\_ind}_t = \text{constant} + \sum_{i=1}^{2} \text{Macro\_ind}_{t-i}$$

$$+ \sum_{i=0}^{2} \text{LTV}_{t-i} + \varepsilon_t \qquad (13.7)$$

Figure 13.13 shows the actual and counterfactual responses of the house price growth, residential investment growth and credit growth. In all cases the actual responses exceed the counterfactuals. This evidence indicates that a declining growth of income inequality amplifies the increase in house price inflation, residential investment growth and credit growth respectively. This shows that the income inequality channel is a potent transmitter of loose LTV shocks to real economic activity.

13.3 Conclusion and Policy Implications

To what extent does a loose loan to value ratio (LTV) shock impact income inequality dynamics in South Africa? Evidence indicates that a loose LTV shock reduces income inequality growth significantly and this is robust to the different model specifications. In addition, an

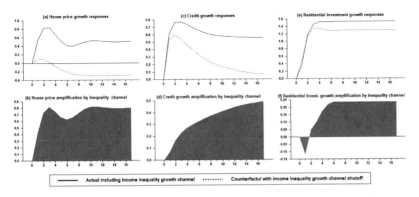

Fig. 13.13 Actual and counterfactual responses to loose LTV shocks and role of income inequality growth channel (*Source* Authors' calculations)

unexpected increase in income inequality leads to a tightening in the LTV ratio. Second, this chapter applies a counterfactual VAR approach to determine if the income inequality channel impact the transmission of a loose LTV shock to house price growth, residential investment growth and credit growth. In all cases, the actual reactions rises higher than the counterfactuals suggest. This evidence indicates that the declining income inequality growth amplifies the increase in house price inflation, increases both residential investment growth and credit growth. This shows that the income inequality channel is a potent transmitter of loose LTV shocks to real economic activity. Policymakers should decisively eliminate the high levels of income inequality as these distort the transmission mechanism of the macroprudential policies.

References

Carpantier, F. F., Olivera, J., & van Kerm, P. (2017, forthcoming). Macroprudential policy and household wealth inequality. *Journal of International Money and Finance*.

Frost, J., & van Stralen, R. (2017). Macroprudential policy and income inequality. *Journal of International Money and Finance, 85*, 278–290.

Gumata, N., & Ndou, E. (2017). *Labour market and fiscal policy adjustments to shocks: The role and implications for price and financial stability in South Africa*. Cham, Switzerland: Palgrave Macmillan.

Monin, P. (2017). *Monetary policy, macroprudential regulation and inequality* (ECP, Discussion note 2017/2).

Punzi, M. T., & Rabitsch, K. (2015). Investor borrowing heterogeneity in a Kiyotaki-Moore style macro model. *Economics Letters, 130*, 75–79.

https://www.investopedia.com/terms/l/loantovalue.asp.

14

Is the Tightening in the National Credit Act a Driver of Growth of Income Inequality?

Main Highlights

- Evidence reveals that the tightening the National Credit Act (NCA) raises income inequality.
- Evidence from counterfactual approaches shows that the rise of growth of income inequality due tightening NCA shock exacerbates the reduction of credit growth, residential investment growth and GDP growth.
- Evidence shows that the income inequality channel is a potent conduit that transmits the NCA shocks to real economic activity and exacerbates their adverse effects.

14.1 Introduction

Access to credit is important for financial inclusion which is necessary for sustainable economic growth. Financial inclusion is necessary for inclusive growth, especially in South Africa, which has the highest

© The Author(s) 2019
E. Ndou and T. Mokoena, *Inequality, Output-Inflation Trade-Off and Economic Policy Uncertainty*,
https://doi.org/10.1007/978-3-030-19803-9_14

income inequalities in the world.[1] This chapter examines the effects of the NCA as part of the macro-prudential toolkit on the evolution of both the level and growth of income inequality.[2] Evidence in Gumata and Ndou (2017) indicates that a tightening in the NCA standards has adverse effects on credit growth and that the repurchase rate complements the NCA. From the redistributive perspective, it is not known how the NCA, through changing the lending standards, influences the income inequality dynamics. For instance, a tightening in the lending standards may make it difficult for lending institutions to finance certain investment projects. So, it is worth asking: To what extent does the NCA influence the income inequality dynamics in the country? Does the income inequality channel impact the transmission of NCA shocks to credit growth, residential investment growth and economic growth?

Recent findings in the literature, although at infant stages, reveal that macroprudential tools do influence income inequality dynamics. It is shown in Ampudia et al. (2014) that caps on the loan to value ratios affect the loss of a given default of the households and more generally the households in distress in the case of a crisis. Evidence in Frost and van Stralen (2017) indicates that macroprudential tools restrict the ability of households with limited financial wealth to purchase a house. However, Carpantier et al. (2017) suggest that well implemented macroprudential tools may be used to smooth credit market and asset price developments over the financial cycle. This may change the redistribution of wealth due to changes in credit delinquencies and asset valuation changes, which influence income and wealth distributions. In addition, Punzi and Rabitsch (2015) reveal that macroprudential policy actions focusing on selected groups can improve individual and social welfare more than a macroprudential policy that targets all households uniformly. Carpantier et al. (2017) shows that caps on loan to value ratios

---

[1]As the Banking Association of South Africa explains on their website: "credit enables people to spend money they don't have, spend more money than they earn, use credit for ordinary purchases, use credit even when they have cash and use debt to pay off debt. The use of credit and poor money management skills often leads people into a situation of over-indebtedness where they are unable to service credit agreements."

[2]The National Credit Act (35 of 2005) was introduced "to promote and advance the social and economic welfare of South Africans, promote a fair, transparent, competitive, sustainable, responsible, efficient, effective and accessible credit market and industry, and to protect Consumers."

can decrease wealth inequality, depending on the underlying structure of the economy.

It is worth pointing out the following: First, research on macroprudential regulation, which includes the effects of the NCA on income inequality in South Africa, is not available. Second, the extent to which income inequality impacts the transmission of the tightening in the NCA is unknown. Third, recent literature suggests that incorporating the link between central bank actions and income inequality can help shape optimal macroprudential regulatory policies. Fourth, some studies suggest that central banks should pay attention to the potential feedback effects of their macroprudential policies on income inequality through impacting other macroeconomic conditions. This will prevent the unintended consequences of their macroprudential policy effects through changes in income distribution.

The chapter fills policy research gaps by determining the extent to which the NCA influences the income inequality dynamics. In addition, this chapter fills policy research gaps by determining the extent to which the income inequality channel impacts the transmission of the NCA shocks to credit growth, residential investment growth, and economic growth.

14.2 Does the National Credit Act Impact Income Inequality?

The empirical analysis begins by determining the impact of the NCA shocks on income inequality growth. Income inequality is measured by the Gini coefficient obtained from Gumata and Ndou (2017). The analysis uses quarterly (Q) data spanning 1993Q1–2016Q3. The NCA dummy equals to one, beginning in 2007Q2 to the end of the sample and zero otherwise. The NCA was implemented in June 2007.

14.2.1 Evidence from Linear Regressions

Figure 14.1 shows the size of the impacts of NCA on income inequality, based on two linear regressions. In the first model, we regress NCA

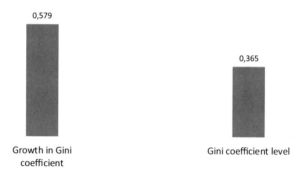

Fig. 14.1 Impacts of NCA on the growth and level of income inequality (*Source* Authors' calculations)

dummy on income inequality. In the second model we regress NCA dummy on income inequality growth. That is, what is the direction of the impact of the NCA dummy on the (1) level of income inequality and (2) income inequality growth? This preliminary evidence indicates that NCA implementation raises income inequality.

14.2.2 Evidence from VAR Analysis

The preceding results based on linear regression indicate that NCA raises both the (1) growth of income inequality and (2) the level of income inequality. The linear regression results refer to the long run effects. This section shows the responses of income inequality to NCA shock using VAR analysis. The VAR model includes the NCA dummy as defined earlier, income inequality growth, credit growth and GDP growth.[3] These are annual growth rates. The VAR model is estimated using one lag and 10,000 Monte Carlo Draws.[4]

The income inequality responses to NCA shocks are shown in Fig. 14.2. The NCA shock is persistent, indicating that its effects linger

---

[3]Based on total loans and advances.
[4]All models include various dummies which control for structural breaks and include the adoption of inflation targeting framework in February 2000 and economic growth recessions.

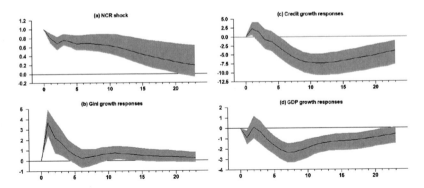

Fig. 14.2 Responses to NCA shock (*Note* The grey shaded area denote the 16th and 84th percentile confidence bands. *Source* Authors' calculations)

for a long time. The NCA shock leads to significant decline in credit growth after four quarters, with a peak decline of 7.5 percentage points occurring in the tenth quarter. In addition, GDP growth declines significantly over all horizons. The income inequality growth rises significantly, reaching a peak in the first quarter. Evidence shows that the NCA shock raises income inequality growth.

How robust is the increase in income inequality growth to NCA shock? The robustness is determined by applying two approaches. The first estimated Eq. (14.1) denoted as (LIN_Model) in Fig. 14.3. The growth of income inequality is denoted by Gini_g_t

$$\text{Gini\_}g_t = \text{constant} + \sum_{i=1}^{4} \text{Gini\_}g_{t-i} + \sum_{i=0}^{3} \text{NCA}_{t-i} + \varepsilon_t \quad (14.1)$$

The other model is an exogenous VAR (EXO_VAR). This model includes the NCA dummy as an exogenous variable, while GDP growth, credit growth and income inequality growth, are endogenous. The model is estimated using one lag and 10,000 Monte Carlo Draws. The income inequality growth rises significantly due to the NCA shocks in both models. Credit growth and GDP growth decline significantly for at least six quarters. The duration of the credit growth contraction exceeds that of GDP growth decline. In addition, the peak magnitude of the decline in credit growth exceeds that of GDP growth.

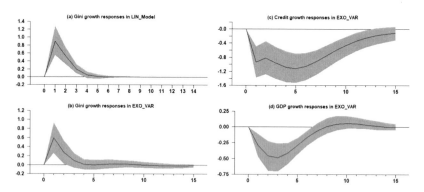

Fig. 14.3 Responses to NCA shock (*Note* The grey shaded area denote the 16th and 84th percentile confidence bands. *Source* Authors' calculations)

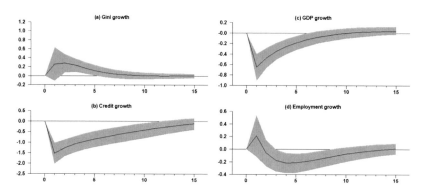

Fig. 14.4 Responses of variables using additional variables (*Note* The grey shaded area denote the 16th and 84th percentile confidence bands. *Source* Authors' calculations)

How robust are the preceding findings to the inclusion of employment growth as an endogenous variable in the Exogenous VAR model? Would the conclusions differ when the wage growth and consumer price inflation variables are included as exogenous variables in other model? The results, based on the model using one lag and 10,000 Monte Carlo Draws, are shown in Fig. 14.4. The income inequality growth rises significantly for nearly six quarters following the NCA

14 Is the Tightening in the National Credit Act ...

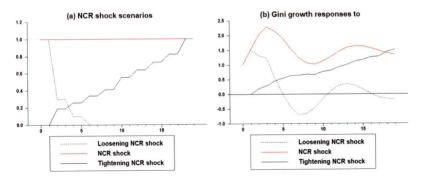

Fig. 14.5 NCA shock scenarios and responses of income inequality growth (*Source* Authors' calculations)

shock. In addition, the NCA shock lowers GDP growth, credit growth and employment growth. This suggests that the transmission of NCA shocks, in raising income inequality, could be transmitted via these channels.

In Fig. 14.4 employment growth declines significantly for nearly nine quarters. At the peak, GDP growth falls by 0.6 percentage points and credit growth decline by 1.5 percentage points. The peak decline in credit growth is achieved in the first quarter. The adverse effects of NCA shocks on real economic activity indicate that these channels may explain the increase in income inequality growth. A counterfactual analysis is used in the following sections to examine the role of these channels in transmitting the NCA shocks to income inequality growth.

However, the preceding analysis did not examine the effects of shock scenarios to show the difference in the changes in lending standards in NCA. Hence, this section performs scenarios of the NCA shocks. The scenarios show a distinction between the effects of loosening in NCA and increasing the tightening in the NCA standards. In Fig. 14.5, the income inequality growth rises due to the increasing tightening in NCA standards. By contrast, the income inequality growth tends to decline to the loosening in the NCA standards. This evidence reveals that policymakers should be aware that changes in the NCA standards matter for the income inequality growth dynamics.

14.2.3 Channels of Transmission of the NCA Shocks to Growth of Income Inequality

This section performs a counterfactual analysis showing the extent to which GDP growth, credit growth, wages growth and inflation regimes may be transmitting the NCA shocks to growth of income inequality. The model shuts off each channel in transmitting the effects of the NCA shocks to income inequality growth. The gaps between the actual response of the income inequality growth and the counterfactual indicate the size of the influence of the indicated channel. The channels include GDP growth, credit growth, wages growth, and consumer price inflation.

The GDP Growth Channel

Determining the relevance of the transmission channels begins by showing the role of economic growth in the transmission of the NCA shocks to income inequality growth. This includes separating between the roles of *negative GDP growth* from the *positive GDP growth*. Two economic growth dummy variables (*GDP_growth_dummy*) are used. The negative GDP growth dummy equals to the negative values of economic growth and zero otherwise. The positive GDP growth dummy equals to the positive values of economic growth and zero otherwise. The effects are estimated using Eqs. (14.2) and (14.3).

$$
\begin{aligned}
\text{Gini\_}g_t = {} & \text{constant} + \sum_{i=1}^{2} \text{Gini\_}g_{t-i} + \sum_{i=0}^{1} \text{NCA}_{t-i} \\
& + \sum_{i=0}^{2} \text{CPI\_inflation}_{t-i} + \sum_{i=0}^{2} \text{Credit\_growth}_{t-i} \quad (14.2) \\
& + \sum_{i=0}^{2} \text{Wages\_growth}_{t-i} + \varepsilon_t
\end{aligned}
$$

$$\text{Gini\_g}_t = \text{constant} + \sum_{i=1}^{2}\text{Gini\_g}_{t-i} + \sum_{i=0}^{1}\text{NCA}_{t-i} + \sum_{i=0}^{2}\text{CPI\_inflation}_{t-i}$$

$$+ \sum_{i=0}^{2}\text{Credit\_growth}_{t-i} + \sum_{i=0}^{2}\text{GDP\_growth\_dummy}_{t-i} \quad (14.3)$$

$$+ \sum_{i=0}^{2}\text{Wages\_growth}_{t-i} + \varepsilon_t$$

In Fig. 14.6, the income inequality growth rises more when the negative GDP growth dummy is included in the model than when this channel is shut off in the model. This suggests that recessions and those periods of negative GDP growth accentuate the increase in income inequality growth, following NCA shocks. This is because NCA shocks tighten lending standards. In contrast, the income inequality growth does not rise as much as the counterfactual suggests when considering the role of positive GDP growth. This suggests that positive or expansionary GDP growth phases help to mitigate the adverse effects of the NCA shocks on the growth of income inequality. The finding shows that the size of amplifications is much enlarged when the economy is in the expansionary GDP growth phases. This implies that policymakers, when tightening the NCA standards, should consider the state of the GDP growth dynamics.

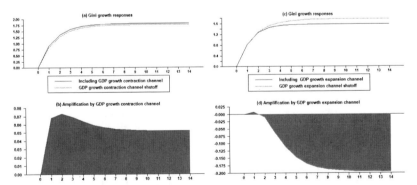

Fig. 14.6 Cumulative responses of income inequality growth to NCA shocks and the role of GDP growth phases (*Source* Authors' calculations)

The Credit Growth Channel

The earlier sections reveal that the NCA shocks lead to significant contraction in credit growth. Such adverse effects of the NCA shocks have been reported in Gumata and Ndou (2017). However, these authors did not examine the influence of credit growth in transmitting the NCA shocks to income inequality. Hence, this is an opportunity to examine: to what extent does the credit growth channel transmits the NCA shocks to the income inequality growth? The effects are estimated using Eqs. (14.4) and (14.5).

$$\text{Gini\_g}_t = \text{constant} + \sum_{i=1}^{2} \text{Gini\_g}_{t-i} + \sum_{i=0}^{1} \text{NCA}_{t-i}$$
$$+ \sum_{i=0}^{2} \text{CPI\_inflation}_{t-i} + \sum_{i=0}^{2} \text{Wages\_growth}_{t-i} + \varepsilon_t \qquad (14.4)$$

$$\text{Gini\_g}_t = \text{constant} + \sum_{i=1}^{2} \text{Gini\_g}_{t-i} + \sum_{i=0}^{1} \text{NCA}_{t-i}$$
$$+ \sum_{i=0}^{2} \text{CPI\_inflation}_{t-i} + \sum_{i=0}^{2} \text{Credit\_growth}_{t-i} \qquad (14.5)$$
$$+ \sum_{i=0}^{2} \text{Wages\_growth}_{t-i} + \varepsilon_t$$

In Fig. 14.7, the income inequality growth rises much higher in the presence of the credit channel than when this channel is shut off in the model. This suggests that a decline in the credit growth following the tightening in the NCA standards amplifies the increase in income inequality growth. Thus, policymakers should consider the distributional effects of tightening in NCA standards.

14 Is the Tightening in the National Credit Act ...

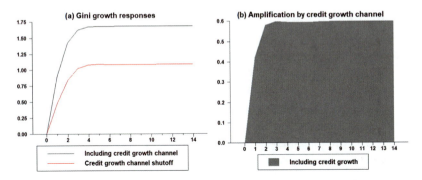

Fig. 14.7 Responses of income inequality growth and role of credit growth channel (*Source* Authors' calculations)

The Wage Growth Channels

The analysis further examines the role of the wage-growth channel in transmitting the tight NCA shocks to income inequality growth. In Fig. 14.8, the actual income inequality growth rises more when the wage growth channel is allowed to operate in the model than when it is shut off. Thus, the decline in the wages growth, following tight NCA standard, exacerbates the increase in income inequality growth.

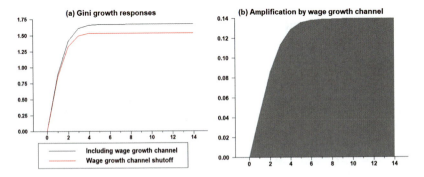

Fig. 14.8 Role of the wage-growth channel in the income inequality growth to a tightened NCA shock (*Source* Authors' calculations)

The Consumer Price Inflation Channel

Since 2017, monetary policymakers have indicated their preference to see consumer price inflation at or below 4.5%. However, this target has not been justified in the public discourse by an economic intuition that considers the redistributive effects. This arises because social commentators and labour unions point out that South Africa is the most unequal society in the world. It is pointed out in Ndou and Gumata (2017) that economic growth tends to be higher when inflation is below the 4.5% threshold. This section offers another perspective by examining the role of the inflation regimes in linking the income inequality dynamics with the NCA standards. The focus is on the consumer price inflation bands: (1) below 4.5%, (2) above 6% and (3) within the 4.5–6%. Three inflation dummy variables are created. The first inflation dummy is equal to the values of consumer price inflation below or equal to 4.5% and zero otherwise. The second inflation dummy is equal to the values of the consumer price inflation above 6% and zero otherwise. The third inflation dummy is equal to the values of consumer price inflation within the 4.5–6% band and zero otherwise. These dummy variables are included in the Eqs. (14.6) and (14.7) separately to capture the role of the inflation bands in influencing the reaction of income inequality to the NCA shocks.

$$
\begin{aligned}
\text{Gini\_g}_t = \text{constant} + \sum_{i=1}^{2} \text{Gini\_g}_{t-i} + \sum_{i=0}^{1} \text{NCA}_{t-i} \\
+ \sum_{i=0}^{2} \text{Credit\_growth}_{t-i} + \sum_{i=0}^{2} \text{GDP\_growth}_{t-i} \quad (14.6) \\
+ \sum_{i=0}^{2} \text{Wages\_growth}_{t-i} + \varepsilon_t
\end{aligned}
$$

14 Is the Tightening in the National Credit Act ...

$$\text{Gini\_g}_t = \text{constant} + \sum_{i=1}^{2} \text{Gini\_g}_{t-i} + \sum_{i=0}^{1} \text{NCA}_{t-i}$$
$$+ \sum_{i=0}^{2} \text{CPI\_inflation\_dummy}_{t-i} + \sum_{i=0}^{2} \text{Credit\_growth}_{t-i} \quad (14.7)$$
$$+ \sum_{i=0}^{2} \text{GDP\_growth}_{t-i} + \sum_{i=0}^{2} \text{Wages\_growth}_{t-i} + \varepsilon_t$$

Figure 14.9 shows the role of inflation regimes. The income inequality growth is lower when inflation is below the 4.5% threshold than when this regime is shut off in the model. This suggests that a low inflation regime may help mitigate the adverse effects of the tightening in the NCA standards on income inequality growth.

In addition, Fig. 14.9e shows the extent to which the high inflation regime (that is, the inflation band above 6%) influences the transmission of the tightening in the NCA standards to income inequality growth. The income inequality growth is higher when inflation is within the 4.5–6% band and when inflation exceeds 6% than when this band is shut off in the model. This suggests that high inflation episodes amplify the increase in the income inequality growth following a tightening in the NCA.

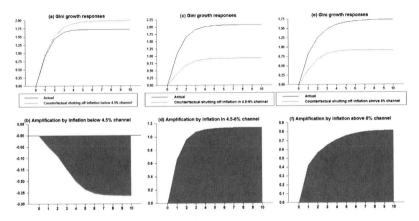

Fig. 14.9 Cumulative responses of the income inequality growth to the NCA shock and the role of inflation regimes (*Source* Authors' calculations)

14.2.4 Does the Income Inequality Channel Impact the Transmission of the NCA Shocks to Credit Growth, Residential Investment Growth, and GDP Growth?

The preceding analysis has shown that the NCA shocks have direct impacts on the evolution of income inequality. In addition, the evidence shows that its effects are transmitted via other channels to impact income inequality dynamics. The missing gap is to determine the extent to which income inequality transmits the NCA shocks to real economic activity. Consequently, this chapter examines the extent to which the income inequality channel impacts the transmission of the NCA shocks to credit growth, residential investment growth, and GDP growth. Various models are estimated to determine whether the role of growth of income inequality impacts the transmission of tight NCA shocks to credit growth, residential investment growth, and GDP growth. This is assessed using Eqs. (14.8.1) and (14.8.2). The robustness is done using models (14.9.1) and (14.9.2) as well as (14.10.1) and (14.10.2). The variables included in the models include credit growth (credit_g), income inequality growth (inequality_g), wages growth (wages_g), GDP growth (GDP_g) and repo rate (Repo_rate).

$$\text{Credit\_}g_t = \text{constant} + \sum_{i=1}^{2} \text{Credit\_}g_{t-i} + \sum_{i=0}^{2} \text{NCA}_{t-i}$$

$$+ \sum_{i=0}^{2} \text{Inequality\_}g_{t-i} + \sum_{i=0}^{2} \text{Wages\_}g_{t-i} \qquad (14.8.1)$$

$$+ \sum_{i=0}^{2} \text{Repo\_rate}_{t-i} + \varepsilon_t$$

$$\text{Credit\_}g_t = \text{constant} + \sum_{i=1}^{2} \text{Credit\_}g_{t-i} + \sum_{i=0}^{2} \text{NCA}_{t-i}$$

$$+ \sum_{i=0}^{2} \text{Wages\_}g_{t-i} + \sum_{i=0}^{2} \text{Repo\_rate}_{t-i} + \varepsilon_t \qquad (14.8.2)$$

$$\text{Credit\_}g_t = \text{constant} + \sum_{i=1}^{2} \text{Credit\_}g_{t-i} + \sum_{i=0}^{2} \text{NCA}_{t-i}$$
$$+ \sum_{i=0}^{2} \text{Inequality\_}g_{t-i} + \varepsilon_t \tag{14.9.1}$$

$$\text{Credit\_}g_t = \text{constant} + \sum_{i=1}^{2} \text{Credit\_}g_{t-i} + \sum_{i=0}^{2} \text{NCA}_{t-i} + \varepsilon_t \tag{14.9.2}$$

$$\text{Credit\_}g_t = \text{constant} + \sum_{i=1}^{2} \text{Credit\_}g_{t-i} + \sum_{i=0}^{2} \text{NCA}_{t-i}$$
$$+ \sum_{i=0}^{2} \text{Inequality\_}g_{t-i} + \sum_{i=0}^{2} \text{GDP\_}g_{t-i} \tag{14.10.1}$$
$$+ \sum_{i=0}^{2} \text{Repo\_rate}_{t-i} + \varepsilon_t$$

$$\text{Credit\_}g_t = \text{constant} + \sum_{i=1}^{2} \text{Credit\_}g_{t-i} + \sum_{i=0}^{2} \text{NCA}_{t-i}$$
$$+ \sum_{i=0}^{2} \text{GDP\_}g_{t-i} + \sum_{i=0}^{2} \text{Repo\_rate}_{t-i} + \varepsilon_t \tag{14.10.2}$$

In Fig. 14.10, the tight NCA shock reduces credit growth, irrespective of the model specification. However, the decline in credit growth is bigger when the income inequality channel is allowed to operate in the model than when it is shut off. This shows that increased income inequality growth, following a tightening in the NCA standards, exacerbates the decline in credit growth.

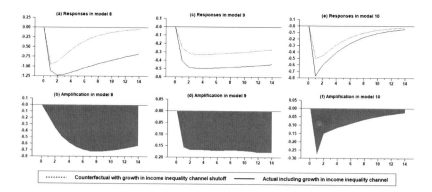

Fig. 14.10 Credit growth responses to the NCA shocks and the role of growth of income inequality (*Note* Models 8, 9, 10, refer to results obtained from Eqs. [14.8.1, 14.8.2, 14.9.1, 14.9.2, 14.10.1, and 14.10.2]. *Source* Authors' calculations)

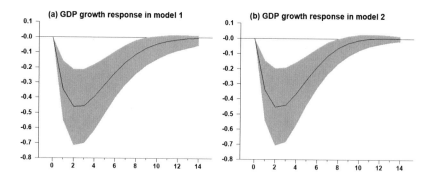

Fig. 14.11 GDP growth responses to tight NCA shocks (*Note* The grey shaded area denote the 16th and 84th percentile confidence bands. *Source* Authors' calculations)

The chapter further shows the extent to which income inequality growth transmits the NCA shocks to GDP growth using models (14.11) and (14.12). In Fig. 14.11, the decline in the actual GDP growth (GDP_g_t) exceeds the counterfactual reaction. This suggests that increased income inequality, following tight NCA shock, worsens the decline in GDP growth.

$$GDP\_g_t = \text{constant} + \sum_{i=1}^{2} GDP\_g_{t-i} + \sum_{i=0}^{2} NCA_{t-i}$$

$$+ \sum_{i=0}^{2} \text{Inequality}\_g_{t-i} + \sum_{i=0}^{2} \text{Wages}\_g_{t-i} \quad (14.11)$$

$$+ \sum_{i=0}^{2} \text{Repo\_rate}_{t-i} + \varepsilon_t$$

$$GDP\_g_t = \text{constant} + \sum_{i=1}^{2} GDP\_g_{t-i} + \sum_{i=0}^{2} NCA_{t-i}$$

$$+ \sum_{i=0}^{2} \text{Wages}\_g_{t-i} + \sum_{i=0}^{2} \text{Repo\_rate}_{t-i} + \varepsilon_t \quad (14.12)$$

In Fig. 14.11, GDP growth declines significantly to a tightening in the NCA. The decline last nearly two years and the peak decline of 0.2 percentage points is achieved in the second quarter. The duration and peak magnitudes are robust to the model specification. GDP growth declines significantly to tightening in the NCA.

Figure 14.12 shows the comparisons of the responses and sizes of amplifications due to the income inequality channel. The gap between the actual and the counterfactual responses indicate the influence of the income inequality channel in transmitting the effects of tightening in the NCA to residential investment growth and GDP growth. GDP growth is replaced by investment growth in the preceding models. In Fig. 14.12a, the tightening in the NCA lowers the residential investment growth. However, the actual residential investment growth declines more than the counterfactual suggest. In Fig. 14.12b, GDP growth declines more than the counterfactual suggests. This evidence shows that the income inequality channel is a potent conduit that transmits the NCA shocks to real economic activity.

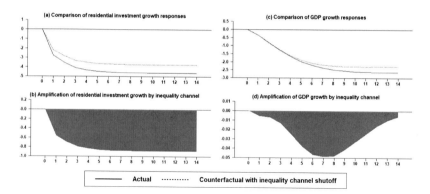

Fig. 14.12 Actual and counterfactual cumulative responses and the role of the income inequality growth channel (*Source* Authors' calculations)

14.3 Conclusion and Policy Implications

This chapter determined the effects of (NCA) on income inequality. Evidence reveals that the NCA raises income inequality. This chapter further determined the extent to which growth of income inequality impacted the transmission of the NCA shock to credit growth, residential investment growth and GDP growth using counterfactual approaches. The counterfactual responses are calculated by shutting off the income inequality channel in transmitting the NCA shock to credit growth, residential investment growth and GDP growth. We saw that tightening in the NCA standards lowers both the actual responses of the credit growth, residential investment growth, and GDP growth more than the counterfactual suggests. This evidence shows that the income inequality channel is a potent conduit that in the transmission of the NCA shocks to real economic activity. This income inequality channel exacerbates the adverse effects. Given the above undesirable outcome, we recommend that policymakers take into account the credit and business cycles in order to attenuate the adverse effects of the tightening of the NCA credit standards.

References

Frost, J., & van Stralen, R. (2017). Macroprudential policy and income inequality. *Journal of International Money and Finance, 85,* 278–290.

Gumata, N., & Ndou, E. (2017). *Labour market and fiscal policy adjustments to shocks: The role and implications for price and financial stability in South Africa.* Cham: Palgrave Macmillan.

Monin, P. (2017). *Monetary policy, macroprudential regulation and inequality* (ECP, Discussion Note 2017/2).

15

Can an Unexpected Loosening in the Labour Market Reforms Reduce the Growth of Income Inequality in South Africa?

Main Highlights

- Evidence indicates that an unexpected loosening in the labour market reforms reduces income inequality growth when complemented by increased government consumption expenditure, income tax cuts, low economic policy uncertainty and inflation below six per cent, but this excludes a weak exchange rate regime. This is because a weak exchange rate mitigates the reduction in the income inequality growth induced by an unexpected loosening in labour market reforms.
- Evidence suggests that the declining consumer price inflation and improvements in economic growth, the increased employment growth, and the declining unemployment rate, following an unexpected loosening in labour market reform, amplifies the reduction in income inequality growth.

© The Author(s) 2019
E. Ndou and T. Mokoena, *Inequality, Output-Inflation Trade-Off and Economic Policy Uncertainty*,
https://doi.org/10.1007/978-3-030-19803-9_15

241

15.1 Introduction

The South African labour market has been described as rigid due to factors such as centralized collective bargaining, legal minimum wages, employment protection laws and unemployment benefits, among others. It has been argued that these rigidities make job creation less attractive for employers and lead to high unemployment and lower participation rates. These rigidities co-exist with high structural unemployment (Pereira 2018). Hence, OECD (2010) suggested it might be beneficial for the agents to adopt labour market reforms. For instance, agents could increase the degree of co-ordination of wage negotiations, weaken legal extension of collective bargaining agreements, and facilitate school to work transitions.[1]

This chapter examines the extent to which an unexpected loosening in the labour market reforms impacts growth of income inequality. We ask: Can an unexpected loosening in the labour market reforms impact the growth of income inequality? In addition, which policy options would combine well with the unexpected loosening in the labour market reforms to reduce growth of income inequality?

Much focus when dealing with income inequality has been on improving the quality of education and skills as well as implementing structural reforms. Nevertheless, the policy mix has received little attention, if nothing at all. This chapter fills policy gaps by examining the policy mix which includes the following: (1) loose labour market reforms and income tax cuts; (2) loose labour market reforms and personal income tax cuts; (3) loose labour market reforms and increased government consumption spending; (4) loose labour market reforms and the exchange rate depreciation; (5) loose labour market reforms and price stability; and (6) loose labour market reforms and expansionary monetary policy. In addition, the chapter fills policy gaps by adding the role of the labour market reforms into the discussion of income inequality in South Africa.

---

[1]For an alternative view that employment protection- which is form of rigidity- reduces income inequality, Campos and Nugent (2015, 2016).

Evidence indicates that an unexpected loosening in the labour market reforms can reduce income inequality. However, this shock needs to be complemented by certain policies to reduce income inequality significantly. The weakened exchange rate policy does not help the reduction in income inequality induced by loosening in labour market reforms. This implies that a weak exchange rate regime may not enable the loosening in the labour market reforms to lower income inequality growth.

15.2 Evidence

The analysis starts by determining the effects of unexpected loosening in the labour market reforms on income inequality. The labour market reforms indicator and the Gini coefficient used in this analysis are obtained from Gumata and Ndou (2017) and other variables are obtained from the South African Reserve Bank. The loose labour market reform shock refers to a one standard deviation shock in the comprehensive index used in Gumata and Ndou (2017). The income inequality level is measured by the Gini coefficient. The analysis uses quarterly (Q) data spanning 1993Q1–2016Q3. Various bivariate VAR models are estimated. The first VAR model (Model 1) includes the labour market reform index and income inequality growth. The second VAR model (Model 2) uses the reverse ordering. The unexpected loosening in labour market reforms leads to a decline in income inequality growth which last nearly five quarters. All growth rates denote year-on-year changes. In Fig. 15.1, the income inequality growth declines by nearly 1.5 percentage points in the third quarter. This finding is robust to the different model specifications (Fig. 15.1).

15.2.1 How Robust Is the Response of Income Inequality Growth to an Unexpected Loosening in the Labour Market Reforms?

This section further examines the robustness of the evidence that unexpected loosening in the labour market reforms reduces income

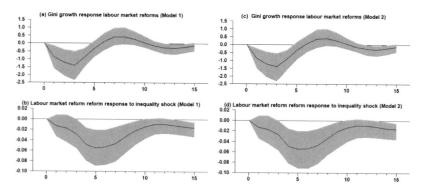

Fig. 15.1 Income inequality responses to unexpected loosening in the labour market reforms (*Note* The grey shaded area denotes the 16th and 84th percentile confidence bands. *Source* Authors' calculations)

inequality growth by estimating four VAR models. The first VAR model (Model 1) includes the labour market reform index, income inequality growth and GDP growth. The exogenous variables include a financial crisis dummy, changes in economic policy uncertainty and consumer price inflation. The second VAR model (Model 2) includes the labour market reform index, income inequality growth and changes in economic policy uncertainty. Exogenous variables include a dummy for financial crisis dummy and consumer price inflation. The third VAR model (Model 3) includes the labour market reform index, income inequality growth and consumer price inflation. Exogenous variables include a dummy for financial crisis, consumer price inflation and economic growth. The fourth VAR model (Model 4) includes the labour market reform index, income inequality growth and employment growth. Again, the exogenous variables include a financial crisis dummy and consumer price inflation. These models are estimated with two lags and 10,000 Monte Carlo draws. The financial crisis dummy equals to one beginning in 2007Q3 to end of sample and includes other periods of economic volatility and zero otherwise.

In Fig. 15.2, the unexpected loosening in the labour market reforms leads to significant reduction in income inequality growth. In addition, income inequality growth declines significantly for nearly five quarters.

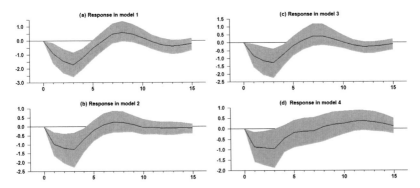

Fig. 15.2 Responses of income inequality growth to unexpected loosening in labour market reforms (*Note* The shaded grey area denotes the 16th and 84th percentile confidence bands. *Source* Authors' calculations)

The peak decline ranges between 1 and 2 percentage points and this occurs in the third quarter.

15.2.2 What Are the Effects of an Unexpected Loosening in the Labour Market Reforms on GDP Growth and Consumer Price Inflation?

The analysis further examines the effects of an unexpected loosening in the labour market reforms on economic growth, consumer price inflation and changes in the unemployment rate. The results from the VAR model, which includes the labour market reform index, economic growth, consumer price inflation, and changes in unemployment rate, are shown in Fig. 15.3. The model is estimated using two lags. The consumer price inflation declines significantly for six quarters. Moreover, economic growth rises significantly between 5 and 12 quarters, and unemployment rates declines significantly for 13 quarters. This shows that an unexpected loosening in the labour market reforms drives consumer price inflation and economic growth.

A counterfactual analysis is performed to show the role of consumer price inflation and GDP growth in transmitting an unexpected loosening

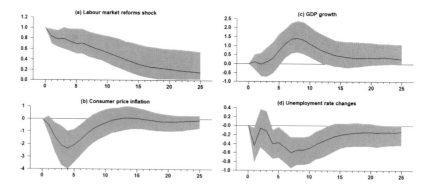

Fig. 15.3 Responses to unexpected loosening in the labour market reforms (*Note* The shaded grey area denotes 16th and 84th percentile confidence bands. *Source* Authors' calculations)

in the labour market reforms to income inequality growth. The counterfactual VAR model shuts off these two channels in transmitting the unexpected loosening in the labour market reforms to income inequality growth. The cumulative impulse responses are shown in Fig. 15.4. Income inequality growth declines. However, the actual income inequality growth declines more than the counterfactual suggests. This suggests that the declining consumer price inflation and improvements in economic growth amplify the decline in income inequality growth.

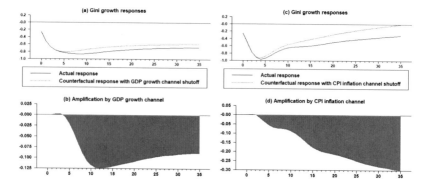

Fig. 15.4 Cumulative responses to unexpected loosening in the labour market reforms and the role of GDP and inflation channels (*Source* Authors' calculations)

15.2.3 Can the Unexpected Loosening in the Labour Market Reforms Be Transmitted Through Other Labour Market Indicators?

This chapter further examines the relevance of unemployment rates and the employment growth channels in transmitting unexpected loosening in labour market reforms to income inequality growth. This is done by estimating a counterfactual VAR model which shuts off the labour market indicator channels (that is, unemployment rate and employment growth) in the model. The VAR models include the labour market reforms indicator, income inequality growth and a labour market indicator channel. The models are estimated using two lags and 10,000 Monte Carlo draws. The results are robust to different model specifications. The gaps between the actual and counterfactual responses denote the role of the labour market indicator channel in transmitting the loose labour market reforms shock to income inequality growth. In Fig. 15.5, the actual income inequality growth declines more than the counterfactual suggest. This shows that increased employment growth and the declining unemployment rate, following a loose labour market reform shock, amplifies the reduction in income inequality growth.

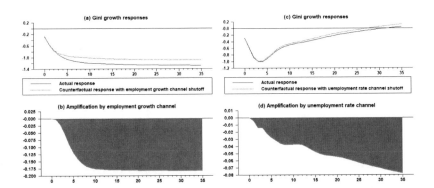

Fig. 15.5 Cumulative responses to unexpected loosening in the labour market reforms and the role of employment and unemployment rate channels (*Source* Authors' calculations)

15.2.4 How Do Labour Market Reforms Interact with Other Policies to Impact Income Inequality?

This section examines the policy combinations that can be used and lead to bigger reductions in income inequality growth. These policy combinations include the following: (1) loose labour market reforms and expansionary monetary policy; (2) loose labour market reforms and price stability based on inflation below six per cent versus inflation being below the 4.5 per cent threshold; (3) loose labour market reforms and low economic policy uncertainty; (4) loose labour market reforms and exchange rate depreciation; and (5) loose labour market reforms and fiscal policy (that is, increased government consumption expenditure and income tax cuts).

These policy channels are shut off in the model to calculate the counterfactual impulses. The models are estimated using two lags and 10,000 Monte Carlo draws. The gaps between the actual and counterfactual responses show the size of the influence of the indicated policy channel. Figure 15.6 shows that the actual income inequality growth declines more than the counterfactual suggests.

In addition, Fig. 15.7 shows a comparison of the sizes of the amplifications induced by the channels indicated above. The income inequality

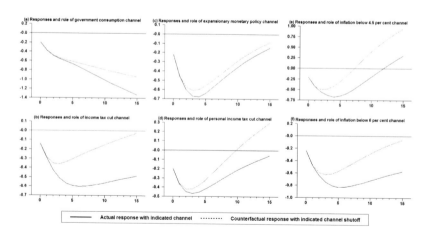

Fig. 15.6 Cumulative responses to unexpected loosening in labour market reforms and the role of income tax and inflation channel (*Source* Authors' calculations)

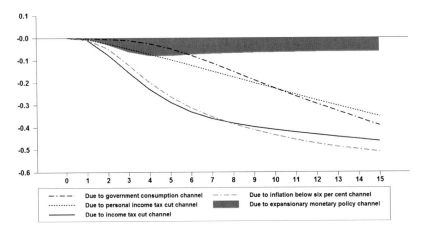

Fig. 15.7 Comparisons of size of the amplifications (*Source* Authors' calculations)

growth is reduced more by amplifications by keeping inflation below the 6 per cent threshold as well as income tax reductions. This shows that maintaining price stability is important. Expansionary monetary policy has the least amplification effects. However, this does not mean it cannot contribute to lowering income inequality growth.

15.2.5 Is the Combination of a Weak Exchange Rate Regime and the Unexpected Loosening in the Labour Market Reforms a Better Policy Option?

This analysis concludes by examining the extent to which the exchange rate depreciation channel influences the effects of loose labour market reforms on income inequality using counterfactual VAR models. Two models are estimated. In the first VAR model the exchange rate depreciation channel is shut off to calculate the counterfactual income inequality response to unexpected loosening in the labour market reforms. The gap between the actual and counterfactual responses denotes the role of the exchange rate depreciation channel. In the second VAR model, the consumer price inflation channel is shut off to calculate the counterfactual income inequality response to the exchange rate depreciation shock.

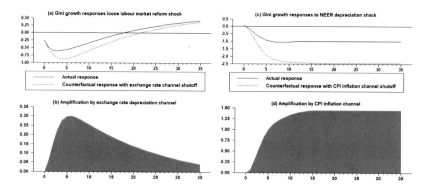

Fig. 15.8 Cumulative income inequality growth responses and the channels of amplification (*Source* Authors' calculations)

In Fig. 15.8a, the actual income inequality declines less than the counterfactual suggests, to an unexpected loosening in the labour market reform. This suggests that the exchange rate depreciation channel mitigates the reduction in the income inequality growth. In addition, Fig. 15.8c shows that income inequality declines less than the counterfactual suggests. This suggests that increased consumer price inflation mitigates the decline in income inequality growth following an exchange rate depreciation shock. This evidence suggests that a combination of loose labour market reforms and the exchange rate depreciation regime may not lead to maximum reduction in the income inequality growth, because of the accompanying inflation pressures.

15.3 Conclusion and Policy Implications

Can an unexpected loosening in the labour market reforms impact the growth of income inequality? Evidence indicates that an unexpected loosening in the labour market reforms reduces significantly the growth of income inequality. In addition, the chapter examined the policy combinations which might work well with loose labour market reforms to lower the income inequality growth. Evidence indicates that unexpected loosening in the labour market reforms reduces income inequality growth when complemented by increased government consumption expenditure, income tax cuts, low economic policy uncertainty and inflation below six per cent, but this excludes a weak exchange rate regime. This is because a weak exchange rate policy mitigates the reduction in the income inequality induced by unexpected loosening in the labour market reforms. This chapter applied a counterfactual approach to assess the role of the consumer price inflation, GDP growth, employment growth and the unemployment rate channels in transmitting the labour market reform shocks to income inequality growth. Evidence suggests that the declining consumer price inflation and the improvement in economic growth, increased employment growth and declining unemployment rate, following an unexpected loosening in labour market reforms, amplify the reduction in income inequality growth. Given the above empirical evidence, policymakers would find it beneficial to substantially increase employment and real economic growth; maintain price stability; and adapt incentive-compatible labour market reforms.

References

Campos, N., & Jeffrey, N. J. (2016). *Labour market reforms, growth and inequality: Evidence from a new dataset*. Voxeu.org.

Campos, N., & Nugent, J. (2015). *The dynamics of labour market reform, growth and inequality: Evidence from a new dataset* (Revised version of IZA DP 6881, October 2012).

Gumata, N., & Ndou, E. (2017). *Labour market and fiscal policy adjustments to shocks: The role and implications for price and financial stability in South Africa*. Cham, Switzerland: Palgrave Macmillan.

Howell, D., & Huebler, F. (2005). Wage compression and the unemployment crisis: Labor market institutions, skill and inequality-unemployment tradeoffs. In D. Howell (Eds.), *Fighting unemployment*. Oxford University Press.

OECD. (2010). *OECD Economic Surveys*. South Africa.

Pereira, M. (2018). The effects of labour market reforms upon unemployment and income inequalities: An agent based model (Discussion Paper 328). Instituto de Economia.

Part VI

**Bank Concentration,
Income Inequality
and Other Channels**

16

Does the Increase in Banking Concentration Impact Income Inequality in South Africa?

Main Highlights

- Evidence reveals that income inequality rises significantly to a positive bank concentration shock.
- In addition, the income inequality fluctuates following the positive bank concentration shock.
- The counterfactual analysis reveals that the increase in income inequality to positive bank concentration shocks is amplified by the declining credit and GDP, as well as rising unemployment.
- Therefore, bank concentration should be reduced to lower income inequality via the indicated channels.

16.1 Introduction

This chapter examines the extent to which positive bank concentration shocks impact income inequality in South Africa. In addition, this chapter shows the extent to which employment, credit, unemployment and GDP transmit positive bank concentration shocks to income

© The Author(s) 2019　　　　　　　　　　　　　　　　　**255**
E. Ndou and T. Mokoena, *Inequality, Output-Inflation Trade-Off and Economic Policy Uncertainty*,
https://doi.org/10.1007/978-3-030-19803-9_16

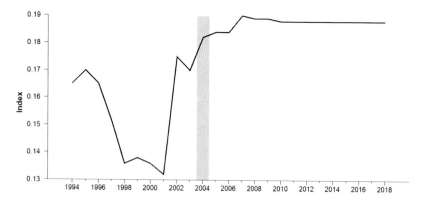

Fig. 16.1 Evolution of competition in the banking sector as measured by the H-index (*Source* South African Reserve Bank)

inequality as measured by the Gini coefficient. The next two chapters examine the effects of bank concentration shocks on GDP and employment growth in South Africa. This analysis is motivated by Feldmann's (2013) articulation that, following the financial crisis, some industrial countries experienced both an increase in bank concentration while their labour market performance deteriorated. Similarly, South Africa exhibits high levels of income inequality before and after the financial crisis that began in 2007.

Figure 16.1 shows the evolution of the Herfindahl-Hirschman Index (H-index) in the South African banking sector. We use the index to measure the effects of bank concentration. It is evident that the H-index was declining between 1995 and 2001. This indicates a reduction in the concentration levels as well as improvements in the competition. This trend has reversed and remained high since 2001, which is an indication of reduced competition with high concentration in the banking sector.[1,2]

---

[1] The index varies between 0 to indicate many banks in the system and 1 to indicate monopoly in the system. Measured this way, the H-index also serves as an indicator that measures the degree of monopoly power in the system or market. A smaller (higher or strong) the H-index indicates that there is greater (low or weak) competition and lower (high) concentration in the banking system. For further details on the methodology to calculate the H-index see https://www.resbank.co.za/Lists/News%20and%20Publications/Attachments/4006/Annual+Report+2001[1].pdf.

[2] See various editions of the South African Reserve Bank Banking Supervision Annual Reports for further reading. Degryse et al. (2009) also consider markets with the H-index below 0.10 to be

16 Does the Increase in Banking Concentration Impact ... 257

Literature on financial regulation points to a link between financial policy regulation and income inequality. One possible way through which finance may influence income inequality may arise as the banks with oligopolistic power will have, at equilibrium, higher loan rates and smaller quantities of loanable funds than that would prevail under perfect competition. The limited supply of loan quantities will reduce economic growth, and this reduction may raise income inequality.[3] This is further supported by a positive link that may arise via the predictions of the banking market's structure-conduct-performance hypothesis (Feldmann 2013; Guzman 2000; Smith 1998). This hypothesis suggests that more concentrated banking system raises the lending rates, leading to higher interest rate margins, thereby restricting credit extension due to reduced competition. The restricted credit extension lowers investment, constrains economic growth, and reduces job created, leading to higher unemployment especially when wages do not adjust downwards. These developments may raise income inequality. By contrast, bank concentration may lead to lower income inequality if the efficient-structure-hypothesis holds. The efficient-structure-hypothesis indicates that high concentration in the banking system may lead to more efficient banks. This leads to higher efficiency in financial intermediation, with favourable effects on the lending rates. Firms will gain access to credit, as banks charge modest lending rates. In the end, this fosters job creation, investment and economic growth, leading to lower unemployment. Under the efficient-structure-hypothesis, all this may lower income inequality.

This chapter fills research policy gaps regarding the studies focusing on the link between bank concentration and income inequality in South Africa. We fill the research policy by examining the extent to which the banking system's concentration impacts on income

---

competitive and markets with an H-index above 0.18 to be concentrated. The authors regard a change in the H-index of 0.10 as a benchmark for marking the transition from a competitive to a concentrated market. Markets in which H-index is in excess of 0.18 are regarded as concentrated.

[3]However, there is greater incentive for monopolistic bank to establish lending relationship to promote firms' access to investment and raise economic growth, raising employment opportunities, and thus lowering income inequality.

inequality. However, other gaps will be examined in the next chapter. The gaps filled include determining the strength of the link between bank concentration and labour market performance. This will show the potency of labour market performance as one of the channels which impact income inequality. In addition, the link between bank concentration and GDP is examined as a separate transmission channel. In assessing the transmission of the positive bank concentration shocks to income inequality, the chapter further utilises the counterfactual approach to determine the influence of the following channels: credit, GDP, employment, and unemployment.

16.2 What Is the Effect of a Positive Banking Concentration Shock on Income Inequality?

This section examines the link between bank concentration and income inequality. We use the Gini coefficient to represent income inequality. The relationship is determined by estimating various models that control for the different aspects of the economy. In addition, the analysis determines the robustness of the findings. Bank concentration and competition (*hereafter referred to as bank concentration*) is measured by the Herfindahl-Hirschman Index. The Gini coefficient is obtained from Gumata and Ndou (2017). All other data is obtained from the South African Reserve Bank. The analysis uses quarterly (Q) data from 1994Q1 to 2018Q2.

16.2.1 Evidence from Bivariate VAR Models

The analysis estimates various bivariate VAR models. The first VAR model (model 1) includes the log bank concentration and log Gini coefficient as endogenous variables. The exogenous variables include the log BER business confidence index and log real effective exchange rate. The second VAR model (model 2) tests the effects of reverse ordering of the endogenous variables in model 1 but adds log GDP to the exogenous

16 Does the Increase in Banking Concentration Impact ...

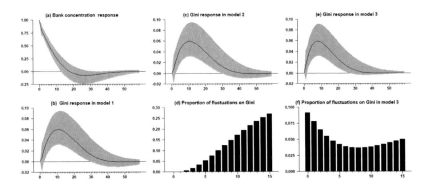

Fig. 16.2 Responses to positive bank concentration shocks (*Note* The grey shaded bands denote the 16th and 84th percentile confidence bands. Gini refers to Gini coefficient. *Source* Authors' calculations)

variables. The third VAR model (model 3) adds a recession dummy as an exogenous variable. The log transformed variables are multiplied by 100 and impulse responses should be interpreted as deviations from their trends. All the three models are estimated using two lags and 10,000 Monte Carlo Draws.

The income inequality impulse responses to one unit positive bank concentration shock are shown in Fig. 16.2. The income inequality rises significantly to a positive bank concentration shock. Inequality rises by nearly 0.6% at the peak impact, which occurs at around ten quarters after the positive bank concentration shock. In addition, the income inequality fluctuates very much due to the positive bank concentration shock. This evidence confirms that bank concentration shocks drive the income inequality. This finding is robust to the different model specifications.

16.2.2 Evidence from Linear Regressions

The analysis further examines the responses of income inequality to a once-off positive bank concentration shock using models 16.1 and 16.2. The cris_dummy equals to one from 2007Q3 to end of sample and zero otherwise. This includes periods of volatile economic growth and recessions.

$$\log \text{Gini}_t = \text{constant} + \sum_{i=1}^{4} \log \text{Gini}_{t-i}$$
$$+ \sum_{i=0}^{4} \log \text{bank concentration}_{t-i}$$
$$+ \text{Cris\_dummy} + \varepsilon_t \quad (16.1)$$

$$\log \text{Gini}_t = \text{constant} + \sum_{i=1}^{4} \log \text{Gini}_{t-i}$$
$$+ \sum_{i=0}^{4} \log \text{bank concentration}_{t-i}$$
$$+ \sum_{i=0}^{4} \log \text{GDP}_{t-i} + \text{Cris\_dummy} + \varepsilon_t \quad (16.2)$$

The impulses responses of income inequality to positive bank concentration shocks are shown in Fig. 16.3. Income inequality rises significantly to positive bank concentration shocks. This evidence shows that the rise in income inequality is robust to different model specifications.

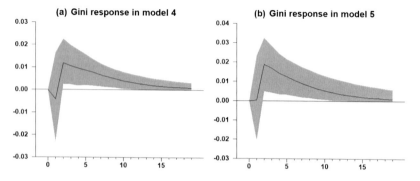

Fig. 16.3 Responses to positive bank concentration shocks (*Note* The grey shaded band denotes the 16th and 84th percentile confidence bands)

16.2.3 How Robust Is the Reaction of Income Inequality to Positive Bank Concentration Shocks?

The analysis further examines the robustness of the responses of income inequality to the positive bank concentration shocks by adding more endogenous variables in the model. This allows for the interactions and feedbacks amongst the variables. Various VAR models are estimated. Figure 16.4 shows that income inequality rises to the positive bank concentration shocks, and the increase is robust to different model specifications. This evidence suggests that the increase in bank concentration contributes to the rise in income inequality. The next section examines various channels through which this may be happening.

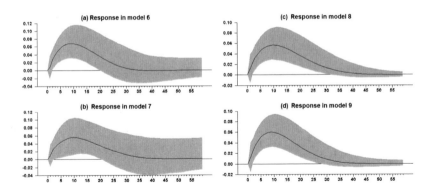

Fig. 16.4 Income inequality responses to positive bank concentration shocks (*Note* The sixth model [model 6] includes log bank concentration, log GDP, log Gini coefficient, labour market reform index and log credit to private sector as endogenous variables. The exogenous variables include log BER business confidence index and log real effective exchange rate. The seventh model [model 7] consists of log bank concentration, log Gini coefficient and log gross fixed capital formation as endogenous variables. The exogenous variables include log BER business confidence index, log real effective exchange rate and repo rate. The eighth model [model 8] consists of log-bank-concentration, log Gini coefficient, log GDP and log gross fixed capital formation as endogenous variables. The exogenous variables include log BER business confidence index and log real effective exchange rate. The models are estimated with two lags and 10,000 Monte Carlo draws) (*Note* The grey shaded band denotes the 16th and 84th percentile confidence bands)

The analysis further examines whether the impact of positive bank concentration shocks differs according to banking concentration regimes. Hence the analysis uses a threshold of 0.18. We use the threshold of 0.18 in the H-index to delineate periods of high and low market concentration. The high competition and low market concentration (high regime) dummy takes on the values of the log-H-index below 0.18 and zero otherwise. The low competition and high market concentration (low regime) dummy takes on the values of the log-H-index above 0.18 and zero otherwise. We estimate two bivariate VAR models. The models consist of a dummy for bank concentration regimes and the log Gini coefficient. The exogenous variables include log GDP, log BER business confidence index, log real effective exchange rate and a crisis dummy. The results are robust to different orderings of the endogenous variables in the model. The log transformed variables are multiplied by 100 and the impulse responses should be interpreted as per cent deviation from the trend. The impulse responses of income inequality measures are shown in Fig. 16.5. The bank concentration shock in the high competition and low concentration regime lowers income inequality in Fig. 16.5a. By contrast, in Fig. 16.5b, the shock in the low competition

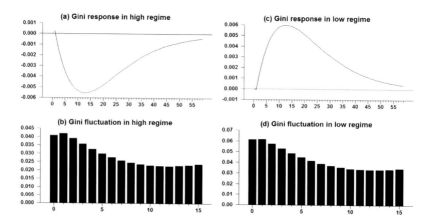

Fig. 16.5 Responses to positive bank concentration shocks according to banking concentration regimes (*Note* Gini refers to the Gini coefficient which measures income inequality. *Source* Authors' calculation)

16 Does the Increase in Banking Concentration Impact ... 263

and high concentration regime raises income inequality. This evidence shows that regimes matter.

16.2.4 Counterfactual Models

The analysis concludes by estimating counterfactual models to determine the roles of credit, GDP and unemployment as channels that transmit positive bank concentration shocks to income inequality. These channels are shut off in transmitting the positive bank concentration shocks to income inequality. The gap between the actual and counterfactual responses measures the role of these channels. The models are given by Eqs. (16.3) and (16.4). The second equation is the baseline model, which gives the counterfactual income inequality response after shutting off the credit and GDP channels in Eq. (16.3) by setting them to zero.

$$\log \text{Gini}_t = \text{constant} + \sum_{i=1}^{4} \log \text{Gini}_{t-i}$$

$$+ \sum_{i=0}^{4} \log \text{bank concentration}_{t-i}$$

$$+ \sum_{i=0}^{4} \log \text{credit}_{t-i} + \sum_{i=0}^{4} \log \text{GDP}_{t-i}$$

$$+ \text{Crisdummy} + \varepsilon_t \qquad (16.3)$$

$$\log \text{Gini}_t = \text{constant} + \sum_{i=1}^{4} \log \text{Gini}_{t-i}$$

$$+ \sum_{i=0}^{4} \log \text{bank concentration}_{t-i}$$

$$+ \text{Cris\_dummy} + \varepsilon_t \qquad (16.4)$$

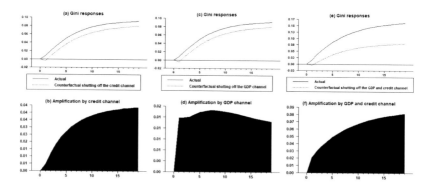

Fig. 16.6 Responses to positive bank concentration shocks (*Note* Gini refers to the Gini coefficient. *Source* Authors' calculation)

The models are robust to the inclusion of the recession dummy. The dummy equals to one for the recession in 2009Q1–2009Q3 and 2018Q1–2018Q2 and zero otherwise. The models are estimated using 10,000 bootstrap draws. Figure 16.6 shows the income inequality responses to a one positive standard deviation shock in bank concentration.

In Fig. 16.6, actual income inequality rises more than the counterfactual suggests. This suggests that credit, GDP and the combined effects of the two channels amplify the rise in income inequality. The adverse effects of bank concentration may arise when the increased cost of financial intermediation reduces investment and the demand for labour. The reduction in the labour demand arises when wages are rigid downwards (Feldman 2013). In addition, bank concentration may have adverse effects on the growth of equity-financed and skill-intensive industries as found by Carlin and Mayer (2003). This has the potential to reduce employment and raise unemployment. Feldmann (2013) found evidence which indicates that the concentrated banking system has adverse effects on labour market performance. They suggest this is consistent with concentrated banking system increasing the costs of financial intermediation, which dampens economic growth, lowers the rate of business formation via the credit channel, or increases the costs of intermediation or restricts credit or imposes higher costs on loans for

16 Does the Increase in Banking Concentration Impact ... 265

starts-ups and other SMEs. These channels are more likely to dampen job creation in the overall economy.

$$\log \text{Gini}_t = \text{constant} + \sum_{i=1}^{4} \log \text{Gini}_{t-i}$$

$$+ \sum_{i=0}^{2} \log \text{bank concentration}_{t-i}$$

$$+ \sum_{i=0}^{4} \log \text{unemployment}_{t-i}$$

$$+ \sum_{i=0}^{4} \log \text{GDP}_{t-i} + \text{Cris\_dummy} + \varepsilon_t \tag{16.5}$$

$$\log \text{Gini}_t = \text{constant} + \sum_{i=1}^{4} \log \text{Gini}_{t-i}$$

$$+ \sum_{i=0}^{4} \log \text{bank concentration}_{t-i}$$

$$+ \text{Cris\_dummy} + \varepsilon_t \tag{16.6}$$

The analysis further examines the role of the unemployment and GDP channels as well as their combined roles in transmitting positive bank concentration shocks to income inequality based on Eqs. (16.5) and (16.6). The channels are shut off in the model by setting their estimated coefficients to zero in Eq. (16.5). The gaps between the actual and counterfactual income inequality measure the influence of these channels. Figure 16.7 shows the income inequality responses to a positive bank concentration shock. In Figs. 16.7a and c, the actual income inequality rises more than the counterfactual, suggesting that unemployment and GDP dynamics, following a positive bank concentration shock, amplify the rise in income inequality.

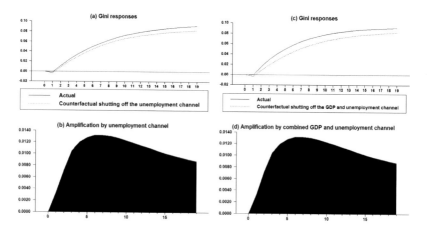

Fig. 16.7 Responses to positive bank concentration shocks (*Note* Gini refers to the Gini coefficient which measures income inequality)

16.3 Conclusion and Policy Implications

Evidence reveals that income inequality rises significantly to positive bank concentration shocks. In addition, the income inequality fluctuates following positive bank concentration shock. The counterfactual analysis reveals that the increase in income inequality to positive bank concentration shocks is amplified by declining credit and GDP, as well as rising unemployment. Therefore, bank concentration should be reduced to lower income inequality via the indicated channels.

References

Carlin, W., & Mayer, C. (2003). Finance, investment and growth. *Journal of Financial Economics, 69*(1), 191–226.

Cetorelli, N., & Gambera, M. (2001). Banking market structure: Financial dependence and growth international evidence from the industry data. *Journal of Finance, 56*(2), 617–648.

Feldmann, H. (2013). Banking systems concentration and labour market performance in industrial countries. *Contemporary Economic Policy, 31*(4), 719–732.

Guzman, M. G. (2000). Bank structure, capital accumulation and growth: A simple macroeconomic model. *Economic Theory, 16*(2), 421–455.

Smith, R. T. (1998). Banking competition and macroeconomic performance. *Journal of Money, Credit and Banking, 30*(4), 793–815.

17

Do Positive Bank Concentration Shocks Impact Economic Growth in South Africa?

Main Highlights

- Evidence shows that GDP declines to positive bank concentration shock. The finding is robust to different model specifications.
- Evidence from the counterfactual analysis shows that actual GDP declines more than the counterfactual suggests. The decline is accentuated by the slowdown in investment, reduction in employment, increased unemployment and reduced credit growth due to the unexpected increase in bank concentration.
- This shows that unexpected increase in the bank concentration has adverse effects on economic growth and this happens via different channels.
- Therefore, it is important for policymakers to lower the entry barriers and introduce a sliding scale of capital adequacy ratios that rise with the size of the banks.

© The Author(s) 2019
E. Ndou and T. Mokoena, *Inequality, Output-Inflation Trade-Off and Economic Policy Uncertainty,*
https://doi.org/10.1007/978-3-030-19803-9_17

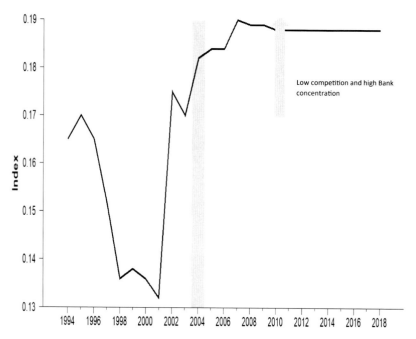

Fig. 17.1 Evolution of competition in the banking sector as measured by the H-index (*Source* South African Reserve Bank)

17.1 Introduction

The preceding chapter examined the extent to which the increase in banking concentration impacts income inequality in South Africa. The finding revealed that, positive bank concentration shocks raise income inequality. The policy implications implied that, bank concentration should be reduced to lower income inequality via the indicated channels. This chapter differs from Chapter 16 by examining the effects of unexpected increase in banking concentration and competition (*hereafter referred to as bank concentration*) on GDP growth in South Africa. By applying a counterfactual approach, the chapter further determines the roles of employment, investment, credit and the unemployment channels in transmitting positive bank concentration shocks to GDP.

17 Do Positive Bank Concentration Shocks Impact ... 271

The chapter measures the banking sector's concentration by the Herfindahl-Hirschman Index (H-index) shown in Fig. 17.1. The H-index declined between 1995 and 2001, indicating a reduction in concentration and improvements in competition. This trend reversed and has remained high since 2001, an indication of reduced competition with high concentration in the banking sector. The findings in this chapter are relevant for policymakers, academics and researchers because the level bank concentration in the South African financial sector is important for economic growth. In addition, the findings are relevant during this period of economic slowdown. Moreover, it is important to examine the link between bank concentration and economic growth, given that South African economic growth has been volatile and low, while the unemployment rate remained high.

Theory predicts different effects of bank concentration shocks on economic growth. For instance, Liu et al. (2014) suggest that the banking system is a mechanism that can convert the impact of financial market development into economic growth. Empirical evidence indicates that competition can drive banks to reduce lending costs, leading to an increase in the demand for bank funds to support business and economic growth. Furthermore, a highly concentrated banking industry may be beneficial to economic developments when banks with oligopolistic power have greater incentive to forge and maintain long-term relationships with firms and thus facilitating their access to credit. This will foster long term investment and economic development. Also, evidence indicates that sectors that are heavily dependent on bank financing grow faster in countries where there is fierce bank competition (Claessens and Laeven 2005).

By contrast, theory alternative suggests that high bank concentration can be detrimental to economic growth. This happens, when imperfect competition is linked to the inefficiencies that hinder firms' access to credit. Thus, a highly concentrated banking sector which reduces competition, will increase inefficiencies and harm firms' access to credit, thereby dampening economic growth. Increased bank concentration increases the cost of intermediation and dampens credit growth. Other studies find that higher bank concentration levels lead to increased collusion and high interest margins for loans and demand deposits. In addition, concentration lowers economic activity (Cetorelli and Gambera 2001), lowers the growth of equity-financed industries (Carlin and Mayer 2003), as well leads to a decline in business formation. These effects are likely to lower employment while raising the unemployment rate.

There are mixed empirical results in literature showing that high bank concentration has different effects on economic growth. Despite the diverse findings, there are no studies that examine the link between bank concentration and economic growth or GDP dynamics and apply a counterfactual approach to show the role of the employment, investment, credit and unemployment channels in transmitting positive bank concentration shocks to GDP.

17.2 Empirical Results

The analysis uses quarterly (Q) data spanning 1994Q1–2018Q2. Data is obtained from the South African Reserve Bank. This empirical analysis starts by examining the reaction of GDP to positive bank concentration shocks using various VAR models. The change in the market structure, competition and concentration in the banking system is measured by the Herfindahl-Hirschman Index (H-index). Hence, this analysis uses the H-index as a proxy for bank concentration. The analysis further estimates various models to determine the robustness of the finding of the impact of a positive bank concentration shock on GDP growth. The models are estimated using two lags and 10,000 Monte Carlo draws. Responses are to a one unit positive bank concentration shock, unless stated otherwise.

The impulse responses to positive bank concentration shocks are shown in Fig. 17.2. GDP declines to a positive bank concentration shock. This finding is robust to different model specifications. Therefore, increased bank concentration has adverse effects on economic growth.

The analysis further examines the reaction of investment and consumption components of GDP. GDP in the preceding models is

17 Do Positive Bank Concentration Shocks Impact ...

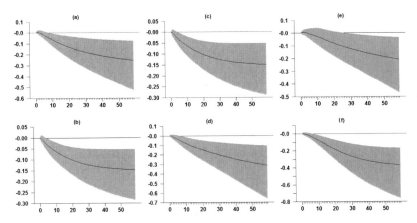

Fig. 17.2 GDP responses to a positive bank concentration shock (*Note* The impulse responses in (a) are from a model consisting of log bank concentration, log GDP and the repo rate as an endogenous variable, whereas the log BER business confidence index and the log real effective exchange rate are exogenous variables. The impulse responses in (b) are from a model containing the log GDP, the repo rate and the log bank concentration and the repo rate as endogenous variables, whereas the log BER business confidence index and the log real effective exchange rate are exogenous variables. The impulse responses in (c) are from a model consisting of the log bank concentration, log GDP, the repo rate and the log BER business confidence index as endogenous variables whereas and consumer confidence index is an exogenous variable. The impulse responses in (d) are from a model consisting of log bank concentration, log GDP, the repo rate, the log consumer price index, the repo rate and the log BER business confidence index as endogenous variables, whereas the log BER consumer confidence index is an exogenous variable. The impulse responses in (e) are from a model consisting of log bank concentration, log GDP and log BER business confidence index as endogenous variables, whereas consumer confidence index is an exogenous variable. The impulse responses in (f) are from a model consisting of log bank concentration and log GDP as endogenous variables, whereas consumer confidence index is an exogenous variable. All models are estimated using two lags and 10,000 Monte Carlo Draws. The grey band denotes the 16th and 84th percentile confidence bands. *Source* Authors' calculations)

replaced with household consumption spending and investment spending, respectively. Investment is measured by the gross fixed capital formation. The variables are used in levels, log transformed and thereafter multiplied by 100. The impulse responses should be interpreted as deviations from the trend.

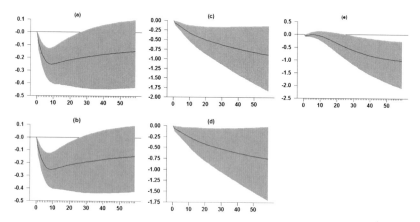

Fig. 17.3 Consumption responses to a positive bank concentration shock (*Note* The impulse responses in (a) are from a model consisting of log bank concentration, log household consumption, and the repo rate as endogenous variables, whereas the log BER business confidence index and the log real effective exchange rate are exogenous variables. The impulse responses in (b) are from a model consisting of log household consumption; the repo rate and log bank concentration as endogenous variables, whereas log BER business confidence index and log real effective exchange rate are exogenous variables. The impulse responses in (c) are from a model consisting of log bank concentration, log household consumption, the repo rate and log-BER-business-confidence index as endogenous variables, whereas and log-consumer-confidence index is exogenous variable. The impulse responses in (d) are from a model consisting of the log bank concentration, log household consumption, the repo rate, the log consumer price index, the repo rate and log BER business confidence index as endogenous variables, whereas the log BER consumer confidence index is an exogenous variable. The impulse responses in (e) are from a model consisting of log bank concentration, log household consumption and log BER business confidence index as endogenous variables, whereas consumer confidence index is an exogenous variable. All models are estimated using two lags and 10,000 Monte Carlo Draws. *Source* Authors' calculations). The grey shaded band denotes the 16th and 84th percentile confidence bands

Figure 17.3 shows that consumption spending declines significantly to a positive bank concentration shock. The consumption decline is robust to different model specifications. This indicates that the decline in GDP is also attributed to the reduction in consumption, following a positive bank concentration shock. This could happen when increased

17 Do Positive Bank Concentration Shocks Impact ... 275

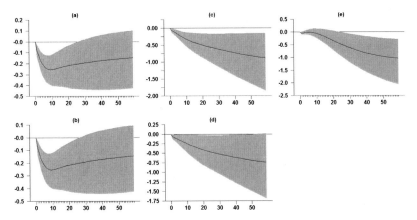

Fig. 17.4 Investment responses to a positive bank concentration shock (*Note* The impulse responses in (a) are from a model consisting of the log bank concentration, log investment and the repo rate as endogenous variable whereas log BER business confidence index and log real effective exchange rate are exogenous variables. The impulse responses in (b) are from a model consisting of log investment, the repo rate and log bank concentration and the repo rate as endogenous variables, whereas the log BER business confidence index and log real effective exchange rate are exogenous variables. The impulse responses in (c) are from a model consisting of log bank concentration, log the investment, the repo rate and the log BER business confidence index as endogenous variables, whereas and the log consumer confidence index is an exogenous variable. The impulse responses in (d) are from a model consisting of the log bank concentration, log investment, the repo rate, the log consumer price index, the repo rate and log BER business confidence index as endogenous variables, whereas the log BER consumer confidence index is an exogenous variable. The impulse responses in (e) are from a model consisting of log-bank-concentration, log-investment and the log BER business confidence index as endogenous variables, whereas consumer confidence index is an exogenous variable. All models are estimated using two lags and 10,000 Monte Carlo Draws. *Source* Authors' calculations). The grey shaded bands denotes the 16th an 84th percentile confidence bands

bank concentration leads to high interest rate margins, which makes it difficult for households to gain access to credit.

Figure 17.4 shows the responses of investment (measured by gross fixed capital formation). Similarly, investment declines significantly to positive bank concentration shocks. The decline is robust to different

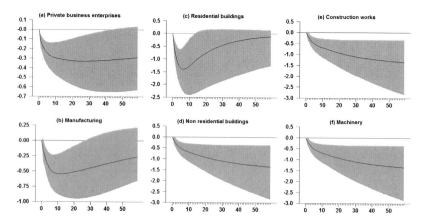

Fig. 17.5 Components of investment responses to a positive bank concentration shock (Note All models are estimated using two lags and 10,000 Monte Carlo Draws. The grey shaded bands denote 16th and 84th percentile confidence bands. Source Authors' calculations)

model specifications. Feldmann (2013) suggests that start-ups and SMEs are less likely to have easy access to loans and the loans are likely to be expensive. This may probably lead to a decline in business formation and lower the rate of growth of young firms and other SMEs.[1]

The analysis further shows the effects of positive bank concentration shocks on disaggregated components of gross fixed capital formation by private business enterprises. These components are included separately in the model. The model includes log bank concentration, the log component of gross fixed capital formation by private business enterprises and the repo rate. The components of private business enterprises are shown by the headings of impulse responses in Fig. 17.5. The components are included separately in the model. However, the results are robust to the different model specifications. The exogenous variables include the log business confidence index and log real effective exchange rate. The models are estimated using two lags and 10,000 Monte Carlo Draws.

---

[1] These small firms create most of the new jobs while the older and larger firms create few and destroy many jobs. As a consequence, a concentrated banking sector may lower employment and raise unemployment, especially by focusing on the latter type of firms.

Figure 17.5 shows the impulse responses. All components of private fixed capital formation decline significantly to a positive bank concentration shock. This may happen when the concentrated banking system increases the cost of financial intermediation, thereby dampening economic growth and lowering the rate of business formation (Feldmann 2013).

17.2.1 Which Channels Transmit Positive Bank Competition Shocks to GDP?

The analysis concludes by estimating a counterfactual VAR model to determine the roles of the investment and employment channels in transmitting the positive bank concentration shocks to GDP. These channels are shut off in transmitting the positive bank concentration shocks to GDP. The gap between actual and counterfactual responses measures the role of these channels. The counterfactual VAR model includes log bank concentration, log GDP and a transmission channel (that is, log employment, log GDP, log credit and the unemployment) as endogenous variables. The model includes a constant, the log BER business confidence index, the log real effective exchange rate and a recession dummy as exogenous variables. The recession dummy equals to one for the recession in 2009Q1–2009Q3 and 2018Q1–2018Q2 and zero otherwise. The channels are included separately in the model. The channels are shut off to calculate the counterfactual GDP responses. The models are estimated using two lags and 10,000 Monte Carlo draws. Figure 17.6, shows the responses to a one positive standard deviation in the bank concentration shock.

In Fig. 17.6, the actual GDP declines more than the counterfactual suggests, indicating that investment dynamics, following the positive bank concentration shocks, amplify the decline in GDP. In addition, the reduction in employment due to increased bank concentration amplifies the decline in GDP. The role of the employment channel supports Feldmann's (2013) evidence which does not support the view that a more concentrated banking industry may improve the labour market performance. Thus, the concentrated banking system has adverse effects

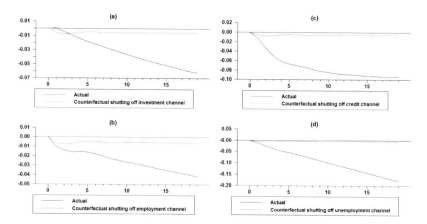

Fig. 17.6 GDP responses to a positive bank concentration shock and the role of different channels (*Source* Authors' calculations)

on the labour market performance. We find that banking concentration has adverse effects on the labour market performance by lowering economic growth.

Figure 17.6, shows the actual and counterfactual GDP responses to a positive bank concentration shock, including the role of labour market indicators. The role of labour market indicators is shown in Figs. 17.6b and d. Figure 17.6b shows that the employment channel amplifies the decline in GDP to a positive bank concentration shock. Figure 17.6d shows that the unemployment rate amplifies the decline in GDP, following a positive bank concentration shock. The analysis further examines the role of the credit channel in transmitting the positive bank concentration shocks to GDP. Figure 17.6c, shows that actual GDP declines more than the counterfactual, indicating the influence in the worsening of credit developments. The worsening via the credit channel could be due to increased cost of intermediation, or insufficient credit, or higher cost of loans and this is more likely to dampen job creation in the overall economy. This happens when banks with oligopolistic power would, in comparisons to perfect competition, have at equilibrium higher loan rates and smaller quantity of loans funds. The limited supply of loan quantities would reduce economic growth.

17.2.2 What Should Policymakers Do?

This analysis concludes by determining the extent to which GDP responds to positive bank concentration shocks in the low and high bank concentration regimes. The regimes are based on the bank concentration threshold of 0.18. The values above this threshold denote high bank concentration. The high bank concentration regime (high regime) takes all values of bank concentration above 0.18 and zero otherwise. The low bank concentration regime (low regime) takes all values of log bank concentration below 0.18 and zero otherwise. The estimated VAR model includes a bank concentration-dummy and the log GDP. The bank concentration dummies are included separately in the model. The other variables included as exogenous variables in the model are the log BER business confidence index and the log the real effective exchange rate. The model is estimated using two lags and 10,000 Monte Carlo Draws.

In Fig. 17.7, positive bank concentration shock lowers GDP in the high bank concentration regime and it increases it in the low regime. This suggests that reducing bank concentration and making the sector competitive enables the GDP to rise.

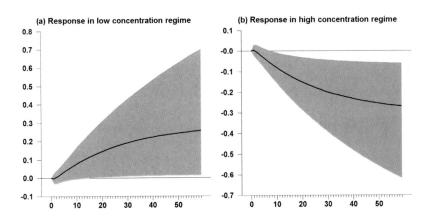

Fig. 17.7 GDP responses to a positive bank concentration shock in the low and high concentration regimes (*Note* All models are estimated using two lags and 10,000 Monte Carlo Draws. The grey shaded band denotes the 16th and 84th percentile confidence bands. *Source* Authors' calculations)

17.3 Conclusion and Policy Implications

This chapter examined the extent to which a positive bank concentration shock impacts on GDP in South Africa? Evidence shows that GDP declines to a positive bank concentration shock. This shows that bank concentration has adverse effects on economic growth. The finding is robust to different model specifications. Evidence from the counterfactual analysis shows actual GDP declines more than the counterfactual suggests, the decline is accentuated by decreases in investment and reduction in employment due to increased bank concentration. As in Diallo and Zhang (2017), the findings have implications for policymakers and academics since they may mean that the low level of bank concentration in the South African financial sector would promote economic growth and these findings are highly relevant in periods of economic slowdown. It is important to examine the link between bank concentration and economic growth, given that the South African economic growth has been volatile and low, and unemployment is high. Therefore, it is important for policymakers to lower the entry barriers and introduce a sliding scale of capital adequacy requirement ratios that rises with the size of the banks.

References

Carlin, W., & Mayer, C. (2003). Finance, investment and growth. *Journal of Financial Economics, 69*(1), 191–226.

Cetorelli, N., & Gambera, M. (2001). Banking market structure, financial dependence and growth: International evidence from the industry data. *Journal of Finance, 56*(2), 617–648.

Feldmannn, H. (2013). Banking systems concentration and labour market performance in industrial countries. *Contemporary Economic Policy, 31*(4), 719–732.

18

Do Positive Bank Concentration Shocks Impact Employment in South Africa?

Main Highlights

- Evidence reveals that employment declines significantly to positive bank concentration shocks and the declines are much bigger to persistently rising shocks than to less persistent shocks.
- In addition, the counterfactual analysis reveals that actual employment declines more than the counterfactual suggests, indicating that the declining credit extension and reduced capital formation amplifies the reduction in employment.
- Thus, policymakers should reduce the degree of banking concentration and make the banking system competitive by lowering entry barriers and by introducing sliding scale of capital adequacy requirement ratios that increase with the size of the banks.

© The Author(s) 2019
E. Ndou and T. Mokoena, *Inequality, Output-Inflation Trade-Off and Economic Policy Uncertainty*,
https://doi.org/10.1007/978-3-030-19803-9_18

281

18.1 Introduction

This chapter continues the discussion of the link between bank concentration and competition (*here after referred to as bank concentration*) and income inequality. Income inequality is measured by the Gini coefficient. In addition, the analysis offers additional explanation through which increased bank concentration may be raising income inequality, by impacting on employment. The objective of this chapter is to examine the extent to which positive bank concentration shock impacts on the labour market performance by looking at the reaction of employment. This is motivated by the high unemployment rate in South Africa and this has not been linked to the effects of increased bank concentration. However, Feldmann (2013) noted that, following the financial crisis, some industrial countries experienced increasing bank concentration, while their labour market performance deteriorated. In addition, the analysis is motivated by the granting of banking licences to new banks, which may induce competition in the banking sector, albeit over time.

According to Feldmann (2013), there are two main hypotheses through which bank concentration impacts employment. The first hypothesis is referred to as the structure-conduct-performance hypothesis. This hypothesis suggests that a more concentrated banking system tends to raise lending rates, leading to higher interest rate margins. The high rates and margins restrict credit extension due to reduced competition (Feldmann 2013; Guzman 2000; Smith 1998). In addition, the reduced credit extension will lower investment, which in turn lowers economic growth and slows job creation, if Okun's law holds. Unemployment will increase if wages are sticky downwards. The adverse effects of bank concentration on the labour market may arise through increased cost of financial intermediation. This may reduce investment and thus demand for labour. The reduction in labour demand raises unemployment when there are wage rigidities (Feldmann 2013).

The second hypothesis is referred to as the efficient-structure hypothesis. This hypothesis suggests that a highly concentrated banking system may lead to more efficient banks which have large market shares. This leads banks to achieve higher efficiency in financial intermediation, leading to favourable effects on lending rates. This happens due to banks having incentives to forge and maintain long-term relationships with large firms and younger firms. Due to lending strategies, banks may charge modest lending rates, thereby enabling more firms to be started and financed. Hence, this may lead to increased job creation, improvements in investment and economic growth, leading to lower unemployment. The beneficial effects arise when the concentrated banking aids the fostering of long-term relationships with firms, which leads to improvements in long-term investment and economic developments. In addition, bank concentration may have adverse effects on growth of equity-financed and skill-intensive industries as found in Carlin and Mayer (2003). This has the potential to reduce employment and raise unemployment.

These preceding discussions indicate that the effects of bank concentration on labour markets performance are ambiguous from a theoretical point of view. Hence, their direction and magnitude must be resolved empirically. Evidence in the literature points to the link between bank concentration and employment dynamics. For instance, Feldmann (2013) found evidence indicating that a more concentrated banking industry worsens labour market performance. This evidence supports the structure-conduct-performance hypothesis, which suggests that a highly concentrated banking system may increase the costs of financial intermediation, which may dampen economic growth and lower the rate of business formation.

This chapter fills policy gaps by showing the effects of positive bank concentration shocks on employment. The chapter further applies counterfactual analysis to examine the role of investment and the credit channel in amplifying the reaction of employment to a positive banking concentration shock. Evidence indicates that a positive bank concentration shock lowers employment, and this is worsened by the credit and investment channels. This points to the role of the credit channel or costs of intermediation or insufficient credit or higher costs of loans and slower capital formation, which dampen job creation in the overall economy.

18.2 Results

The analysis begins by determining the response of employment to a positive bank concentration shock using quarterly (Q) data from 1994Q1 to 2018Q2. The banking sector's concentration and competition is measured by the Herfindahl-Hirschman Index (H-index). All data used in this paper is obtained from the South African Reserve Bank. To show the differential effects of the shocks, we show the effects of different bank concentration shock scenarios on employment dynamics. The three shock scenarios capture the following; (1) persistently increasing bank concentration; (2) unchanged bank concentration; and (3) less persistent positive bank concentration shock.

The bank concentration shock effects are determined by estimating a bivariate VAR model. The model is estimated with variables in levels. The basic model includes bank concentration and total non-agricultural employment as endogenous variables. The exogenous variables include GDP, BER business confidence index, the real effective exchange rate, and the repo rate. Apart from the repo rate, all other variables are logarithm transformed and multiplied by 100, hence the results should be interpreted as percentage deviation from the trend. The repo rate is expressed in per cent. The model uses two lags.

Figure 18.1 shows employment responses to a positive bank concentration shock. In Fig. 18.1a, bank concentration increase tends to be persistent. Employment declines significantly after four quarters in Fig. 18.1b. It declines by about 0.06% after 8 quarters. Based on shock scenarios, employment declines are much bigger to a persistently rising bank concentration shock than to a less persistent shock in Fig. 18.1d. The decline in employment is robust to when the variables in the basic model are ordered in reverse.

How robust is the reaction of employment to a positive bank concentration shock? To determine the sensitivity of the employment reaction, the analysis determines the robustness of the employment decline to a positive bank concentration shock using different VAR models. Four models are estimated, and the reaction of employment is shown

18 Do Positive Bank Concentration Shocks Impact ...

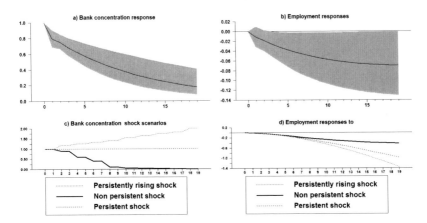

Fig. 18.1 Employment responses to a positive bank concentration shock (*Note* The grey shaded bands denote the 16th and 84th percentile confidence bands. *Source* Authors' calculations)

in Fig. 18.2. In Fig. 18.2, employment declines significantly to a positive bank concentration shock. This suggests that employment reacts to a positive bank concentration shock and the finding is robust to the different model specifications. This finding suggests the prevalence of structure-conduct-performance hypothesis. Hence, the effects of more concentration and less competition in the banking sector may be working by raising the lending rate, which leads to higher interest rate margins, and restriction on the credit extension due to reduced competition (Feldmann 2013; Guzman 2000; Smith 1998). Therefore, the reduced credit extension will likely lower investment, economic growth, and job creation. The reduction in job creation rate may raise unemployment when wages are sticky.

Would the employment reaction vary according to different sector-specific employment categories included in the model? We extend the analysis to determine how a positive bank concentration shock impacts employment by sectors. This is assessed by estimating a bivariate VAR model. The model consists of the log of the bank concentration measure and the log sector-specific employment as endogenous variables.

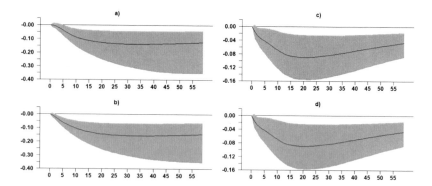

Fig. 18.2 Employment responses to a positive bank concentration shock (*Note* The impulses in (a) are from a model consisting of log bank concentration, log GDP, log employment and the repo rate as endogenous variables, with log BER business confidence index and log real effective exchange rate as exogenous. The impulses in (b) are from a model consisting of log bank concentration, log GDP and log employment as endogenous variables, while log BER business confidence index and log real effective exchange rate as exogenous. The impulses in (c) are from a model consisting of log bank concentration, log employment and the repo rate as endogenous variables, while log BER business confidence index, log GDP and log real effective exchange rate as exogenous. The impulses in (d) are from a model consisting of log employment, log bank concentration and the repo rate as endogenous variables, while log BER business confidence index, log GDP and log real effective exchange rate as exogenous. The models are estimated using two lags. The bands denote the 16 and 84th percentiles. *Source* Authors' calculations)

The exogenous variables include the log BER business confidence index, a recession dummy, and the log credit extension to the private sector. All the log transformed variables are multiplied by 100. The results are robust to different orderings of the endogenous variables in the bivariate VAR model and to estimating a three-variable VAR model.

Figure 18.3 shows the employment responses to a positive bank concentration shock. The employment rate declines for a prolonged period in most cases. This indicates that a positive bank concentration shock also depresses sector-specific employment.

18 Do Positive Bank Concentration Shocks Impact ...   287

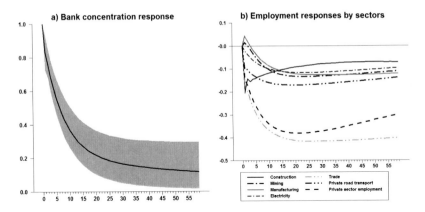

Fig. 18.3 Sector-specific employment responses to a positive bank concentration shock (*Note* The grey shaded bands denote the 16th and 84th percentile confidence bands. *Source* Authors' calculations)

18.3 Counterfactual Analysis

The analysis concludes by estimating a counterfactual VAR model to determine the role of gross fixed capital formation (investment) and credit extension in transmitting positive bank concentration shocks to employment. These channels are shut off in transmitting the shock to employment; hence, the gap between the actual and counterfactual responses measures the role of these channels. The counterfactual VAR model includes the log of the bank concentration measure, the log of employment and specified channel. The channels are log investment and log credit. The model includes a log BER business confidence index and a recession dummy as exogenous variables. The recession dummy equals to one for the recession during the periods 2009Q1–2009Q3 and 2018Q1–2018Q2 and zero otherwise. The channels are included separately in the model. The channels are shut off to calculate the counterfactual employment responses. The models are estimated using two lags and 10,000 Monte Carlo draws. The responses to a one positive standard deviation shock in bank concentration are shown in Fig. 18.4. In both instances the actual employment declines

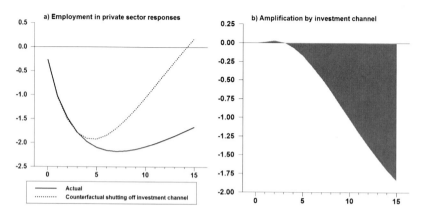

Fig. 18.4 Employment responses to positive bank concentration shock and role of investment (*Source* Authors' calculations)

more than the counterfactual suggests, indicating that investment, following the positive bank concentration shocks amplifies the decline in employment.

We further show the role of the credit channel in transmitting a positive bank concentration shock to employment in the manufacturing sector, using the preceding three-variable VAR model. The employment variable in the preceding model is replaced with the log employment

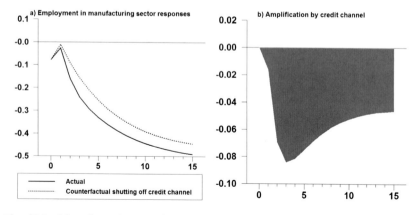

Fig. 18.5 Manufacturing employment responses to a positive bank concentration shock (*Source* Authors' calculations)

in the manufacturing sector. The model uses the log credit extension to the private sector as a channel. This channel is shut off in the model in transmitting the positive bank concentration shocks to employment in the manufacturing sector. In Fig. 18.5, the actual employment in the manufacturing sector declines more than the counterfactual suggests. This suggests that the declining credit extension due to the unexpected increase in bank concentration amplifies the reduction in employment in the manufacturing sector. We therefore conclude that this evidence is robust that the decline in employment is transmitted via other channels, following a positive bank concentration shock (Fig. 18.5).

18.4 Conclusion and Policy Implications

Evidence reveals that employment declines significantly to a positive bank concentration shocks and the declines are much bigger to a persistently rising shock than to less persistent shock. Counterfactual analysis reveals that actual employment declines more than the counterfactual suggests, indicating that the declining credit extension and reduced capital formation amplify the reduction in employment. The fact that increased bank concentration leads to a deterioration in labour markets and lowers the employment suggests that policymakers should reduce the degree of banking sector concentration and make the banking system competitive. Therefore, it is important to lower entry barriers and to impose stricter limits on mergers that would create or enhance one bank's dominant market position. In addition, we recommend that a sliding scale of capital adequacy ratios that rise with the size of the banks should be introduced.

References

Carlin, W., & Mayer, C. (2003). Finance, investment and growth. *Journal of Financial Economics, 69*(1), 191–226.
Cetorelli, N., & Gambera, M. (2001). Banking market structure, financial dependence and growth: International evidence from the industry data. *Journal of Finance, 56*(2), 617–648.

Feldmann, H. (2013). Banking systems concentration and labour market performance in industrial countries. *Contemporary Economic Policy, 31*(4), 719–732.

Guzman, M. G. (2000). Bank structure, capital accumulation and growth: A simple macroeconomic model. *Economic Theory, 16*(2), 421–455.

Smith, R. T. (1998). Banking competition and macroeconomic performance. *Journal of Money, Credit and Banking, 30*(4), 793–815.

Part VII

Output-Inflation Trade-Off and the Role of Inflation Regimes

19

Is There Evidence of the Trade-Off in Output and Inflation Volatilities in South Africa?

Main Highlights

- Evidence shows there is trade-off between output and inflation volatilities. The volatilities of inflation and the output were minimised in the inflation-targeting period.
- Evidence reveals that periods when the macroeconomic performance was superior coincided with the periods of minimal volatilities in both the inflation rates and the output gap.

19.1 Introduction

This chapter presents evidence based on the trade-off between inflation and output volatilities in South Africa. This evidence is extracted from Ndou and Gumata (2017). This is the first segment in the sequence of chapters that analyze the prevalence of the output-inflation trade-off in South Africa. The achievement of the primary objective of price stability on a sustainable basis implies tough choices regarding the output and inflation trade-off. This is particularly a compelling case when

© The Author(s) 2019
E. Ndou and T. Mokoena, *Inequality, Output-Inflation Trade-Off and Economic Policy Uncertainty,*
https://doi.org/10.1007/978-3-030-19803-9_19

293

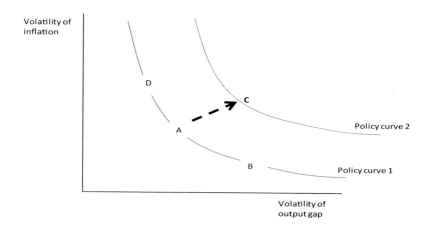

Fig. 19.1 The output-inflation trade-off (*Source* Authors drawing adapted from Ndou and Gumata [2017])

the domestic economy is subjected to several severe supply side shocks and at a time when the output gap is persistently negative. The policy choices open to policymakers are depicted in the movements along the efficiency policy frontier in Fig. 19.1. This chapter shows that the policy efficiency frontier, which measures the trade-off, has shifted over time and the periods of high economic growth were associated with minimum inflation and output volatilities.

The standard output-inflation trade-off depicted in Fig. 19.1 begins with a central bank trying to minimise the expected value of the loss function (L) where, π_t denotes the inflation rate, π^* denotes the inflation target and λ is the central bank's weight given to inflation, y_t is output and y^* is the target output level.

$$L = \lambda(\pi_t - \pi^*)^2 + (1 - \lambda)(y_t - y^*)^2 \qquad (19.1)$$

By varying λ we can plot the efficiency frontier as the locus indicating the smallest variance of inflation obtainable for any given variance of the output gap.[1] A zero weight on the inflation term reduces the bank's objective to output alone, while a zero weight on output reduces the objective to inflation alone. As the weight varies between inflation and the output gap, the bank's objectives also shift. As a result, the greater the weight put on inflation, the lower the implied variance of inflation and the higher the implied variance of output. Theoretically, any point on the output-inflation trade-off reflects optimal monetary policy choices subject to the structural model of the economy and the weights assigned to the stabilisation of inflation and output. The output-inflation trade-off can therefore be seen as an efficient policy frontier which connects the efficient trade-off between the unconditional variances of inflation and the output gap.[2]

The trade-off between the volatilities of inflation and output is known as the output-inflation trade-off or the Taylor curve. Taylor (1979) also refers to the output-inflation trade-off as the second-order Phillips curve in which case there is a permanent trade-off between the variance of inflation and the variance of the output gap. The trade-off arises because monetary policy cannot simultaneously offset both types of variability. Based on the description in Taylor (1979), the positions on the output-inflation trade-off that best describe policy choices available to policymakers are shown in Fig. 19.1. The policy choices can be summed up as follows:

Strict inflation targeting—For policymakers more concerned about the variability in inflation, the choice to aggressively lower the variability in inflation and deviations from the targeted path means that they will be located in a position such as B on the policy curve. This results in an outcome whereby the variability of output gap is relatively high, whereas that of the inflation rate is low.

---

[1]Taylor (1979), Chatterjee (2002), Olson et al. (2012), Ndou et al. (2013), and Ndou and Gumata (2017).

[2]Moreover, theoretically the optimal point on the output-inflation efficiency frontier can only be achieved when a central banker has the independence to set policy without political backlash. Hence, discretionary policymaking translates to the central banker being able to choose the appropriate inflation variability aversion parameter to solve the minimisation problem and make independent policy decisions with a positive influence on a country's stability and growth.

296   E. Ndou and T. Mokoena

Output targeting—This is a choice of less aggressive policy actions in lowering deviations in inflation from the targeted path. Hence, the variability in output is low whereas that of the inflation rate is relatively high as in point D.

Flexible inflation targeting—This happens along points like A and C. These points represent a variability combination for which there is likely to be consensus. The variability combinations near these points brings closer the diversity of views about the relative demerits of inflation and output variability represented by the extreme lying points. Movements from A to C reflect a change in the policy framework.

19.2   Evidence of the Output-Inflation Trade-Off

19.2.1 Initial Evidence Indicating the Output-Inflation Volatility Trade-Off Shifts in South Africa

As indicated earlier, this chapter presents evidence of the output-inflation trade-off and macroeconomic performance based on Ndou and Gumata (2017). The aim is to give insight on the nature of the correlations in the volatilities between the output gap and inflation over the business cycle phases. Table 19.1 shows the average volatilities of inflation and the output gap. These are based on the quarterly (Q) data from 1975Q1 to 2012Q2. The lowest inflation volatility and output gap volatilities occurred in the period 2000Q1–2007Q2 and the

Table 19.1   Average volatilities, trade-off and economic growth

Periods	Inflation volatility	Output gap volatility	Correlation	GDP growth
1975Q1–1999Q4	0.930	1.431	−0.153	1.985
2000Q1–2007Q2	**0.791**	**1.153**	**−0.306**	**4.286**
2007Q3–2012Q3	0.832	1.238	−0.079	2.352
1975Q1–2012Q3	0.888	1.348	−0.175	2.493

Note Bold shows the period with lowest volatilities and higher average economic growth
Source South African Reserve Bank and authors' calculations

19 Is There Evidence of the Trade-Off ...   297

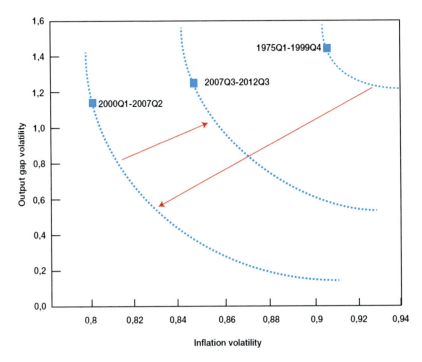

Fig. 19.2 Shifts in the South African output-inflation trade-offs (*Source* Authors' calculations and drawing)

accompanying correlation was more negative than in other periods.[3] This period also achieved the highest average GDP growth rate of 4.3%. The lowest average growth of 1.98% appears in 1975Q1–1999Q4 periods which has the highest inflation and output gap volatilities. This suggests that high macroeconomic performance in terms of higher average GDP growth tends to be associated with periods of more negative trade-off in volatilities.

Figure 19.2 visualises these relationships graphically by showing the average conditional volatilities for the output gap and inflation for the periods; 1975Q1–1999Q4, 2000Q1–2007Q2, and 2007Q3–2012Q2. In Fig. 19.2 the average volatilities for the period 1975–1999 show the

---

[3]The two-year correlations approach is consistent with monetary policy being implemented in a forward looking way, such that the interest rates affect the economy in 18–24 months.

298 E. Ndou and T. Mokoena

contrasting performance relative to those observed in the period from 2000 to 2007. Vast literature documents that better policy conduct can take some credit for this improvement. The anchoring of inflation expectations led to a huge reduction in inflation volatility, indicating that a period of double digit inflation and high variability in output was consigned to the past (King 2013).

The adoption of inflation targeting framework in South Africa on February 2000 was subsequently followed by a prolonged period of macroeconomic stability before the beginning of the financial crisis that started in 2007. This is shown in Fig. 19.2, by the output-inflation curve which shifted inwards as the lower level of inflation volatility was achieved for any given level of output volatility. While causality remains an area of debate, inflation targeting was at least consistent with economic stability.

However, following the financial crisis, the variance of the output gap and inflation has been much higher and the policy curve has shifted outwards for the period 2007–2012 as shown in Fig. 19.2. The causes of this outward shift can be considered to be due to the change in the structure of the economy. Hence, the coefficients of the output-inflation variability have changed. It is also possible that a series of large unanticipated shocks that have hit the economy, of which the global financial crisis has been relatively persistent, are the contributing factors to the shift. From the results, these shocks have heightened macroeconomic instability and have contributed to the volatilities of both output and inflation moving in the same direction.

19.2.2 The Second Evidence of Output-Inflation Trade-Off Based on the Manufacturing Monthly Data

Evidence from Ndou and Gumata(2017) based on monthly (M) data from 1990M1 to 2016M12 is shown in Fig. 19.3. Figure 19.3a shows that output growth volatility decline with varying magnitudes due to an unexpected positive inflation volatility shock. In addition, Fig. 19.3b shows that output volatility decline when preceded by high inflation

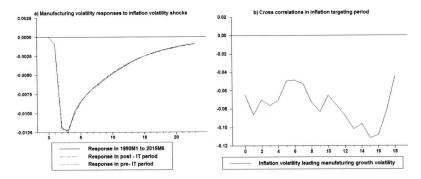

Fig. 19.3 The trade-off between output growth volatility and inflation volatility (*Note* IT means the inflation-targeting period. *Source* Authors' calculations)

volatility. The trade-off is more pronounced in the first ten months and retracts towards the pre-shock level. This suggests that the trade-off weakens over time. This trade-off is most evident in both the post and pre-inflation targeting framework.

19.2.3 The Third Evidence of Output-Inflation Trade-Off Based on a Scatterplot

Is the trade-off between inflation volatility and output growth volatility dependent on the techniques used? Not so. Figure 19.4b further corroborates the negative responses of output growth volatility due to elevated inflation volatility during the inflation targeting period. The bilateral scatterplots in Fig. 19.4 also confirm a negative relationship between inflation volatility and output growth volatility.

19.2.4 The Fourth Evidence of the Output-Inflation Trade-Off and the Effects of the Persistence of Shocks

The analysis is extended to include various scenarios of inflation volatility shocks. These scenarios are separated into persistent, non-persistent, and persistently rising inflation volatility shock as shown in Fig. 19.5a.

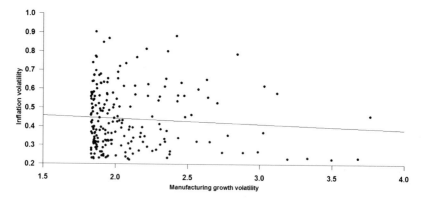

Fig. 19.4 Scatterplot between output growth volatility and inflation volatility (*Source* Authors' calculations)

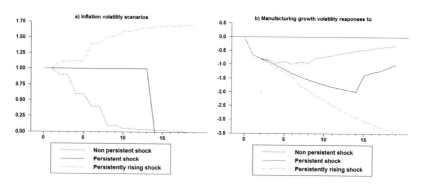

Fig. 19.5 Trade-off between output growth volatility and inflation volatility for various volatility scenarios (*Source* Authors' calculations)

We show the reactions of the manufacturing growth volatility during the inflation targeting period to given scenarios of inflation volatility shocks. This evidence indicates that manufacturing growth volatility declines irrespective of the inflation volatility shock. The persistently rising inflation volatility shock worsens the manufacturing growth volatility more than the less persistent inflation volatility shock.

These results confirm a negative trade-off between inflation and growth volatility. This evidence suggests that anti-inflation policies to lower inflation minimise the inflation volatility and the loss function.

19.3 Conclusion and Policy Implications

The results show that the output-inflation trade-off has shifted over the sample period. The output-inflation trade-off shifted inward under the inflation targeting regime. Furthermore, macroeconomic performance is superior during the periods in which the output-inflation trade-off relationship led to minimum volatilities. In policy terms, the shift to the inflation-targeting regime minimised the inflation volatility and managed to achieve price stability. The conduct of policy managed to minimise both the anticipated and unanticipated deviations in inflation. However, the results of the outward shifts in the output-inflation trade-off since the onset of the financial crisis suggest that policymakers should aim at reducing the inflation and output gap volatilities. This may minimise the volatilities and result in an inward shift of the output-inflation trade-off. Furthermore, the results show that positive trade-off tends to be followed by a slowdown in economic growth. This means that when both volatilities move in the same direction economic growth tends to slowdown. The positive trade-off, in less stricter terms, implies shifts, rather than movements, along the efficient frontier curve. The implication is that periods of positive trade-offs indicate sub-optimal monetary policy settings and these may adversely impact economic growth performance (Friedman 2006).

References

Chatterjee, S. (2002). The Taylor curve and the unemployment-inflation trade off. *Business Review*. Federal Reserve Bank of Philadelphia. www.phil.frb.org/researchreview/2002/q3/brq302sc.pdf.

Friedman, M. (2006). *Tradeoffs in monetary policy*. Paper presented as Unpublished Manuscript. Stanford University. www.nber.org/chapters/c0074.pdf.

King, M. (2013). *Monetary policy: Many targets, many instruments. Where do we stand?* Remarks at the IMF Conference on 'Rethinking Macro Policy II: First Steps and Early Lessons', Washington, DC.

Ndou, E., & Gumata, N. (2017). *Inflation dynamics in South Africa: The role of thresholds exchange rate pass-through and inflation expectations on policy trade-offs*. Cham: Palgrave Macmillan.

Ndou, E., Gumata, N., Ncube, M., & Olson, E. (2013). *An empirical estimation of the Taylor curve in South Africa* (African Development Bank Working Paper No. 183). https://www.afdb.org/fileadmin/uploads/afdb/Documents/Publications/Working_Paper_189_An_Empirical_Investigation_of_the_Taylor_Curve_in_South_Africa.pdf.

Taylor, J. B. (1979). Estimation and control of a macroeconomic model with rational expectations. *Econometrica, 47*(5), 1267–1286.

20

To What Extent Does the Output-Inflation Trade-Off Exist in South Africa and Is It Impacted by the Six Per Cent Inflation Threshold?

Main Highlights

- The chapter determines the extent to which elevated nominal volatilities make expansionary policy ineffective in achieving maximum real output and low inflation.
- Evidence shows that elevated nominal demand and inflation volatility shocks reduce the output-inflation trade-off, and this reduces policy effectiveness in achieving desirable outcomes. The magnitudes of the reduction in the output-inflation trade-off effects are larger in the high inflation regime than in the low inflation regime.
- In addition, a combination of increases in both inflation and nominal demand volatilities is bad for the output-inflation trade-off.
- In policy terms, this evidence confirms the new Keynesian hypothesis, which implies that demand policy is less effective in countries with both high inflation and demand volatilities. Therefore, policymakers should minimise the volatility of inflation when implementing demand policy and ensure that price stability is enforced to minimise inflation volatility.

© The Author(s) 2019   303
E. Ndou and T. Mokoena, *Inequality, Output-Inflation Trade-Off and Economic Policy Uncertainty,*
https://doi.org/10.1007/978-3-030-19803-9_20

20.1 Introduction

Another approach to testing the effectiveness of an expansionary policy shock on output is to determine the output-inflation trade-off following a shock. This chapter focuses on the reaction of output to an expansionary policy shock. The analysis is based on inflation regimes and this differs from the approach applied in Chapter 19. We revisit the policy ineffectiveness propositions posited by the new Keynesian and new Classical theories regarding the effects of nominal demand policy shocks. As shown in Fig. 20.1, the policy effectiveness of an expansionary shock depends on the slope of the aggregate supply curve (S). A nominal demand shock such as an expansionary policy (for example increased government spending ΔG or monetary stimulus ΔR) will shift the aggregate demand (D) curve from D1 to D2, resulting in three output outcomes. The outcomes indicate a trade-off between output and inflation outcomes. In this case, the outcomes are dependent on the slope of the supply curve.

Given the supply curve S1, output does not change and prices react fully, suggesting that an expansionary policy shock is fully passed

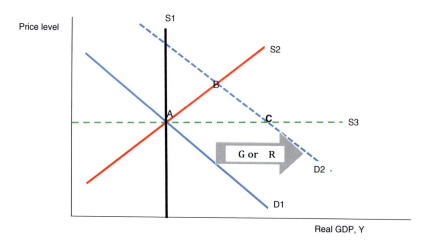

Fig. 20.1 Theoretical effects of an expansionary policy shock on output and inflation (*Source* Authors' drawing)

20 To What Extent Does the Output-Inflation Trade-Off ...

through to prices. Based on the supply curve S3, the expansionary policy is fully passed onto output without any effect on prices. Using the supply curve S2, it is seen that both the real output and prices respond to an expansionary policy shock. Theoretically, there is an output-inflation trade-off induced by an expansionary policy shock but is this supported by data analysis and does price stability impact the trade-off?[1]

The determination of the size of the output-inflation trade-off can either refute or ascertain the prevalence of the policy ineffectiveness proposition. Does output-inflation trade-off exists in South Africa and to what extent is it impacted by the role of the six per cent inflation threshold? Does trend inflation impact the transmission of positive nominal demand shocks on the output-inflation trade-off? This chapter, in determining the policy ineffectiveness hypothesis tests the new Keynesian theory on nominal rigidities by investigating whether trend inflation has an impact on the magnitudes of demand policy on real GDP.

In point of fact, Ball et al. (1988) pointed out the importance of menu costs in the new Keynesian theory and showed that the real effects of nominal demand shocks depend on how often adjustments were made to prices.[2] According to these authors, the faster (slower) the speed of adjustment of prices, the smaller (larger) the real effects of such nominal demand shocks, therefore the steeper (flatter) the Philips curve. In addition, they postulated that a demand policy would be less effective in countries with high trend inflation because prices are less rigid, which leads agents to alter prices rather than change quantities.

The analysis of the output-inflation trade-off concept is spread over three chapters. This includes determining what weakens the output-inflation trade-off. The next section shows how in the short run the output-inflation trade-off is measured in the literature and this could be linked to theoretical predictions based on Fig. 20.1.

---

[1]During high inflation prices are less rigid.

[2]The new classical economics suggests that policy intervention should not exist because inflation is costlier than unemployment, and that the short-run Philips curve is very steep and the economy, being self-correcting, works smoothly and quickly. By contrast, the new Keynesian theory suggests that policy interventions, because unemployment is costlier than inflation, the Philips curve becomes flat and the self-correcting mechanism is rather slow and unreliable.

20.2 How Is the Short-Run Output-Inflation Trade-Off Measured?

To capture the theoretical predictions in Fig. 20.1, Ball et al. (1988) showed that the short-run output-inflation trade-off (τ) can be derived by running Eq. (20.1). Some studies criticised the econometrics behind such estimations. However, the validity of such results, based on theoretical assumptions made, are taken into consideration in the following sections. In Eq. (20.1), ΔNominal GDPgrowth$_t$ captures the nominal demand shock.

$$\text{Real GDP}_t = \text{constant} + \tau * \Delta\text{Nominal GDPgrowth}_t$$
$$+ \beta * \text{trend} + \varepsilon_t \qquad (20.1)$$

Equation (20.1) implies that output movements can be decomposed into long-run time trend and short-run fluctuations due to aggregate demand disturbances. It is the intuition of this equation that matters for this analysis as τ captures the short-run effects of nominal disturbance on real output. The τ measures the output-inflation trade-off, which is a kind of a slope of the Philips curve.

The change in aggregate demand can be transmitted to real output or to prices or both. When $\tau = 1$, this implies that nominal demand shocks are passed onto real output for one to one. However, when $\tau = 0$ this implies a full pass-through of nominal demand shock to prices. When $0 < \tau < 1$ implies that changes in nominal demand shock falls partly on real output and partly on the price level.[3]

---

[3]The larger the τ the larger the effect of a change in demand on the real economy. The smaller τ refers to the proportion that is passed into prices. Thus, a small τ implies that nominal disturbances have more effects on prices.

20.3 Does a Positive Nominal Demand Shock Exert Any Real Effect on GDP or Induce the Output-Inflation Trade-Off?

This chapter determines the effectiveness of positive nominal demand policy changes by examining the size and significance of the output-inflation trade-off as measured by the response of real output to a change in nominal demand as in Lucas (1973) and Ball et al. (1988). This literature suggests that the output-inflation trade-off measures the slope of the Philips curve.

The analysis determines whether the output-inflation trade-off is impacted by the six per cent inflation threshold. The results are analysed according to two inflation regimes. The low inflation regime refers to inflation below the six per cent threshold level. The high inflation regime refers to inflation above six per cent threshold. The chapter uses quarterly (Q) data that spans 1960Q1 to 2017Q2 obtained from the South African Reserve Bank.

20.3.1 Evidence from the Bivariate VAR Models

Two regime-dependent VARs are estimated under three model assumptions to deal with econometric issues raised in the literature regarding Eq. (20.1). This tests the robustness of the results to different transformations of real GDP. Model 1 uses both the growth rates on real and nominal GDP. Model 2 uses the real GDP in levels and growth in the nominal GDP. The second model utilises the specification of variables as in Ball et al. (1988). The first model deals with criticism that Model 2 is a spurious regression. Literature permits the estimation of models allowing the inclusion of both nonstationary and stationary variables. Model 3 uses real GDP gap and growth in nominal GDP following Odedokun (1991). The real GDP growth gap is derived from the difference between actual real GDP and the Hodrick Prescott filter trend. Hence, the analysis uses growth rates, levels, and the gap of real GDP to show robustness of the results.

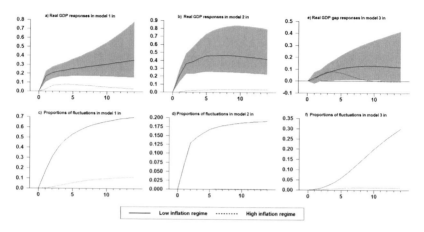

Fig. 20.2 Responses to positive nominal demand shock (*Note* The grey shaded area band denotes the 16th and 84th percentiles confidence bands. *Source* Authors' calculations)

Figure 20.2 shows the responses of real output to a positive nominal demand shock or the output-inflation trade-off parameter. Evidence in Fig. 20.2 shows the differential responses of output between the low and high inflation regimes. The real GDP growth rises to a positive nominal demand shock. The increase in the real GDP happens irrespective of model specifications and inflation regimes. Abstracting from model specifications, the real output rises much higher in the low inflation regime than in the high inflation regime. This finding indicates that the output-inflation trade-off is much higher in the low inflation regime relative to the high inflation regime. This suggests that a nominal demand policy shock affecting nominal demand will have bigger effect on real output in the low inflation regime than in the high inflation regime. As in Fig. 20.2, the low output-inflation trade-off in the high inflation regime implies the nominal demand shock is passed more into inflationary pressures than to real output. That is, the nominal demand shock raises inflation rather than stimulate real output growth.

In addition, Fig. 20.2c and d shows the proportion of fluctuations in real output induced by the nominal demand shock. A nominal demand shock induces more fluctuations in real output in the low inflation regime than in the high inflation regime. This evidence further shows that more output-inflation trade-off movements occur in the low inflation regime. This shows that policy initiatives that stimulate nominal demand will have much bigger real effect in the low inflation regime. Thus, both the impulse response and fluctuation decomposition approaches conclude similarly that inflation regimes play an important role in explaining the trade-off dynamics.

20.3.2 Evidence from a Three-Variable VAR Model

The robustness test of the preceding evidence is carried out by including the inflation variable in the analysis to determine whether inflation regimes play an important role in impacting the output-inflation trade-off. A number of studies use the real and nominal GDP variables without inflation. This analysis includes inflation in the two models specified above for robustness checks. Irrespective of the model specifications, evidence in Fig. 20.3 shows that inflation regimes play an important role in the output-inflation trade-off. The trade-off is significantly higher in the low inflation regime than in high regime. Thus, evidence is robust to the inclusion of inflation in the model.

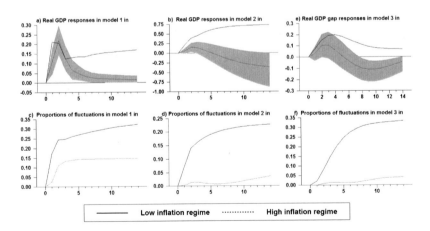

Fig. 20.3 Responses to positive nominal demand shock (*Note* The grey shaded area band denotes the 16th and 84th percentiles confidence bands. *Source* Authors' calculations)

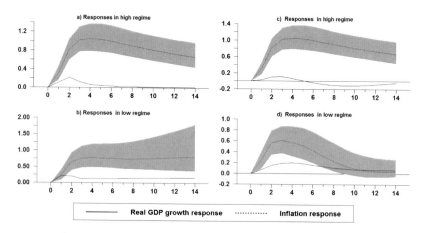

Fig. 20.4 Responses to positive nominal demand shocks (*Note* The grey shaded area band denotes the 16th and 84th percentiles confidence bands. *Source* Authors' calculations)

In addition, Fig. 20.4 compares the responses of real GDP and inflation to a positive nominal demand shock. The responses in Fig. 20.2a and b are based on a model which includes real GDP growth, while the results in Fig. 20.2c and d are based on the model which includes real GDP gap. A positive nominal demand shock affects the inflation rate more than the real output. Peak inflation increases are smaller in the low inflation regime than in the high inflation regime. In addition, real output rises persistently higher in the low inflation regime than in the high inflation regime. This suggests that a positive nominal demand shock is likely to stimulate real output in the low inflation regime together with low inflationary pressures.

20.4 Evidence from Single Regression Equations

20.4.1 Evidence from Regime-Dependent Regression Equations

The two-regime dependent linear regressions given by Eqs. (20.2) and (20.3) are estimated to determine the extent to which inflation regimes impact positive nominal demand shocks on real GDP. The effects are

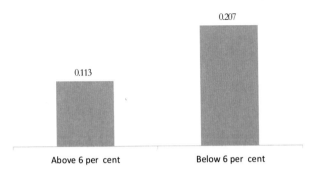

Fig. 20.5 Responses to positive nominal demand shocks (*Source* Authors' calculations)

estimated using the data whereby inflation exceeds six per cent and where inflation is below or equal to six per cent.

$$\text{Real GDP growth} = \text{constant} + \beta * \text{Real GDP growth}_{t-1} \\ + \delta * \text{Nominal GDP growth}_t \\ + \varepsilon_t, \text{Inflation} > 6 \quad (20.2)$$

$$\text{Real GDP growth} = \text{constant} + \beta * \text{Real GDP growth}_{t-1} \\ + \delta * \text{Nominal GDP growth}_t \\ + \varepsilon_t, \text{Inflation} \leq 6 \quad (20.3)$$

Figure 20.5 shows the magnitudes of real GDP growth responses to a positive nominal demand shock. The magnitudes differ according to inflation regimes. The impact of a positive nominal demand shock is larger in the low inflation regime than in the high regime. This finding is further tested using a different approach in the next section.

Evidence from Dummy Variable Approach

This section explores further the extent to which inflation regimes impact the magnitudes of positive nominal demand shocks on real GDP growth using two equations. Dabove6_NGDPgrowth denotes nominal GDP growth when inflation exceeds the 6% inflation threshold and zero otherwise. Dbelow6_NGDPgrowth denotes Nominal GDP growth when inflation is below or equal to 6% inflation threshold and zero otherwise.

$$\text{RGDP growth} = c + \delta * \text{Dabove6\_NGDPgrowth}_t + \rho * \text{Dbelow6\_NGDPgrowth}_t + \varepsilon_t \quad (20.4)$$

$$\text{RGDP growth} = \delta * \text{Dabove6\_NGDPgrowth}_t + \rho * \text{Dbelow6\_NGDPgrowth}_t + \varepsilon_t \quad (20.5)$$

$$\text{RGDP growth} = c + \beta * \text{RGDP growth}_{t-1} + \delta * \text{Dabove6\_NGDPgrowth}_t + \rho * \text{Dbelow6\_NGDPgrowth}_t + \varepsilon_t \quad (20.6)$$

$$\text{RGDP growth} = \beta * \text{RGDP growth}_{t-1} + \delta * \text{Dabove6\_NGDPgrowth}_t + \rho * \text{Dbelow6\_GDPgrowth}_t + \varepsilon_t \quad (20.7)$$

Irrespective of the model estimated, the results in Table 20.1 show that the positive nominal demand shock has bigger impact on real GDP growth in low inflation regime than in high inflation regimes. This evidence further ascertains that inflation regimes play a significant role (Table 20.1).

What is the threshold value of inflation leading to differential impacts of the nominal shock to real GDP growth? The analysis is extended to determine where the threshold lies using various variants of the logistic smooth transition autoregression (LSTR) model. The results, based on the various models, are shown in Table 20.2. The results indicate that nominal GDP growth shocks have bigger impact in the low inflation regime than in the high inflation regime. The threshold values are below 5%.

20.4.2 Price Changes

Ball et al. (1988) argue that menu costs cause prices to adjust infrequently and for a given frequency of individual adjustment and

20 To What Extent Does the Output-Inflation Trade-Off ... 313

Table 20.1 Impact of inflation regimes

Variable	Equation 20.4		Equation 20.5		Equation 20.6		Equation 20.7	
	Coefficient		Coefficient		Coefficient		Coefficient	
Dbelow6_ NGDPgrowth	0.30	(0.00)	0.17	(0.00)	0.02	(0.50)	0.02	(0.26)
Dbelow6_ NGDPgrowth$_t$	0.51	(0.00)	0.36	(0.00)	0.07	(0.01)	0.06	(0.01)

Note (.) denotes the *p*-values
Source Authors' calculations

Table 20.2 Estimated coefficients

	Model 1		Model 2		Model 3	
Linear part	Coefficient		Coefficient		Coefficient	
Rgdpg{1}	0.790	(0.00)	0.533	(0.00)	0.712	(0.00)
Ngdpg	0.250	(0.00)	0.228	(0.00)	0.158	(0.00)
Ngdpg{2}	−0.133	(0.00)				
Non linear part						
Rgdpg{1}			0.258	(0.19)		
Ngdpg	−0.086	(0.00)	−0.205	(0.01)	−0.112	(0.00)
Speed of transition	2.602	(0.16)	2.976	(0.05)	2.695	(0.06)
Threshold	4.442	(0.00)	4.557	(0.00)	4.570	(0.00)
Centred R^2					0.882	
Impacts						
Impact below threshold	0.117		0.228		0.158	
Impact above threshold	0.031		0.023		0.046	

Note (.) denotes the *p*-values. Rgdpg implies real GDP growth. Ngdpg implies nominal GDP growth. The model is estimated using variables indicated in each column
Source Authors' calculations

staggering, there is a slowdown in the adjustment of the price level. In addition, Sun (2012) shows that price inflation is state dependent. Indeed, some studies show evidence suggesting that in the high inflation environment consumer prices tend to change more often. This section examines whether the price adjustments differ when they are above and below the six per cent inflation threshold. Using the preceding three-variable VAR model based on real GDP growth, evidence in Fig. 20.6 shows that inflation rises much higher in the high inflation regime than in the low inflation regime following a positive nominal demand shock. Furthermore, inflation fluctuates much more in the

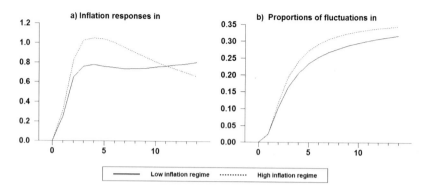

Fig. 20.6 Inflation responses and fluctuations to a positive nominal demand shock (*Source* Authors' calculations)

high inflation regime than in the low inflation regime. The results are robust to using the second model specification.

20.4.3 What Are the Implications of the Trend-Inflation Channel on the Output-Inflation Trade-Off?

The implications of the inflation dynamics on impacting the output-inflation trade-off are further determined by estimating a regime-dependent counterfactual VAR model based on inflation regimes. The inflation regimes are based on the six per cent inflation threshold. A high inflation regime refers to inflation above six per cent. The model estimated includes growth in real and nominal GDP, as well as inflation. The inflation rate is shut off in the model to determine the counterfactual real output response to a positive nominal demand shock. The gap between the actual and counterfactual measures the size of the amplification effect induced by the inflation dynamics. The models are estimated using two lags and 10,000 Monte Carlo draws.

The actual and counterfactual responses are shown in Fig. 20.7. Evidence in Fig. 20.7 shows that the amplification effects by inflation differs between the low and high inflation regimes. In the high inflation regime in Fig. 20.7a, inflation has a dampening role on the impact of positive nominal GDP shocks on real GDP growth. By contrast, in

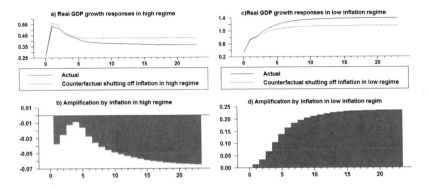

Fig. 20.7 Cumulative responses to a nominal demand shock and the role of trend inflation (*Source* Authors' calculations)

Fig. 20.7c inflation amplifies the real GDP growth reaction to a positive nominal demand shock. Evidence shows that a positive nominal GDP growth shock has a bigger effect on real GDP in the low inflation regime than in the high inflation regime. Thus low inflation regime matters for the pass-through effects of the positive nominal demand policy shocks. This evidence confirms the new Keynesian hypothesis, which implies that demand policy is less effective in countries with high trend inflation and where prices are less rigid.

20.5 Conclusion and Policy Implications

This chapter examined the following questions: Does output-inflation trade-off exist in South Africa and to what extent is it impacted by the role of the six per cent inflation threshold? Does inflation impact the transmission of positive nominal demand shocks to impact the output-inflation trade-off parameter? Evidence shows the existence of output-inflation trade-off. The inflation regimes are based on the six per cent inflation threshold. A high inflation regime refers to inflation above six per cent. The real output rises much higher in the low inflation regime than in the high inflation regime. This finding indicates that the output-inflation trade-off is much higher in the low inflation regime relative to the high inflation regime. This suggests that a positive nominal demand policy shock that affect nominal demand will have a bigger effect on the real output in the low inflation regime than in the high regime. The weak output-inflation trade-off in the high inflation regime implies that positive nominal demand shock is passed more into inflationary pressures than to real output. That is, a positive nominal demand shock raises inflation rather than stimulate the real output growth in high inflation regime.

This evidence shows that inflation rises and fluctuates much higher in the high inflation regime than in the low inflation regime following a positive nominal demand shock. Thus, evidence confirms the new Keynesian hypothesis, which implies that demand policy is less effective in countries with high trend inflation and where prices are less rigid.

In policy terms, since the output-inflation trade-off is much higher in the low inflation regime relative to the high inflation regime there is a need for an incentive-compatible policy to maintain welfare improving price stability mandate.

References

Ball, L., Mankiw, N. G., & Romer, D. (1988). The new Keynesian economics and the output-inflation tradeoff. *Brooking Papers on Economic Activity, 1,* 1–65.

Lucas, Robert. (1973). Some international evidence on output-inflation tradeoffs. *American Economic Review, 63*(3), 326–334.

Odebokun, O. (1991). Evidence on the inflation-output trade off in developing and industrial countries. *Applied Economics, 23,* 731–742.

Sun. (2012). *Nominal rigidity and some new Keynesian evidence on the new Keynesian theory of the output-inflation trade off* (MPRA Chapter No. 45021).

21

Do Inflation Regimes Affect the Transmission of Positive Nominal Demand Shocks to the Consumer Price Level?

Main Highlights

- Evidence reveals that real output rises much higher in the low inflation regime than in the high inflation regime. Thus, a positive nominal demand policy shock affecting aggregate demand will have a bigger effect on real output in the low inflation regime than in the high inflation regime.
- We find that inflation rises and fluctuates much higher in the high inflation regime than in the low inflation regime, following a positive nominal demand shock.
- Evidence confirms the new Keynesian hypothesis, which implies that a positive demand policy shock is less effective in countries with high trend inflation and where prices are less rigid.

© The Author(s) 2019
E. Ndou and T. Mokoena, *Inequality, Output-Inflation Trade-Off and Economic Policy Uncertainty*,
https://doi.org/10.1007/978-3-030-19803-9_21

317

318   E. Ndou and T. Mokoena

21.1 Introduction

This chapter continues the theme of output-inflation trade-off from the price level reaction perspective, following an expansionary demand policy shock. Due to low inflationary pressures, economic agents have pointed to the need for a loosening monetary policy stance to stimulate economic growth. Surprisingly, the calls neither pointed out the dilemma that may be caused by an expansionary policy shock, nor motivated what could make the demand management policy stance produce the desired effects. Theoretically speaking, an expansionary policy shock may stimulate economic growth transitorily as this depends on the persistence of policy changes. The same policy stance may pose a risk to the price stability mandate as it raises consumer price inflation. The increase in the inflation rate may be problematic if it is closer to the upper end of the inflation target band of 3–6%.

It is the objective of this analysis to show policymakers that magnitudes of price changes, following an expansionary policy shock, differ depending on whether inflation is above or below the 6% threshold. In addition, it is the objective of this chapter to show that price rigidities, which are important for the real effects of policy changes, differ depending on whether inflation is above or below 6%. It is the purpose of this chapter to show policymakers that there exists an inflation band that is consistent with minimising the pass-through of a positive nominal demand shock to the consumer price level. Hence, an expansionary policy may have real effects even when inflation is close to the upper end of the target band provided there are price rigidities. When prices do not adjust then quantities should adjust.

It is ideal to revert to economic theory as in Fig. 21.1 to show that a pass-through of a positive nominal demand shock to the price level depends on the slope of the supply curve. Three possible outcomes arise depending on the slope of supply curve. The nominal demand shock impacts price (P) only if the supply curve is perfectly inelastic as in Fig. 21.1a. In contrast, there can be no pass-through to the price level if the supply curve is perfectly inelastic as in Fig. 21.1c. The pass-through of a nominal demand shock can be distributed to both the price level

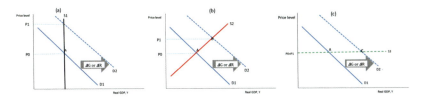

Fig. 21.1 Theoretical depiction of the price level response to a positive nominal demand shock (*Source* Authors' drawing)

and real GDP, as in Fig. 21.1b, when the supply curve is upward sloping, although with varying degrees. The problem faced by policymakers is: Under which inflation rate will the pass-through of a positive nominal demand shock (e.g. increased government spending ΔG or expansionary monetary policy ΔR) to the consumer price level be minimised? For instance, Fig. 21.1c shows that when the consumer price level reacts very little or not at all, real output reacts significantly.

When the consumer price level rises as in Fig. 21.1a real output does not react. These dispositions seem to concur with the predictions of the role of menu costs as argued in Ball et al. (1988)'s new Keynesian theory that the real effects of nominal demand shocks depend on the frequency of price adjustments and the speed of adjustment.[1] According to these authors, the faster the speed of adjustment of prices, the smaller the real effects of such nominal demand shocks. Alternatively, the slower the speed of adjustment of prices, the larger are the real effects of such nominal demand shocks. Figure 21.1 does not show the role of the inflation regimes. Hence, it is convenient to ask: Do the inflation regimes affect the transmission of positive nominal demand shocks to the consumer price level?

---

[1] The new classical economics suggests that policy intervention should not exist because inflation is costlier than unemployment, and that the short-run Philips curve is very steep and a self-correcting economy works smoothly and quickly. By contrast, the new Keynesian theory suggests that there should be policy interventions, because unemployment is costlier than inflation. In this context, the Philips curve is flat and a self-correcting mechanism is rather slow and unreliable.

This analysis fills policy and research gaps by examining the long run pass-through of nominal demand shocks to consumer price level and the speed of correction towards the long run equilibrium. The effects are examined when (1) inflation is above and (2) below the 6% threshold. In addition, the analysis shows policymakers the implications of the pass-through of the nominal demand shock to inflation, when inflation is below 4.5%. The implications of the midpoint of the inflation target range in this analysis differ from those appearing in Ndou and Gumata (2017). This chapter further shows the implications for the real GDP growth, following a nominal demand shock and whether the effects differ when inflation is below 6% relative to those below 4.5%. This analysis applies a cointegration analysis to determine the long run impact of a nominal demand shock and permits the determination of an error correcting impact.

This chapter shows policymakers that a positive nominal demand shock will have relatively bigger real effects in the inflation region where price changes are determined to be rigid or less flexible. This determination matters because the expected outcome from an expansionary policy shock is to achieve maximum real effects, while minimising inflation pressures.[2] Holmes (2000) argued that price flexibility allows the adjustment of prices rather than quantities, which leads to no real effects, following a nominal demand shock.

This analysis finds that the effectiveness of an expansionary policy shock depends on the price rigidities. The low inflation regime is ideal for an expansionary policy shock to have a bigger real effect with accompanying low inflation pressures relative to what happens in a high inflation regime.

---

[2] This follows the new Keynesian hypothesis, which implies that a demand policy is less effective in high-trend inflation, especially where prices are less rigid. In addition, due to nominal rigidities arising from the adjustment costs or staggered contracts, prices do not adjust fully to compensate for the shifts in nominal demand such that changes in the nominal demand have real effect (Sun 2012).

21.2 Methodology

The chapter follows Holmes (2000) to estimate the long run relationship between the consumer price level P_t and nominal GDP using Eq. (21.1) and ε_t represents the deviation from long run equilibrium.

$$P_t = \text{constant} + \beta * \text{Nominal GDP}_t + \varepsilon_t \qquad (21.1)$$

There are four possible values for β. First, a situation whereby $\beta = 0$; this implies that there is zero price flexibility, suggesting that the movements in the nominal demand shocks are not associated with movements in the consumer price level. Second, a situation whereby $\beta < 1$; implies long run price rigidities. In this context, theory suggests that nominal demand changes will have real effects. Third, when $\beta = 1$, leads to a situation whereby movements in nominal demand are matched by changes in the price level. Fourth, when $\beta > 1$ this suggests that nominal demand shocks are matched by much larger increases in the price level changes. Holmes (2000) suggests this is consistent with increases in nominal income which causes a wage-price spiral, and this ends up putting a downward pressure on real output.

This analysis is based on variables appearing in Fig. 21.1. To properly estimate Eq. (21.1), we begin by testing the stationarity properties of the consumer price level and nominal GDP in levels. We use quarterly (Q) data spanning 1960Q1–2017Q1. The data is obtained from the South African Reserve Bank. Evidence shows that the consumer price level and nominal GDP are nonstationary and become stationary after first differencing.[3] This enables the estimation of the cointegration relationship. The cointegration tests are done using the Johannsen cointegration test and the results are reported in Tables 21.1 and 21.2 based on the trace and maximum eigenvalue tests. The trace approach indicates that there is one cointegration relationship.

---

[3]Literature points that inflation is either I(0) or I(1).

322 E. Ndou and T. Mokoena

Table 21.1 Unrestricted cointegration rank test (Trace)

Hypothesised No. of CE(s)	Eigenvalue	Trace Statistic	0.05 Critical value	Prob.**
None*	0.371039	58.80378	20.26184	0.0000
At most 1	0.072997	8.262043	9.164546	0.0740

Note Trace test indicates 1 cointegrating equation at the 0.05 level
*Denotes rejection of the hypothesis at the 0.05 level
**MacKinnon-Haug-Michelis (1999) *p*-values
Source Authors' calculations

Table 21.2 Unrestricted cointegration rank test (Maximum Eigenvalue)

Hypothesised No. of CE(s)	Eigenvalue	Max-Eigen Statistic	0.05 Critical value	Prob.**
None *	0.371039	50.54174	15.89210	0.0000
At most 1	0.072997	8.262043	9.164546	0.0740

Note Max-eigenvalue test indicates 1 cointegrating equation at the 0.05 level
*Denotes rejection of the hypothesis at the 0.05 level
**MacKinnon-Haug-Michelis (1999) *p*-values
Source Authors' calculations

In addition, the maximum eigenvalue in Table 21.2 concludes similarly that there is one cointegration relationship. Hence, in the next section we estimate the long run relationship and the speed of adjustment.

21.2.1 In Which Inflation Regime Do Consumer Prices React the Most? Evidence from the VECM Approach

The vector error correction (VECM) approach enables the estimation of both the long run relationship and error correction terms. What are the pass-through magnitudes of positive nominal demand GDP shocks on the consumer price level in the long run? The impacts of nominal demand shocks on the consumer price level are shown in Table 21.3. In Table 21.3, the pass-through is less than one. This is a robust finding to different estimation periods. The pass-through magnitudes exhibit a

Table 21.3 Estimates of long run coefficient or pass-through according to inflation regimes in given periods

Inflation regime	1960Q1–2017Q1		1970Q1–2017Q1		1980Q1–2017Q1		1990Q1–2017Q1	
No regime	0.702	(0.004)	0.727	(0.005)	0.693	(0.008)	0.566	(0.007)
High regime	0.748	(0.007)	0.748	(0.007)	0.708	(0.010)	0.566	(0.008)
Low regime	0.684	(0.004)	0.695	(0.010)	0.524	(0.011)	0.524	(0.011)
Below 4.5% regime	0.683	(0.004)	0.521	(0.018)	0.521	(0.018)	0.521	(0.018)

Note p values are in (.)
Source Authors' calculations

declining trend from big values in the high inflation regime to smaller values in the low inflation regime. The smallest values occur when inflation is below 4.5%. Across all sample periods, the pass-through is smaller when inflation is below 4.5%. This shows that the pass-through of positive nominal demand shocks to consumer prices is bigger in the high inflation regime.

Evidence reveals price rigidities in the low inflation regime. Hence, it is possible that the pass-through to real GDP is much higher in the low inflation regime than in high inflation regime. Any evidence in support of this outcome would suggest that policymakers have considerable scope to engage in the short run demand management policies in the low inflation regimes than in the high inflation regime. This suggests there is a substantial degree of policy effectiveness that can be achieved in the low inflation regime. Overall, the consumer prices become more rigid as inflation moves below the 4.5% inflation threshold.

The speed of adjustment provides information on the short run responsiveness of inflation to nominal demand. The closer to zero is the speed of adjustment, the less flexible are prices in the short run (Holmes 2000). In Table 21.4, the speed of adjustment is relatively large in the high inflation regime than in the low inflation regime. This suggests that there is more price level flexibility in the high inflation regime than in the low inflation regime. This indicates that positive nominal demand shocks are unlikely to generate much inflation in the low inflation regime relative to that in the high inflation regime.

Table 21.4 Speed of price adjustment

	1960–2017		1980–2017		1990–2017	
No regime	−0.022	(0.006)	−0.018	(0.008)	−0.064	(0.017)
High regime	−0.012	(0.006)	−0.016	(0.007)	−0.065	(0.019)
Low regime	−0.010	(0.006)	−0.015	(0.011)	−0.024	(0.025)

Note P-values are in (.)
Source Authors' calculations

21.2.2 In Which Inflation Regime Does Inflation React Mostly? Evidence from Regime-Dependent VARs

The analysis further shows the effects of nominal demand shocks on inflation according to inflation regimes. Regime-dependent bivariate VAR models are estimated using two lags and 10,000 Monte Carlo draws. One lag is used in model that use 4.5% inflation threshold. The first VAR model (Model 1) includes the annual consumer price inflation rate and annual growth in nominal GDP. A second VAR model (Model 2) is estimated to test the robustness of the results using the reverse ordering of variables in the preceding model. The annual growth in nominal GDP captures the nominal demand shock emanating from either expansionary fiscal or monetary policies. The three inflation regimes are as follows: (1) high regime when inflation exceeds the 6% inflation rate; (2) low regime when inflation is below 6%; and (3) below the 4.5% regime.

Figure 21.2a, c show that a positive nominal demand shock is passed more into the consumer price inflation in the high inflation regime than in the low regime. Overall, inflation rises much less when inflation is below or equals to 4.5%. This means inflation regimes matter for the impact of a positive nominal demand shock on inflation.

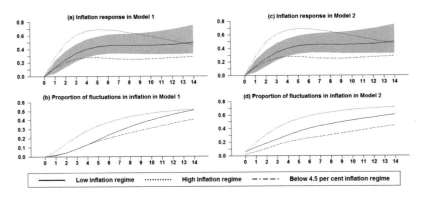

Fig. 21.2 Inflation responses and fluctuations to a positive nominal demand shock in the 1990Q1–2017Q1 period (*Note* The grey shaded area denote the 16th and 84th percentile confidence bands. *Source* Authors' calculations)

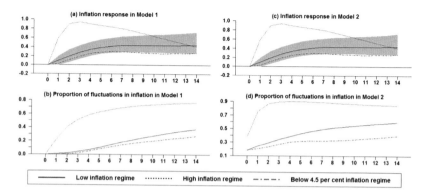

Fig. 21.3 Inflation responses and fluctuations to a positive nominal demand shock during the inflation-targeting period (*Note* The grey shaded area denotes the 16th and 84th percentile confidence bands. *Source* Authors' calculations)

In addition, Fig. 21.2b, d show the proportions of inflation fluctuations explained by a positive nominal demand shock according to high inflation regime and low regime as well as inflation below the 4.5% threshold. Evidence shows that inflation fluctuates significantly in the high inflation regime than when it is below 4.5%. This shows that inflation tends to be rigid in the low inflation regime than in the high regime. Evidence is robust to using the inflation targeting period in Fig. 21.3 and the sample spanning from 1980Q1–2017Q1.

21.2.3 What Are the Implications for Real GDP Growth?

This question is investigated by applying the preceding regime-dependent bivariate VAR models but we replace inflation with real GDP growth. The objective is to determine if there is a relationship between low inflation and high real GDP growth responses to a positive nominal demand shock. In Fig. 21.4 a positive nominal demand shock raises real GDP growth much less in the high inflation regime than in the low regime or below the 4.5% inflation threshold. However, there are no significant differential responses in the real GDP growth based on whether inflation is below 6 or 4.5%. In addition, the real GDP growth fluctuations

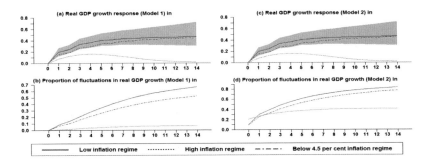

Fig. 21.4 Real GDP growth responses to a positive nominal demand shock and the role of inflation regimes during the inflation-targeting period (*Note* The grey shaded area denotes the 16th and 84th percentile confidence bands. *Source* Authors' calculations)

are much bigger in the low inflation regime than in the high inflation regime. Both fluctuations show that positive nominal demand shocks induce real effects in the low inflation regime than in the high regime. This finding supports the intuition that weak inflationary pressures in the low inflation regime are accompanied by high real GDP growth, following a positive nominal demand shock. This suggests that a positive nominal demand shock has real effects when prices are rigid in a low inflation environment, suggesting that adjustment happens via quantities.

Does it matter whether inflation is just below 6% or 4.5%? This arises because there has been much talk regarding the relevance of the midpoint of the inflation target band. The reference to midpoint of target band has neither been backed by facts regarding its role in explaining the real GDP growth dynamics, nor has there been a demonstration of its amplification ability in passing through the nominal demand shocks to real activity. As a result, the analysis further performs a counterfactual analysis to determine the role of inflation when it is in the region of 4.5% inflation and below in transmitting the nominal demand shocks to real GDP growth. This section compares the effects to those in the inflation region below the 6% threshold. This is achieved by estimating a three-variable VAR model which includes nominal GDP growth, real GDP growth and inflation dummy. We create inflation dummies for each of the inflation regimes. The inflation dummy regime equals to the value of inflation in a specific regime and zero otherwise.

The VAR models are estimated using one or two lags depending on the regime. The models are estimated using 10,000 Monte Carlo draws. The counterfactual responses are calculated by shutting off inflation in transmitting the positive nominal demand shocks to real GDP growth. The size of amplification is determined by the gap between the counterfactual and actual responses. In Fig. 21.5, real GDP growth rises much higher in the low inflation environment than what the counterfactual suggests. This shows that a low inflation regime amplifies the reaction of real GDP growth to a positive nominal demand shock. However, the amplifications are much bigger when inflation is below 4.5% than just considering inflation when it is below the 6% inflation threshold. This shows that a low inflation regime matters for positive nominal demand shocks to stimulate real GDP growth.

The robustness of the preceding results is done based on the counterfactual analysis using data spanning 1990Q1–2017Q1. The impulse responses in Fig. 21.6 show that a high inflation regime dampens the real GDP growth response to a positive nominal demand shock. By contrast, low inflation magnifies the response of real GDP growth to a positive nominal demand shock. This finding is robust to the extension of the sample period used in the estimations.

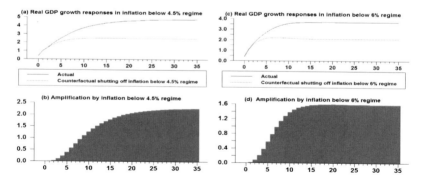

Fig. 21.5 Accumulated real actual and counterfactual real GDP growth responses to a positive nominal demand shock and the role of inflation in 2000Q1–2017Q1 (*Source* Authors' calculations)

21 Do Inflation Regimes Affect the Transmission ...

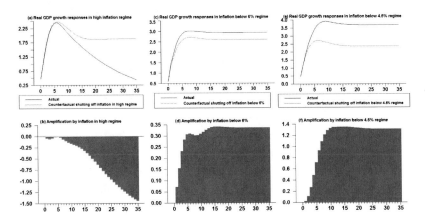

Fig. 21.6 Accumulated real actual and counterfactual real GDP growth responses to a positive nominal demand shock and the role of inflation in 1990Q1–2017Q1 (*Source* Authors' calculations)

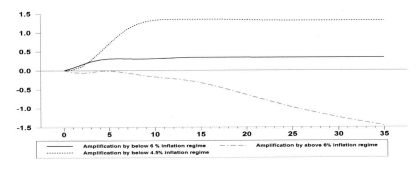

Fig. 21.7 Comparisons of real GDP growth amplifications by inflation regimes (*Source* Authors' calculations)

Figure 21.7 compares the amplifications by inflation regimes as shown in Fig. 21.6. The comparison shows that inflation below 4.5% leads to bigger amplifications of real GDP growth responses to a positive nominal demand shock.

21.3 Conclusion and Policy Implications

The chapter determined in which inflation region relative to the 6% inflation threshold are consumer price levels less responsive to a positive nominal demand shock (e.g. expansionary fiscal or monetary policy shock). Theory suggests that positive nominal demand shock will have bigger real effects in the region where prices are less responsive, because quantities will adjust more than prices. The relevance of inflation regimes is assessed based on three regimes defined as (1) high regime when inflation exceeds 6%, (2) low regime when inflation is below 6%, and (3) below 4.5%. We find that inflation regimes affect the transmission of positive nominal demand shocks to the consumer price level. Evidence shows that the pass-through of a positive nominal demand shock through to inflation is bigger in the high inflation regime than in the low inflation regime. In addition, the speed of inflation adjustment is relatively large in the high inflation regime than in the low regime.

In policy terms, these findings suggest that there is more price rigidity in the low inflation regime than in the high regime, following a positive nominal demand shock. This suggests that an expansionary demand policy shock will have bigger real effects in the low inflation regime since the price levels exhibit rigidities relative to much flexibility inherent in the high regime. Therefore an expansionary demand policy shock will be more effective in raising real output much higher in the low inflation regime than in the high regime. The implication of this evidence is that policymakers have considerable scope to engage in the short run demand management policies in the low inflation regimes than in high inflation regime. Alternatively, this suggests there is a substantial degree of policy effectiveness that can be achieved in the low inflation regime. Overall, the prices become more rigid, following a positive nominal demand shock as inflation moves below the 4.5% inflation regime.

References

Ball, L., Mankiw, N. G., & Romer, D. (1988). The new Keynesian economics and the output-inflation tradeoff. *Brooking chapters on Economic Activity, 1,* 1–65.

Ndou, E., & Gumata, N. (2017). *Inflation dynamics in South Africa, the role of thresholds, exchange rate pass-through and inflation expectations on policy trade offs.* Palgrave Macmillan.

Sun. (2012). *Nominal rigidity and some new Keynesian evidence on the new Keynesian theory of the output-inflation trade off.* (MPRA Chapter No. 45021).

22

Do Positive Nominal Volatility Shocks Reduce the Output-Inflation Trade-Off and Is There a Role for Inflation Regimes?

Main Highlights

- The chapter determines the extent to which elevated nominal volatilities make expansionary policy ineffective in achieving maximum real output and low inflation. Evidence shows that elevated nominal demand and inflation volatility shocks reduce the output-inflation trade-off and this reduces policy effectiveness in achieving desirable outcomes.
- The magnitudes of the reduction in the output-inflation trade-off effects are larger in the high inflation regime than in the low inflation regime. In addition, a combination of increases in both inflation and nominal demand volatilities is bad for the output-inflation trade-off.
- In policy terms, this evidence confirms the new Keynesian hypothesis, which implies that demand management policy is less effective in countries with both high inflation and demand volatilities. Therefore, policymakers should minimise these volatilities when implementing demand management policies and ensure that price stability is enforced to minimise inflation volatility.

© The Author(s) 2019
E. Ndou and T. Mokoena, *Inequality, Output-Inflation Trade-Off and Economic Policy Uncertainty,*
https://doi.org/10.1007/978-3-030-19803-9_22

333

22.1 Introduction

Policymakers with price stability mandate often argue that a low inflation environment is needed for sustainable and high economic growth. This reasoning indicates the existence of an inverse relationship between the two economic indicators. This chapter continues the theme of output-inflation trade-off, but the focus is to show the role of nominal volatilities in deriving this trade-off. It is also possible that the volatilities can minimise the effectiveness of an expansionary policy in attaining the ideal output-inflation trade-off. The ideal policy intervention should induce much trade-off, such as achieving high GDP growth accompanied by low inflation.

To what extent are both the inflation and nominal demand volatilities impacting the output-inflation trade-off? Is the impact dependent on whether inflation is above or below six per cent threshold? Determining the strength of the supposed trade-off would be much needed in assessing guidance on whether any policy intervention could achieve the expected effects in any period. This may be more pertinent when forecasts indicate weak and low economic growth. This chapter argues that it is possible that economic growth weakness is compounded by the elevated nominal demand and inflation volatilities. Despite the contradictory theoretical policy outcomes from some opposing economic theories, it is important to show the role of the volatilities in the dynamics of the output-inflation trade-off.

Not all theories advocate for a policy interventionist approach. The new Classical economics suggests policy intervention should not exist because inflation is costlier than unemployment. In this theory, the self-correcting mechanism of the economy works very smoothly and fast.[1] In contrast, the new Keynesian theory recommends policy interventions, because unemployment is considered costlier than inflation. In addition, this theory postulates that the self-correcting mechanism operates very slowly and is unreliable.[2] It is noteworthy to indicate that

---

[1] That is, the short-run Philips curve is very steep.

[2] The Philips curve is flat.

the new Keynesian and the new Classical theories suggest that, under certain conditions, there exists a possibility of policy ineffectiveness due to adverse volatility effects. Ball et al. (1988) (*hereafter referred to as BMR*), as well as Lucas (1973) point out that both the inflation and aggregate demand volatilities impact negatively on the output-inflation trade-off dynamics. Does the output-inflation trade-off react to positive inflation and aggregate demand volatility shocks and what is the role of inflation regimes?

This chapter argues that during volatile nominal GDP episodes, an expansionary demand policy shock is less effective on stimulating real output.[3] This arises when higher variance of aggregate demand induces more uncertainty in the firms' determination of future optimal price. This uncertainty shortens the firm's time interval taken between price changes.

The hypothesis of negative associations between the volatilities of both aggregate demand and inflation and output-inflation trade-off has been tested in a cross-country context, which included South Africa. However, none of the studies examined the role of the six per cent inflation threshold on impacting the output-inflation trade-off, following a nominal demand shock. This chapter fills both academic and policy research gaps by showing the role of the six per cent inflation threshold on impacting the hypothesis. In addition, the analysis examines the extent to which inflation volatility propagates the impacts of the nominal demand volatility shocks on the output-inflation trade-off. The analysis uses regime-dependent counterfactual VAR approach.

22.2 Short Run Output-Inflation Trade-Off

This analysis requires the estimation of the output-inflation trade-off parameter in Eq. (22.1). The 20-quarter rolling windows of the output-inflation trade-off (τ) parameter is estimated using a modified

---

[3]This chapter tests three hypotheses below to determine the extent to which nominal demand policy impacts real output and the extent to which the output-inflation trade-off is impacted by inflation regimes.

version of Ball et al. (1988) specification using Eq. (22.1). The rolling period gives enough degrees of freedom and is consistent with the average duration of the business cycle reported in many studies. The rolling estimate of the output-inflation trade-off (τ) parameter is used in the next sections. Equation (22.1) links annual real GDP growth to annual nominal GDP growth. In this context, literature uses real GDP in levels as in Ball et al. (1988). However, other variants use the growth of real GDP and the gap between real and trend real GDP for the dependent variable. Existing evidence in these studies points to the same conclusions irrespective of the transformations done on real GDP. This study uses the real GDP growth. It is the intuition of this Eq. (22.1) that matters for this analysis as τ captures the short run effects of nominal disturbance on real output.

$$\Delta\text{Real GDP}_t = \text{constant} + \tau * \Delta\text{Nominal GDP}_t + \beta * \text{trend} + \varepsilon_t \quad (22.1)$$

22.3 Evidence from Regime-Dependent VAR Models

The analysis estimates regime-dependent VAR models. The first VAR model includes inflation, the output-inflation trade-off parameter and inflation volatility. The second VAR model includes inflation, the output-inflation trade-off parameter and nominal demand volatility. The inflation and nominal demand volatilities are calculated using a four-quarter moving variance of the inflation rate and nominal GDP growth, respectively. The models are estimated using one lag and 10,000 Monte Carlo draws. Two inflation regimes are considered based on the six per cent inflation threshold. The high (low) inflation regime refers to inflation above (below) 6%. The regime-dependent VAR models are estimated using quarterly (Q) data spanning 1990Q1–2016Q4.

22.3.1 Evidence from Positive Nominal Demand Volatility

Figure 22.1, shows the effects of positive inflation volatility shocks on the short-run output-inflation trade-off. The output-inflation trade-off

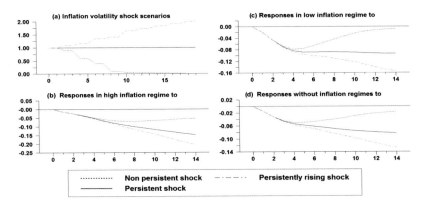

Fig. 22.1 Output-inflation trade-off parameter response to positive inflation volatility shocks

declines due to positive inflation volatility shock. The decline is robust to the different inflation volatility shock scenarios and happens in both inflation regimes. However, the negative impact is less severe in the low inflation regime than in the high inflation regime. This finding suggests that elevated inflation volatility reduces the output-inflation trade-off. From a policy perspective, this implies that inflation volatility should be minimised to mitigate its effects on impacting the nominal demand policy shock on real output.

22.3.2 Evidence on the Interaction Between Nominal Demand and Inflation Volatilities

This section looks at the effects of a positive nominal demand volatility shock on the output-inflation trade-off. In Fig. 22.2 the positive nominal demand shock has a negative effect on the output-inflation trade-off. This shows that elevated nominal demand volatility reduces the output-inflation trade-off. The effects are severe in the high inflation regime than in the low inflation regime. This suggests that policymakers should minimise volatility when implementing a specific demand policy. In addition, the results show that inflation regimes play a role in minimising the adverse effects of nominal demand volatility shocks on output-inflation trade-off (Fig. 22.2).

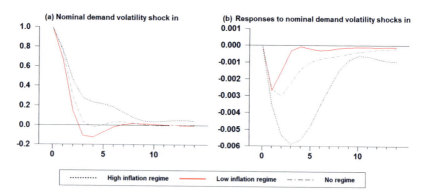

Fig. 22.2 Positive nominal demand volatility shock and output-inflation trade-off parameter responses

In addition, the analysis shows the extent to which inflation regimes influence the role of inflation volatility in transmitting the positive nominal demand volatility shocks onto the output-inflation trade-off parameter. The high inflation regime refers to inflation above six per cent. This analysis is based on regime-dependent counterfactual VAR models that include nominal GDP growth volatility, the output-inflation trade-off parameter, and inflation volatility. The inflation volatility channel is shut off in the model to calculate the counterfactual output-inflation trade-off impulse responses. The gap between the actual and counterfactual responses gives the size of the role of inflation volatility in transmitting nominal demand volatility shocks. The models are estimated using one lag and 10,000 Monte Carlo draws. In Fig. 22.3, the output-inflation trade-off declines more when inflation volatility is included in the model than when it is shut off in the model. The peak decline is more pronounced in the high inflation regime relative to that prevailing in the low inflation regime. This evidence shows that inflation regimes matter in mitigating the adverse effects of the inflation volatility channel in accentuating the reduction in the output-inflation trade-off, following nominal demand volatility shock.

A comparison of the sizes of amplifications from inflation volatility channel according to inflation regimes is shown in Fig. 22.4. In the high inflation regime, the prevailing inflation volatility exacerbates the reduction in the output-inflation trade-off.

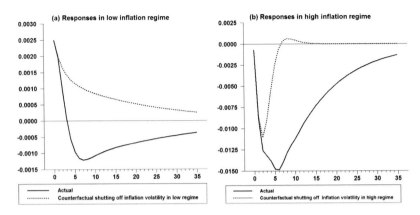

Fig. 22.3 Positive nominal demand volatility shock and output-inflation trade-off parameter responses and amplifications by inflation volatility

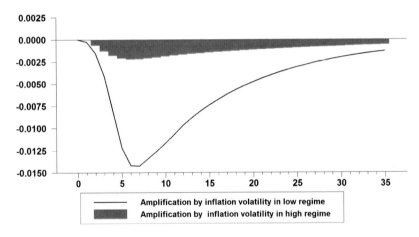

Fig. 22.4 Comparison of amplification by inflation volatilities according to inflation regimes

22.4 Conclusion and Policy Implications

Both positive nominal demand and inflation volatility shocks have negative effects on the output-inflation trade-off parameter. This shows that elevated nominal demand and inflation volatilities reduce the output-inflation trade-off and this reduces policy effectiveness in achieving desirable outcomes. The magnitudes of reduction in the output-inflation trade-off parameter are larger in the high inflation regime than in the low regime. In addition the result shows that inflation regimes play a significant role in minimising the adverse effects of the two volatility shocks on the output-inflation trade-off. This evidence confirms the new Keynesian hypothesis, which implies that demand policy shock is less effective in countries with both high inflation and demand volatilities. In addition, a combination of increases in both the inflation and nominal demand volatilities is bad for the output-inflation trade-off. This evidence suggests policymakers should minimise volatility when implementing demand policies, while the price stability mandate should be enforced to minimise inflation volatility.

References

Ball, L., Mankiw, N. G., & Romer, D. (1988). The new Keynesian economics and the output-inflation trade off. *Brookings Papers on Economic Activity, 1*, 1–65.

Lucas, R. (1973). Some international evidence on output-inflation tradeoffs. *American Economic Review, 63*(3), 326–334.

Part VIII

Output Growth Persistence and Inflation

23

Does the Persistence of Output Growth Depend on Inflation Regimes?

Main Highlights

- Evidence reveals that the sizes of output persistence measures are smaller when inflation is above the 6% threshold relative to when inflation is less or equal to 6%.
- We also determine whether the average frequency of price changes based on Kiley (2000) differs between the high and low inflation regimes. Evidence shows that the average frequency of price changes is relatively shorter in the high inflation regime than in the low regime.
- Evidence shows that increased price flexibility in the high inflation regime weakens the responses of household consumption growth to an expansionary monetary policy shock. However, the reduced price flexibility in the low inflation regime magnifies the household consumption growth increase due to expansionary monetary policy shocks.
- From a policy perspective, this implies that an expansionary monetary policy shock, when inflation is below 6%, will stimulate household consumption growth more than raising the inflation rate because prices are less flexible.

© The Author(s) 2019
E. Ndou and T. Mokoena, *Inequality, Output-Inflation Trade-Off and Economic Policy Uncertainty*,
https://doi.org/10.1007/978-3-030-19803-9_23

343

23.1 Introduction

This chapter investigates whether the output growth persistence differs between high and low inflation regimes. The identification of the inflation regime in which output growth persistence is high would help policymakers when implementing stimulatory policy interventions to magnify and increase the output growth persistence effect. We ask: how relevant are the inflation regimes based on the 6% inflation threshold in determining output growth persistence? In addition, how relevant is the price flexibility measure based on Kiley (2000) in impacting the transmission of expansionary monetary policy shocks to household consumption growth? Do inflation regimes matter?

This chapter uses the Ball et al. (1988) and Kiley's (2000) postulation to link price stickiness (or sluggish price adjustment) and output persistence in South Africa, as to answer the preceding questions. It is worth agreeing on the foundations of these authors' hypotheses, which are based on how nominal policy changes impact nominal variables in Eq. (23.1). Based on Eq. (23.1) there are several outcomes that can arise. For instance, the price level (P) can remain unchanged or change slowly in Eq. (23.1) following an expansionary monetary policy shock which raises nominal output (NY) to achieve increased persistence in the real GDP (RG). Showing where output persistence is higher is important for the expansionary monetary policy shocks to (1) potentially raise the persistence effects directly, or (2) indirectly enable the enlargement of the shock propagation effects. By agreeing with the above mentioned authors' foundation does not mean the number of possible outcomes cannot be extended. This chapter therefore brings into the discussion the role of inflation thresholds.

$$RG_t = \frac{NY_t}{P_t} \tag{23.1}$$

It will be an incomplete motivation for this analysis to rely only on Eq. (23.1), which offers the foundations for the discussion. Hence, Fig. 23.1 depicts the link between output persistence and inflation, as well as related amplification dynamics.

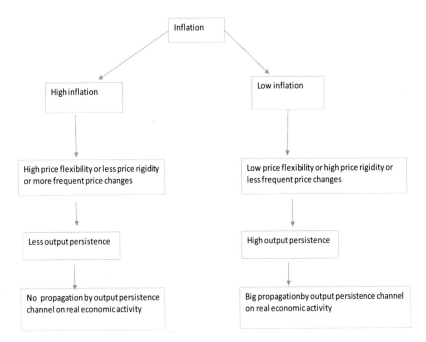

Fig. 23.1 Theoretical depiction of the link between inflation and output persistence (*Source* Authors' drawing)

While earlier evidence in Ball (1988), Kiley (2000) and Khan (2004) indicates that output fluctuations around the trend are less persistent in high inflation economies, it is possible this depends on an inflation threshold. Neither Eq. (23.1) nor Fig. 23.1 shows the ideal inflation threshold that leads to the differential effects. Hence, this chapter contextualises the analysis within the confines of the upper part of the inflation target band. The analysis uses the 6% inflation rate (which is the upper part of the inflation target band) as the threshold. The depiction in Fig. 23.1 indicates that inflation regimes have different implications for the price flexibility or output persistence, and the amplification effects of shocks to the real economic activity. The persistence of real output growth movements is entirely

346   E. Ndou and T. Mokoena

determined by the degree of price stickiness. In addition, the propagation of shocks to real economic activity depends on the output persistence.[1]

This chapter contributes to the discussions on the output-inflation trade-off by filling various policy research and academic gaps indicated below. This chapter examines the extent to which inflation impacts the magnitudes of output persistence, when it is above or below the 6% threshold. In addition, the analysis shows the extent to which inflation, which at any time, may be above or below 6%, impacts price flexibility. Furthermore, the analysis shows the extent to which inflation below 6% determines how price flexibility impacts the transmission of expansionary monetary policy shocks to household consumption growth. Moreover, this chapter shows policymakers the inflation regime in which output persistence effects are bigger. Hence, such realisation may help policymakers embarking on policy initiatives to stimulate economic growth to facilitate further propagation of the impacts of real shocks to real economic activity by strengthening the output persistence channel.

Evidence reveals that the sizes of output persistence measures are smaller above the 6% threshold relative to when inflation is below or equals to 6%. The average frequency of price changes is relatively shorter in the high inflation regime than in the low regime. This indicates that prices are less rigid in the high inflation regime, which is consistent with evidence in the Ball et al. (1988). Evidence shows that increased price flexibility in the high inflation regime weakens the response of household consumption growth to an expansionary monetary policy shock. By contrast, price flexibility in the low inflation regime magnifies the household consumption growth to an expansionary monetary policy shock.

---

[1]When aggregate demand process is persistent and prices are sticky, the persistence of the aggregate demand shocks leads to persistent output fluctuations (Kiley 2000) and this indicates real effects of the shock.

23.2 In Which Inflation Regime, Based on the 6% Threshold, Is Real Output Persistence Higher?

23.2.1 Evidence from the Threshold Approach Using the 6% Inflation Threshold

The investigation begins by estimating a threshold equation to determine the effects of the inflation threshold on impacting the persistence of output growth. The analysis uses quarterly (Q) data spanning 1990Q1–2016Q1 obtained from the South African Reserve Bank. Output persistence is determined by the impact of lagged real GDP growth ($RGDPG_{t-1}$) on current real GDP growth ($RGDPG_t$). This is consistent with the specifications of capturing persistence in the literature, but the role of inflation regimes has not been applied. Hence, the analysis determines the effects of inflation regimes based on the 6% threshold. Equations (23.2) and (23.3) are estimated to compare the effects based on the inclusion and exclusion of the constant.[2] In addition, the inclusion or exclusion of the constant, determines the robustness of the results.

$$RGDPG_t = \text{constant} + \beta * RGDPG_{t-1} * (\text{inflation} > 6)$$
$$+ \gamma * RGDPG_{t-1} * (\text{inflation} \leq 6) + \varepsilon_t \qquad (23.2)$$

$$RGDPG_t = \beta * RGDPG_{t-1} * (\text{inflation} > 6) + \gamma * RGDPG_{t-1}$$
$$* (\text{inflation} \leq 6) + \varepsilon_t \qquad (23.3)$$

Table 23.1 shows the magnitudes of output persistence based on the two inflation regimes. The output persistence magnitudes are less than one. In both models, the output persistence impacts are smaller above the 6% threshold relative to when inflation is less or equal to 6%. This evidence suggests that the magnitudes of output persistence differ according to the two inflation regimes.

---

[2]This due to certain studies not including a constant in the estimation.

Table 23.1 Magnitudes of output persistence measures according to inflation regimes and model specifications

	Equation (23.2) Coefficient		Equation (23.3) Coefficient	
$RGDPG_{t-1} * (\text{inflation} > 6)$	0.62	(0.00)	0.71	(0.00)
$RGDPG_{t-1} * (\text{inflation} \leq 6)$	0.78	(0.00)	0.85	(0.00)

Note p-values in (.)
Source Authors' calculations

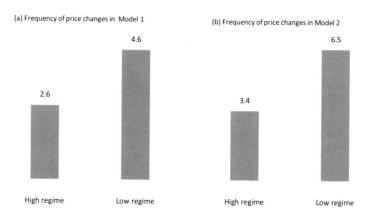

Fig. 23.2 Frequency of price changes in quarters based on Kiley (2000) approach (*Source* Authors' calculations)

This analysis further relies on the theoretical link between output persistence and average frequency of the price changes derived by Kiley (2000). Consequently, we use the Kiley approach to calculate the average frequency of price changes,[3] given by $(1/[1 - \text{output persistence coefficient}])$ in the low and high inflation regimes. In Fig. 23.2, it is seen that, on average, prices change nearly 2.6–3.4 quarters in the high-inflation regime compared to 4.6–6.5 quarters in the low inflation regime. Thus, the frequency

---

[3]In addition, we have not seen articles that have criticised this approach despite widespread uses of micro data.

of price changes is relatively shorter in the high inflation regime than in the low inflation regime. This evidence indicates prices are less rigid in the high inflation regime, which is consistent with evidence in Ball et al. (1988).

23.2.2 Evidence from the Logistic Smooth Transition Autoregression Analysis

The analysis further examines the role of inflation regimes in impacting the magnitudes of output persistence using a logistic smooth transition autoregression (LSTR) model based on Terasvirta (1994). This approach indicates that real GDP growth can be modelled as a nonlinear process. Hence, it is important to determine the inflation threshold value that leads to the differential output persistence effects using the nonlinear models as in Terasvirta (1994). In the LSTR models the threshold is determined endogenously in the model. Since the focus is on inflation regimes, the inflation rate is used as a transition variable to show the low and high output persistence regimes.

The LSTR model determines a threshold of nearly 4.2% inflation rate as shown in Table 23.2. The results show that there is no significant evidence of increased output persistence when inflation exceeds

Table 23.2 Evidence from logistic smooth transition autoregression

Variable	Coefficient	p-value
Linear part		
Constant	1.56	(0.01)
$RGDPG_{t-1}$	0.73	(0.00)
Nonlinear part		
Constant	−1.50	(0.02)
$RGDPG_{t-1}$	0.16	(0.24)
Speed of transition	3.28	
Inflation threshold values	4.2%	
R^2	0.86	

Note Dependent variable is real GDP growth ($RGDP_t$). $RGDP_{t-1}$ denotes lagged real GDP growth
Source Authors' calculations

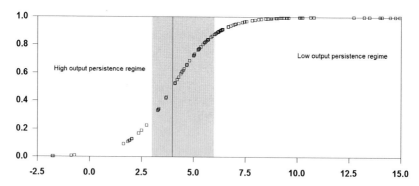

Fig. 23.3 Output persistence, regimes, and inflation (*Note* The light shaded area denotes 3–6% inflation-target band. *Source* Authors' calculations)

the estimated threshold. The output persistence effect is larger in the low-inflation regime below the threshold of 4.2%. Figure 23.3 shows the transition function depicting the output persistence regimes and links them to inflation dynamics.

23.3 Is the Relationship Between Inflation and Output Persistence and Price Flexibility Dependent on the Inflation Regimes?

23.3.1 Evidence from the Output Persistence Based on the Moving Cross Correlation Approach

This section examines the relationship between the output persistence measure based on 20 quarters rolling window correlation between real GDP growth and its first lag. In addition, the section estimates the 16 and 12 quarters of the rolling window output persistence measure. The scatterplots in Fig. 23.4 shows a negative relationship between output persistence and inflation. This evidence supports the findings appearing in Kiley (2000).

23 Does the Persistence of Output Growth Depend ...

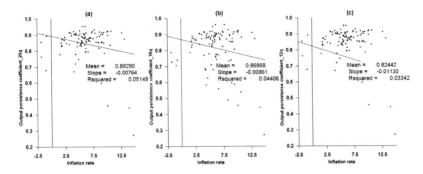

Fig. 23.4 The relationship between output persistence and the consumer inflation rate (*Source* Authors' calculations)

However, the above scatterplots do not show the effects of inflation on output persistence based on whether inflation is above or below the 6% inflation threshold. Hence, this section examines the role of inflation regimes in impacting the output persistence coefficient. Equations (23.4) and (23.5) are estimated for the two inflation regimes, respectively.

$$\text{Output persistence}_t = \text{constant} + \beta * \text{inflation}_t + \varepsilon_t, \quad \text{inflation} > 6 \quad (23.4)$$

$$\text{Output persistence}_t = \text{constant} + \beta * \text{inflation}_t + \varepsilon_t, \quad \text{inflation} \leq 6 \quad (23.5)$$

The magnitudes of the inflation effects on output persistence for the two inflation regimes are shown in Fig. 23.5. The impact is positive in the low inflation regime but negative in the high regime. In addition, the absolute size of the impact is larger in the high inflation regime. This finding shows that the 6% inflation threshold leads to different signs and magnitudes of the impact of inflation on output persistence. Evidence indicates that the prediction of less persistent output fluctuations depends on the inflation regimes. This indicates that inflation regimes matter for the impact of inflation on output persistence dynamics.

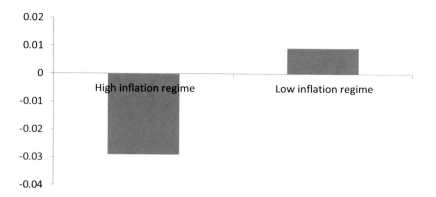

Fig. 23.5 Impacts of inflation on output persistence according to inflation regimes (*Source* Authors' calculations)

23.4 Evidence from the Output Persistence Based on Recursive Least Squares Approach

The section further examines whether the relationship between output persistence and inflation is robust to the techniques used to estimate output persistence. The recursive least squares approach is applied rather than the rolling regression to estimate the output persistence measure. At the same time, the Kiley approach is used to link output persistence to price flexibility. Kiley defines *one minus output persistence measure* as price flexibility. Scatterplots in Fig. 23.6 show the relationships between output persistence or price flexibility measures and the inflation rate. The relationships are separated between the high and low inflation regimes. In Fig. 23.6a, inflation leads to much steeper decline in the output persistence in the high inflation regime than in the low inflation regime. In addition, in Fig. 23.6b, the rising inflation rate leads to steep increase in the price flexibility in the high inflation regime than in the low regime. This evidence supports the results presented in Fig. 23.2.

In addition, a number of bivariate VAR models are estimated to show the robustness of the relationships between inflation rate and the output persistence and price flexibility measures. The first VAR model (first ordering) uses inflation and output persistence or the price

23 Does the Persistence of Output Growth Depend ...

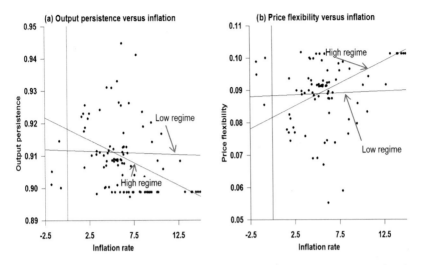

Fig. 23.6 Relationship between inflation versus output persistence and price flexibility (*Source* Authors' calculations)

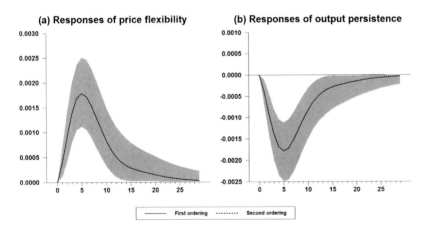

Fig. 23.7 Responses to positive inflation shocks (*Note* The shaded area denote the 16th and 84th percentile confidence bands. *Source* Authors' calculations)

flexibility parameter. The second VAR model (second ordering) uses the reverse ordering in which the output persistence or price flexibility parameter is placed before the inflation rate. All models are estimated using two lags and 10,000 Monte Carlo draws. Figure 23.7, shows the output persistence and price flexibility responses to positive inflation shocks. A positive inflation shock raises price flexibility significantly for long periods. In addition, a positive shock to inflation lowers output persistence significantly.

23.5 Does Price Flexibility Matter for the Transmission of the Expansionary Monetary Policy Shocks?

We further examine the role of price flexibility in the transmission of expansionary monetary policy shocks to household consumption growth. This is achieved by estimating a three-variable counterfactual VAR model which includes changes in the repo rate, household consumption growth, and the price flexibility parameter. The price flexibility variable is shut off to determine the counterfactual response of the household consumption variable to monetary policy shocks. The models are estimated using two lags and 10,000 Monte Carlo draws. Figure 23.8c shows that

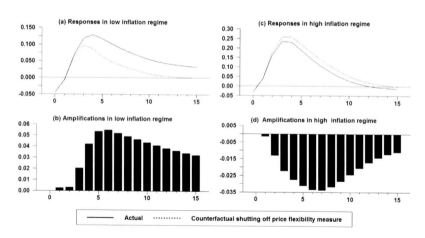

Fig. 23.8 Responses of household consumption growth to an expansionary monetary policy shock and the amplification by the price flexibility measure (*Note* The amplification is due to price flexibility measure. *Source* Authors' calculations)

expansionary monetary policy shocks raise the counterfactual response of household consumption growth more than the actual response. This shows that increased price flexibility weakens the responses of household consumption growth to an expansionary monetary policy shock as shown in Fig. 23.8d. However, as shown in Fig. 23.8a, b price flexibility in the low inflation regime magnifies the household consumption growth to expansionary monetary policy shock.

23.6 Conclusion and Policy Implications

This chapter examined the relevance of the inflation regimes based on the 6% threshold in determining output growth persistence. In addition, the analysis determined the relevance of the price flexibility measure based on Kiley (2000) in impacting the transmission of expansionary monetary policy shocks to household consumption growth and whether inflation regimes matter.

Evidence reveals that the sizes of output persistence measures are smaller when inflation is above the 6% threshold relative to when inflation is less than or equals to 6%. The chapter further determined whether the average frequency of price changes based on Kiley (2000) differed between the high and low inflation regimes. Evidence shows that the average frequency of price changes is relatively shorter in the high inflation regime than in the low inflation regime. The analysis concludes by showing the role of price flexibility in transmitting expansionary monetary policy shocks to household consumption growth. Evidence shows that increased price flexibility in the high inflation regime weakens the responses of household consumption growth to expansionary monetary policy shocks. However, the reduced price flexibility in the low inflation regime magnifies the increase in the household consumption growth due to expansionary monetary policy shocks. From the policy perspective, this implies that expansionary monetary policy shocks, happening when inflation is below 6%, will stimulate household consumption growth more than raising inflation because prices are less flexible. In addition price stability matter in the above context.

References

Ball, L., Gregory Mankiw, G., & Romer, D. (1988). The new Keynesian economics and the output-inflation trade-off. *Brookings Papers on Economic Activity*, Economic Studies Program, The Brookings Institution, *19*(1), 1–82.

Khan, H. (2004). Price stickiness, trend inflation and output dynamics: A cross country analysis. *The Canadian Journal of Economics, 37*(4), 999–1020.

Kiley, M. T. (2000). Endogenous price sickness and business cycle persistence. *Journal of Money, Credit and Banking, 32*, 28–53.

Terasvirta. (1994). Specification, estimation and evaluation of smooth transition autoregressive models. *Journal of American Statistical Association, 89*, 208–218.

24

Do the Effects of Expansionary Monetary Policy Shocks on Output Persistence Depend on Inflation Regimes?

Main Highlights

- Evidence shows that expansionary monetary policy shocks raise output persistence more when inflation is below or equal to six per cent than when it is above six per cent. Output persistence rises more to a scenario of successive policy rate cuts of varying magnitude than a constant policy rate change scenario.
- The findings indicate that low economic policy uncertainty magnifies the output persistence response to the expansionary monetary policy shocks. By contrast, high economic policy uncertainty lowers the output persistence response to an expansionary monetary policy shock.
- In policy terms, this implies that a larger expansionary monetary policy shock than expected will raise output persistence significantly and the amplification effects will be enlarged when inflation is in the low inflation regime.

© The Author(s) 2019
E. Ndou and T. Mokoena, *Inequality, Output-Inflation Trade-Off and Economic Policy Uncertainty,*
https://doi.org/10.1007/978-3-030-19803-9_24

358 E. Ndou and T. Mokoena

24.1 Introduction

This chapter investigates the extent to which expansionary monetary policy shocks impact real GDP growth persistence (*hereafter referred to as output persistence*), and whether the effects differ between the high inflation regime and low inflation regime. The regimes are based on the six per cent inflation threshold, with inflation above (below) this threshold as high (low) inflation regime. The IMF and credit ratings agencies have pointed out to the prevalence of high economic policy and political uncertainty, which has implications for economic growth, and possibly the implementation of structural reforms. Structural reforms have been envisaged as a potential source to achieving high economic growth rates, while monetary policy is deemed as having little influence. The communications from these institutions happen when inflation is below six per cent, hence the role of price stability cannot be left out of this analysis. In addition, we investigate the extent to which expansionary monetary policy shock effects on output persistence are impacted by economic policy uncertainty regimes?

Under certain conditions monetary policy as a demand management tool, may have limited influence in raising economic growth to higher levels. This chapter postulates that expansionary monetary policy may raise output persistence and the increase may amplify the effects other stimulatory shock on real economic activity. The stimulatory effects of monetary policy on output persistence are vital in triggering the multiplier effects in the economy. The amplification ability of output persistence has not been articulated in policy discourse.

The chapter fills policy and research gaps by examining the extent to which inflation, when it is above or below the six per cent threshold, impacts the magnitudes of output persistences to expansionary monetary policy shocks. In addition, the analysis fills policy research gaps by determining the extent to which the economic policy uncertainty channel affects the transmission of expansionary monetary policy shocks to output persistence. Furthermore, the analysis contrasts the effects of three repo rate cut shock scenarios on output persistence responses in the low and high inflation regimes. Thereafter, the chapter further examines the extent to which output persistence matters for the transmission of expansionary monetary policy and positive wage growth shocks to household consumption growth.

Evidence indicates that inflation regimes matter for the size of output persistence response to an expansionary monetary policy shock. The findings further reveal that the sizes of output persistence measures, following the expansionary monetary policy shocks, are smaller when inflation is above six per cent, relative to when inflation is below or equals to six per cent. Thus, expansionary monetary policy shocks drive output persistence and the reaction is bigger in the low inflation regime than in the high one. The emphasis on policy pronouncements has been on transitory effects of monetary policy on output growth. However, evidence in this chapter shows that expansionary monetary policy shocks impact output persistence and the effects depend on inflation regimes and trajectory policy rate path. In addition, evidence indicates that output persistence is an amplifier of positive wage shocks on household consumption growth. The effects are bigger when inflation is below six per cent inflation than when no inflation regime is considered in the model. This suggests that some inflation is needed to enable amplification effects.

24.2 Do Inflation Regimes Impact the Response of Expansionary Monetary Policy Shocks on Output Persistence?

This section determines the extent to which expansionary monetary policy shocks impact output persistence responses based on inflation regimes. Regime-dependent bivariate VAR models are estimated and these are based on inflation regimes. The inflation regimes are based on whether inflation exceeds or is below six per cent. A high inflation regime refers to inflation above the six per cent threshold. Low inflation regime refers to inflation below or equal to six per cent. The estimated model includes the repo rate changes and an output persistence measure based on the recursive least squares approach. The two

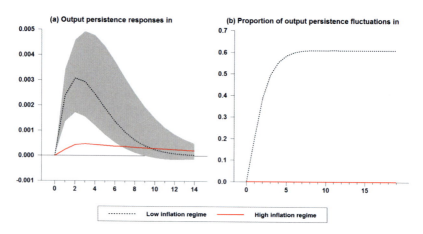

Fig. 24.1 Output persistence responses and fluctuations due to an expansionary monetary policy shock (*Note* The shaded area in (**a**) denotes the 16th and 84th percentile as confidence bands. *Source* Authors' calculations)

regime-dependent VAR models are estimated using 2 lags and 10,000 Monte Carlo Draws. The models are estimated using quarterly (Q) data spanning 1990Q1 to 2017Q1 obtained from the South African Reserve Bank. However, in the following section when using economic policy uncertainty variable the sample ends in 2016Q1 since the uncertainty series was obtained from Hlatshwayo and Saxegaard (2016).[1]

Impulse responses in Fig. 24.1a show that expansionary monetary policy shocks raise output persistence much higher in the low inflation regime than in the high regime. Expansionary monetary policy shocks induce more fluctuations in output persistence in the low inflation regime than in the high regime in Fig. 24.1b. This evidence is robust to the reverse ordering of variables in the preceding model. This evidence shows that expansionary monetary policy shocks do impact the evolution of output persistence but the bigger increase is achieved in the low inflation regime.

---

[1]The latter economic uncertainty variable is based on search algorithms that were employed via the Dow Jones Factiva news aggregator.

24 Do the Effects of Expansionary Monetary Policy Shocks ...

We perform scenario analysis of the expansionary monetary policy shocks to determine the reaction of output persistence following an initial 0.25 percentage points reduction in the repo rate. Three scenarios are simulated. The *first scenario* depicts a once-off policy loosening followed by a tightening shock. This scenario shows that an initial 0.25 percentage points decrease in the repo rate is followed by a tightening of similar magnitude. The *second scenario* depicts two periods of loosening shock. This scenario shows an initial 0.25 percentage points reduction in repo rate is followed by a 0.5 percentage points decrease. The *third scenario* shows three periods of policy loosening shock. This scenario shows three consecutive reductions in the repo rate of increasing magnitudes. The results of scenarios are shown according to the inflation regimes estimated from regime-dependent VAR models. The high inflation regime refers to regions where inflation is above the six per cent threshold.

In Fig. 24.2, evidence shows that an expansionary monetary policy shock raises output persistence, irrespective of the shock scenario and inflation regime. However, two differences are visible. First, the sizes of output persistence reactions are higher in the low inflation regime than

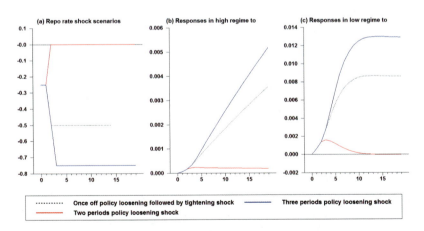

Fig. 24.2 Output persistence responses to expansionary monetary policy shocks and the role of inflation regimes (*Note* High regime denotes high inflation regime. Low regime denotes low inflation regime. *Source* Authors' calculations)

362 E. Ndou and T. Mokoena

in the high regime. Second, the consecutive policy rate cuts shock scenario, leads to a bigger increase in the output persistence relative to that achieved by once-off loosening followed by a tightening shock scenario.

24.2.1 Does the Economic Policy Uncertainty Channel Matter for Transmitting Expansionary Monetary Policy Shocks to Output Persistence in the Low Inflation Regime?

We examine the role of economic policy uncertainty in impacting the transmission of expansionary monetary policy shocks to output persistence. But the focus is on when inflation is below or equals to six per cent (low inflation regime) and we distinguish between the roles of negative economic policy uncertainty and positive uncertainty changes. The negative economic policy uncertainty dummy is equal to negative values of annual growth in economic policy uncertainty and zero otherwise. The positive economic policy uncertainty dummy is equal to positive values of annual growth in uncertainty and zero otherwise. We estimate counterfactual VAR models which shut off the economic policy uncertainty channel to calculate the counterfactual responses. The estimated models include changes in the repo rate, output persistence, and either negative or positive economic policy uncertainty dummy. The models are estimated using 1 lag and 10,000 Monte Carlo draws.

Figure 24.3, shows that expansionary monetary policy shocks raise output persistence, irrespective of whether economic policy uncertainty is included or not in the model. However, the negative and positive economic policy uncertainty channels have different effects on transmitting expansionary monetary policy shocks to output persistence. In Fig. 24.3a the actual output persistence rises more than the counterfactual reaction. This suggests that negative economic policy uncertainty channel magnifies the increase in output persistence following an expansionary monetary policy shock. In Fig. 24.3b, the counterfactual output persistence rises more than the actual response. This suggests that the elevated economic policy uncertainty reduces the output persistence reaction to expansionary monetary policy shocks.

24 Do the Effects of Expansionary Monetary Policy Shocks ...

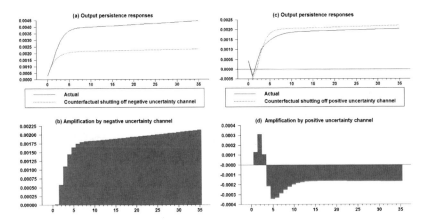

Fig. 24.3 Output persistence responses to expansionary monetary policy shocks and the role of the economic policy uncertainty channels (*Source* Authors' calculations)

24.2.2 Does the Output Persistence Matter for the Amplification of Expansionary Monetary Policy and Positive Wage Shocks to Household Consumption Growth?

The chapter performs another counterfactual analysis to show the role of the output persistence channel in the transmission of an expansionary monetary policy shock to household consumption growth. The counterfactual approach shuts off the output persistence channel in transmitting an expansionary monetary policy shock to household consumption growth. The counterfactual reaction refers to the impulse responses after shutting off the output persistence channel. We show the impulse responses in the low inflation regime and when there are no inflation regimes.

Figure 24.4 shows the household consumption growth responses to an unexpected one standard deviation cut in the repo rate. Impulse responses show that expansionary monetary policy shocks have bigger effects on household consumption growth in the low inflation regime than when no inflation regimes are considered.

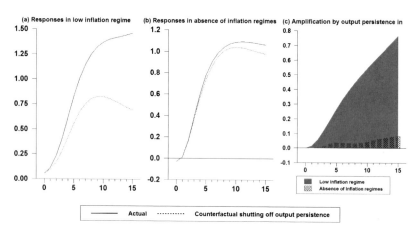

Fig. 24.4 Responses of household consumption growth to expansionary monetary policy shocks and amplification effects by output persistence (*Source* Authors' calculations)

The endogenous-exogenous VAR approach is used to determine the role of output persistence in impacting the responses of household consumption growth to a positive wage growth shock. The output persistence is an endogenous variable in one model, while being exogenous in the other model. The gap between the household consumption growth responses to positive wage shocks measures the role of output persistence in transmitting shocks. Figure 24.5, shows that high output persistence amplifies the increase in household consumption growth following a positive wage growth shock. The amplification is much bigger in the low inflation regime than in the absence of inflation regimes. This evidence is robust to the assumption regarding the role of output persistence in transmitting wage growth shocks to household consumption.

24.3 Conclusion and Policy Implications

This chapter investigates the extent to which expansionary monetary policy shocks impact output persistence and whether the effects differ between the high and low inflation regimes based on the six per cent

24 Do the Effects of Expansionary Monetary Policy Shocks ...

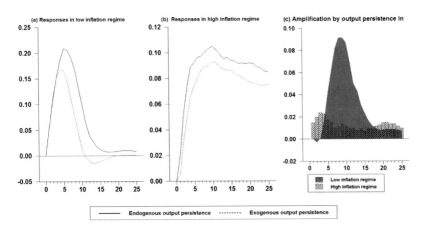

Fig. 24.5 Responses of household consumption growth to a positive wage growth shock and amplification by output persistence (*Source* Authors' calculations)

threshold. The chapter investigates, given a low inflation regime, the extent to which expansionary monetary policy shock effects on output persistence are influenced by the low and high economic policy uncertainty regimes. First, evidence shows that expansionary monetary policy shocks raise output persistence more when inflation is below or equal to six per cent than when it is above six per cent. Second, evidence indicates that low economic policy uncertainty magnifies the output persistence response to expansionary monetary policy shocks. By contrast, high economic policy uncertainty lowers the output persistence response to expansionary monetary policy shock. Third, output persistence rises more to successive policy rate cuts of varying magnitude than a constant policy rate change scenario. Fourth, evidence indicates that output persistence is an amplifier of household consumption growth increase due to positive wage shocks and the effects are bigger below six per cent inflation than when no inflation regime is considered in the model. In policy terms, the finding implies that a larger expansionary monetary policy shock than expected will raise output persistence very much and the amplification effects will be enlarged in the low inflation regime.

Reference

Hlatshwayo, S., & Saxegaard, M. (2016). *The consequences of policy uncertainty: Disconnects and dilutions in the South African real effective exchange rate-export relationship* (IMF Working Paper No. 16/113).

25

Output and Policy Ineffectiveness Proposition: A Perspective from Single Regression Equations

Main Highlights

- This analysis shows that the increase in nominal GDP has a small impact on the real GDP growth when inflation is above the six per cent threshold (high inflation regime) compared to below this limit (low inflation regime). Thus, the impact of a one percentage point increase in nominal GDP growth on real GDP growth is larger in the low inflation regime than in the high inflation regime. Evidence from the logistic smooth transition autoregression model indicates that the optimal inflation threshold values are around 4.4–4.57% and these values are within the current 3–6% inflation band.
- In policy terms, this evidence suggests that price stability matters for the size of the impact of a positive nominal demand shock (such as expansionary monetary policy shocks) on real GDP growth based on the six per cent inflation threshold. Therefore, there is high likelihood that expansionary monetary policy shocks in the low inflation regime will raise real GDP growth more than in the high inflation regime, ceteris paribus.

© The Author(s) 2019

E. Ndou and T. Mokoena, *Inequality, Output-Inflation Trade-Off and Economic Policy Uncertainty*,
https://doi.org/10.1007/978-3-030-19803-9_25

25.1 Introduction

This chapter continues the discussion on output-inflation trade-off, but the focus is on determining the relevance of the policy ineffectiveness proposition based on the inflation regimes. The analysis uses threshold approaches based on the inflation threshold of six per cent, which is the upper part of the current inflation target band. Do the inflation thresholds lead to different impacts of one percentage point increase in nominal GDP growth on real GDP growth?

This chapter fills policy research gaps by applying threshold autoregression approaches to determine whether there is a change in the impact of nominal GDP growth on real GDP growth after crossing the threshold. At the same time, the analysis is aware that it may not be ideal to use the six per cent inflation rate, because there may be a different threshold existing either within or outside the inflation target band. This bespeaks the need to estimate three logistic smooth transition autoregressive models under three different assumptions to determine whether the inflation threshold leads to differential effects of the increase in nominal demand on real GDP growth. Alternatively, if thresholds are different, this may indicate the need for a justification to use the inflation target band.

Evidence indicates that the size of the reaction of the real GDP growth to a one percentage point increase in nominal GDP growth (nominal demand shock) differs according to inflation regimes. The coefficient measuring the impact of a one percentage point increase in the nominal GDP growth on the real GDP growth is larger in the lower inflation regime than in the high inflation regime. In policy terms, this indicates that the six per cent inflation threshold matters for the response of the real GDP growth to nominal demand increase. The logistic smooth transition autoregression model indicates that the inflation threshold values are around 4.4–4.57% and these values are within the current 3–6% inflation band. The one percentage point increase in nominal GDP growth significantly raises the real GDP growth below the thresholds while it has negative effect above the threshold.

25.2 Theoretical Links Between Nominal GDP and Nominal Policy Shocks

Ball et al. (1988) and other authors have linked the real GDP (RY_t) and the ratio of nominal GDP (NY_t) to price level (P_t) in Eq. (25.1).

$$(RY_t = NY_t/P_t) \tag{25.1}$$

Equation (25.2) shows that real GDP could be linked to real money balances M_t/P_t. And M_t denotes nominal money supply.

$$RY_t = M_t/P_t \tag{25.2}$$

It can be shown through mathematical derivations based on logarithmic transformations that changes in nominal GDP (ΔNY_t) equals to changes in nominal money supply (ΔM_t).

$$\Delta NY_t = \Delta M_t \tag{25.3}$$

This shows changes in nominal GDP could be assumed to arise from changes in monetary policy. This offers a direct link that any nominal policy shocks (such as expansionary monetary or fiscal policy shock) impacts nominal GDP.

Three possibilities arise from Eq. (25.1) regarding the effects of the nominal policy shock that impacts GDP (NY_t). It is possible that an increase in nominal GDP can be fully passed through to real GDP (RY_t) if the price level (P_t) does not react at all. Or it may be that changes in nominal GDP can be offset by similar changes in the price level, leaving real GDP unchanged. Alternatively, changes in nominal GDP can be partially offset by changes in the price level, leading to some changes in the real GDP.

25.3 Do Threshold Autoregressive Approaches Matter for Determining the Differential Policy Effectiveness Based on the Inflation Regimes?

25.3.1 Evidence from Regime-Dependent Regression Equation Results

Empirical estimation begins by estimating regime-dependent linear regressions to determine the extent to which inflation regimes lead to the differential impacts of one percentage point increase in nominal GDP growth on real GDP growth. Literature on output-inflation trade-off uses nominal GDP to capture nominal demand shocks. A similar interpretation is adopted in this analysis. The regime-dependent effects are estimated using Eqs. (25.4) and (25.5). The effects depend on whether (1) inflation (π_t) exceeds six per cent and (2) inflation is below or equals to six per cent. All the estimations use quarterly (Q) data spanning 1990Q1 to 2017Q1 obtained from the South African Reserve Bank. All growth rates are annual rates calculated using log transformations.

$$
\begin{aligned}
\text{Real GDP growth} = \text{constant} &+ \beta * \text{Real GDP growth}_{t-1} \\
&+ \delta * \text{Nominal GDP growth}_t \\
&+ \varepsilon_t, \ (\pi_t > 6)
\end{aligned}
\tag{25.4}
$$

$$
\begin{aligned}
\text{Real GDP growth} = \text{constant} &+ \beta * \text{Real GDP growth}_{t-1} \\
&+ \delta * \text{Nominal GDP growth}_t \\
&+ \varepsilon_t, \ (\pi_t \leq 6)
\end{aligned}
\tag{25.5}
$$

Figure 25.1 compares the magnitudes (δ) of real GDP growth changes to a one percentage point increase in nominal GDP growth. The real GDP growth magnitudes differ according to inflation regimes. The coefficient of real GDP growth to a one percentage point increase in the nominal GDP growth is larger in the lower inflation regime compared to that in the high inflation regime. This is the first evidence indicating that the six per cent inflation threshold matters for the response of the real GDP growth to a one percentage point increase in the nominal GDP growth.

25.3.2 Evidence from the Modified Hansen (1999) Threshold Regression

The analysis applies a second approach based on the Hansen (1999) threshold regression analysis. The analysis further examines the robustness of the results to different threshold approaches. Equations (25.6)–(25.9) are used to determine the extent to which inflation regimes impact the effect of a one percentage point increase in the nominal GDP growth $\left(\text{NGDPgrowth}_t\right)$ on the real GDP growth $\left(\text{RGDPgrowth}_t\right)$.

$$\text{RGDPgrowth} = c + \delta * \text{NGDPgrowth}_t * (\pi_t > 6) \\ + \gamma * \text{NGDPgrowth}_t * (\pi_t \leq 6) + \varepsilon_t \quad (25.6)$$

$$\text{RGDPgrowth} = \delta * \text{NGDPgrowth}_t * (\pi_t > 6) \\ + \gamma * \text{NGDPgrowth}_t * (\pi_t \leq 6) + \varepsilon_t \quad (25.7)$$

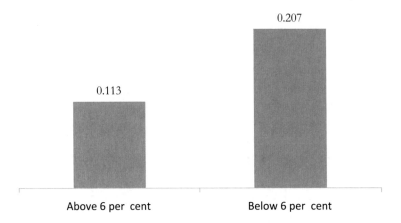

Fig. 25.1 Impacts of nominal GDP on real GDP (*Source* Authors' calculation)

$$\text{RGDPgrowth} = c + \beta * \text{RGDPgrowth}_{t-1}$$
$$+ \delta * \text{NGDPgrowth}_t * (\pi_t > 6)$$
$$+ \gamma * \text{NGDPgrowth}_t * (\pi_t \leq 6) + \varepsilon_t \quad (25.8)$$

$$\text{RGDPgrowth} = \beta * \text{RGDPgrowth}_{t-1}$$
$$+ \delta * \text{NGDPgrowth}_t * (\pi_t > 6)$$
$$+ \gamma * \text{NGDPgrowth}_t * (\pi_t \leq 6) + \varepsilon_t \quad (25.9)$$

Irrespective of the model estimated, in Table 25.1, the one percentage point increase in nominal GDP growth has bigger impact on real GDP growth in the low inflation regime (γ) compared to that in the high inflation regime (δ). This evidence further ascertains the important role of inflation regimes (Table 25.1).

25.3.3 Evidence from Terasvirta's (1994) Logistic Smooth Transition Autoregression Model

A third approach is applied to determine where the inflation threshold value is located relative to the inflation target band using the logistic smooth transition autoregression (LSTR) based on Terasvirta (1994). The estimations use the inflation rate as a transition variable. In addition, various models are estimated to determine the robustness of the results. The results based on three LSTR non-linear models are shown in Table 25.2. The results indicate that a one percentage point increase in nominal GDP growth (*Ngdpg*) leads to bigger impact on the real GDP growth (*Rgdpg*) in the low inflation regime than in the high regime. In addition, all the threshold values are below 5%.

The smooth transition graphs are shown in Fig. 25.2. Figure 25.2 depicts a smooth transition from the low inflation regime to the high inflation regime. All three thresholds are within the inflation target band as shown by the light grey shaded portion.

Table 25.1 Impacts of nominal GDP growth on Real GDP growth based on Eqs. (25.6)–(25.9)

Variable	Equation (25.6)		Equation (25.7)		Equation (25.8)		Equation (25. 9)	
$NGDP\,growth_t * (\pi_t > 6)$	0.30	(0.00)	0.17	(0.00)	0.02	(0.50)	0.02	(0.26)
$NGDP\,growth_t * (\pi_t \leq 6)$	0.51	(0.00)	0.36	(0.00)	0.07	(0.01)	0.06	(0.01)

Note p value in (.)
Source Authors' calculations

Table 25.2 Impacts of nominal GDP growth on real GDP growth

	Model 1		Model 2		Model 3	
	Coefficient		Coefficient		Coefficient	
Linear part						
Rgdpg$_{t-1}$	0.790	(0.00)	0.533	(0.00)	0.712	(0.00)
Ngdpg	0.250	(0.00)	0.228	(0.00)	0.158	(0.00)
Ngdpg$_{t-2}$	−0.133	(0.00)				
Non-linear part						
Rgdpg$_{t-1}$			0.258	(0.19)		
Ngdpg	−0.086	(0.00)	−0.205	(0.01)	−0.112	(0.00)
Speed of transition	2.602		2.976		2.695	
Inflation threshold (%)	*4.44*		*4.56*		*4.57*	
Impacts						
Impact below threshold	0.117		0.228		0.158	
Impact above threshold	0.031		0.023		0.046	

Note P value in (.)

Source Authors' calculations

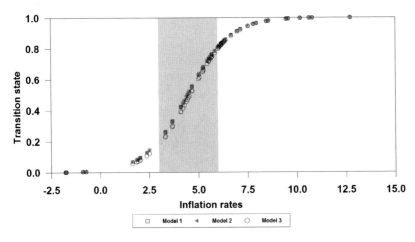

Fig. 25.2 Transition graphs (*Source* Authors' calculations)

25.4 Conclusion

This analysis showed that the impact of a one percentage point increase in nominal GDP growth on real GDP growth is larger in the lower inflation regime than in the high inflation regime. In policy terms, this indicates that the six per cent inflation threshold matters for the response of the real GDP growth to nominal demand increase. The logistic smooth transition autoregression model indicates that inflation threshold values are around 4.4–4.57% and these values are within the 3–6% inflation band. The increase in nominal GDP has a small impact on real GDP growth above these thresholds compared to the ones below them. In policy terms, this evidence suggests that price stability matters for the size of the impact of a positive nominal demand shock (such as expansionary monetary policy shocks) on real GDP growth based on the current inflation threshold. Therefore, there is high likelihood that expansionary monetary policy shock in the low inflation regime will uplift real GDP growth more than in the high inflation regime, ceteris paribus.

References

Ball, L., Gregory Mankiw, G., & Romer, D. (1988). The new Keynsesian economics and the output-inflation trade-off. *Brookings Chapters on Economic Activity, 19* (1), 1–82.

Hansen, B. E. (1999). Threshold effects in non-dynamic panels: Estimation, testing, and inference. *Journal of Econometrics, 93*(2), 345–368.

Holmes, M. J. (2000). The output-inflation trade-off in African less developed countries. *Journal of economic developments, 25*(1), 41–55.

Terasvirta. (1994). Specification, estimation and evaluation of smooth transition autoregressive models. *Journal of American Statistical Association, 89*, 208–218.

Part IX

Economic Policy Uncertainty, Expansionary Monetary Policy and Fiscal Policy Multipliers

26

Does the Economic Policy Uncertainty Channel Impact the Influence of Expansionary Monetary Policy Changes on Output Dynamics?

Main Highlights

- Evidence shows that elevated economic policy uncertainty shock reduces economic growth, which is consistent with the real option theories predictions.
- Evidence shows that low economic policy uncertainty amplifies the economic growth reaction to an unexpected cut in the repo rate. By contrast, the actual economic growth response rise less than the counterfactual responses in the high economic policy uncertainty regime.
- From policy perspective, policymakers anticipating a certain magnitude of the impact from stimulatory policy shock, should consider economic policy uncertainty regimes in their policy decisions; otherwise policy effects may fall short of their expectations and induce more uncertainty.

© The Author(s) 2019
E. Ndou and T. Mokoena, *Inequality, Output-Inflation Trade-Off and Economic Policy Uncertainty*,
https://doi.org/10.1007/978-3-030-19803-9_26

26.1 Introduction

This chapter examines whether economic policy uncertainty can alter the influence of an expansionary monetary policy shock to stimulate economic growth. Given, the price stability mandate, this chapter determines whether the effects of an expansionary monetary policy shock on economic growth vary according to whether uncertainty is high or low in an environment where inflation is below the 6% level. Does the economic policy uncertainty channel impact the influence of an expansionary monetary policy shock on output dynamics? What are implications for the required size of policy rate adjustments that is expected to influence economic growth?

Theory is ambiguous about the effects of uncertainty shocks on economic growth, and this depends on whether investment is reversible or irreversible. This suggests that the overall effects of elevated uncertainty on real economic activity require an empirical investigation, given that uncertainty can enhance or retard economic growth. Figure 26.1 shows two possible outcomes linked to the adverse effects of macroeconomic uncertainty shocks on economic growth. For instance, the real option and growth option theory propose different theoretical outcomes on economic growth due to how uncertainty influences investment.

The real option channel argues that increased uncertainty reduces investment due to the irreversibility of investment (Bernanke 1983) and this leads to reduced output growth. These theoretical models are premised on the role of physical adjustment frictions (Bernanke 1983; Dixit et al. 1994).[1] Thus, high uncertainty together with non-smooth adjustment frictions lead firms to behave cautiously, slowing down or pausing in hiring and investment. Thus, when firms are uncertain about how the future unfolds, and adopt a "*wait and see*" behaviour, this generates a drop in economic activity. Moreover, investment is irreversible according to this theory. The growth option theory argues that elevated uncertainty

---

[1]However, Bloom (2009) argues that these models predict that high uncertainty should be followed by a quick bust boom cycle. Evidence in Bloom (2009), based on using exogenous shock to changes in volatility, indicated the postponement of irreversible investment. This postponement leads to a fall in the current level of economic activity.

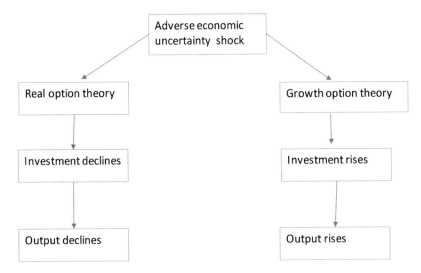

Fig. 26.1 The depiction of the transmission of elevated uncertainty shocks (*Source* Authors' drawing)

may increase investment thereby raising output growth.[2] This arises because investment is reversible. The growth-enhancing effects of positive uncertainty shocks are based on the idea that potential losses of investment projects are bounded at their initiation costs, while potential revenue is unbounded (Kraft et al. 2013; and Stein and Stone 2013).

Thus, if the growth option channel is important, then a stimulatory policy shock during a period of high uncertainty should amplify output expansion. By contrast, the dominance of the real option channel should dampen the stimulatory effects of policy shocks on output expansion. So, which channel explains the effects of the uncertainty shock in South Africa and are there implications for the size of policy rate adjustments?

This chapter fills policy research gaps by determining the relevance of the indirect channel of economic policy uncertainty in transmitting

---

[2]This is hinged on investment being reversible, firms operating in perfectly competitive markets and firms having long time span. All these conditions may lead uncertainty shock to enhance investment activity. The evidence supporting this growth enhancing effects of theory has been found in R&D intensive firms (Kraft et al. 2013; Stein and stone 2013).

382 E. Ndou and T. Mokoena

an expansionary monetary policy shock to real output. For instance, Aastveit et al. (2017) found evidence that US monetary policy shocks affect economic activity less when uncertainty is high, in line with the real option theory. This chapter adds to the literature and policy debates as it differs from Aastveit et al. (2017) by applying a counterfactual approach and further distinguishes the role of economic policy uncertainty in the low inflation regime (that is, when inflation is below 6%).

26.2 What Are the Effects of Economic Policy Uncertainty Shocks on Economic Growth?

This analysis uses quarterly (Q) data from 1990Q1 to 2015Q4. The data is obtained from the South African Reserve Bank. The investigation begins by estimating a bivariate VAR model which includes both annual growth in economic policy uncertainty and GDP. The model is estimated using two lags and 10,000 Monte Carlo draws. Being cognisant of the different measures of economic uncertainties, it is worth mentioning that determining the best measure of uncertainty is not the objective of this chapter. The objective is to determine whether the effects of uncertainty shocks on economic growth in South Africa can be described as being consistent with the predictions of real option or the growth option theory. This chapter further separates the effects between those linked to the persistent and non-persistent uncertainty shocks for both positive and negative uncertainty shocks.

Figure 26.2 shows the economic growth responses to positive and negative economic policy uncertainty shocks. A positive economic policy uncertainty shock lowers economic growth. By contrast, a negative economic policy uncertainty shock raises economic growth. This evidence is consistent with the real option theory which elaborates that a given level of elevated uncertainty induces caution and this lowers the sensitivity of the real output. Thus, economic policy uncertainty shocks drive economic growth and the effects differ, because they depend on the persistence of the shock effects. Evidence so far points to the direct effects. However, in practice, it might well be the case that uncertainty may indirectly transmit monetary policy shocks.

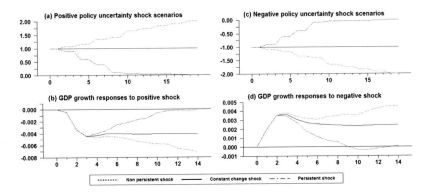

Fig. 26.2 GDP growth responses to economic policy uncertainty shocks (*Source* Authors' calculations)

The relevance of the indirect role is examined in more detail in the next sections.

26.3 Does the Economic Policy Uncertainty Channel Affect the Impact of an Expansionary Monetary Policy Shock on Economic Growth?

Evidence in the preceding sections showed that elevated economic policy uncertainty directly lowers economic growth, and this is consistent with the predictions of the real option theory. This analysis further examines the indirect role of economic policy uncertainty regimes in impacting the reaction of economic growth to an expansionary monetary policy shock. The expansionary monetary policy shock refers to a one standard deviation shock which is equivalent to a 50 basis point cut in the repo rate. The economic policy uncertainty changes are divided into two regimes based on whether the annual growth in economic policy uncertainty is positive or negative. A high (low) uncertainty regime refers to positive (negative) annual growth in the economic policy uncertainty index.

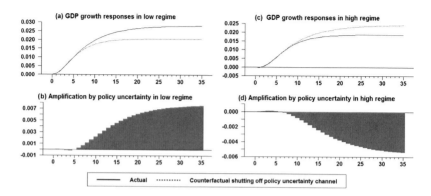

Fig. 26.3 Accumulated GDP growth responses to an expansionary monetary policy shock and the role of economic policy uncertainty regimes (*Source* Authors' calculations)

Figure 26.3 shows the accumulated economic growth responses to an expansionary monetary policy shock. An expansionary monetary policy shock stimulates economic growth. However, the overall effects depend on the economic policy uncertainty regimes. Figures 26.3a and b shows that a low economic policy uncertainty amplifies the economic growth reaction to an unexpected cut in the repo rate. By contrast, in Fig. 26.3c the actual economic growth rises less than the counterfactual responses in the high economic policy uncertainty regime. As shown in Fig. 26.3d, elevated economic policy uncertainty in the high economic policy uncertainty regime dampens the economic growth responses to an expansionary monetary policy shock.

Overall evidence shows that an unexpected repo rate cut has stimulatory effects on economic growth, but the economic policy uncertainty regimes matter. The small increase in economic growth in the high economic policy uncertainty regime implies that a much larger than expected repo rate cut may achieve a desirable outcome in stimulating economic growth. Thus, the economic policy uncertainty regime impacts the magnitude of the repo rate required to stimulate economic growth. This implies that when policymakers have an expected magnitude of impact from stimulatory policy shock, they should consider economic policy uncertainty regimes in their policy decisions, otherwise the policy effects may fall short of their expectations and induce more uncertainty.

This analysis belongs to the chapters that debate whether monetary policy is either more or less effective in recessions and considers the regime-dependent effects of policy shocks on business cycle dynamics. Studies find mixed evidence of the potency of expansionary policy shocks during recessions and booms. However, the potency of the policy effects during recessions indicates the relevance of theories pointing to time-varying policy effects, such as economic slack, bank-lending, and bank-capital channels (Aastveit et al. 2017). These channels predict stronger effects during recessions. Recent empirical evidence indicates that economic uncertainty is a potential explanation of why expansionary monetary policy could be less effective in recessions (Ndou et al. 2017) and in periods of slow economic growth. Evidence in this section shows that an expansionary monetary policy may fail to stimulate real output if uncertainty is high.[3]

Does the role of the economic policy uncertainty matter for the expansionary monetary policy shock effects even in a low inflation regime (that is, inflation below 6%)? This is due to episodes in which heightening in the economic policy uncertainty can happen while inflation is within the target band. Consequently, this analysis examines the role of economic policy uncertainty regimes in impacting the pass-through of the repo rate cuts to economic growth in a low inflation regime.

Figure 26.4 shows the accumulated responses of economic growth to an expansionary monetary policy shock in the low inflation regime (that is, below 6%) and roles of high and low economic policy uncertainty channels in the inflation targeting period (that is, 2000Q1–2015Q4).

An unexpected cut in the repo rate stimulates economic growth in the low inflation regime despite the economic policy uncertainty regimes. However, the impact is much bigger in the presence of the low economic policy uncertainty than when it is elevated. In Fig. 26.4a and b, the low economic policy uncertainty channel amplifies the increase in economic growth following an expansionary monetary policy shock. In Fig. 26.4d, the high economic policy uncertainty channel dampens the increase in economic growth following an expansionary monetary policy shock.

---

[3]This conclusion is consistent with, Aastveit et al. (2017) evidence that US monetary policy shocks affect economic activity less when uncertainty is high, in line with real option theory.

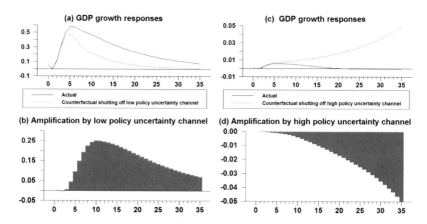

Fig. 26.4 Accumulated responses to expansionary monetary policy shock in the low inflation regime (*Source* Authors' calculations)

26.4 Conclusion and Policy Implications

This chapter determines the relevance of the indirect channel of economic policy uncertainty in transmitting expansionary monetary policy shocks to real output. Evidence shows that elevated economic policy uncertainty has negative effects on economic growth, consistent with the real option theory. The analysis further examines the indirect role of the economic policy uncertainty regimes in impacting the reaction of economic growth to an expansionary monetary policy shock.[4] An expansionary monetary policy shock stimulates economic growth, despite the prevailing policy uncertainty levels. However, the sizes of the overall economic growth responses depend on the economic policy uncertainty regimes. Counterfactual evidence shows that the low economic policy uncertainty amplifies the economic growth reaction to an unexpected cut in the repo rate. Counterfactual analysis reveals that the elevated economic policy uncertainty dampens the economic growth responses to an expansionary monetary policy shock.

---

[4]The expansionary monetary policy shock refers to a one standard deviation shock equivalent to 50 basis points cut in repo rate.

Does the role of economic policy uncertainty matter for an expansionary monetary policy shock effects, even in the low inflation regime? Consequently, this analysis examined the role of economic policy uncertainty regimes in impacting the pass-through of the repo rate cuts to economic growth. Evidence shows that an unexpected cut in the repo rate has stimulatory impact on economic growth in low inflation regime despite the economic policy uncertainty regimes. However, the impact is much bigger in the presence of low economic policy uncertainty than when it is high. The low economic policy uncertainty channel amplifies the increase in economic growth, following an expansionary monetary policy shock.

The policy implication is that a low inflation regime is ideal for an expansionary monetary policy shock to raise economic growth much higher, and this requires a low economic policy uncertainty environment. Hence, policymakers should implement policies that minimise policy uncertainty. Economic policy uncertainty regimes matter. The small increase in economic growth in the high economic policy uncertainty regime imply that a much larger than expected repo rate cut may achieve a desirable outcome on stimulating economic growth. Thus, economic policy uncertainty regimes do impact the magnitude of the repo rate adjustment required to stimulate economic growth. In case policymakers have an expected magnitude of impact from stimulatory policy shock, they should consider economic policy uncertainty regimes in their policy decisions, otherwise policy effects may fall short of their expectations and induce more uncertainty.

References

Aastveit, K. A., Natvik, G.J., & Sola, S. (2017). Economic uncertainty and the influence of monetary policy. *Journal of International Money and Finance, 76*, 50–67.

Baker, S. R., Bloom, N., & Davis, S. J. (2015). *Measuring economic policy uncertainty* (NBER Working Paper 21633).

Bernanke, B. S. (1983). Irreversibility, uncertainty, and cyclical investment. *The Quarterly Journal of Economics, 98*(1), 85–106.

Dixit, A. K., Robert S. S., & Pindyck, R. S. (1994). *Investment under uncertainty*. Princeton, NJ: Princeton University Press.

Hlatshwayo, S., & Saxegaard, M. (2016). *The consequences of policy uncertainty: Disconnects and dilutions in the South African real effective exchange rate-export relationship* (International Monetary Fund Working Paper/16/113).

Kraft, H., Schwartz, E. S., & Weiss, F. (2013). *Growth options and firm valuations* (NBER Working Paper w18836).

Ndou, E., Gumata, N., & Ncube, M. (2017). *Global economic uncertainties and exchange rate shocks, Transmission Channels to the South African Economy*. Basingstoke: Palgrave Macmillan.

Stein, L. C. R., & Stone, E. C. (2013). *The effect of uncertainty on investment, hiring and R&D: Casual evidence from equity options*.

27

How Does Inflation Impact the Effects of Expansionary Monetary Policy and Fiscal Policies on Real GDP Growth?

Main Highlights

- Evidence indicates the magnitudes of the multiplier effects of expansionary monetary and fiscal policies on output are bigger in the low inflation environment and low economic policy uncertainty regime than in the high inflation regime. The high trend inflation and elevated economic policy uncertainty dampen the multiplier effects of expansionary policies.
- Therefore a low inflation and low economic policy uncertainty regime matters in the propagation of the stimulatory effects of expansionary policies on GDP growth.

27.1 Introduction

The current economic landscape is characterised by the concurrence of the heightened economic policy and political uncertainty, recurring credit ratings downgrades, recessionary growth environment, and subdued GDP growth outlook. At the same time, given that the economy

© The Author(s) 2019
E. Ndou and T. Mokoena, *Inequality, Output-Inflation Trade-Off and Economic Policy Uncertainty*,
https://doi.org/10.1007/978-3-030-19803-9_27

389

Fig. 27.1 The link between expansionary policy, inflation, and economic growth (*Source* Authors' drawing)

has entered the period where inflation is below 6%, there are calls to loosen monetary and fiscal policy stance. It is against this background which motivates us to revisit the theoretical foundations of expansionary monetary and fiscal policy multiplier effects on output. In addition, we ask: Does inflation impact the multiplier effects of expansionary monetary and fiscal policies on GDP growth? In addition, the chapter explores the role of the price stability mandate by using inflation regimes based on the 6% threshold. This requires a clear distinction between the high and the low inflation regimes.

In Fig. 27.1, an expansionary policy shock can have either a direct or indirect impact on economic growth. Indirectly, the transmission or pass-through of the expansionary policy effects may be impacted by inflation regimes, thereby also impacting the pricing behaviour of firm and inflation persistence before affecting economic growth. Hence, this analysis considers the role of inflation regimes.

Why is it important to revisit the subject of the policy multiplier effects on economic growth? Koelln et al. (1996) examined the extent to which fiscal and monetary policy multipliers decrease with rising trend inflation.[1] Ball et al. (1988) tested whether fiscal and monetary policy multipliers are smaller in countries with high inflation rates. These studies conclude that rising trend inflation impacts fiscal and monetary policy multiplier effects on economic growth. Hence, the objective of this chapter is to show that the fiscal and monetary policy multiplier effects

---

[1]Their work differed from that of Ball et al. (1988) and Defina (1999) by allowing for the differential effects of monetary policy and government spending. They test the new Keynesian proposition that sticky prices increase the effects of government spending and monetary policy on gross national product. They found little evidence of the new Keynesian sticky price model.

27 How Does Inflation Impact the Effects of Expansionary ... 391

on output depend on the inflation regimes. When inflation exceeds the 6% threshold, it is possible that the fiscal and monetary policy effects may be neutralised. The problem with generalising the inflation effects is similar to the *"sand"* and *"grease"* arguments of inflation. Hence, the analysis in this chapter shows that inflation effects cannot be generalised but should be contextualised within the 6% inflation threshold.

27.2 Empirical Evidence from Regime-Dependent Effects of Policy Multipliers

The analysis begins by estimating a bivariate VAR model using quarterly (Q) data from 1990Q1 to 2017Q4. The data is obtained from the South African Reserve Bank. The variables include annual GDP and either government consumption spending growth or changes in the repo rate. Government consumption spending captures the fiscal policy stance while the repo rate signifies the monetary policy stance. The models are estimated using two lags as selected by Akaike information criterion (AIC). To determine the role of inflation, the analysis uses a regime-dependent VAR model based on the inflation threshold of 6%. The models are estimated using 10,000 Monte Carlo draws. Two inflation regimes are considered: the low (high) inflation regime refers to inflation below or equal to (above) 6%. In addition, this approach captures the interaction between fiscal and monetary policies via the role of price stability based on inflation thresholds.

The impulse responses to expansionary monetary and fiscal policy shocks are shown in Fig. 27.2. GDP growth increases significantly due to expansionary fiscal and monetary policy shocks in the low inflation regime compared to the high inflation regime. In addition, the responses in the high inflation regime, although positive on impact, are insignificant. A three-variable model is also estimated and captures the direct interaction between fiscal and monetary policy variables. Evidence shows that allowing for the interaction between fiscal and monetary policy does not alter the results.

Does the inclusion of economic policy uncertainty impact the robustness of the preceding findings? To answer this question, the

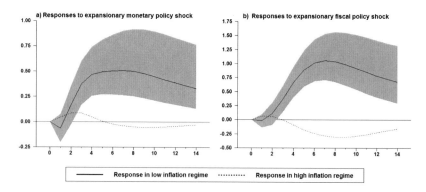

Fig. 27.2 GDP growth responses to expansionary policies (*Note* The grey shaded bands denote the 16th and 84th percentile confidence bands. *Source* Authors' calculations)

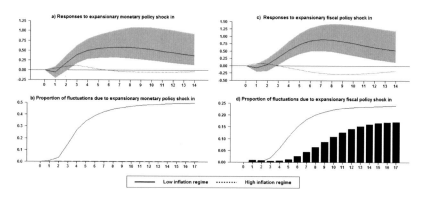

Fig. 27.3 Responses and the proportion of fluctuations due to expansionary policies (*Note* The grey shaded bands denote the 16th and 84th percentile confidence bands. *Source* Authors' calculations)

model is extended to include the role of annual growth in the South African economic policy uncertainty. Figure 27.3 confirms that expansionary monetary and fiscal policies have a pronounced positive impact on GDP growth in the low inflation regime compared to the high regime.

In addition, the proportion in fluctuations induced by these shocks in Fig. 27.3c and d is larger in the low inflation regime. This shows that the low inflation regime plays an important role in the transmission of the stimulatory effects to GDP growth. Therefore, the inflation threshold and the resulting inflation regimes matter. It follows that inflation levels exert differential effects on the transmission of policy effects on economic growth.

27.3 Evidence from a Counterfactual VAR Approach

This chapter further applies a counterfactual VAR approach to determine what would have happened to GDP growth, following an expansionary policy shock, when inflation is shut off in the model compared to when it is allowed to operate. This section estimates a three-variable VAR model which includes GDP growth, either a fiscal or monetary policy variable and inflation. The policy variable refers to either annual growth in government consumption spending or changes in the repo rate, which are included individually in the model. The inflation rate is shut off in the model not to transmit the expansionary shock effects to economic growth when calculating a counterfactual VAR impulse response. The VAR model is estimated using two lags and 10,000 Monte Carlo draws.

Evidence in Fig. 27.4a and c indicates that the counterfactual GDP growth responses increase more than the actual responses to expansionary policy shocks. This shows that high inflation lowers the policy multiplier effects. The amplification effects in Fig. 27.4b and d due to inflation are negative, indicating that high inflation dampens the fiscal and monetary policy multipliers. This evidence confirms that low inflation is ideal for the realisation of maximum effects of expansionary policy shocks on GDP growth.

Furthermore, Fig. 27.5 shows the role of the low inflation regime in transmitting expansionary policy shocks to GDP growth. The results are based on a similar model used for estimating the preceding results but the responses are conditioned on the low inflation regime. Actual GDP growth responses increase more than the counterfactual responses, indicating that the low inflation regime enhances the stimulatory and multiplier effects of expansionary policies.

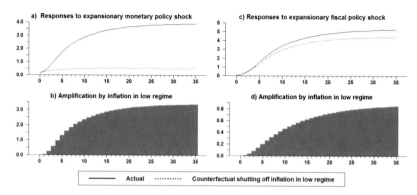

Fig. 27.4 Accumulated effects of inflation on monetary and fiscal policy multipliers (*Source* Authors' calculations)

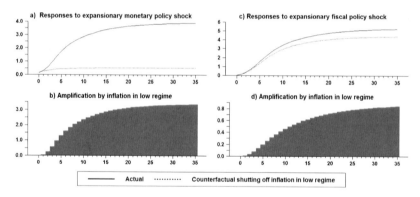

Fig. 27.5 GDP growth responses and the role of the low inflation regime (*Source* Authors' calculations)

27.4 The Multiplier Effects of Expansionary Monetary Policy and the Inflation Regimes

What are the direct effects of inflation on the size of multipliers effects of expansionary monetary policy shocks on GDP growth? This section explores this via three shock scenarios: (1) less persistent, (2) constant change, and (3) persistently rising shocks.

27 How Does Inflation Impact the Effects of Expansionary ...

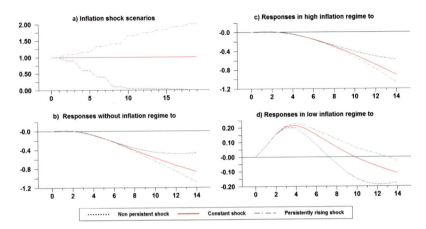

Fig. 27.6 Responses of expansionary monetary policy multiplier effects on positive inflation shock (*Source* Authors' calculations)

This approach distinguishes whether the effects based on the shock scenarios matter and the implications for policy rate adjustments. Furthermore, to capture the effects of positive inflation shocks on the multiplier effects requires estimating a two-year rolling window impact of the (1) negative repo rate changes on GDP growth and (2) the effect of government consumption spending on GDP growth. Thereafter, bivariate VAR models with inflation and the rolling expansionary monetary policy multiplier coefficients are estimated. The bivariate VAR model is estimated using two lags and 10,000 Monte Carlo draws.[2]

The responses of the expansionary monetary policy multiplier effects on economic growth to positive inflation shocks are shown in Fig. 27.6. They indicate that positive inflation shocks have different effects on policy multipliers in different inflation regimes. Positive inflation shocks reduce the multiplier effects in the high inflation regime, in contrast to the positive effects in the low inflation regime. This indicates that the inflation threshold of 6% matters for the transmission of expansionary monetary policy shocks to real output.

---

[2]This approach differs from Ball et al. (1988) and other studies that uses cross-country analysis.

27.5 Inflation Effects on the Expansionary Fiscal Policy Multiplier Effects

Similarly, Fig. 27.7 shows that positive inflation shocks impact the multiplier effects of expansionary fiscal policy on output growth based on the bivariate VAR model results.

A positive inflation shock has a negative impact on expansionary fiscal policy multiplier effects without imposing inflation regimes. On the other hand, a positive inflation shock reduces the fiscal policy multiplier effects in the high inflation regime. This contrasts with the positive effects in the low inflation regime.

27.6 Economic Policy Uncertainty and the Transmission of Expansionary Policy Shocks

Given the low inflation regime, do economic policy uncertainty regimes impact the multiplier effects of expansionary policy shocks on GDP growth? The economic policy uncertainty is obtained from Hlatshwayo and Saxegaard (2016) as indicated in the previous chapters.

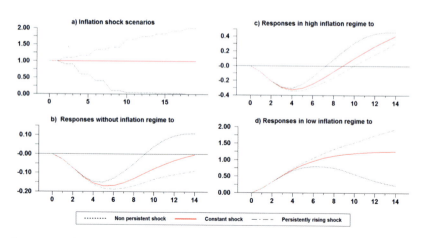

Fig. 27.7 Inflation effects on the impact of expansionary fiscal policy on GDP (*Source* Authors' calculations)

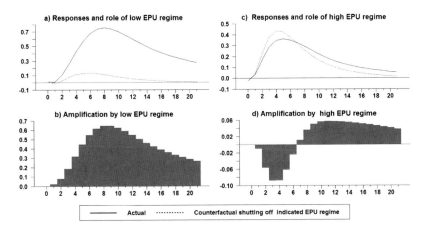

Fig. 27.8 GDP growth responses to monetary policy shocks in the low inflation regime (*Note* EPU denotes economic policy uncertainty. *Source* Authors' calculations)

The economic policy uncertainty changes are divided into two regimes based on whether growth in economic policy uncertainty is positive or negative. A high (low) uncertainty regime refers to positive (negative) annual growth in economic policy uncertainty index. Figure 27.8 shows that in the low inflation regime the reduced (or low) economic policy uncertainty magnifies the multiplier effects of the expansionary monetary policy on GDP growth.

This means that low inflation and low economic policy uncertainty reinforce each other and have a positive effect in the transmission of expansionary fiscal and monetary policy shocks on real economic activity.

27.7 Conclusion and Policy Implications

This chapter determined whether the multiplier effects of expansionary monetary and fiscal policy multipliers on output are affected by the (1) inflation regimes, (2) trend inflation and (3) the economic policy uncertainty regimes. We find that GDP growth increases significantly in the low inflation regime compared to the high regime, following expansionary policy shocks. In addition, the proportion in fluctuations induced by these shocks is larger in the low inflation regimes. This shows that the low inflation regime is important for the transmission of stimulatory effects of expansionary monetary and fiscal policy to GDP growth. Counterfactual analysis shows that trend inflation reduces the size of multiplier effects of expansionary policies on GDP growth. The evidence in this chapter asserts that low inflation below the 6% threshold, combined with low economic policy uncertainty, is ideal for the realisation of maximum effects of expansionary policy shocks on GDP growth. Thus low inflation and low economic policy uncertainty regimes reinforce each to magnify the real activity reaction to expansionary fiscal and monetary policy shocks.

The policy implication is that lower inflation than 6%, coupled with the low economic policy uncertainty, magnifies the stimulatory effects of expansionary policies on GDP growth. Persistently high and rising inflation dampen the policy multipliers. In policy terms, this suggests that price stability matters for the realisation of maximum size of policy multipliers.

References

Ball, L., Mankiw, N. G., & Romer, D. (1988). The new Keynesian economics and the output-inflation tradeoff. *Brooking Papers on Economic Activity, 1,* 1–65.

Defina, R. H. (1999). International evidence on a new Keynesian theory of the output-inflation trade-off. *Journal of Money, Credit and Banking, 23*(3), 410–422.

Hlatshwayo, S., & Saxegaard, M. (2016). *The consequences of policy uncertainty: Disconnects and dilutions in the South African real effective exchange rate-export relationship* (IMF WP Number 16/113).

Koelln, K., Rush, M., & Walso, D. (1996). Do government policy multipliers decrease with inflation? *Journal of Monetary Economics, 38,* 495–505.

28

The Time-Varying Pass-Through of the Lending Rate Responses to the Repo Rate Changes and Loan Intermediation Mark-Ups

Main Highlights

- We find that the interest rate pass-through and the loan intermediation mark-up move in opposite directions.
- A high (low) mark-up is accompanied by a low (high) pass-through. The interest rate pass-through coefficient is higher pre-2009M1 and the mark-up is lower pre-2009 compared to other samples.
- The reduced interest rate pass-through and higher loan intermediation mark-up post-2009 might indicate the role of the risk premium attached to weak and low economic growth and the accompanying instabilities during this period.
- In addition, the results show that the size of the interest rate pass-through and loan intermediation mark-up differs across the monetary policy tightening and loosening cycles.

© The Author(s) 2019
E. Ndou and T. Mokoena, *Inequality, Output-Inflation Trade-Off and Economic Policy Uncertainty*,
https://doi.org/10.1007/978-3-030-19803-9_28

399

28.1 Introduction

This chapter estimates the time-varying association between loan intermediation mark-ups and the interest rate pass-through and shows the nature of their associations. Second, we determine whether the sizes of interest pass-through and loan intermediation mark-ups during the policy rate tightening and loosening periods are similar or different.

The transmission of monetary policy shocks to the real sector depends in part on the bank behaviour and the monetary policy cycle. As far as the bank behaviour is concerned, the nature of how banks change lending rates in response to changes in the banks' cost of funds is influenced by the changes in the monetary policy stance. For monetary policy actions to be effective, changes in the repo rate should, ideally, be completely passed through to the lending rates after the announcement of the monetary policy stance. Depending on the interest rate cycle, the pass-through may not be complete in the sense that changes in the repo rate may not be fully passed through to the bank lending rates. A complete and symmetric pass-through will support monetary policy objectives. Moreover, the manner in which banks set lending rates will affect their margins, profitability and the soundness of the financial system, bank decisions regarding yields paid on their assets and liabilities influence expenditure and investment decisions by depositors and borrowers (de Bont 2005).

The adjustment of lending rates to policy rates may be rigid and asymmetric. This is due to factors that include fixed menu costs, adjustment costs, high switching costs, imperfect competition, credit rationing and the outcome of implicit risk-sharing arrangements between banks and their customers. Several studies in the pass-through literature generally find that lending rates adjust sluggishly to changes in money-market rates, for various reasons. For instance, Stiglitz and Weiss (1981) argue that due to asymmetric information problems banks may choose to, instead of raising lending rates, set their interest rate below the equilibrium rate and ration credit. Therefore, credit rationing would lead to upward stickiness in lending rates. Hannah and Berger (1991) and Cottarelli and Kourelis (1994), however, suggest that given the adjustment costs associated with re-quoting prices of financial products, banks may be reluctant to filter changes in market rates. Klemperer (1987) provides that the switching costs borne by customers when switching financial products or institutions may tend to make them less likely to change products even when lending rates are slow to adjust. Berger and Udell (1992) and Burgstaller and Schaler (2010), however, contend that loan rate stickiness may be the outcome of implicit risk-sharing arrangements between banks and their customers, with banks insuring their customers against interest rate risk. All of the literature, however, points out that the existence of such rigidities may impede the speed of monetary policy transmission and ultimately alter its desired effects on the real economy.[1]

The theory of an asymmetric pass-through has been investigated by authors such as Hannan and Berger (1991), Neumark and Sharpe (1992) and later Scholnick (1996). These papers suggest that there may be an asymmetric pass-through from an increase in a money-market rate and a decrease in a money-market rate.[2] A downward rigidity in lending rates has been reasoned by the collusion or similar uncompetitive market practices, the reasoning being that banks expect high costs from the possible breakdown in collusive arrangements and this can lead

---

[1]Studies such as Mojon (2000), Heinemann and Schüler (2002), Sander and Kleimeier (2004), Cottarelli and Kourelis (1994) and Borio and Fritz (1995) have examined differences in the pass-through across countries. Their findings suggest that the differences in the pass-through across countries are generally associated with differences related to structural factors such as the level of concentration or financial market characteristics. While studies that have focused on micro-level analysis within countries, such as De Graeve et al. (2004) relate the pass-through to factors such as an institution's size, refinancing conditions and the extent of business conducted with non-bank institutions within the economy.

[2]With regard to pass-through studies conducted in South Africa, Sander and Kleimeier (2006) find a small degree of stickiness in lending rates in response to changes in money-market rates on impact; owever, they observe that anticipated changes were adjusted almost immediately. Aziakpono and Wilson (2010) found that South African commercial banks are more rigid in adjusting their lending rates upwards in response to positive shocks in the official rate. This finding supports the negative customer reaction hypothesis.

to downward rigidity in lending rates. On the contrary, an upward rigidity in lending rates may arise from the adverse customer reaction hypothesis, which is based on the notion that the greater upward rigidity is associated with customers' unfavourable reaction to unstable lending rates.[3]

28.2 What Is the Nature of the Association Between Loan Intermediation Mark-Ups and the Interest Rate Pass-Through?

As shown in Fig. 28.1, the spread between the lending rate and the repo rate increased post-2009. In addition, the size of the spread during the tightening phase in the 2006–2008 period is lower relative to that in the 2014–2017 period. We determine the existence of a long-run relationship between the lending rate and the repo rate using the Engle-Granger and Johansen cointegration tests. First, we test for the stationarity of the variables and test for the existence of a cointegrating relationship. We use monthly (M) data from 2000M1 to 2017M7. The unit root test confirms that the lending rate and the repo rate are non-stationary. All data used in this analysis are obtained from the South African Reserve Bank.

The Engle-Granger and Johansen cointegration tests in Table 28.1 in the appendix indicate that the lending rate and the repo rate are cointegrated. Hence, it is appropriate to use the OLS approach to estimate the pass-through of the policy rate to lending rate in using Eq. (28.1). In Eq. (28.1), θ measures the loan intermediation mark-up,

---

[3]The results showed that, on average, mortgages rates responded more quickly to changes in the costs of funds than business lending rates. The speed at which the lending rates go back to their equilibrium relationship with funding costs differed across the lending markets. Chong et al. (2006) found that the adjustment speeds of administered rates in response to changes in the benchmark market rate in Singapore varied across financial products and were asymmetric. Based on their findings, they concluded that upward rigidity in lending rates in Singapore was consistent with the credit rationing hypothesis as opposed to menu costs, imperfect competition or the switching costs hypothesis. In New Zealand, Liu et al. (2011) found asymmetries in the initial short-run response of bank lending rates to changes in funding rates. They found asymmetries in the initial short-run response of bank rates and mortgage rates adjusted downwards more rapidly than upwards.

28 The Time-Varying Pass-Through of the Lending Rate ...

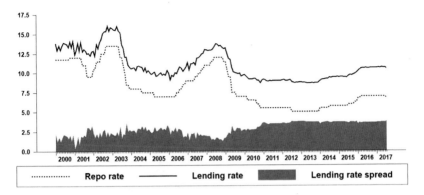

Fig. 28.1 Weighted lending rate and repo rate (*Source* Authors' calculations and South African Reserve Bank)

δ measures the degree of the pass-through in the long run. If the interest rate pass-through is complete then $\delta = 1$, whereas if it is incomplete when $\delta < 1$, and u_t is the disturbance term measuring the deviations of the lending rate from its equilibrium path. The Crisis_dummy$_t$ refers to dummy which equals to one from 2007M7 to the end of the sample and zero otherwise. The dummy captures periods of economic instability, volatile and weak economic growth, heightened economic policy and political uncertainty, and periods of credit rating downgrades.

The existence of an incomplete pass-through may indicate that banks have some degree of market power. Factors that affect market power include the existence of switching costs, asymmetric information costs, and the preconditions for a degree of monopoly power and administrated pricing (Niggle 1987).

$$\text{lending\_rate}_t = \theta + \delta * \text{Reporate}_t + \rho * \text{Crisis\_dummy}_t + u_t \quad (28.1)$$

The interest rate pass-through and the loan intermediation mark-up are estimated using Eq. (28.1). To establish whether there have been significant changes in the relationship between the repo rate and the lending rate, we divide the full sample of 2000M1–2017M7 into 2000M1–2008M12 and 2009M1–2017M7. The tests reject that the pass-through is equal to one for the whole sample and sub-samples. This means that the interest rate pass-through is incomplete.

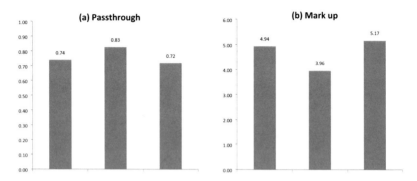

Fig. 28.2 The size of the interest rate pass-through and loan intermediation mark-ups (*Note* Second bar is pre-2009M1 samples. First bar is full sample. The third bar is post-2009 sample. *Source* Authors' calculations)

Figure 28.2 shows the sizes of the interest rate pass-through and the loan intermediation mark-ups for the full sample and sub-samples. The results show that the pass-through coefficient is higher pre-2009M1 and the mark-up is lower pre-2009 compared to other samples. These estimates indicate the pass-through and mark-up move in different directions. A high (low) mark-up is accompanied by a low (high) pass-through. The reduced pass-through post-2009 might indicate the role of the risk premium attached to weak and low economic growth and the accompanying instabilities during this period.

28.3 Are the Sizes of the Interest Rate Pass-Through and Loan Intermediation Mark-Up Coefficients Similar During the Episodes of Monetary Policy Tightening and Loosening?

This section estimates the interest rate pass-through and loan intermediation mark-ups during phases of monetary policy tightening and loosening. In Fig. 28.3a, the interest rate pass-through coefficient is bigger in the second tightening period compared to other periods. The statistical tests do not reject a complete interest rate pass-through of

28 The Time-Varying Pass-Through of the Lending Rate ...

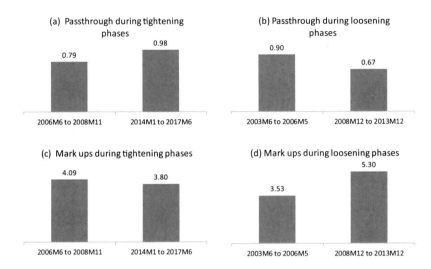

Fig. 28.3 The size of pass-through and mark-ups during the tightening and loosening phases (*Source* Authors' calculations)

the repo rate changes to the lending rates during the 2014M1–2017M6 tightening period. However, the complete pass-through is not rejected during the 2006M6–2008M11 episode. These results may partly explain why credit growth was higher prior to the tightening episode of 2006M6–2008M11. Furthermore, the results suggest that the pricing of credit may have been slightly cheaper pre-2009 as shown by the lower loan intermediation mark-up in Fig. 28.3.

We ask: during the policy rate loosening phases, are there differential interest rate pass-through and loan intermediation mark-up effects? In Fig. 28.4b the interest rate pass-through (loan intermediation mark-up) coefficient is higher (lower) during the period 2003M6–2006M5 compared to the 2008M12–2013M12 policy rate loosening period. This analysis reveals that the size of the interest rate pass-through and loan intermediation mark-up differs across the monetary policy tightening and loosening cycles. Furthermore, Fig. 28.4 shows that there is a high interest rate pass-through during periods of policy rate tightening than policy rate loosening phases. Loan intermediation mark-ups increase during the policy rate loosening compared to the policy-tightening

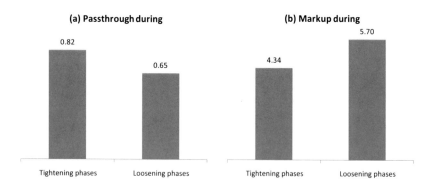

Fig. 28.4 The size of interest pass-through and loan intermediation mark-ups during the policy rate tightening and loosening periods (*Source* Authors' calculations)

phases. This suggests that banks pass on cost increases more than cost decreases. In addition, banks find it easier to increase loan intermediation mark-ups during periods of policy loosening compared to policy tightening. This is indicative of the asymmetric effects in the lending rate adjustment to increases and decreases in the repo rate changes. This motivates the need to determine the extent of the amount asymmetry and adjustment asymmetries which is done in later sections.

28.4 Evidence from Time-Varying Approach

We established that the sizes of the interest rate pass-through and loan intermediation mark-up coefficients differed across monetary policy cycles. This suggests that the assumption of the constant pass-through and loan intermediation mark-up coefficients (1) might not be realistic and (2) might not fully capture the transmission of policy rate changes to lending rates. Hence, we use a time-varying Eq. (28.2) using the state space approach to estimate the time-varying pass-through and loan intermediation mark-up coefficients. Where β_{0t} is mark-up, β_{1t} is the pass-through coefficients of the repo rate and β_{2t} is impact of a crisis dummy. This approach differs from the rolling window regression which uses an arbitrary choice of the number of rolling windows which can impact the results.

$$\text{lending\_rate}_t = \beta_{0t} + \beta_{1t} * \text{Repo\_rate}_t$$
$$+ \beta_{2t} * \text{Crisis\_dummy}_t + \varepsilon_t \quad (28.2)$$

$$\beta_{it} = \beta_{it-1} + \varepsilon_t$$

The estimated time-varying interest rate pass-through and loan intermediation mark-up coefficients are shown in Fig. 28.5a. In general, the results show that the interest rate pass-through was high during the 2003–2007 period. Thereafter, it declined slightly in the 2007–2010 period and further declined in 2011–2013. However, the interest rate pass-through increased after 2014 until 2017M6 which coincided with the interest rate tightening cycle. Generally, the results of the time-varying interest rate pass-through and loan intermediation mark-ups confirm earlier findings that they tend to move in opposite direction. It is also evident that, whereas the margin between the time-varying interest rate pass-through and loan intermediation mark-up narrowed post-2011, it seems to be widening again since 2016, although it is still below the levels recorded during the 2001–2006 period.

For the reasonableness test, Fig. 28.5b–f shows the relationship between (i) the repo rate and time-varying loan intermediation mark-up, and (ii) the time-varying interest rate pass-through and the repo rate. The results show that the interest rate pass-through moved

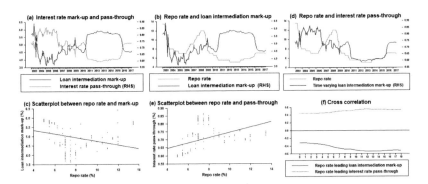

Fig. 28.5 Time-varying interest rate pass-through, loan intermediation mark-up and the repo rate (*Source* Authors' calculations)

in the opposite direction of the changes in the repo rate especially during the 2003–2008 period. Thereafter, the interest rate pass-through seemed to be moving in tandem with the policy rate changes. We established that there was an inverse relationship between time-varying interest rate pass-through and the loan intermediation mark-up. It is shown in Fig. 28.5b that the loan intermediation mark-up moves in the opposite direction to the policy rate changes, especial post-2009. In Fig. 28.5c, d, there is a generally negative association between the repo rate and the loan intermediation mark-up; and the interest rate pass-through is positively associated with the repo rate.

Furthermore, the lead-lag relationships in Fig. 28.5f indicate that increases in the repo rate precede the increase in the interest rate pass-through, while increases in the repo rate lead to a decline in the loan intermediation mark-up. These results corroborate earlier findings that banks also find it easier to increase loan intermediation mark-ups during periods of policy loosening compared to policy tightening. Whereas, banks pass-through more of the repo rate increases to lending rates compared to the repo rate declines.

28.4.1 The Relationship Between the Time-Varying Interest Rate Pass-Through with the Prevailing Economic Conditions?

This section conducts further reasonableness tests by assessing how the time-varying interest rate pass-through is associated with the selected economic indicators. We assess the relationship between the time-varying interest rate pass-through, the lending rate spread, the credit conditions, the credit growth, and the retail sales growth. The scatterplots in Fig. 28.6b shows that there is a negative relationship between the time-varying pass-through coefficient and the lending rate spread (defined as the difference between the weighted lending rate and the repo rate). The negative relationship indicates that an increase in the lending rate spread is accompanied by a decrease in the interest rate pass-through.

28 The Time-Varying Pass-Through of the Lending Rate … 409

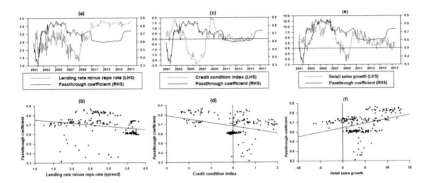

Fig. 28.6 The relationship between lending rate spread and time-varying pass-through (*Source* Authors' calculations)

Furthermore, Fig. 28.6d shows that there is a negative relationship between the credit conditions index[4] and the time-varying interest rate pass-through. The negative relationship is consistent with tight credit conditions resulting in a decline in the interest rate pass-through effects. Alternatively, this may mean that loosening in the credit conditions will raise the pass-through. Similarly, Fig. 28.6f shows that there is a positive relationship between retail sales and the time-varying interest rate pass-through. Thus, improved economic activity results in an increase in the time-varying interest rate pass-through.

To conclude the reasonableness tests, Fig. 28.7 shows that there is a positive relationship between the time-varying interest rate pass-through and credit growth. Furthermore, Fig. 28.7b, d shows that periods of a low (high) interest rate pass-through are associated with low (high) credit growth. Low interest rate pass-through during monetary policy loosening periods implies that credit is still expensive, and this dampens credit growth. These relationships indicate that business cycles, policy rate cycles, and the credit conditions cycles, play an important role in determining the extent of the interest rate pass-through of the repo rate changes to the lending rates. Thus, this analysis confirms that the time-varying interest rate pass-through is reasonable and can be used for policy analysis.

---

[4]The credit conditions index is sourced from Gumata and Ndou (2018). Bank credit extension and real economic activity in South Africa.

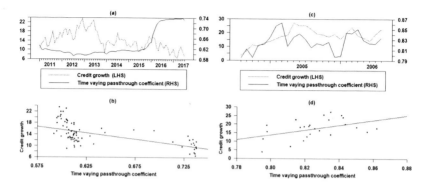

Fig. 28.7 The relationship between credit growth and the time-varying interest rate pass-through (*Source* Authors' calculations)

28.5 Conclusion and Policy Implications

We find that the interest rate pass-through and the loan intermediation mark-up move in opposite directions. A high (low) mark-up is accompanied by a low (high) pass-through. Furthermore, the interest rate pass-through coefficient is higher pre-2009M1 and the mark-up is lower pre-2009 compared to other samples. The reduced interest rate pass-through and higher loan intermediation mark-up post-2009 might indicate the role of the risk premium attached to the weak and low economic growth and the accompanying instabilities during this period. In addition, the results show that the size of the interest rate pass-through and loan intermediation mark-up differs across the monetary policy tightening and loosening cycles. Banks also find it easier to increase loan intermediation mark-ups during periods of policy loosening compared to policy tightening. This is indicative of the asymmetric effects in the lending rate adjustment to increases and decreases in the repo rate changes. Nonetheless, the results show that the magnitudes of asymmetry are not significantly large.

Appendix

See Tables 28.1 and 28.2.

Table 28.1 Cointegration tests

Null hypothesis: Series are not cointegrated
Automatic lags specification based on Schwarz criterion (maxlag = 14)

Dependent	tau-statistic	Prob.*	z-statistic	Prob.*
Lending rate	−3.556110	0.0307	−26.55645	0.0116
Repo rate	−3.510921	0.0346	−25.69323	0.0142

*MacKinnon (1996) *p*-values
Source Authors calculations

Unrestricted cointegration rank test (Trace)

Hypothesised No. of CE(s)	Eigenvalue	Trace Statistic
None *	0.078969	19.47302
At most 1	0.010852	2.280421

Note Trace test indicates 1 cointegrating eqn(s) at the 0.05 level
*Denotes rejection of the hypothesis at the 0.05 level
**MacKinnon-Haug-Michelis (1999) *p*-values

Unrestricted cointegration rank test (Maximum Eigenvalue)

Hypothesised No. of CE(s)	Eigenvalue	Max-Eigen Statistic
None *	0.078969	17.19260
At most 1	0.010852	2.280421

Note Max-eigenvalue test indicates 1 cointegrating eqn(s) at the 0.05 level
*Denotes rejection of the hypothesis at the 0.05 level
**MacKinnon-Haug-Michelis (1999) *p*-values
Source Authors calculation

Table 28.2 Cointegration and asymmetry tests based on MTAR

	Coefficient (std-error)	Decision
Direction of adjustment in change in spreads		
Impact when $\Delta Spread_{t-1} \geq -0.0402$ ($_1$)	−0.0237 (0.0467)	
Impact when $\Delta Spread_{t-1} < -0.0402$ ($_2$)	−0.2326 (0.0806)	
Threshold of $\Delta Spread_{t-1}$	−0.0402	
Null hypothesis of no cointegration		
[b]ϕ ... $\rho_1 = \rho_2 = 0$	4.1060	There is cointegration
Null hypothesis of symmetry		
[c]$\rho_1 = \rho_2$	5.0481	There is asymmetric adjustment

[a]T-max exceeds EG statistics at 5%, [b]ϕ exceeds EG statistics at 10%, [c]Testing equality which implies symmetric adjustment
Source Authors calculation

References

Aziakpono, M. J., & Wilson, M. K. (2010). *Interest rate pass-through and monetary policy regimes in South Africa*. University of Stellenbosch Business School and University of Johannesburg.

Berger, A., & Udell, G. (1992). Some evidence on the empirical signifcance of credit rationing. *Journal of Political Economy, 100*(5), 1047–1077.

Borio, C. E. V., & Fritz, W. (1995). *The response of short-term bank lending rates to policy rates: A cross country perspective*. Bank of International Settlements.

Burgstaller, J., & Scharler, J. (2010). How do bank lending rates and the supply of loans react to shifts in loan demand in the UK? *Journal of Policy Modelling, 32*(2010), 778–791.

Chan, K. S. (1993). Consistency and limiting distribution of the least squares estimator of a threshold autoregressive model. *Annals of Statistics, 21*(1), 520–533.

Chong, B. S., Liu, M.-H., & Shrestha, K. (2006). Monetary transmission via the administered interest rate channel. *Journal of Banking & Finance, 30*, 1467–1484.

Cottarelli, C., & Kourelis, A. (1994, December). Financial structure, bank lending rates, and the transmission mechanism of monetary policy. *Staff Papers—International Monetary Fund (IMF) 41*(4), 587–623.

28 The Time-Varying Pass-Through of the Lending Rate ... 413

de Bont, G. J. (2005). Interest rate pass-through: Empirical results from the Euro Area. *German Economic Review, 6*(1), 37–78.

De Graeve, F., De Jonghe, O., and Vander Vennet, R. (2004). *The determinants of pass-through of market conditions to bank retail interest rates in belgium* (Working Paper 261), Ghent University.

Enders, W., & Siklos, P. (2001). Cointegration and threshold adjustment. *Journal of Business and Economic Statistics, 19*(2001), 166–176.

Hannan, T., & Berger, A. (1991). The rigidity of prices: Evidence from the banking industry. *American Economic Review, 81,* 938–945.

Heinemann, F., & Schüller, M. (2002) *Integration benefits on EU retail credit markets—Evidence from interest rate pass-through* (Zentrum für Europäische Wirtschaftsforschung GmbH [ZEW] Discussion Paper No. 02–26).

Klemperer, P. (1987). Markets with consumer switching costs. *Quarterly Journal of Economics, 102*(2), 375–394.

Liu, M.-H., Dimitruis, M., & Alireza, T. (2011). Asymmetric information and price competition in small business lending. *Journal of Banking & Finance, 35,* 2189–2196.

Mojon, B. (2000). *Financial structure and the interest rate channel of ECB monetary policy* (European Central Bank, Working Paper Series—Working Paper No. 40).

Neumark, D., & Sharpe, S. A. (1992, May). Market structure and the nature of price rigidity: Evidence from the market for consumer. *The Quarterly Journal of Economics, 107*(2), 657–680.

Niggle, C. J. (1987). A comment on the markup theory of bank loan rates. *Journal of Post Keynesian Economics, 9*(4), 629–631.

Sander, H., & Kleimeier, H. S. (2004). Convergence in euro-zone retail banking? What interest rate pass-through tells us about monetary policy transmission, competition and integration. *Journal of International Money and Finance, 23*(3), 461–492.

Sander, H., & Kleimeier, S. (2006). *Interest rate pass-through in the common monetary area of the SACU countries.* METEOR (Maastricht research school of Economics of Technology and Organizations). Maastricht University, Tongersestraat 53, 6211 LM Maastricht, The Netherlands.

Scholnick. (1996). Asymmetric adjustment of commercial bank interest rate in Malaysia an Singapore. *Journal of International Money and Finance, 15*(3), 485–496.

Scholnik, B. (2006). Asymmetric adjustment of commercial bank interest rate in Malaysia and Singapore. *Journal of International Money and Finance, 15*(3), 485–496.

Stiglitz, J. E., & Weiss, A. (1981). Credit rationing in markets with imperfect information. *The American Economic Review, 71*(3), 393–410.

Valadkhani, A., & Anwar, S. (2012). Interest rate pass-through and the asymmetric relationship between cash rate and the mortgage rate. *Economic record, 88*(282), 341–350.

Yildrim, D. (2012). *Interest rate pass-through to Turkish lending rates: A threshold cointegration analysis* (EC Working Chapters in Economics 12/7).

29

Do Economic Policy Uncertainty Shocks Impact the Bank Lending Rate Margins?

Main Highlights

- Evidence indicates that positive economic policy uncertainty shocks raise bank lending rate margins. By contrast, the negative economic policy uncertainty shocks lower bank lending rate margins.
- Counterfactual VAR evidence shows that inflation below 6% dampens the actual rise in the bank lending rate margins following positive economic policy uncertainty shocks.
- Thus policymakers should consider that, a large reduction in the repo rate than expected is needed to overcome the mitigating effects of elevated economic policy uncertainty in raising the bank lending rate margins even in a low inflation environment.

29.1 Introduction

The repo rate was reduced by 25 basis points in the Monetary Policy Committee meeting held in July 2017. Under normal circumstances this reduction should translate into an equivalent decrease in

© The Author(s) 2019
E. Ndou and T. Mokoena, *Inequality, Output-Inflation Trade-Off and Economic Policy Uncertainty*,
https://doi.org/10.1007/978-3-030-19803-9_29

the lending rate, ceteris paribus. However, at the time of the unexpected policy rate cut, based on market reactions, the economic policy and political uncertainty was deemed to be high. At the same time, the South African Reserve Bank (SARB) forecasts indicated an expectation of low inflation outlook. Could it be that high economic policy uncertainty impacted the bank lending rate margins, thereby preventing the reduction in these margins? Is there a possibility that inflation above 6% affects the way the bank lending rate margins respond to positive economic policy uncertainty shocks relative to when inflation is below 6%? This chapter brings together the link between economic policy uncertainty (EPU) and the lending rate margins and shows the role of inflation thresholds above and below 6%.

It is important to look at EPU and bank lending rate margins relationship for several reasons. The bank lending rate margins are an important component of the overall cost of capital, which is negatively related to investment. Yet, an increase in the cost of capital due to high political uncertainty may force firms to postpone the hard to reverse investment decisions until significant political uncertainty is dissolved (Bloom et al. 2007). In addition, when political uncertainty affects firms' cash flow, lenders may demand extra compensation for bearing the additional political risk (Pastor and Veronesi 2013). Furthermore, increased political uncertainty affects changes in firms' future cash flow and the associated firm's default risk (Nini et al. 2012). The cost of debt is also related to firm's investment decisions and performance.[1] The bank lending rate margins do not depend on the repo rate adjustment alone. Given the high economic policy and political uncertainty environment, it is plausible that the pass-through and efficacy of the lending rate channel of expansionary monetary policy transmission can be

---

[1]Indeed, evidence in Francis et al. (2014) indicates that elevated political uncertainty impacts the firms' level of investments. In addition, elevated political uncertainty influences firms' costs of bank loans by adding extra basis points on margins. These authors further show that lenders have additional advantage in pricing a borrower's future political exposure. Moreover, from the credit supply side, those lenders with higher political exposure will demand additional loan margins.

impacted by increased EPU. It is possible that the size of either the mitigating or magnifying effects on the pass-through of the reduction in the policy rate to the lending rate by elevated economic policy uncertainty depends on the inflation regimes.

This analysis differs from Francis et al.'s (2014) objective and methodology by filling the following gaps. None of the earlier analysis has shown, that EPU effects on bank lending rate margins could be constrained by the inflation regimes. The chapter fills academic gaps by showing the extent to which the inflation regimes matter for the transmission of economic policy uncertainty shocks to the bank lending rate margins using counterfactual VAR analysis.

Evidence shows that price stability, as measured by where inflation is relative to 6%, matters for the transmission of economic policy uncertainty shocks to the bank lending rate margins. In addition, evidence shows that the bank lending rate margins response to positive economic policy uncertainty shock would rise less when inflation is below 6% than when inflation is above 6%.

29.2 Do Bank Lending Rate Margins React to Economic Policy Uncertainty Shocks?

This chapter begins the analysis by examining the direct effects of economic policy uncertainty shock on the bank lending rate margins given by the gap between weighted lending rates and the repo rate. The analysis uses quarterly (Q) data spanning 2001Q1 to 2016Q1 obtained from the SARB. The section estimates bivariate VAR models which include quarter-on-quarter growth in the EPU and bank lending rate margins as endogenous variables. GDP growth and consumer price inflation (*inflation*) are exogenous variables. The models are estimated using 1 lag and 10,000 Monte Carlo draws. The EPU index is obtained from Hlatshwayo and Saxegaard (2016) as indicated in the previous chapters.

Do the low and high economic policy uncertainty regimes matter? To answer this question, the analysis separates the EPU regimes into

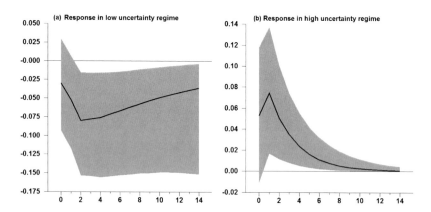

Fig. 29.1 Bank lending rate margins responses to economic policy uncertainty shocks according to uncertainty regimes (*Note* The grey shaded area denotes the 16th and 84th percentile confidence bands. *Source* Authors' calculations)

low and high uncertainty regimes. The low uncertainty regime denotes a region of *negative* EPU growth. By contrast, the high uncertainty regime denotes the region of positive EPU growth. In Fig. 29.1, the negative EPU shock lowers the bank lending rate margins in the low uncertainty regime. By contrast, positive EPU shocks raise the bank lending rate margins in the high EPU regime. This evidence shows that EPU regimes matter for the evolution of the bank lending rate margins.

We apply a robustness test of the results by using EPU dummy indicators rather than uncertainty regimes. We create a negative (positive) uncertainty dummy which equals to negative (positive) annual growth in EPU and zero otherwise. These two dummy variables are included in the model separately when replacing the EPU variable in the preceding models. Figure 29.2 shows the responses to negative and positive EPU shocks based on the dummy variable approach. A negative EPU shock lowers the bank lending rate margins significantly. By contrast, a positive EPU shock raises the bank lending rate margins.

Thus, evidence in this section concludes that EPU dynamics drive the bank lending rate margins. In policy terms, this implies that

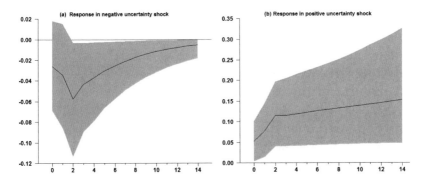

Fig. 29.2 Bank lending rate margins responses to negative and positive economic policy uncertainty shocks (*Note* The grey shaded area denotes the 16th and 84th percentile confidence bands. *Source* Authors' calculations)

bank lending rate margins may fail to decline very much following an expansionary monetary policy shock when EPU is high. This evidence indicates that the effects of EPU shocks on the bank lending rate margins are robust to using EPU regimes and dummy variable approaches.

29.3 Do Inflation Regimes Impact the Bank Lending Rate Margin Responses to Positive Uncertainty Shocks?

It is possible that inflation may interact with the EPU dynamics. We determine the extent to which inflation matters for the pass-through of the EPU shocks to the bank lending rate margins. Counterfactual VAR models are estimated to examine the effects of inflation regimes on the transmission of positive EPU shocks to the bank lending rate margins. The counterfactual impulse responses are calculated by shutting off the inflation channel in transmitting the positive EPU shocks to the bank lending rate margins. The counterfactual VAR model includes EPU growth, bank lending margins, and inflation dummy. The dummy is for the high and low inflation regimes. The dummies for financial crisis in 2007 and recession in 2009 are included as exogenous variables. The model is estimated using one lag and 10,000 Monte Carlo draws. Shock refers to one positive standard deviation in EPU shock.

Does the inflation channel's transmission of positive EPU shocks to bank lending rate margins depend on the inflation threshold of 6%? A low inflation regime dummy equals to the value of inflation below or equal to 6% and zero otherwise. A high inflation regime dummy equals to value of inflation exceeding 6% and zero otherwise. In determining the role of the inflation regimes based on 6% in the transmission of uncertainty shocks to bank lending rate margins, we show the effects of positive EPU shocks. The estimated regime-dependent counterfactual VAR models are based on inflation regimes.

Figure 29.3 shows the effects of positive EPU shocks on the bank lending rate margins and the role of inflation regimes. The actual and counterfactual bank lending rate margins rise following positive EPU shocks. In Fig. 29.3a, inflation in the low regime dampens the increases in bank lending rate margin to positive EPU shocks. In Fig. 29.3c, inflation magnifies the rise in the bank lending rate margins to positive EPU shocks in high inflation regime. The sizes of positive

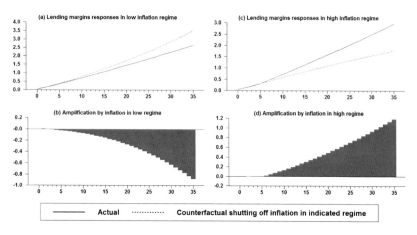

Fig. 29.3 Accumulated bank lending rate margins responses to positive uncertainty shocks (*Source* Authors' calculations)

amplifications induced by inflation in the high inflation regime are shown in Fig. 29.3d.

Evidence shows that EPU's impact on the bank lending rate margins depend on the inflation regimes. The role of inflation channels in transmitting the effects of EPU shock on the bank lending rate margins varies with the inflation regimes. This evidence indicates the need for the enforcement of price stability through keeping inflation below 6% levels to dampen the increase in the bank lending rate margins due to positive EPU shocks.

The chapter further performs a counterfactual VAR analysis by showing that a negative EPU shock may fail to stimulate real GDP growth significantly. This happens when the bank lending rate margins are elevated than when these are shut off in the model. The counterfactual VAR model includes negative EPU dummy, GDP growth, and bank lending margins. The dummies for financial crisis in 2007 and recession in 2009 are included as exogenous variables. The model is estimated using one lag and 10,000 Monte Carlo draws. This implies that low economic policy uncertainty needs to be accompanied by low bank lending rate margins to achieve high real GDP growth (Fig. 29.4).

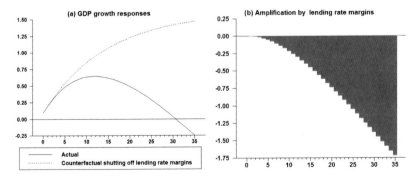

Fig. 29.4 Accumulated real GDP growth responses to negative uncertainty shocks and the role of bank lending rate margins (*Source* Authors' calculations)

29.4 Conclusion and Policy Implications

This chapter investigated the extent to which high economic policy uncertainty impacted the bank lending rate margins in South Africa. In addition, the chapter examined whether there was a possibility that inflation above the 6% threshold affected the way the bank lending rate margins responded to positive economic policy uncertainty shocks relative to when inflation was below 6%. Evidence indicates that a positive economic policy uncertainty shock raises the bank lending rate margins. By contrast, the negative economic policy uncertainty shock lowers the bank lending rate margins. As indicated above, the bank lending rate margins refer to the difference between weighted lending rates and the repo rate.

Counterfactual VAR analysis is used to determine if inflation regimes impact the transmission of economic policy uncertainty shocks to the bank lending rate margins. Evidence shows that when inflation is below 6%, it dampens the actual rise in the bank lending rate margins, following positive economic policy uncertainty shocks. By contrast, when inflation is above 6%, it magnifies the lending rate margins increases due to positive economic policy uncertainty shocks. In policy terms, this evidence shows that elevated levels of EPU prevent the bank lending rate margins from falling as expected in the context of an expansionary monetary policy stance. This implies a large reduction in repo rate than expected may overcome the mitigating effects of elevated economic policy uncertainty in raising the bank lending rate margins despite a low inflation environment.

The analysis concludes by performing a counterfactual analysis showing that a negative economic policy uncertainty shock may fail to raise real GDP growth rates. This happens when the bank lending rate margins are elevated than when these are shut off in model. This implies that low economic policy uncertainty needs to be accompanied by low bank lending rate margins to achieve high real GDP growth.

References

Bloom, N., Stephen, B., & Van Reenen, J. (2007). Uncertainty and investment dynamics. *Review of Economics Studies, 74*(2), 391–415.

Francis, B. B., Hasan, I., & Zhu, Y. (2014). Political uncertainty and bank loan contracting. *Journal of Empirical Finance, 29,* 281–286.

Hlatshwayo, S., & Saxegaard, M. (2016). *The consequences of policy uncertainty: Disconnects and dilutions in the South African real effective exchange rate-export relationship* (IMF Working Chapter WP/16/113).

Nini, G., Smith, D. C., & Amir, S. (2012). Credit control rights, corporate governance, and firm value. *Review of Financial Studies, 25*(6), 1713–1761.

Pastor, L., & Veronesi, P. (2013). Political uncertainty and risk premia. *Journal of Financial Economics, 110*(3), 520–554.

30

Does Economic Policy Uncertainty Impact the Pass-Through of the Repo Rate to the Bank Lending Rates?

Main Highlights

- First, evidence shows that economic policy uncertainty (EPU) shocks directly impact the lending rate dynamics and the effects differ, depending on the persistence of the EPU shock. The persistently rising (declining) EPU shock leads to persistent increase (decrease) in the lending rates. This finding implies that the persistence of the EPU shocks matters for the evolution of the lending rates.
- Second, evidence shows that the actual lending rate responses exceed the counterfactual, following the repo rate tightening shocks, when the elevated EPU channel is operational in the model. This suggests that the positive EPU channel amplifies the increase in the lending rates, following a positive repo rate shock.
- By contrast, the negative EPU channel dampens the increases in lending rates to positive repo rate shocks.

© The Author(s) 2019

E. Ndou and T. Mokoena, *Inequality, Output-Inflation Trade-Off and Economic Policy Uncertainty,*
https://doi.org/10.1007/978-3-030-19803-9_30

425

- Third, evidence shows that EPU played different roles in the two policy loosening periods. Despite the lending rate declining very much to the repo rate loosening during the 2008Q4–2013Q4 period, the EPU mitigated the decline in the lending rates. By contrast, the EPU in the period 2003Q4–2006Q1 accentuated the decline in the lending rate to expansionary monetary policy shocks.

30.1 Introduction

Chapter 28 estimated the time-varying pass-through of the repo rate changes to lending rates and the pass-through post-2010 was found to be high during the period 2015–2017 as shown in Fig. 30.1. Many factors could explain the increased pass-through over this period. These include weakened economic growth outlook, the possibility of credit rating downgrades, heightened economic policy, and political uncertainty. Policymakers pointed out the prevalence and persistence of elevated economic policy and political uncertainty (EPU). First, policymakers did not indicate the extent to which EPU impacts the pass-through of the repo rate to lending rates. Second, policymakers' communications neither elaborated on how EPU may be impacting on the transmission of the repo rate shocks to lending rates during the policy tightening

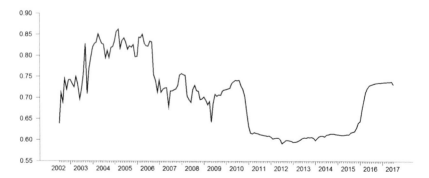

Fig. 30.1 Estimated time varying pass-through of the repo rate to lending rate (*Source* Authors' calculations)

phase; nor are the effects different in the loosening phases. Is it enough only to point at the elevated economic policy and political uncertainty and not indicate its likely impact on the efficacy of the monetary policy transmission mechanism when enforcing the price stability mandate?

This is an appropriate time to put forth the view that Economic policy uncertainty (EPU) may impact the efficacy of the monetary policy transmission mechanism during the policy loosening and tightening cycles, such that the expected outcomes are either realised or not realised over the affected period. In addition, the chapter investigates the possibility that high EPU impacts the pass-through of policy rate loosening shock into the lending rates, thereby preventing the reduction in these rates. Is it possible that high EPU might have impacted the pass-through of the repo rate tightening into the lending rates?

We further argue that it may be important to incorporate the EPU channel into the policy discussions that link the transmission of the repo rate effects to the lending rate dynamics. This is because an increase in the cost of capital due to risk premia attached to high political uncertainty may force firms to postpone investment decisions, until significant political uncertainty is dissolved (Bloom et al. 2007). The persistence of elevated economic and political uncertainty may dampen the stimulatory effects of the policy rate loosening shock via the weakened investment channel. Alternatively, this may worsen the adverse effects of policy tightening shocks. In addition, Pastor and Veronesi (2013) conclude that political uncertainty affects firms' cash flow and lenders may demand extra compensation for bearing the additional political risk. This shows that, the lending rate is not determined only by the repo rate changes.

This chapter fills policy research gaps by showing that EPU impacts the policy rate dynamics during the monetary policy loosening and tightening phases. In addition, the analysis shows that EPU impacted monetary policy loosening shock effects differently in the period 2003–2006 in relation to the 2008Q4–2013Q4 period. In addition, evidence shows that EPU may mitigate as well as reinforce the magnitudes of the pass-through of the repo rate to lending rates.

30.2 Economic Policy Uncertainty and the Lending Rate Dynamics

To properly disentangle the role of the EPU channel, the analysis begins by showing the direct effects of the EPU shocks on the lending rate dynamics. Does the impact of elevated EPU on the lending rates differ from those of their unexpected reductions in the uncertainty? Hence, the analysis examines the responses of the lending rates to positive and negative EPU shocks using bivariate VAR models. The models use quarterly (Q) data spanning 2000Q1–2016Q1. The EPU is obtained from Hlatshwayo and Saxegaard (2016) and other data is obtained from the South African Reserve Bank (SARB). The models are estimated using annual growth of EPU and weighted lending rate. The models are estimated using one lag and 10,000 Monte Carlo draws. The EPU variable is further separated into positive and negative annual growth rates. The positive uncertainty dummy equals to positive values of the annual growth of EPU and zero otherwise. In addition, the negative uncertainty dummy equals to values of negative annual growth of EPU and zero otherwise. These values are used separately in the model. The results shown in Fig. 30.2 are based on one standard deviation shocks.

In Fig. 30.2a, a negative EPU shock lowers significantly the lending rate. In contrast, in Fig. 30.2b, a positive EPU shock raises the lending rate significantly. In general, a positive uncertainty shock raises the lending rate (Fig. 30.2c). In addition, Fig. 30.2d reveals that negative EPU shocks induce more fluctuations in the lending rate than positive EPU shocks. So far, evidence shows that EPU is a driver of the lending rate dynamics.

Does the persistence of the EPU shock matter for the evolution of the lending rate dynamics? Yes, the lending rate responds differently to the various scenarios of elevated (positive) and subsiding (negative) EPU shocks. The positive EPU shock scenarios are depicted in Fig. 30.3a. The scenarios include non-persistent, constant, and persistently rising EPU shocks. The lending rate responses are shown in Fig. 30.3b.

The impact of EPU shocks on the lending rate differs based on the persistence of the shocks. The persistently rising EPU shock leads to persistently rising lending rates. By contrast, the less persistent EPU shock leads to less persistent lending rate increase. Alternatively, the bigger the

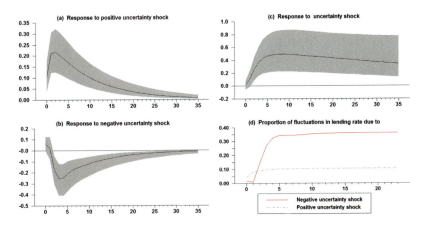

Fig. 30.2 Lending rate responses to negative and positive economic policy uncertainty shocks (*Note* The grey shaded bands denote 16th and 84th percentile confidence bands. *Source* Authors' calculations)

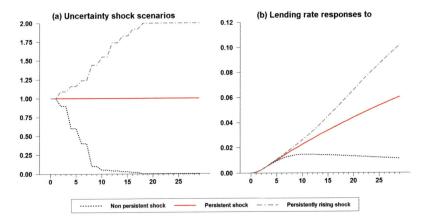

Fig. 30.3 Positive economic policy uncertainty shock scenarios and lending rate responses (*Source* Authors' calculations)

unexpected decline in EPU the lower the lending rate becomes. These findings imply that the persistence of the uncertainty shocks matter for the evolution of the lending rates. Would the preceding findings differ when assessing scenarios of negative EPU shocks? Figure 30.4a shows the negative uncertainty shock scenarios and lending rate responses.

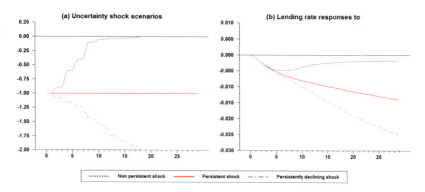

Fig. 30.4 Negative economic policy uncertainty shock scenarios and the lending rate responses (*Source* Authors' calculations)

Evidence shows that persistently declining EPU shocks lead to persistently lower lending rates. In addition, a less subsiding EPU shock leads to a highly transitory decline in the lending rates in comparison to that achieved by persistently declining uncertainty shock.

30.3 The Role of Economic Policy Uncertainty in the Transmission of the Repo Rate Shocks to Lending Rate

The analysis further estimates a counterfactual VAR model *(baseline model)* which includes the repo rate, the lending rate, and annual growth of EPU. All these variables are expressed in percentages. The EPU channel is shut off to calculate the counterfactual responses. The gap between actual and counterfactual responses measures the role of the EPU channel in transmitting the repo rate shocks to lending rates. Figure 30.5 shows that unexpected tightening in the repo rate leads to an increase in the lending rate, irrespective of whether EPU channel is shut off or not. However, the lending rate rises much higher when the EPU channel is operational than when it is shut off in the model. The sizes of the amplification effects are shown in Fig. 30.5b.

30 Does Economic Policy Uncertainty Impact ...

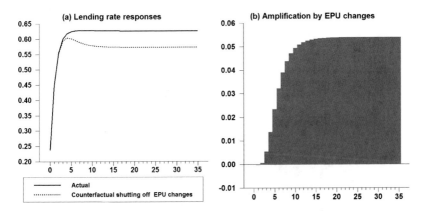

Fig. 30.5 Accumulated lending rate responses to positive repo rate shocks and the role of the economic policy uncertainty changes (*Note* EPU denotes economic policy uncertainty. *Source* Authors' calculations)

30.3.1 The Effects After Decomposing Annual Growth of the Economic Policy Uncertainty into Positive and Negative Changes

The chapter further decomposes the annual growth of EPU into negative and positive annual growth rates. The negative uncertainty dummy is equal to the negative value of annual growth of EPU and zero otherwise. The positive uncertainty dummy is set to be equal to a positive value of annual growth of EPU and zero otherwise. The uncertainty variable in the preceding section's model is replaced with these two uncertainty dummy variables which are used interchangeably in the model. Similarly, these variables are shut off in the model to calculate the counterfactual responses. The lending rate responses are shown in Fig. 30.6. The actual lending rate rises higher than the counterfactual in Fig. 30.6a. This suggests that the positive EPU channel amplifies the increase in the lending rate, following a positive repo rate shock. By contrast, Fig. 30.6c shows that the counterfactual reactions exceeds the actual lending rate responses. This evidence shows that negative EPU channel dampens the lending rate responses to positive repo rate shocks. The amplification is bigger due to the negative EPU channel in relation to positive uncertainty changes.

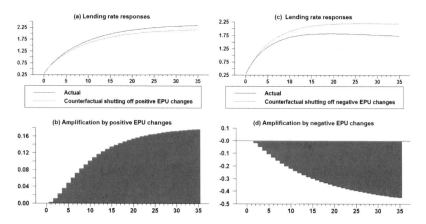

Fig. 30.6 Accumulated lending rate responses to positive repo rate shocks and the role of the economic policy uncertainty changes (*Note* EPU denotes EPU. *Source* Authors' calculations)

Contrasting the Effects of Economic Policy Uncertainty

The investigation continues to examine the role of positive EPU changes post 2008Q4 in transmitting the positive repo rate shocks to the lending rates. This is captured using a dummy which equals to the positive values of annual growth of EPU beginning in 2009Q1 to end of the sample and zero otherwise. This variable replaces the uncertainty variable in the baseline model. In Fig. 30.7, the actual lending rate exceeds the counterfactual response. This shows that elevated EPU post 2008Q4 contributed to the increase in the lending rate to be higher than what the counterfactual suggests.

We further examine the extent to which negative EPU changes before 2009Q1 influenced the repo rate tightening effects. We create a new dummy, which equals to the value of negative annual growth of EPU before 2009Q1 and zero otherwise. This dummy replaces the EPU changes in the baseline model. Figure 30.8b shows that the counterfactual exceeds the actual lending rate responses. This shows that negative EPU shocks before 2009Q1 dampened the actual increase in the lending

30 Does Economic Policy Uncertainty Impact ...

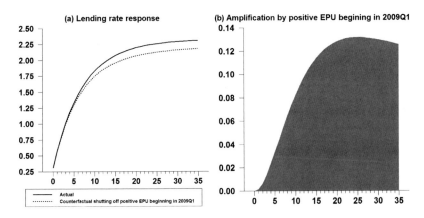

Fig. 30.7 Accumulated lending rate responses to positive the repo rate shocks and the role of economic policy uncertainty changes (*Source* Authors' calculations)

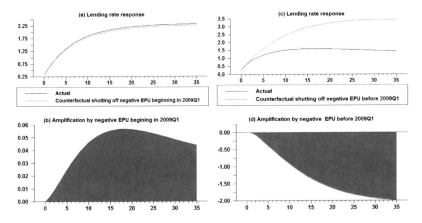

Fig. 30.8 Accumulated lending rate responses to positive repo rate shocks and the role of the economic policy uncertainty changes (*Note* EPU denotes EPU. *Source* Authors' calculations)

rates to be less than what the counterfactual suggests, following the repo rate shock. However, in Fig. 30.8a the negative EPU beginning in the 2009Q1 period fails to mitigate the rise in the lending rate following the repo rate tightening shock.

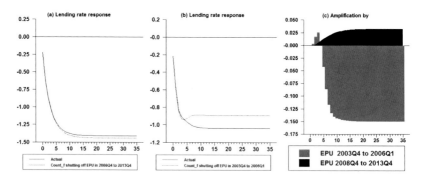

Fig. 30.9 Accumulated lending rate responses to repo rate loosening shock (*Source* Authors' calculations)

The analysis concludes by showing the role of the EPU channel during the two monetary policy loosening periods. Figure 30.9 shows the responses of the lending rate to an expansionary monetary policy shock when assessing the role of the EPU changes in the periods 2003Q4–2006Q1 and 2008Q4–2013Q4. We create two dummy variables, which equals to the value of annual growth of EPU in each period and zero otherwise. Despite the lending rate declining significantly to the repo rate loosening in Fig. 30.9a, the uncertainty in 2008Q4–2013Q4 mitigated the decline. By contrast, the uncertainty in the period 2003Q4–2006Q1 accentuated the decline in the lending rate. This evidence shows that uncertainty played different roles in the two monetary policy loosening periods.

30.4 Conclusion and Policy Implications

Does EPU impact the pass-through of the repo rate changes to lending rates? First, evidence shows that EPU shocks directly impact the lending rate dynamics and the effects differ based on the persistence of the EPU shock. The persistently rising (declining) uncertainty shock leads to persistently rising (declining) lending rates. This implies the persistence of the EPU shocks matter for the evolution of the lending rates.

Second, evidence shows that the actual increase in the lending rate to the repo rate tightening shock exceeds the counterfactual when the elevated EPU channel is operational than when it is shut off in the model. This suggests that the positive EPU channel amplifies the increase in the lending rate, following a positive repo rate shock. By contrast, the negative EPU channel dampens the increase in the lending rate, following positive repo rate shocks. This chapter showed the responses of the lending rate to expansionary monetary policy shocks, when assessing the role of EPU, changes in the periods 2003Q4–2006Q1 and 2008Q4–2013Q4. Despite the lending rate declining significantly to the repo rate loosening shock in the 2008Q4–2013Q4 period, EPU mitigated the decline in this period. By contrast, EPU in the period 2003Q4–2006Q1 accentuated the decline in the lending rate. This evidence shows that EPU played different roles in the two policy loosening periods.

References

Baum, C., Caglayan, M., & Ozkan, N. (2013). The role of uncertainty in the transmission of monetary policy effects on bank lending. *Manchester School, University of Manchester, 81*(2), 202–225.

Bloom, N., Stephen, B., & Van Reenen, J. (2007). Uncertainty and investment dynamics. *Review of Economics Studies, 74*(2), 391–415.

Francis, B. B., Hasan, I., & Zhu, Y. (2014). Political uncertainty and bank loan contracting. *Journal of Empirical Finance, 29,* 281–286.

Hlatshwayo, S., & Saxegaard, M. (2016). *The consequences of policy uncertainty: Disconnects and dilutions in the South African real effective exchange rate-export relationship* (IMF Working Chapter WP/16/113).

Nini, G., Smith, D. C., & Amir, S. (2012). Credit control rights, corporate governance, and firm value. *Review of Financial studies, 25*(6), 1713–1761.

Pastor, L., & Veronesi, P. (2013). Political uncertainty and risk premia. *Journal of Financial Economics, 110*(3), 520–545.

Part X

**Economic Policy Uncertainty
and the Lending Rates, Credit
and Corporate Cash Holding Channels**

31

Are Credit Growth Reactions to Expansionary Monetary Policy Shocks Weakened by Heightened Economic Policy Uncertainty?

Main Highlights

- Evidence indicates that positive (negative) economic policy uncertainty shocks lower (raise) credit extension and tighten (loosen) credit conditions.
- Evidence shows that expansionary monetary policy shocks lead to bigger increases in credit growth in the low economic policy uncertainty regime through amplifications from loosening credit conditions.
- The findings show that elevated economic policy uncertainty directly weakens the transmission of the effects of expansionary monetary policy shocks onto credit growth.
- Thus economic policy uncertainty regimes matter for the efficacy of the credit conditions channel in transmitting expansionary monetary policy shocks to credit growth. Hence a large reduction in the policy rate by more than expected may be required to achieve a similar impact and this may lead to extensive loosening in the credit conditions.

© The Author(s) 2019
E. Ndou and T. Mokoena, *Inequality, Output-Inflation Trade-Off and Economic Policy Uncertainty,*
https://doi.org/10.1007/978-3-030-19803-9_31

31.1 Introduction

During the recent financial crisis, credit growth did not increase as much as expected following expansionary monetary policy shocks. One explanatory reason is due to adverse effects of tight regulatory changes as shown in Gumata and Ndou (2017).[1] This chapter assesses if there is an additional conduit via which the elevated economic policy uncertainty can explain weak credit growth. It is the objective of this chapter to determine whether elevated levels of economic policy uncertainty may impede the transmission of expansionary monetary policy shocks to credit growth. It is also important to determine the extent to which high and low economic policy uncertainty regimes impact the transmission of expansionary monetary policy shocks to credit growth. It is the purpose of this research to determine whether financial frictions, as captured by the credit conditions index, can mitigate or amplify the credit growth responses to expansionary monetary policy shocks.

This chapter examines the following aspects regarding the link between economic policy uncertainty and credit growth: Do economic policy uncertainty shocks impact credit dynamics? Do the periods of elevated economic policy uncertainty environment impact the pass-through of expansionary monetary policy shocks to credit growth? What are the implications for size of policy rate adjustments?

The analysis fills policy research gaps by examining the role of the economic policy uncertainty channel on credit dynamics from three viewpoints. First, the chapter determines the direct effects of economic policy uncertainty shocks on credit growth dynamics. Second, it determines the role of economic policy uncertainty regimes in impacting the reaction of credit growth to expansionary monetary policy shocks. Third, the chapter determines the amplification effects of economic policy uncertainty in transmitting expansionary monetary policy shocks to credit growth. These last two issues are important in determining the size of the repo

---

[1]https://www.palgrave.com/de/book/9783319435503.

31 Are Credit Growth Reactions to Expansionary Monetary Policy ...

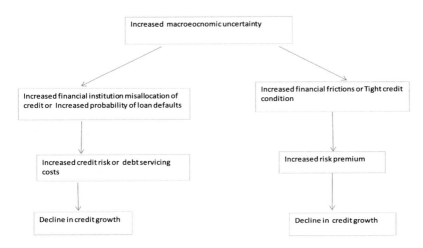

Fig. 31.1 Theoretical depictions of elevated macroeconomic effects on credit dynamics (*Source* Authors' calculations)

rate adjustments. In addition, the chapter shows that economic policy uncertainty regimes affect the ability of credit conditions index to transmit expansionary monetary policy shocks to credit growth.

Figure 31.1 shows a theoretical depiction of the transmission mechanism of uncertainty shocks to credit dynamics via two channels, but this is not exhaustive of all the channels. The first channel shows that elevated macroeconomic uncertainty impacts the strategies of financial institutions' lending decisions, the screening of customers, and the decisions on how best to allocate credit (Chi and Wi 2017).[2] Thus, heightened macroeconomic uncertainties make it difficult for lending institutions to allocate credit. In addition, due to the asymmetric information, banks may allocate scarce credit loans to those borrowers with poor prospects for future gains. As a result, increased information asymmetry can directly increase credit risks and raise the cost of debt, leading

---

[2] It must be pointed out that theory predicts different effects of macroeconomic uncertainty shocks on economic growth via different channels. For instance, the real-option and growth-option theories propose different theoretical outcomes on economic due to how these uncertainty channels may influence investment.

442   E. Ndou and T. Mokoena

to reduced credit extension.[3] In the second channel, the elevated uncertainty shocks lead to increased financial frictions, a factor that raises the risk premium and reduces credit growth.

Evidence reported in the literature points to the prolonged negative responses of output to positive policy uncertainty shocks. This is consistent with the "wait and see" hypothesis.[4] It follows logically that the depressing effects of uncertainty shocks on output growth should have implications for credit dynamics, and the latter's reactions to expansionary monetary policy shocks. Hence, it is important to determine how credit dynamics are impacted in the following ways: First, we determine how credit growth reacts directly to economic policy uncertainty shocks. Second, we determine how credit growth is indirectly affected by the expansionary monetary policy shocks that are being transmitted via the economic policy uncertainty channel. Third, we determine whether credit growth responses to the expansionary monetary policy shocks depend on whether growth of economic policy uncertainty is either below zero or above it.

31.2 Does Economic Policy Uncertainty Impact Credit Growth Dynamics?

This analysis begins by examining the responses of annual growth of total loans and advances (*credit growth*) to economic policy uncertainty shocks. The economic policy uncertainty is obtained from Hlatshwayo and Saxegaard (2016). The other data are obtained from the South

---

[3]Increased macroeconomic uncertainties leading to deterioration of firms' financial conditions will influence the operating performance of financial lending firms. The deterioration in the financial conditions increases operational risk leading to unstable financial situation.

[4]Recent explanation indicates these dynamics are potent when combined with endogenous growth mechanism which includes the R&D investment or those that embody technological change or human capital investment. Bachmann et al. (2013) suggest that when R&D sectors exhibit feature of the wait and see mechanism particularly, then persistent and not transitory uncertainty shocks could lead to prolonged if not permanent effects on economic uncertainty.

African Reserve Bank. The investigation begins by estimating bivariate VAR models. The models include annual growth of economic policy uncertainty and annual growth of total loans and advances. The analysis tests the robustness of the results using the reverse orderings in the VAR model. The analysis uses quarterly data from 2000Q1 to 2016Q1.

This chapter further examines the relationship between economic policy uncertainty and the lending rate spread between the weighted lending and deposit rates. Data for the lending rate spread spans from 2001Q3 to 2016Q1. In the other VAR models, the credit growth variable is replaced with the lending rate spread. The lending rate spread captures a financing wedge and is an indicator of financial frictions in the credit markets. The economic policy uncertainty shocks are separated between negative and positive uncertainty shocks.

Does an economic policy uncertainty shock drive credit growth and do the effects depend on whether the uncertainty shock is negative or positive? Answering this question requires separating the effects of negative and positive economic policy uncertainty to determine the extent of asymmetric effects. In Fig. 31.2, a positive economic policy uncertainty shock exerts adverse effects on credit extension. By contrast, a negative economic policy uncertainty shock uplifts credit growth significantly. Are there asymmetric shock effects?

Yes, negative economic policy uncertainty shocks lead to large peak credit growth responses than positive shocks of similar size. The negative economic policy uncertainty shocks lower the lending rate spread significantly for a longer period. By contrast, the positive uncertainty shock raises lending rate spread significantly over medium-term horizons.

Thus, evidence so far indicates that an unexpected decline in economic policy uncertainty is important in lowering the lending rate spread and in raising credit growth. In policy terms, this evidence suggests that credit growth will remain very subdued due to high economic policy uncertainty and this may counter the stimulatory effects of expansionary monetary policy shocks. This suggests that a large reduction in the policy rate may be required to achieve a similar impact. These aspects are explored in the sections to follow.

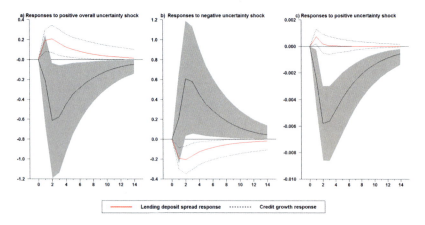

Fig. 31.2 Responses of credit growth and lending rate spread dynamics to uncertainty shocks (*Note* The grey shaded bands denote 16th and 84th percentile confidence bands. *Source* Authors' calculations)

31.2.1 Robustness of the Evidence of Credit Reaction to Uncertainty Shock from Endogenous-Exogenous VAR Models

How robust are the responses of credit growth to both negative and positive economic policy uncertainty shocks? The robustness tests of the preceding findings are carried out using quarterly (Q) data spanning 2000Q1–2016Q1 to estimate various VAR models. These models include either positive or negative annual growth of economic policy uncertainty, changes in the repo rate or annual growth of total loans and advances.[5] Thus, the positive and negative economic policy uncertainty measures are included separately in the model. The second model estimated is the exogenous VAR model. In the exogenous VAR model the positive and negative economic policy uncertainties are used as exogenous variables and enter separately in the model. These models are estimated using 1 lag and 10,000 Monte Carlo draws.

---

[5]The results are robust to the inclusion of credit conditions index, inflation and annual changes in rand per US exchange rate.

31 Are Credit Growth Reactions to Expansionary Monetary Policy ...

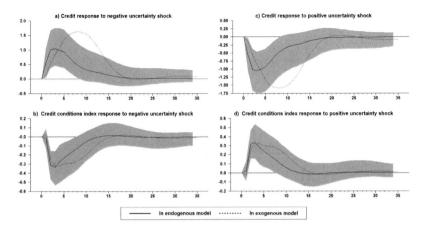

Fig. 31.3 Responses of credit growth and credit condition index to uncertainty shocks (*Note* The grey shaded bands denote 16th and 84th percentile confidence bands. *Source* Authors' calculations)

In Fig. 31.3a, a negative economic policy uncertainty shock raises credit growth significantly for at least 10 quarters. In addition, in Fig. 31.3b the credit conditions index is loosened to negative economic policy uncertainty shock. In contrast, a positive economic policy uncertainty shock lowers credit growth significantly in Fig. 31.3c while credit conditions tighten significantly for at least eight quarters in Fig. 31.3d.

31.2.2 Do Economic Policy Uncertainty Regimes Affect the Ability of Credit Conditions Index to Transmit Expansionary Monetary Policy Shocks to Credit Growth?

Evidence from the preceding section shows that policy uncertainty shocks directly impact credit growth. This section examines the second aspect of the linkage between economic policy uncertainty and credit growth. Does credit growth's reaction to the expansionary monetary policy shocks differ between the low and high economic policy

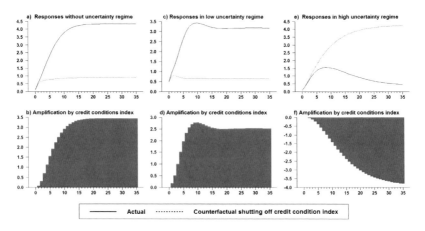

Fig. 31.4 Credit growth responses to expansionary monetary policy responses (*Source* Authors' calculations)

uncertainty regimes? This is answered by estimating a regime-dependent counterfactual VAR model using 1 lag and 10,000 Monte Carlo draws. The low uncertainty regime refers to negative annual growth of economic policy uncertainty. The counterfactual VAR models use changes in the repo rate, credit conditions index, and annual growth of total loans and advances. The counterfactual impulse responses are determined by shutting off the credit conditions index channel in transmitting expansionary monetary policy shocks to growth of credit. Figure 31.4 shows results (1) in the absence of uncertainty regime and according to (2) low uncertainty regime and (3) high uncertainty regime.

In the absence of economic policy uncertainty regimes, Fig. 31.4a shows that the actual credit growth responses increase more in the presence of the credit conditions index than when it is shut off in the model. This suggests the loosening in the credit conditions index, following an expansionary monetary policy shock, magnifies the growth of credit.

Do economic policy uncertainty regimes matter for the credit growth responses to expansionary monetary policy shocks? In a low economic policy uncertainty regime, the actual credit growth impulse responses exceed the counterfactual reaction as shown in Fig. 31.4c. This is because loosened credit condition index amplifies credit growth in Fig. 31.4d. However, the credit conditions index tightens in the high economic policy uncertainty regime, making the counterfactual response to be below the actual credit growth response. As shown in Fig. 31.4f, the tightening credit conditions index lowers the credit growth. Thus, economic policy uncertainty regimes matter for the efficacy of the credit condition index channel in transmitting expansionary monetary policy shocks to credit growth.

31.2.3 Does the Economic Policy Uncertainty Channel Affect the Transmission of Expansionary Monetary Policy Shocks to Growth of Credit?

The analysis further looks at the last aspect of the economic policy uncertainty channel. This involves determining the size of amplifications induced by economic policy uncertainty on credit growth, following expansionary monetary policy shocks. This is answered by using quarterly (Q) data spanning 1990Q1–2016Q1 and tests the robustness of the evidence using 2000Q1–2016Q1 period.

The purpose is to determine the extent to which the economic policy uncertainty regimes impact the pass-through of expansionary monetary policy shocks to credit growth. Therefore, the regime-dependent counterfactual VAR models are estimated. The model includes change in the repo rate, annual credit growth, and annual growth of economic policy uncertainty. The model is estimated using 1 lag and 10 000 Monte Carlo draws. We shut off the growth of the economic policy uncertainty in each uncertainty regime to determine the counterfactual impulse responses of credit growth. The low (high) uncertainty regime refers to regions when annual growth of economic policy uncertainty is negative (positive).

Does the efficacy of the economic policy uncertainty channel in transmitting expansionary monetary policy shocks to credit growth depend on the economic policy uncertainty regimes? In Fig. 31.5a the increase in actual credit growth exceeds the counterfactual reaction. This

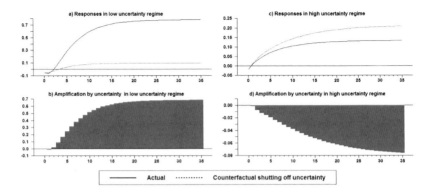

Fig. 31.5 Credit growth responses to expansionary monetary policy responses and role of uncertainty (*Source* Authors' calculations)

suggests that the economic policy uncertainty channel in the low uncertainty regime magnifies the credit growth increase, following an expansionary monetary policy shock. In Fig. 31.5c, the actual credit growth rises less than the actual reaction. This suggests that economic policy uncertainty channel in the high uncertainty regime dampens the credit growth, following an expansionary monetary policy shock.

Are the preceding findings robust to changes in the sample size and using dummy variables to define positive and negative annual growth of economic policy uncertainty? We test the robustness of the results using quarterly data spanning 2000Q1–2016Q1. A negative uncertainty dummy equals to one when annual growth of economic policy uncertainty is negative and zero otherwise. In addition, a positive uncertainty dummy equals one when annual growth of economic policy uncertainty is positive and zero otherwise.

In Fig. 31.6a, the actual credit growth rises more when negative economic policy uncertainty operates in the model than when it is shut off in the model. By contrast, in Fig. 31.6c the actual credit growth rises less than the counterfactual response. This shows that the positive economic policy uncertainty channel dampens credit growth, following an expansionary monetary policy shock. This evidence shows that the economic policy uncertainty channels and the uncertainty regimes matter.

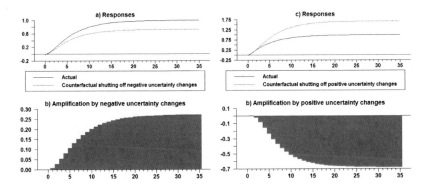

Fig. 31.6 Credit growth responses to expansionary monetary policy responses and the role of the economic policy uncertainty channels (*Source* Authors' calculations)

31.2.4 What Are Implications for Monetary Policy?

This is answered by comparing the amplification effects of the lending rate and credit conditions index channels. Figure 31.7 compares the credit growth responses in the presence and absence of the lending rates and credit conditions index used in separate estimations, but subjected to the same size of an expansionary monetary policy shock. Evidence indicates both these variables have similar amplification roles, however, their amplifying magnitudes differ. Credit growth rises more to an expansionary monetary policy shock in the presence of credit conditions index than when using lending rate. This is due to the greater magnifying effect of the credit conditions index than the lending rate on raising credit growth, following an expansionary monetary policy shock.

Based on these findings, it can be argued that it is the wider loosening in the aggregate financial indicators that is very important than just the mere reduction in the lending rate alone. One lesson from the recent financial crisis is that policy rate reductions did not stimulate credit growth very much despite reductions in the lending rates, because the financial condition indicators pointed to tighter conditions. This tightening could emanate from an elevated policy uncertainty as shown here. Hence, based on this section's evidence, it is important that

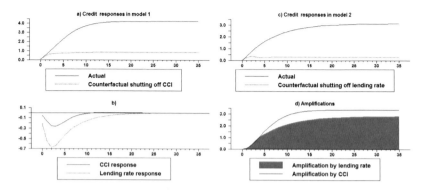

Fig. 31.7 Credit growth responses to an expansionary monetary policy shock (*Note* CCI denotes credit condition index. *Source* Authors' calculations)

policymakers ensure that future expansionary monetary policy decisions are accompanied by significant loosening of aggregated financial conditions. One possibility is to induce a larger than expected cut in the policy rate. Another possibility is to loosen other prudential tools which banks control that impact on other financing conditions. Evidence shows that high uncertainty regime makes credit conditions index tighter, hence the reliance on the lending rate channel alone may fail to deliver the expected pass-through of expansionary monetary policy shocks to credit growth.

31.3 Conclusion and Policy Implications

This chapter examined the link between economic policy uncertainty and credit growth of various ways. This included determining whether economic policy uncertainty shocks impact credit dynamics. The chapter also investigated the effects of an elevated economic policy uncertainty environment in impacting the pass-through of expansionary monetary policy shocks to growth of credit and the implications for the size of policy rate adjustments. First, evidence indicates that positive (negative) economic policy uncertainty shocks lower (raise) credit extension and tighten (loosen) credit conditions. Second, evidence shows that expansionary monetary policy shock leads to bigger (smaller) increase in credit growth in the low (high) economic policy uncertainty regimes through amplifications from loosening (tightening) in the credit conditions index.

Third, evidence shows that credit growth would rise by less than that would prevail in the absence of economic policy uncertainty. Thus, elevated economic policy uncertainty directly weakens the transmission of the effects of expansionary monetary policy shocks onto credit growth. In policy terms, economic policy uncertainty regimes matter for the efficacy of the credit condition index channel in transmitting expansionary monetary policy shocks to credit growth. This implies that credit growth will remain very subdued due to high economic policy uncertainty, which tightens credit conditions. This counters the stimulatory effects of expansionary monetary policy shocks. This suggests that a large reduction in the policy rate than expected may be required to achieve a similar impact and this may lead to extensive loosening in the credit conditions.

References

Bachmann, R., Elstner, S., & Sims, E. R. (2013). Uncertainty and economic activity: Evidence from business survey data. *American Economic Journal: Macroeconomics, 5*(2), 217–249.

Chi, Q., & Wi, W. (2017). Economic policy uncertainty, credit risks and banks' lending decisions: Evidence from Chinese commercial banks. *China Journal of Accounting Research, 10,* 33–50.

Gumata, N., & Ndou, E. (2017). *Bank credit extension and real economic activity in South Africa: The impact of capital flow dynamics, bank regulation and selected macro-prudential tools.* Cham: Palgrave Macmillan.

Hlatshwayo, S., & Saxegaard, M. (2016). *The consequences of policy uncertainty: Disconnects and dilutions in the South African real effective exchange rate-export relationship* (IMF Working Paper WP/16/113).

32

Do Companies' Cash Holdings Impact the Transmission of Economic Policy Uncertainty Shocks to Capital Formation?

Main Highlights

- Evidence shows that positive (negative) economic policy uncertainty raises (reduces) growth of companies' deposits. Increases in the growth of companies' deposits accentuate the decline in capital formation following a positive economic policy uncertainty shock. The decline is large when inflation exceeds the 6% threshold than below this limit.
- The reduction in the growth of companies' deposits in the low inflation regime amplifies the increase in capital formation following a negative economic policy uncertainty shock.
- From policy perspective, price stability matters as the low inflation environment makes the growth of companies' deposits to cushion the decline in the capital formation growth due to positive economic policy uncertainty shocks.

© The Author(s) 2019

E. Ndou and T. Mokoena, *Inequality, Output-Inflation Trade-Off and Economic Policy Uncertainty,*
https://doi.org/10.1007/978-3-030-19803-9_32

32.1 Introduction

During the recent financial crisis that began in 2007, companies increased their holdings of cash, including deposits with banks. Cash hoarding was accompanied by reduced investment growth, which delayed recovery of economic growth. The likelihood of the adverse effects of such phenomenon happening may be due to the increased policy and political uncertainty, and threats of possible further sovereign credit downgrades from credit rating agencies. All this happens when inflation is within the inflation target band and monetary policy has been loosened. In addition, the Bank's forecasts indicate expectation of low inflation and weaker economic growth outlook in the future. It seems inadequate and incomplete to talk about the benefits of low economic policy uncertainty without including price stability. It will be incomplete analysis to focus on the benefits of low economic policy uncertainty without including company's cash holdings and inflation regimes. Monetary policy cycles determine the costs of capital, which is key to capital formation growth.

Hence, this chapter examines the following aspects: To what extent does an economic policy uncertainty shock drive cash holdings of companies as measured by deposits held at the banks? To what extent do inflation regimes impact the relationship between economic policy uncertainty and companies' deposits held at the banks? Do the companies' cash holdings impact the transmission of economic policy uncertainty shocks to gross fixed capital formation? Is there a real option channel of economic policy uncertainty shock and is there a role of inflation regimes?

Theoretically, there are three motives for holding cash. These are the transactions, precautionary, and speculative motives. The transaction motive refers to cash for daily business activities. The precautionary motive implies accumulating cash to meet unanticipated contingencies that may arise. The speculative motive argues for accumulating cash to be used for profit-making opportunities that may arise. Figure 32.1, depicts the transmission mechanism of elevated uncertainty on how it affects the value of cash holdings through financial constraints, agency conflicts, and real option channels. The last channel's effect is further

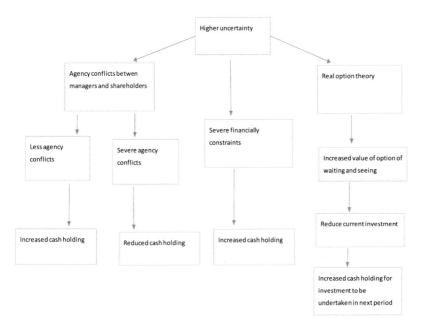

Fig. 32.1 Link between higher uncertainty and companies' cash holding (*Source* Authors' drawing)

attributed to the increased value of the option to "wait and see" strategy. The less severe agency conflicts, severe financially constraints, and real option theory channels predict increased cash holding after elevated uncertainty. Despite showing all these channels, the analysis focuses on the relevance of the real options theory channel in South Africa.

Bloom (2009) show that uncertainty reduces corporate investment by increasing the value of the option to wait and see. This causes the firms to wait for additional information before taking actions.[1] Im et al. (2017), found that in North America increased firms' levels of uncertainty affects the value of cash holdings, indicating the influence of real option effects, agency and financially constraints channels. So, is there a real option channel in South Africa?

---

[1]Bernanke (1983).

This chapter contributes to studies that assess the effects of uncertainty on corporates' cash holdings. These studies on uncertainty effects focused on firms' level uncertainty or aggregate uncertainty as driver of corporate cash holdings. This analysis does not focus on the effects of policy uncertainty by decomposing them into idiosyncratic and permanent shocks. The analysis shows the differential effects between transitory and unchanged, negative, and positive uncertainty shocks' impacts on growth of companies' deposits. In addition, Im et al. (2017) and Baum et al. (2002) examined the link between uncertainty and the value of cash holdings by testing the three channels depicted in Fig. 32.1.

This chapter differs from Im et al. (2017) and other studies by showing the effects of positive and negative economic policy uncertainty shocks. This study differs further by including the role of price stability based on the 6% inflation threshold, to show the influence of low and high inflation regimes. The analysis further shows the effects of shock scenarios distinguishing between the transitory and unchanged, negative, and positive economic policy uncertainty shock. The counterfactual policy analysis is applied to determine a number of policy relevant matters.

32.2   Is There a Link Between Economic Policy Uncertainty and Companies' Cash Holdings?

This analysis starts by examining the bilateral relationships in (1) levels and (2) annual growth rates between economic policy uncertainty and companies' deposits. This chapter uses quarterly(Q) data from 1993Q1 to 2016Q1 obtained from the South African Reserve Bank. The economic policy uncertainty data is obtained from Hlatshwayo and Saxegaard (2016). The scatterplots in Fig. 32.2 depicts a positive relationship between economic policy uncertainty and companies' deposits.

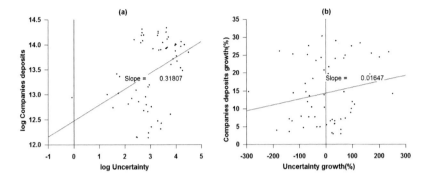

Fig. 32.2 Relationship between economic policy uncertainty and companies' deposits (*Source* Authors' calculations)

This suggests that an increase in economic policy uncertainty leads to an increase in companies' deposits. However, this section's analysis does not show the relationship between negative growth of economic policy uncertainty and growth of companies' deposits. This relationship will be examined in a later section.

32.2.1 Evidence from Negative and Positive Economic Policy Uncertainty Effects

Evidence from Cross Correlations

Figure 32.3 shows the lead relationships between annual growth of economic policy uncertainty and growth of companies' deposits. That is, what happens to the growth of companies' deposits when preceded by elevated economic policy uncertainty? In general, the elevated economic policy uncertainty precedes the rise in the growth of companies' deposits. Positive growth of economic policy uncertainty precedes the rise in growth of companies' deposits. Negative growth of economic policy uncertainty precedes the decline in growth of companies' deposits. So far evidence supports the wait and see which is consistent with the real option channel of uncertainty.

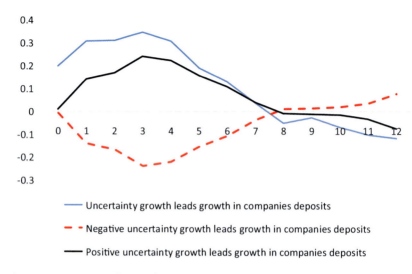

Fig. 32.3 Cross correlations (*Source* Authors' calculations)

32.2.2 Evidence from Linear Regressions and Role of Inflation Regimes

The chapter further estimates the regime-dependent linear regressions Eqs. (32.1)–(32.3) to determine the effects of inflation regimes on impacting the sizes of positive and negative economic policy uncertainty effects on the growth of the companies' deposits (Deposits$_t$).

$$\text{Deposits}_t = \beta * \text{Positive\_unc}_t + \gamma * \text{Negative\_unc}_t, \quad \text{inflation} > 6 \quad (32.1)$$

$$\text{Deposits}_t = \beta * \text{Positive\_unc}_t + \gamma * \text{Negative\_unc}_t, \quad \text{inflation} \leq 6 \quad (32.2)$$

$$\text{Deposits}_t = \beta * \text{Positive\_unc}_t + \gamma * \text{Negative\_unc}_t \quad (32.3)$$

The Positive_unc$_t$ is a dummy referring to positive annual growth of economic policy uncertainty and zero otherwise. The Negative_unc$_t$ is a dummy referring to negative annual growth of economic policy uncertainty and zero otherwise.

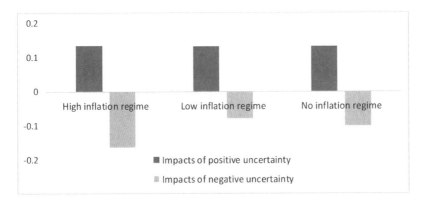

Fig. 32.4 Impacts of negative and positive economic policy uncertainty on growth of companies' deposits and role of inflation regimes (*Source* Authors' calculations)

The results are shown in Fig. 32.4. The positive economic policy uncertainty raises growth of companies' deposits. In contrast, the negative economic policy uncertainty reduces growth of companies' deposits. The effects happen irrespective of inflation regimes. This suggests that economic policy uncertainty developments are drivers of growth of companies' deposits. However, the magnitudes are smaller in the low inflation regimes.

32.3 Evidence from Pentecôte and Rondeau (2015) Approach

The chapter further estimates the reaction of growth of companies' deposits (Deposit) to uncertainty shocks using the modified approaches of Cerra and Saxena (2008) and Pentecôte and Rondeau (2015). The growth rates of economic policy uncertainty are separated into positive and negative uncertainty changes. Positive uncertainty dummy equals to the positive values of annual growth of economic policy uncertainty and zero otherwise. Negative uncertainty dummy equals to the negative values of annual growth of economic policy uncertainty and zero otherwise.

$$\text{Deposit} = \text{constant} + \beta * \sum_{i=1}^{4} \text{Deposit}_{t-i} + \gamma * \sum_{i=0}^{4} \text{Crisdum}_{t-i}$$

$$+ \tau * \sum_{i=0}^{4} \text{Uncertainty\_dum}_{t-i} + \varepsilon_t \qquad (32.4)$$

The economic policy uncertainty dummies are captured by Uncertainty_dum$_{t-i}$ in Eq. (32.4) and are included separately in the model. An additional dummy, that captures the recession in 2009Q1–2009Q3 and periods of subsequent turbulence in economic growth and zero otherwise is included in the model. The Crisdum$_{t-i}$ is equal to one for period beginning in 2007Q3 to end of sample and zero otherwise. The dummy also captures periods of elevated global turbulence, low and volatile economic growth. These equations are estimated using 10,000 Monte Carlo Draws. The responses of growth of companies' deposits to positive and negative economic policy uncertainty shocks are shown in Fig. 32.5. A negative economic policy uncertainty shock lowers significantly the growth of companies' deposits. By contrast, a positive economic policy uncertainty shock raises companies' deposits significantly for seven quarters. This evidence shows that economic policy uncertainty dynamics matters for changes in companies' deposits.

The analysis further shows the effects of scenarios of both positive and negative economic policy uncertainty shocks based on Eq. (32.4). The

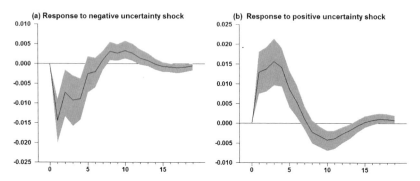

Fig. 32.5 Responses of growth of companies' deposit to negative and positive economic policy uncertainty shocks (*Note* The grey shaded area denotes 16th and 84th percentile confidence bands. *Source* Authors' calculations)

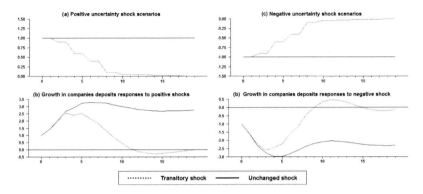

Fig. 32.6 Growth of companies' deposits to different economic policy uncertainty shock scenarios (*Source* Authors' calculations)

shock scenarios distinguish between transitory and unchanged shocks and responses are shown in Fig. 32.6. The growth of companies' deposits rises more to the unchanged positive economic policy uncertainty shock than to less persistent shock. This shows that more heightened economic policy uncertainty shocks lead to bigger growth of companies' deposits. In contrast, a large negative economic policy uncertainty shock leads to big reduction in the growth of companies' deposit than less persistent negative uncertainty shock. Thus, evidence shows that the nature of economic policy uncertainty shock matters for dynamics in growth of companies' deposits (Fig. 32.6).

Therefore evidence so far is robust to the technique used. Thus, negative economic policy uncertainty shock lowers growth of companies' deposits. By contrast, positive economic policy uncertainty shocks raise the growth of companies' deposits.

32.4 Evidence from the VAR Approach

The chapter extends the analysis to using bivariate VAR models to determine the responses of growth of companies' deposits to positive and negative economic policy uncertainty shocks. These economic policy uncertainty shocks are as defined in the preceding section. The models include growth of economic policy uncertainty and growth of companies' deposits. The models are estimated using two lags and

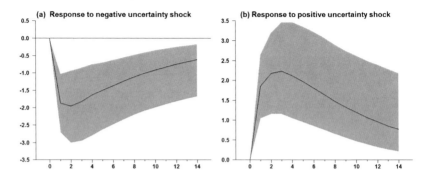

Fig. 32.7 Growth of companies' deposits responses to economic policy uncertainty shocks (*Note* The shaded grey band denotes the 16th and 84th percentile confidence bands. *Source* Authors' calculations)

10,000 Monte Carlo Draws. Like the preceding findings, evidence in Fig. 32.7, shows that negative economic policy uncertainty shocks lower significantly the growth of companies' deposits. By contrast, positive economic policy uncertainty shock raises growth of companies' deposits. The results are robust to the reverse ordering.

The analysis is extended to determine the robustness of the preceding findings through including growth of total loans and advances (credit) in the preceding VAR model. The impulse responses in Fig. 32.8, shows that both growth of credit and companies deposits react differently to

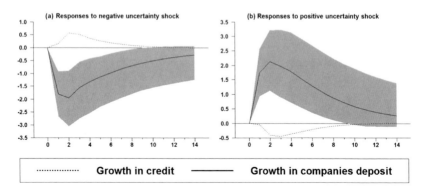

Fig. 32.8 Growth of companies' deposits and credit responses to economic policy uncertainty shocks (*Note* The grey shaded area denotes the 16th and 84th percentile confidence bands. *Source* Authors' calculations)

similar economic policy uncertainty shocks of the same magnitude. Thus, growth of credit increases to negative economic policy uncertainty shocks while growth of companies' deposits decline. In addition, a positive uncertainty shock raises growth of companies' deposits significantly whereas growth of credit declines.

32.5 Is There a Real Option Channel of Economic Policy Uncertainty Shock?

The real option theory suggests that elevated uncertainty has adverse effects on capital formation growth because investment is irreversible, hence agents adopt a cautious wait and see approach. Additional VAR models are estimated, and these include annual growth of economic policy uncertainty, annual capital formation growth and repo rate. The consumer price inflation (inflation), real GDP growth, and crisis dummy for the post-2008 period are used as exogenous variable in the model. The models are estimated using two lags and 10,000 Monte Carlo Draws. The quarterly (Q) data spans from 1990Q1 to 2016Q1. Figure 32.9a shows the trajectory of positive economic policy uncertainty shock which is highly transitory. This shock lowers

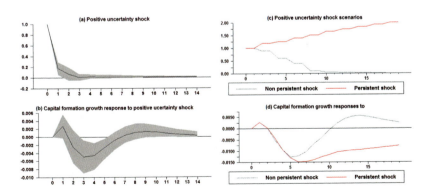

Fig. 32.9 Response of capital formation growth to positive economic policy uncertainty shocks (*Note* The grey shaded area denotes the 16th and 84th percentile confidence bands. *Source* Authors' calculations)

capital formation growth significantly between two and six quarters. This suggests that elevated economic policy uncertainty retards capital formation. Figure 32.9 shows scenarios for positive economic policy uncertainty shocks. The persistent economic policy uncertainty shock lowers capital formation growth more than the non-persistent shock in Fig. 32.9d. This evidence further shows that elevated economic policy uncertainty retards capital formation growth.

While positive economic policy uncertainty shock retards capital formation growth, what are the effects of negative uncertainty shocks? This is answered by bringing in the role of the inflation regimes and growth of companies' deposits. The repo rate is replaced with growth of companies' deposits in the preceding VAR models. Figure 32.10 shows the responses of capital formation growth and companies' deposits to negative economic policy uncertainty shocks. Negative economic policy uncertainty shocks raise capital formation (Capital_for) growth significantly over six quarters in the low inflation regime. By contrast, a negative economic policy uncertainty shock lowers capital formation growth significantly in the high inflation regime. This evidence shows that the 6% inflation threshold matters for the effects of negative economic policy uncertainty shock on capital formation growth.

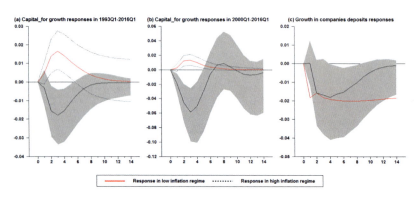

Fig. 32.10 Responses to negative uncertainty shocks and role of inflation regimes (*Note* The grey shaded area denotes the 16th and 84th percentile confidence bands. *Source* Authors' calculations)

32 Do Companies' Cash Holdings Impact the Transmission ...   465

Thus, capital formation only benefits from low economic policy uncertainty only in the low inflation regime; hence policymakers should note such developments and that price stability needs to be accompanied by low economic policy uncertainty. Irrespective of inflation regimes, negative economic policy uncertainty lowers growth of companies' deposits. The variations in the different responses of capital formation growth are due to the interest rate variable which increases in higher inflation regime compared to low inflation regime. Thus, it would be incomplete and inadequate to talk about benefits of low economic policy uncertainty without including price stability, since the latter is linked to monetary policy cycles.

We perform counterfactual analysis to show the role of growth of companies' deposits channel in transmitting positive economic policy uncertainty shocks to capital formation growth. The counterfactual VAR models use annual growth of economic policy uncertainty, annual capital formation growth and annual growth of companies' deposit. Both a counterfactual VAR model and the accompanying regime-dependent version are estimated. This will show the role of inflation regimes based on the 6% inflation threshold. The low inflation regime refers to inflation below or equal to 6%. High inflation regime refers to inflation above 6%. The models are estimated using 2 lags and 10,000 Monte Carlo Draws. The growth of companies' deposits channel is then shut off to calculate the counterfactual capital formation growth responses.

The responses of annual capital formation growth to positive economic policy uncertainty shocks are shown in Fig. 32.11. The decline in actual capital formation growth exceeds the counterfactual response. This indicates that growth of companies' deposits worsens the decline in capital formation growth following a positive economic policy uncertainty shock. However, the decline differs between the low and high inflation regimes. The growth of companies' deposits leads to smaller amplification in capital formation growth contraction in the low inflation regime than in the high inflation regime. This indicates that price stability matters for the transmission of positive economic policy uncertainty shocks to capital formation growth.

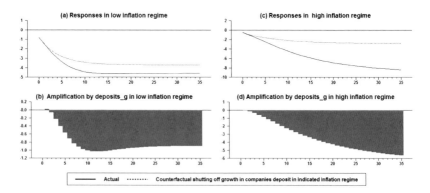

Fig. 32.11 Accumulated capital formation growth responses to positive uncertainty shocks and the role of inflation regimes (*Note* Deposits_g refers annual growth of companies' deposits. *Source* Authors' calculations)

The analysis further shows the role of inflation regimes in impacting the growth of companies' deposit channel in transmitting negative economic policy uncertainty shocks to capital formation growth. But the focus is on the inflation targeting period. The preceding model is used, and the annual growth of economic policy uncertainty is replaced with a dummy which equals to the values of negative growth of economic policy uncertainty and zero otherwise.

Figure 32.12a shows that negative economic policy uncertainty shocks raise capital formation growth in the low inflation regime. In addition, the actual growth exceeds the counterfactual in the low inflation regime. This suggests that a decrease in growth of companies' deposits magnifies the capital formation growth following negative economic policy uncertainty shock. This suggests that companies increase their capital formation. Figure 32.12c shows that negative economic policy uncertainty shocks have a delayed positive impact on capital formation growth in the high inflation regime. This is because a decrease in the growth of companies' deposit dampens the decline in capital formation growth that would be achieved in the absence of companies' deposits channel. In addition, the growth of the companies' deposit decline is much larger in the high inflation regime than in the low regime.

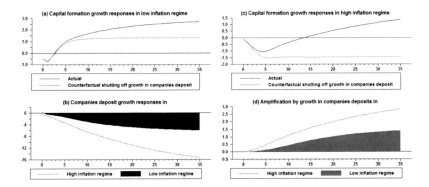

Fig. 32.12 Accumulated capital formation growth responses to negative uncertainty shocks and the role of inflation regimes (*Source* Authors' calculations)

This shows that inflation regimes matter. This indicates that price stability matters for the overall effects of negative economic policy uncertainty onto capital formation growth.

32.6 What Are the Implications for Expansionary Monetary Policy Shocks on Driving Capital Formation Dynamics When Inflation Is Below or Equal to 6%?

The analysis shows the role of economic policy uncertainty in the transmission of expansionary monetary policy shocks to capital formation growth in the low inflation regime. A counterfactual VAR model is estimated, and this includes changes in the repo rate, capital formation growth, companies' deposits growth and annual growth of economic policy uncertainty. The regime dependent counterfactual VAR shut off the economic policy uncertainty channel in transmitting expansionary policy shocks to capital formation growth. The model is based on inflation below or equal to 6%. In Fig. 32.13, the actual capital formation growth

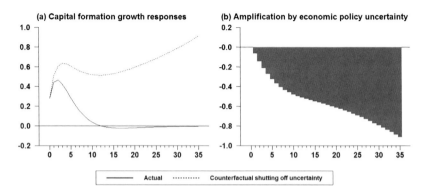

Fig. 32.13 Capital formation responses to expansionary monetary policy shock and role of economic policy uncertainty (*Source* Authors' calculations)

rises less than the counterfactual. This suggests elevated economic policy uncertainty dampens the capital formation growth reaction to the expansionary monetary policy shocks as shown in Fig. 32.13b. This suggests that a large expansionary monetary policy shock than expected maybe required to achieve the same effect to that due to a smaller-size shock in the absence of the economic policy uncertainty channel.

32.7 Conclusion and Policy Implications

This chapter examined whether economic policy uncertainty shock drives cash holding of companies measured by deposits held at the banks. In addition, we determine the extent to which inflation regimes impact the relationship between economic policy uncertainty and companies' deposits held at the banks. We extended the analysis to investigating if the companies' cash holdings impact the transmission of economic policy uncertainty shocks to capital formation. We also showed the extent to which the real option channel of economic policy uncertainty shock holds and this depends on inflation regimes

First, evidence shows that positive economic policy uncertainty raises growth of companies' deposits. In contrast, the negative economic policy uncertainty reduces the growth of companies' deposits. Second, a

32 Do Companies' Cash Holdings Impact the Transmission ... 469

positive economic policy uncertainty shock retards capital formation growth which is consistent with the predictions of real options theory. However, negative economic policy uncertainty shock raises capital formation only when inflation is below or equal to 6% and lowers it above this threshold. This evidence shows that the 6% inflation threshold matters for the effects of negative economic policy uncertainty shock on capital formation growth. In policy terms, this implies that capital formation growth benefits from low economic policy uncertainty shock only when inflation is below or equal to 6%. Hence, policymakers should note that price stability need to be accompanied by low economic policy uncertainty to raise capital formation growth. Fourth, evidence shows that increases in growth of companies' deposits accentuate the decline in the capital formation following a positive economic policy uncertainty shock. The decline is large when inflation exceeds the 6% threshold than below it. The reduction in growth of companies' deposits in the low inflation regime amplifies the increase in the capital formation following a negative economic policy uncertainty shock. In policy terms, this implies price stability matters as the low inflation environment makes the growth of companies' deposits to cushion the decline in capital formation growth due to positive economic policy uncertainty shocks. Fifth, evidence shows that elevated economic policy uncertainty dampens the rise in capital formation growth to expansionary monetary policy shocks. This suggests that a large expansionary monetary policy shock than expected maybe required to achieve the same effect as a small-sized shock in the absence of economic policy uncertainty channel.

References

Baum, C. F., Caglayan, M., & Ozkan, N. (2002). *The impact of macroeconomic uncertainty on bank lending behavior* (Computing in Economics and Finance, No. 94). Society for Computational Economics.

Baum, C. F., Caglayan, M., & Talavera, O. (2010). On the sensitivity of firms' investment to cash flow and uncertainty. *Oxford Economic Papers*, New Series, *62*(2), 286–306.

Bernanke, Ben S. (1983). Irreversibility, uncertainty, and cyclical investment. *The Quarterly Journal of Economics, 98*(1), 85–106.

Bloom, N. (2009). The impact of uncertainty shocks. *Econometrica, 77*(3), 623–685.

Cerra, V., & Saxena, S. C. (2008). Growth dynamics: The myth of economic recovery. *The American Economic Review, 98*(1), 439–457.

Hlatshwayo, S., & Saxegaard, M. (2016). *The consequences of policy uncertainty: Disconnects and dilutions in the South African real effective exchange rate-export relationship* (IMF Working Paper WP/16/13).

Im, H. J., Park, H., & Zhao, G. (2017). Uncertainty and the value of cash holdings. *Economics Letters, 155*, 43–48.

Pentecôte, J., & Rondeau, F. (2015). Trade spillovers on output growth during the 2008 financial crisis. *International Economics, CEPII Research Center, 143*, 36–47.

33

Does an Increase in the Value of Companies' Cash Holdings Impact the Transmission of Expansionary Monetary Policy Shocks? Counterfactual Policy Analysis

Main Highlights

- Evidence indicates that expansionary monetary policy shocks raise credit growth more than the counterfactual suggests in the low uncertainty regime. This suggests that in the low economic policy uncertainty environment, the slowdown in companies' deposits growth due to expansionary monetary policy shock amplifies increases in the credit growth.
- By contrast, expansionary monetary policy shock raises credit growth less than the counterfactual in the high uncertainty regime. This is due to an increase in the growth of companies' deposits in the high uncertainty regime, which dampens credit growth.
- The multiplier mechanism in the credit creation based on deposits is weakened in the high economic policy uncertainty periods and this weakens the stimulatory effects of expansionary monetary policy shocks. This suggests that a higher than expected policy stimulus may induce improvements in the multiplier effects.

© The Author(s) 2019
E. Ndou and T. Mokoena, *Inequality, Output-Inflation Trade-Off and Economic Policy Uncertainty,*
https://doi.org/10.1007/978-3-030-19803-9_33

471

33.1 Introduction

Evidence in the preceding chapter indicates that an unexpected elevation in economic policy uncertainty induces companies to increase their cash holdings as measured by deposits in banks. In addition, the chapter showed that increased cash holdings during high economic policy uncertainty periods leads to slowdown in the growth of gross fixed capital formation, consistent with increased value of the option to wait and the ultimate postponement of investment.[1] This analysis is an extension of the preceding chapter but focuses on showing the implications of increased cash holdings for the transmission of expansionary monetary policy shock effects. Is it possible that the increased growth of companies' cash holdings (measured by deposits) could impact the transmission of expansionary monetary policy shocks to credit growth? Is it possible that, the slowdown in credit growth could be linked to the weakened role of deposits in credit creation in the high economic policy uncertainty regimes?

This chapter brings the view, that, they may be unintended macroeconomic consequences, if the growth of companies' deposits mitigates or reduces the transmission of the expansionary monetary policy shocks to credit growth during periods of elevated economic policy uncertainty. Thus, the link between credit growth and deposits may be broken down depending on whether economic policy uncertainty is high or low. Under normal conditions, an increase in deposits should translate into an increase in credit extended, *ceteris paribus*. Hence, the chapter tests whether the role of growth of companies' deposits in passing through expansionary monetary policy shocks differs between low and high economic policy uncertainty. The chapter submits a view that inflation regimes may influence the growth of companies' deposits to either mitigate or magnify the transmission of expansionary monetary policy shocks to credit growth.

---

[1] This slowdown in growth in gross capital formation is consistent with predictions of the real option theory in which increased uncertainty, make agents to be cautious and adopt a "*wait and see approach*".

33.2 How Important Is the Growth of Companies' Deposit Channel in Transmitting Expansionary Monetary Policy Shocks to Credit Dynamics?

This question is answered by examining the importance of the growth of companies' deposits in transmitting negative economic policy uncertainty shocks to the growth of credit. The analysis uses quarterly (Q) data from 1993Q1 to 2016Q1 to estimate VAR models. The Economic Policy Uncertainty index data is obtained from Hlatshwayo and Saxegaard (2016). The other data is obtained from the South African Reserve Bank. The VAR model includes changes in the repo rate, annual growth of credit and annual growth of companies' deposits. The annual real GDP growth and crisis dummy are used as exogenous variables in the model. The crisis dummy equals one beginning in 2009Q1 to the end of sample and zero otherwise. The VAR model is estimated using 1 lag and 10,000 Monte Carlo draws. In addition, the analysis calculates the quarter-on-quarter growth of economic policy uncertainty index obtained from Hlatshwayo and Saxegaard (2016). The negative (positive) values of growth of economic policy uncertainty denote a low (high) uncertainty regime.

This chapter estimates regime-dependent counterfactual VAR models based on economic policy uncertainty regimes. This includes shutting off the growth of companies' deposits channel to determine the counterfactual credit growth reaction. The gap between the actual and counterfactual credit growth responses measures the importance of the growth of the companies' deposit channel.

Do economic policy uncertainty regimes matter for the expansionary monetary policy effects on credit growth? Evidence in Fig. 33.1a indicates that in the low uncertainty regime the actual credit growth response exceeds the counterfactual. This evidence suggests that the growth of companies' deposits magnifies the credit increase due to an expansionary monetary policy shock. By contrast, in Fig. 33.1c expansionary monetary policy shocks raise actual credit growth less than the counterfactual in the high economic policy uncertainty regime. This is because growth of companies' deposits has a dampening effect on credit

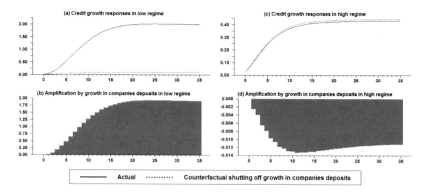

Fig. 33.1 Accumulated credit growth responses to expansionary monetary policy shocks according to uncertainty regimes (*Source* Authors' calculations)

growth, following an expansionary monetary policy shocks as shown in Fig. 33.1d. This shows that economic policy uncertainty regimes impact the way expansionary monetary policy shocks get transmitted via the growth of companies' deposits to impact credit growth.

33.3 How Important Is Price Stability for Growth of Companies' Deposits Channels in Transmitting Expansionary Monetary Policy Shocks to Credit Dynamics?

The analysis further examines the extent to which inflation regimes impact the transmission of expansionary monetary policy shocks to credit dynamics. Hence, the need to estimate regime-dependent counterfactual VAR models based on inflation regimes. A high (low) inflation regime refers to inflation above (below or equal to) 6%. The economic policy uncertainty variable is then replaced with annual consumer price inflation in the preceding VAR models. The counterfactual credit growth response is determined by shutting off the growth of companies deposits in transmitting expansionary monetary policy shocks to credit in each inflation regime.

Evidence in Fig. 33.2a shows that expansionary monetary policy shocks raise actual credit growth much higher than the counterfactual

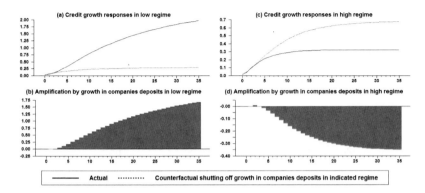

Fig. 33.2 Accumulated responses to expansionary monetary policy shocks according to inflation regimes (*Source* Authors' calculations)

indicates. This suggests that the growth of companies' deposits magnifies the increase in credit to an expansionary monetary policy shock in the low inflation regime. Can a similar credit growth reaction be seen in the high inflation regime? No, because in Fig. 33.2c the counterfactual exceeds the actual credit growth in the high inflation regime. This evidence indicates that the growth of companies' deposits depresses the credit extension in the high inflation regime as shown in Fig. 33.2d. Evidence concludes that inflation regimes matter for the growth of companies' deposit channel to pass through the expansionary monetary policy shocks to credit growth.

33.4 Low Uncertainty Matters for the Interaction Between Real GDP Growth and Growth of the Companies' Deposits

The analysis concludes by determining the extent to which negative economic policy uncertainty shocks get transmitted via the growth of the companies' deposits to impact both annual growth of real GDP and credit. The model estimated includes negative economic policy uncertainty dummy, annual real GDP growth, annual credit growth and annual companies' deposits growth. The inflation rate and crisis

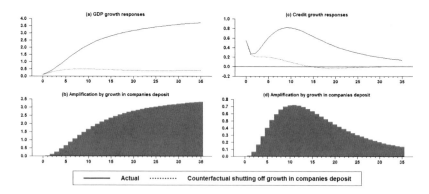

Fig. 33.3 Accumulated responses to negative economic policy uncertainty shocks (*Source* Authors' calculations)

dummies are included as exogenous variables in the model. The model is estimated using 1 lag and 10,000 Monte Carlo Draws. The negative economic policy uncertainty dummy equals to the value of the negative growth of the economic policy uncertainty and zero otherwise. The counterfactual VAR approach shuts off the growth of companies deposits in transmitting negative economic policy uncertainty shocks to real economic activity. In Fig. 33.3a, c, the negative economic policy uncertainty shocks raise actual GDP and credit growth rates more than the counterfactual suggests. This shows that the growth of companies' deposits magnifies the increases in the growth of credit and GDP, following negative economic policy uncertainty shocks.

33.5 Conclusion and Policy Implications

This chapter examined the importance of growth of companies' deposits in transmitting expansionary monetary policy shocks to credit growth and how this is impacted by economic policy uncertainty regimes. We show the effects based on low and high uncertainty regimes. Evidence indicates expansionary monetary policy shocks raise credit growth more than the counterfactual suggests in the low uncertainty regime. This suggests that in the low economic policy uncertainty environment, the slowdown in companies' deposits growth due to the expansionary monetary policy shocks, amplify increases in the credit growth. By contrast, expansionary monetary policy shocks raise credit growth less than the counterfactual in the high uncertainty regime. This is due to an increase in the growth of companies' deposits in the high uncertainty regime that dampens credit growth. We conclude that economic policy uncertainty regimes impact the way expansionary monetary policy shocks get transmitted via growth of companies' deposits to impact credit growth. From policy perspective, the slowdown in credit growth could be linked to a weakened role of deposits in credit creation in the high economic policy uncertainty regime. The policy implication is that the multiplier mechanism in credit creation based on deposits is weakened in the high economic policy uncertainty periods and this weakens the stimulatory effects of expansionary monetary policy shocks. This suggests that a higher than expected policy stimulus may induce an improvement in the multipliers effects.

The analysis further examined the extent to which the inflation regimes impact the transmission of expansionary monetary policy shocks to credit dynamics. Evidence shows that expansionary monetary policy shocks raise actual credit growth much higher than the counterfactual reaction in the low inflation regime. By contrast, the counterfactual exceeds actual credit growth in the high inflation regime. We therefore conclude that inflation regimes matter for the growth of companies' deposit channel to pass through expansionary monetary policy shocks to credit growth.

References

Baum, C. F., Caglayan, M., & Ozkan, N. (2002). *The impact of macroeconomic uncertainty on bank lending behavior* (Computing in Economics and Finance 94). Society for Computational Economics.

Bloom, N. (2009). The impact of uncertainty shocks. *Econometrica, 77*(3), 623–685.

Hlatshwayo, S., & Saxegaard, M. (2016). *The consequences of policy uncertainty: Disconnects and dilutions in the South African real effective exchange rate-export relationship* (IMF Working Chapter WP/16/113).

Im, H. J., Park, H., & Zhao, G. (2017). Uncertainty and the value of cash holdings. *Economics Letters, 155,* 43–48.

34

Does an Unexpected Reduction in Economic Policy Uncertainty Impact Inflation Expectations?

Main Highlights

- Evidence indicates that an unexpected reduction in the economic policy uncertainty lowers all the categories of inflation expectations. This suggests that an unexpected reduction in economic policy uncertainty has a direct impact on the inflation expectations and may lead to anchoring of inflation expectations.
- We perform counterfactual analysis to determine what would have happened to inflation expectations when the exchange rate, economic growth, and consumer price inflation channels are shut off in transmitting unexpected reduction in economic policy uncertainty. Evidence from counterfactual analysis shows that the actual inflation expectations decline more than the counterfactual response.
- This suggests that an exchange rate appreciation and reduction in the consumer price inflation, following an unexpected reduction in the economic policy uncertainty, lead to further reduction in the inflation expectations.

© The Author(s) 2019 **479**
E. Ndou and T. Mokoena, *Inequality, Output-Inflation Trade-Off and Economic Policy Uncertainty,*
https://doi.org/10.1007/978-3-030-19803-9_34

34.1 Introduction

The central bank indicated on several occasions that it is comfortable with both consumer price inflation and inflation expectations being lower than 4.5%, which is the midpoint of the inflation target band. The emphasis of the midpoint target gained momentum since the uncertainty about economic policy has been deemed to be elevated. The missing policy gap in the communication has been the continuous lack in the clarity regarding whether uncertainty about economic policy is a hindrance or limits the speed at which inflation and inflation expectations should fall towards the 4.5%. This is not surprising given that literature which includes Baker et al. (2015) who constructed various economic policy indices for selected countries, have used these indices to show that elevated uncertainty explains depressed economic growth and sluggish economic recovery. However, these studies did not link economic policy uncertainty on impacting the attainment of price stability.

Is the decline in economic policy uncertainty the missing link needed to stimulate economic growth, while enabling the attainment of price stability via the inflation expectations channel? As a result, this analysis examines whether the unexpected reduction in the economic policy uncertainty impacts the inflation expectations dynamics.

It seems, theoretically at least, there is no ambiguity about the effects of the unexpected reduction in the economic policy uncertainty on the exchange rate appreciations. But they maybe differing sizes of exchange rate appreciations. The overall effects of the economic policy uncertainty on the expected price level are ambiguous, and, this may pose policy dilemmas, especially when the effects of the exchange rate on aggregate supply and demand are not looked at. The ambiguity would be less of an issue if it could be determined whether it is the demand or the supply channel that does most of adjustment. The unexpected reduction in economic policy uncertainty (EPU) in Fig. 34.1a, is supposed to shift outwards the domestic demand (DD) schedule from DD (EPU0) to DD (EPU1) thereby raising output

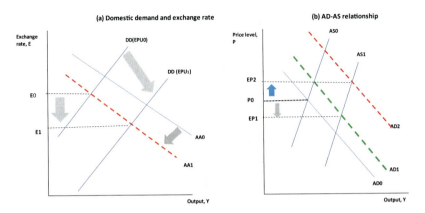

Fig. 34.1 A depiction of the transmission of the unexpected reduction in the economic policy uncertainty (*Source* Authors' calculations)

following an increase in investment. In addition, the exchange rate appreciates from E0 to E1.

The exchange rate affects both the aggregate supply and demand. In Fig. 34.1b, the exchange rate appreciation may lower the price of imported intermediated goods, thereby shifting the aggregate supply (AS) curve from AS0 to AS1. At the same time, the low price of domestic goods may shift the aggregate demand curve (AD) outwards, thereby raising output. The shift in aggregate demand may lead to lower (EP1) or higher (EP2) expected price relative to that at P0. To what extent would the unexpected reduction in the economic policy uncertainty impact inflation expectations in the direction desired by policymakers?

First, the uncertainty regarding the final expected price level outcome induces policy response dilemmas. Second, theory and evidence suggest that in an environment of well-anchored inflation expectations, temporary news or shocks to economic variables should not influence the inflation expectations. Figure 34.1 illustrates the theoretical prediction due to uncertainty caused by economic policy in affecting economic agents' inflation expectations. Third, the recent studies such as Ghosh et al. (2017) as well as Istrefi and Piloiu (2014) report that elevated economic policy uncertainty shocks pose upside risks to the anchoring of long-term inflation expectations is new to the literature.[1] Fourth, studies find that elevated economic uncertainty tend to move GDP growth and inflation expectations in different directions and this may impair monetary policy decisions. Theoretically, elevated uncertainty is supposed to reduce hiring, investment, and consumption of durables in the presence of adjustment costs.

This chapter differs from Ghosh et al. (2017) as well as Istrefi and Piloiu (2014). We fill policy research gaps by showing that the unexpected reduction in the economic policy uncertainty impacts inflation expectations directly and indirectly via other channels. Second, the study fills policy gaps by applying a counterfactual approach to determine how GDP growth, the exchange rate, and the consumer price inflation channel, transmit uncertainty shocks to inflation expectations.

Evidence indicates that an unexpected reduction in the economic policy uncertainty lowers all categories of the inflation expectations. This indicates that an unexpected reduction in the economic policy uncertainty has direct impact on inflation expectations. Thus, the reduction may lead to the anchoring of inflation expectations. The chapter performs a counterfactual analysis, which shuts off the exchange rate, consumer price inflation, and the GDP growth channels in transmitting economic policy uncertainty shocks to inflation expectations. Evidence shows that actual inflation expectations decline more than the counterfactual response. This suggests that an exchange rate appreciation and the subsequent reduction in the consumer price inflation, following an unexpected reduction in the economic policy uncertainty, leads to further reduction in the inflation expectations. There is need for a clear communication on what policymakers can do and what they know, how they can respond to the present challenges. Also, a long-term consistency of policies would help reduce economic policy uncertainty, leading to anchoring of lower inflation expectations.

---

[1]And these studies indicate that monetary policy appears to face a trade-off between responding to the state of the economy and to long-run inflation expectations. This is because the unexpected increase in economic policy uncertainty leads central banks to lower interest rates strongly. They suggest this resembles the response of a central bank that follows a typical Taylor rule, accommodating the economy in response to falling output and prices.

34.2 Are the Effects of Unexpected Reduction in Economic Policy Uncertainty Depicted in a Model Applicable to the South African Economy?

The analysis begins by examining various channels in which the unexpected reduction in economic policy uncertainty is transmitted to the economy based on variables in Fig. 34.1. The estimated baseline VAR model is based on the variables in the preceding theoretical model. The baseline VAR model includes GDP growth, nominal effective exchange rate (NEER) growth, consumer price inflation and economic policy uncertainty growth. These are annual rates. The model is estimated using one lag and 10,000 Monte Carlo Draws using quarterly (Q) data spanning 1995Q1 to 2015Q4. The economic policy uncertainty is obtained from Hlatshwayo and Saxegaard (2016). The other data is obtained from the South African Reserve Bank. The objective is to determine the effects of the unexpected reduction in the economic policy uncertainty. The results are shown in Fig. 34.2. An unexpected reduction in economic policy uncertainty raises economic growth significantly for over two years. The exchange rate appreciates while the

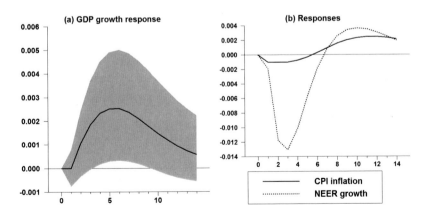

Fig. 34.2 Responses to unexpected reduction in economic policy uncertainty (*Note* The grey shaded band denotes the 16th and 84th percentile confidence bands. *Source* Authors' calculations)

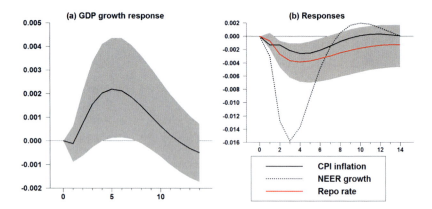

Fig. 34.3 Evidence from the expanded model (*Note* The grey shaded band denotes the 16th and 84th percentile confidence bands. *Source* Authors' calculations)

consumer price inflation declines. Thus, the effects of the unexpected reduction in the economic policy uncertainty are consistent with the predictions in the model in Fig. 34.1.

The chapter further performs several robustness tests to determine whether the preceding findings are sensitive to the inclusion of the repo rate. Evidence in Fig. 34.3 shows that GDP growth rises significantly for eight quarters. In addition, the exchange rate appreciates while consumer price inflation declines. The decline in consumer price inflation is accompanied by a reduction in the repo rate. This suggests that the reduction in the economic policy uncertainty may lower the risk premium on the exchange rate. This evidence shows that the unexpected reduction in the economic policy uncertainty is directly transmitted via economic growth, consumer price inflation, exchange rate, and policy rate.

34.2.1 Evidence from Economic Policy Uncertainty Shock Scenario Analysis

The analysis further determines whether, the persistence of the reduction in the economic policy uncertainty shock matters. Figure 34.4 shows three scenarios of unexpected reduction in economic policy uncertainty shocks. The scenarios include the constant change, persistent

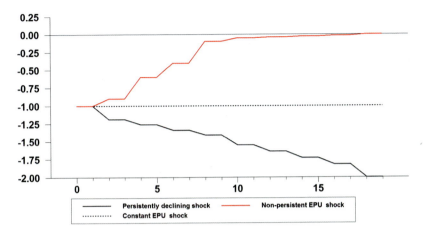

Fig. 34.4 Depictions of the unexpected reduction in the economic policy uncertainty shock scenarios (*Source* Authors' calculations)

decline and transitory decline. This analysis will reveal the extent to which the persistence of the economic policy uncertainty shock matters.

The responses of variables to the unexpected reduction in economic policy uncertainty are shown in Fig. 34.5. The persistent decline in economic policy uncertainty leads to a big appreciation in the exchange

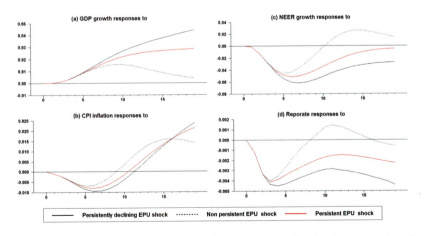

Fig. 34.5 Responses to various shocks of unexpected reduction in economic policy uncertainty (*Note* EPU refers to economic policy uncertainty. *Source* Authors' calculations)

486 E. Ndou and T. Mokoena

rate relative to that induced by transitory decline in the uncertainty shock. In addition, the consumer price inflation declines more to a persistently declining economic policy uncertainty shock than to a transitory shock. Furthermore, the policy rate declines irrespective of the size of the economic policy uncertainty shocks, while the real economic growth rises. The reaction indicates that the persistence of the economic policy uncertainty shocks matters for the maximum responses.

34.3 Do the Economic Policy Uncertainty Shocks Impact Inflation Expectations?

The preceding evidence revealed that an unexpected reduction in the economic policy uncertainty leads to an increase in output, a reduction in both the consumer price inflation and the policy rate. However, little is known about how economic policy uncertainty affects inflation expectations. This section investigates the dynamic relationship between policy related uncertainty and measures of inflation expectations. Does an unexpected reduction in economic policy uncertainty impact inflation expectations?

The chapter further estimates the bivariate VAR models using annual growth in economic policy uncertainty and inflation expectations. The categories of the inflation expectations are included separately in the model. The models are estimated using quarterly data from 2002Q3 to 2016Q1. The model is estimated using 10,000 Monte Carlo Draws and two lags. The negative economic policy uncertainty shock lowers all the inflation expectations variables in Fig. 34.6. However, the current and one year ahead inflation decline much more than the two years ahead inflation expectations. This suggests that economic policy uncertainty has direct influence on the inflation expectations.

In addition, Fig. 34.7 shows the economic policy uncertainty shocks scenarios and the responses of inflation expectations and GDP growth. Inflation expectations decline much more to the persistent reduction in the economic policy uncertainty shock than to a non-persistent shock. This shows that the subsiding economic policy uncertainty may be an

34 Does an Unexpected Reduction in Economic Policy ...   487

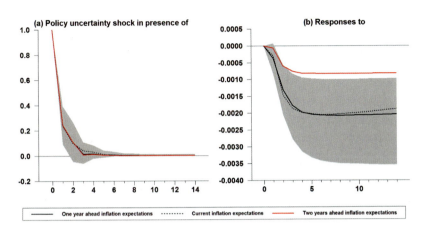

Fig. 34.6 Responses to unexpected reduction in economic policy uncertainty (*Note* The grey shaded band denotes the 16th and 84th percentile confidence bands. *Source* Authors' calculations)

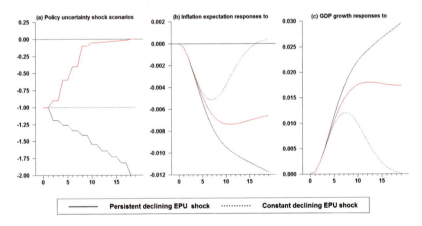

Fig. 34.7 Economic policy uncertainty shock scenarios and inflation expectations (*Note* EPU refers to economic policy uncertainty. *Source* Authors' calculations)

additional channel that is needed to lower the inflation expectations. The reduction would be enlarged if the negative economic policy uncertainty shock is much larger. In addition, GDP growth increases to all scenarios of unexpected reductions in economic policy uncertainty.

34.3.1 Can the Unexpected Reduction in the Economic Policy Uncertainty Lower Inflation Expectations?

This section performs three counterfactual VAR analysis. This is used to determine what would happen to the inflation expectations when the exchange rate, economic growth, and the consumer price inflation channels are shut off in transmitting economic policy uncertainty shocks to inflation expectations. The analysis examines the relevance of the exchange rate, the consumer price inflation and GDP growth channels in transmitting the unexpected reduction in economic policy uncertainty to inflation expectations. The counterfactual refers to the impulse responses after shutting off the indicated channels individually in the model.

The Role of the Exchange Rate Channel in Transmitting the Unexpected Reduction in Economic Policy Uncertainty to Inflation Expectations

In Fig. 34.8 actual inflation expectations decline more than the counterfactual response. This suggests that the exchange rate appreciation,

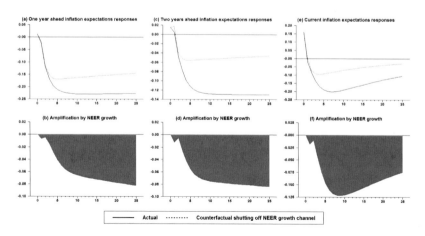

Fig. 34.8 Responses to unexpected economic policy uncertainty shock and the role of the exchange rate channel (*Source* Authors' calculations)

34 Does an Unexpected Reduction in Economic Policy ...

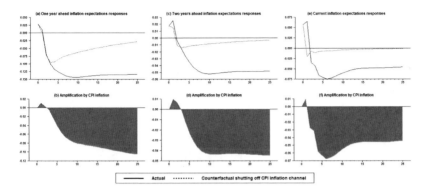

Fig. 34.9 Responses to unexpected economic policy uncertainty shock and the role of CPI inflation (*Source* Authors' calculations)

following an unexpected reduction in the economic policy uncertainty, leads to further reduction in the inflation expectations.

The Role of the CPI Inflation Channel in Transmitting the Unexpected Reduction in Economic Policy Uncertainty to Inflation Expectations

The section further examines the relevance of the consumer price inflation channel in transmitting the unexpected reductions in the economic policy uncertainty to inflation expectations. In Fig. 34.9 the actual inflation expectations decline more than the counterfactual response. This suggests that the decline in consumer price inflation, following an unexpected reduction in the economic policy uncertainty, leads to further reduction in inflation expectations.

The Role of the GDP Growth Channel in Transmitting the Unexpected Reduction in Economic Policy Uncertainty to Inflation Expectations

The chapter concludes by examining further the relevance of the GDP growth channel in transmitting unexpected reduction in economic policy uncertainty to the inflation expectations. In Fig. 34.10, the actual

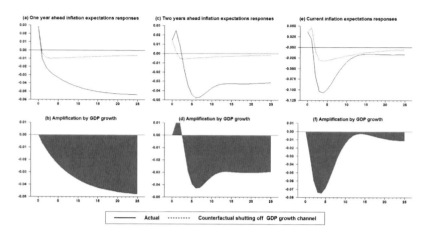

Fig. 34.10 Responses to unexpected economic policy uncertainty shock and the role of the GDP channel (*Source* Authors' calculations)

inflation expectations decline more than the counterfactual response. This suggests that the decline in GDP growth, following an unexpected reduction in the economic policy uncertainty, leads to further reduction in inflation expectations.

34.4 Conclusions

Theory and evidence suggest that, in an environment of well-anchored inflation expectations temporary news or shocks to economic variables should not influence long-run inflation expectations. Does an unexpected reduction in economic policy uncertainty impact inflation expectations dynamics in South Africa? Evidence indicates that an unexpected reduction in economic policy uncertainty lowers the inflation expectations. This suggests that a lower economic policy uncertainty has a direct impact on inflation expectations and this leads to the anchoring of inflation expectations. The chapter performed counterfactual analysis to determine what would have happened to inflation expectations when the exchange rate, economic growth and the CPI channels are shut off in transmitting an unexpected reduction in economic policy uncertainty to inflation expectations. The counterfactual refers to inflation expectations impulse responses after shutting off the exchange rate channel and the consumer price inflation channel, respectively. Evidence shows that all the categories of the actual inflation expectations decline more than the counterfactual response. This suggests that an exchange rate appreciation and reduction in the consumer price inflation, following an unexpected reduction in the economic policy uncertainty, leads to further reduction in the inflation expectations. Overall, these results support our hypothesis that, in an environment of increased policy uncertainty, agents begin to question the ability and the commitment of policymakers to deliver on their promises (Istrefi and Piloiu 2014). The credibility of a central bank's commitment in the eyes of the public becomes crucial for the success of monetary policy implementation. But this credibility is in doubt when there exists uncertainty about the details of the policy put in place, its effectiveness, the firmness of the commitment to future policies but also about other policies such as fiscal policy. A clear communication on what policymakers can do and what they know should prompt a strong response to prevailing challenges, and a long-term consistency of policies would help reduce policy uncertainty.

References

Baker, S. R., Bloom, N., & Davis, S. J. (2015). *Measuring economic policy uncertainty* (NBER Working Paper 21633).

Ghosh, T., Sahu, S., & Chattopadhyay, S. (2017). *Household inflation expectations in India: Role of economic policy uncertainty and global financial uncertainty spill-over* (WP-2017-007). Mumbai: Indira Gandhi Institute of Development Research.

Istrefi, K., & Piloiu, A. (2014). *Economic policy uncertainty and inflation expectations* (Document No. 51.1).

Index

A

Aastveit, K.A. 382, 385
above 4.5 percent 43, 61, 63, 65
additional loan margins 416
adverse income inequality effects theory 4, 36
adverse inflationary effects 118
aggregate households' consumption inequality 182, 185
aggregate supply curve 13, 304
Albanesi, S. 54
Alireza, T. 402
Amir, S. 416
amplification effects 5, 10, 15, 16, 19, 52, 249, 345, 357, 359, 364, 365, 393, 430, 440, 449
amplified by the high income inequality 80
Ampudia, M. 222

anchoring of inflation expectations 24, 29, 298, 479, 482, 490
Areosa, M.B.M. 77
Areosa, W.D. 77
Atems, B. 38
Attanasio, O. 176
Average volatilities 296, 297
Aziakpono, M.J. 401

B

Bachmann, R. 442
Baker, S.R. 480
Ball, L. 14, 15, 17, 305–307, 312, 319, 335, 336, 344–346, 349, 369, 390, 395
banking concentration 255, 258, 262, 270, 278, 281, 283
banking regulation 162

© The Editor(s) (if applicable) and The Author(s), under exclusive license to Springer Nature Switzerland AG 2019
E. Ndou and T. Mokoena, *Inequality, Output-Inflation Trade-Off and Economic Policy Uncertainty*,
https://doi.org/10.1007/978-3-030-19803-9

494 Index

bank lending rate margins viii, xi,
28, 415–422
Baum, C.F. 23, 456
below 3 percent ix, 5, 7, 24, 25, 51,
61–65, 71, 87, 101
below 4.5 percent vi, 5, 7, 24, 25,
43–46, 49, 51, 55, 61–65,
67, 69, 71, 87, 101, 232, 320,
324, 326, 328–330
below 4.5 percent threshold ix, 4, 5,
24, 35, 37, 45, 46, 49, 51–55,
59, 63, 66, 67, 69–71, 91,
232, 233, 326
below 6 percent 51, 62, 63, 65,
71, 138, 143, 147, 148, 318,
320, 325, 327, 330, 385, 390,
415–417, 421, 422
Berger, A. 401
Bernanke, B.S. 21, 380, 455
Bertrand, M. 163
Bilbie, F.O. 77
bivariate VAR asymmetric approach
59, 97
bivariate VAR model 38, 40, 56, 57,
65, 108, 111, 124, 151, 164,
169, 178, 194, 210, 211, 243,
258, 262, 284–286, 325, 326,
352, 359, 382, 391, 395, 396,
417, 428, 443, 461, 486
Bivens, J. 90, 121
Bloom, N. 21, 380, 416, 427, 455,
480
Borio, C.E.V. 401
Bulir, A. 5, 53, 54, 78
Burgstaller, J. 401
business cycles 11, 95, 101, 238, 409

C

Caglayan, M. 23, 456
Campos, N. 242
capital formation ix, 20, 21, 23, 29,
47, 261, 277, 281, 283, 289,
453, 464–466, 468, 469, 472
capital formation growth xii, 23, 29,
453, 454, 463–469
Carlin, W. 264, 272, 283
Carney, M. 7, 88
Carpantier, F.F. 191, 192, 208, 222
Cash hoarding 454
cash holding of companies 468
cash holdings ix, 1, 20, 21, 452–454,
470
categories of consumption expenditure 176
cautious wait and see approach 463
central bank 2, 7, 77, 78, 88, 90,
207, 208, 223, 294, 480, 482,
491
Cerra, V. 459
Cetorelli, N. 272
Chatterjee, S. 295
Chattopadhyay, S. 481, 482
Chi, Q. 19, 441
Chong, B.S. 402
Coibion, O. 90, 121
cointegrating relationship 402
Cojocaru 78
Colciago, A. 90
Collie, S. x, 26, 162, 189, 192, 204,
206
companies' cash holdings viii, ix, 3,
20, 22, 453, 454, 456, 468,
471

Index 495

companies' deposits growth 29, 467, 471, 475, 477

Components of investment responses 276

consumer price inflation vi, 5, 13, 24, 35, 37, 40, 43, 45, 46, 52, 56, 57, 69, 89, 91, 101, 106–108, 117, 119, 125, 127, 128, 130, 135, 136, 138, 142, 144, 146, 148, 151, 157, 178, 181–183, 190, 202, 226, 228, 232, 241, 244–246, 250, 251, 318, 325, 417, 463, 474, 479, 480, 482–484, 486, 489, 491

consumer price inflation channel 43, 124, 125, 151, 172, 181–183, 185, 232, 249, 479, 482, 488, 489, 491

consumption inequality channel vii, 161, 163, 168, 170, 172, 175

consumption inequality response 180, 181

contractionary monetary policy dummy 83, 145

contractionary monetary policy shocks 6, 24, 75, 79, 80, 82–84, 88, 90, 92, 99, 100, 105, 106, 108, 112–115, 120

Cottarelli, C. 401

counterfactual analysis 3, 7, 11, 12, 24–26, 35, 44, 49, 52, 54, 56, 66, 87, 98, 101, 117, 130, 149, 189, 192, 197, 206, 215, 227, 228, 245, 255, 266, 269, 280, 281, 283, 287, 289, 327, 328, 363, 386, 422, 465, 479, 482, 490

counterfactual approaches 10, 49, 75, 84, 88, 221, 238

counterfactual consumption inequality response 181

Counterfactual policy analysis 456, 471

counterfactual VAR x, 26, 27, 45, 79, 113, 125, 144, 145, 147, 156, 158, 175, 181, 185, 205, 213, 220, 246, 247, 277, 287, 354, 393, 415, 417, 421, 422, 430, 467, 476

counterfactual VAR models 47, 69, 100, 105, 115, 142, 158, 161, 162, 170, 173, 192, 249, 362, 419, 446, 465

CPI inflation channel 489

credit condition index 445, 447

credit conditions 19, 20, 29, 408, 409, 439–441, 444–447, 449–451

credit conditions cycles 409

credit conditions index channel 446, 449

credit conditions index tightens 447

credit creation 23, 471, 477

credit dynamics viii, 3, 8, 18–20, 161–166, 168–170, 172, 173, 175, 176, 209, 440–442, 450, 474, 477

credit extension 19, 20, 26, 161, 257, 281, 282, 285–287, 289, 409, 439, 442, 443, 450, 475

credit growth xii, 2, 9, 10, 18–20, 23, 26, 27, 29, 38, 40, 45, 55, 162, 163, 168, 169, 192, 194–197, 200, 202, 203, 205, 212, 213, 215, 217–225, 227, 228, 230, 234–236, 238, 269, 271, 405, 408–410, 439–451, 471–477

496 Index

credit growth channel 197, 198, 216, 230, 231
credit ratings downgrades 389
Cross correlations 457, 458

D

Davis, S.J. 480
de Bont, G.J. 400
Defina, R.H. 390
De Graeve, F. 401
de Haan, J. 90
De Jonghe, O. 401
demand management tool 358
demand volatilities 27, 303, 333–336, 340
Demirgüç-Kunt, A. 9, 191
deposits in banks 472
deposits in credit creation 23, 472, 477
Diallo 280
Di Bella, G. 36
Dimitruis, M. 402
direct inflow 124
disposable income growth 6, 7, 25, 54, 55, 66, 67, 75, 82, 84, 98, 99, 101
distributional effects vi, 5, 7, 51, 52, 58, 59, 88, 90, 120, 207, 208, 230
Dixit, A.K. 380
Duesenberry 164
durable goods 171, 178

E

economic growth vii, 1, 2, 4, 7, 16–18, 26, 28, 55, 59, 63, 67, 87, 89, 90, 93, 94, 99–101, 117, 118, 120, 128, 130, 137, 192, 198, 221–224, 228, 232, 241, 244–246, 251, 257, 264, 269, 271, 272, 277, 278, 280, 282, 283, 285, 294, 296, 301, 318, 334, 346, 358, 379, 380, 382–387, 390, 393, 395, 399, 403, 404, 410, 426, 441, 454, 460, 479, 480, 483, 484, 486, 488, 490
economic growth channel 198
economic policy uncertainty channel viii, 17, 18, 20, 37, 41–43, 358, 362, 363, 379, 380, 383, 385, 427, 428, 430, 431, 434, 435, 440, 442, 447–449, 467–469
economic policy uncertainty (EPU) v, viii, ix, xi, 3, 18–20, 28, 29, 37, 41, 42, 49, 244, 360, 362, 380–383, 385–387, 391, 396, 397, 416–419, 421, 422, 425–435, 440, 442–445, 447, 448, 450, 451, 453, 454, 456–461, 463, 466–468, 472–474, 479–484, 486–491
economic policy uncertainty regimes xi, 19, 28, 29, 358, 379, 383–387, 398, 439–441, 445–447, 451, 473, 474, 476, 477
economic policy uncertainty shocks 18, 20, 21, 29, 382, 383, 415, 417, 418, 422, 428, 429, 434, 439, 440, 442–444, 450, 453, 454, 462, 463, 465, 468, 476, 482, 486, 488–490
economic policy uncertainty shock scenarios 428–430, 461, 484, 485, 487

efficacy of the credit condition index channel 29, 439, 447, 451
elevated economic policy uncertainty xi, 4, 18, 20, 28, 35, 42, 49, 379, 383, 384, 386, 389, 415, 417, 422, 428, 435, 439, 440, 450, 451, 457, 464, 468, 469, 472, 481
Elstner, S. 442
employment channel 37, 99, 199, 270, 272, 277, 278
employment growth 5–7, 24, 25, 38, 40, 45, 46, 51, 54, 55, 61–64, 66, 67, 69, 71, 75, 79–84, 87, 89, 91, 95, 96, 98–101, 123, 190, 192, 197, 199, 207, 213–215, 217, 226, 227, 241, 244, 247, 251, 256
employment shares of the services sector 149
endogenous-exogenous VAR approach 364, 444
endogenous-exogenous VAR models 444
Engle-Granger 402
episodes of monetary policy tightening 404
EPU_growth 42
excess CAR x, 9, 26, 189–203, 206
exchange rate channel 120, 125, 126, 151, 157, 158, 488, 491
exogenous VAR 109, 166, 169, 179, 193, 225, 444
exogenous VAR (Exo_VAR) model 40
exogenous VAR model 40, 45, 95, 96, 110, 123, 166, 167, 169, 196, 226, 444
expansionary fiscal policy multiplier effects 396

expansionary monetary policy viii, ix, xi, xii, 6, 7, 15–17, 19–21, 23, 25, 27–29, 69, 75, 82–84, 87, 89–99, 101, 107, 114, 115, 120, 135, 138, 144–148, 242, 248, 249, 343, 344, 346, 354, 355, 357–365, 367, 375, 379, 380, 382–387, 394, 395, 397, 416, 419, 422, 426, 434, 435, 439–443, 445–451, 467–469, 471–475, 477
expansionary monetary policy dummy 83, 145
expansionary monetary policy multiplier effects 395
Expansionary monetary policy shock scenarios 96
expected price level 480, 481
exports 106–109, 111, 112, 114

F

favorable income inequality effects theory suggest 4, 36
Feldmann, H. 256, 257, 264, 276, 277, 282, 283, 285
financial conditions 442, 450
financial frictions 19, 440, 442, 443
financial globalisation vi, 25, 118
fiscal policy multiplier effects 390, 396
Flexible inflation targeting 296
Francis, B.B. 416, 417
Frank, R.H. 163
Friedman, M. 301
Fritz, W. 401
Frost, J. 206, 208, 222
Furceri, D. 90, 91, 121

498 Index

G

Gabraith, J.K. 191
Gambera, M. 272
GDP growth vi, viii, ix, 1, 3–7, 10,
17, 24–26, 28, 35–52, 54, 55,
57–60, 63, 64, 66–69, 71, 75,
79–84, 87, 91, 93, 95, 96, 98,
99, 101, 109, 123, 128, 129,
149, 153, 154, 169, 179, 189,
190, 192, 194–197, 199–203,
206, 213–217, 221, 224, 225,
227–229, 234, 236–238, 244,
245, 251, 270, 272, 296, 297,
307, 308, 310–314, 320,
326–329, 334, 336, 347, 349,
350, 358, 367–371, 375, 383,
384, 389–398, 417, 421, 422,
463, 473, 475, 482–484, 486,
487, 490
GDP growth channel 67, 198, 228,
488, 489
Ghosh, T. 481, 482
Gini coefficient 8, 11, 38, 55, 57,
79, 90, 91, 108, 121, 122,
138, 151, 164, 178, 190, 193,
207, 209, 223, 243, 256, 258,
261, 262, 266, 282
Grigoli, F. 36
gross fixed capital formation 1, 261,
273, 275, 276, 287, 454, 472
growth of companies' deposit channel 466, 473, 475, 477
growth of companies' deposits mitigate,
growth of companies' deposits
xii, 29, 453, 456, 457, 459–466,
468, 469, 471–474, 476, 477

growth of income inequality vii,
ix, 8, 24, 26, 56, 58, 59, 68,
70, 89, 91, 92, 96–99, 101,
105, 106, 108–115, 117, 118,
122–130, 152, 154, 178–184,
192, 193, 209, 217–219, 221,
222, 224, 225, 228, 229, 234,
236, 238, 242, 250
growth option channel 381
Guerrello, C. 78, 90, 120, 121
Gumata, N. 19, 38, 55, 79, 91, 138,
190, 193, 207, 209, 222, 223,
230, 232, 243, 293–296, 298,
320, 385, 409, 440
Guzman, M.G. 257, 282, 285

H

Hannan, T. 401
Hansen, B.E. 371
Hasan, I. 416, 417
Hasset, K. 176
Heckschler-Ohlin-Samuelson 106
heightened economic policy and
political uncertainty 389, 403,
426
Heinemann, F. 401
Herfindahl-Hirschman Index 256,
258, 271, 272, 284
high economic policy uncertainty xi–
xii, 20, 23, 27–29, 357, 365,
384, 416, 422, 427, 443, 451,
471, 472, 477
high economic policy uncertainty
regime 23, 28, 379, 384, 387,
447, 472, 473

high inflation regime xi, 14–17, 27, 28, 54, 126, 127, 147, 171, 183, 184, 233, 303, 308, 310, 312–317, 320, 324–328, 330, 333, 337, 338, 340, 343, 346, 348, 349, 351, 352, 355, 358, 359, 361, 367, 368, 370, 372, 375, 389, 391, 395, 396, 420, 456, 464–466, 475, 477
high output persistence 349, 364
high uncertainty regime 29, 418, 446, 448, 450, 471, 476, 477
Hlatshwayo, S. 41, 360, 396, 417, 442, 456, 473
Holmes, M.J. 320, 321, 324
Hölscher, J. x, 26, 162, 189, 192, 203, 206
household consumption growth xi, 16, 27, 79–82, 162, 343, 344, 346, 354, 355, 359, 363–365
household disposable income growth 7, 83, 87, 89, 95, 96, 101
house price growth 27, 192, 197, 199, 200, 205, 213, 218–220
house price growth channel 199, 200
house prices 207, 215
Hurst, E. 176

Im, H.J. 21, 455, 456
import and export channels 107
imports 106–109, 111, 114
Inaba, K. 90, 121
income inequality channel vi, 6, 9–11, 24, 26, 55, 59, 75–84, 88, 120, 192, 201, 202, 205, 206, 208, 218–223, 234, 235, 237, 238

income inequality shock scenarios 49, 166
income tax cuts xi, 27, 241, 242, 248, 251
income tax cut shock 5, 52, 70, 71
increased government consumption xi, 27, 51, 53, 71, 241, 242, 248, 250
increased growth of companies' cash holdings 472
increased income inequality growth x, 26, 189, 203, 206, 235
inflation below or equal to six percent 126, 359
inflation channel 8, 43, 45, 46, 70, 125, 171, 178, 181–183, 185, 419–421
inflation exceeds the six percent threshold, inflation expectations 13, 23, 24, 29, 190, 479–482, 486–491
inflation regime below the 4.5 percent threshold 5, 44, 51, 71
inflation regimes vi–viii, 3, 12, 15–18, 23, 37, 53, 64, 91–93, 95, 101, 135, 147, 157, 183, 184, 228, 232, 233, 304, 307–315, 317, 319, 323–325, 327, 329, 330, 333, 335–340, 343–345, 347–352, 355, 357, 359, 361, 363, 364, 368, 370–372, 390, 391, 393–398, 417, 419–422, 454, 458, 459, 464–468, 472, 474, 475, 477
inflation target band 2, 5, 51, 71, 142, 327, 345, 368, 372, 454, 480
inflation target band of 3 to 6 percent 318

Index

inflation targeting 224, 293, 298–301, 326, 385, 466
inflation-targeting period 38, 299, 326, 327
inflation thresholds 59, 156, 344, 368, 391, 416
inflation volatility 15, 27, 296, 298–301, 303, 333, 335–340
inflation volatility shocks 299, 300, 303, 333, 336, 337, 339
interest pass-through 400, 406
Istrefi, K. 481, 482, 491

J

Johansen cointegration tests 402
Johansson, A.C. 9, 191
Jones, J. 38

K

Kaldor, N. 4, 36
Khan, H. 345
Kiley approach 348, 352
Kiley, M.T. 15, 343–346, 348, 350, 352, 355
Killian 59, 97
King, M. 298
Kleimeier, S. 401
Klemperer, P. 401
Koelln, K. 17, 390
Kourelis, A. 401
Kraft 381
Kumhof, M. 163

L

labour income 89, 90, 121, 137

labour market reforms vii, x, xi, 27, 241–251
large negative economic policy uncertainty shock 461
Lazear, E. 36
Lebarz, C. 163
lending rates viii, 3, 18, 257, 282, 283, 400–402, 405, 406, 408, 409, 417, 422, 425–428, 430, 432, 434, 449
less persistent economic policy uncertainty shock 428
less persistent negative uncertainty shock 461
less persistent shock 281, 284, 289, 461
less rigid in the high inflation regime 346, 349
less subsiding economic policy uncertainty shock 430
Levine, A.S. 163
Levine, R. 9, 191
life cycle hypothesis 177
Liu 271, 402
Liu, M.-H. 402
loan intermediation mark-up(s) viii, 399, 400, 402–408, 410
logistic smooth transition autoregression (LSTR) 312, 349, 367, 368, 372, 375
logistic smooth transition autoregression model 349
loose loan to value ratio shock, loose LTV shock 10, 205, 206, 209–220
loosening credit conditions index 20, 28, 409, 439, 446, 451
loosening loan to value ratio 190

Index

Loungani, P. 90, 121
Lovin 78
low and high economic policy uncertainty 365, 417, 445, 472
low economic policy uncertainty xi, xii, 27–29, 241, 248, 251, 357, 365, 379, 384, 385, 387, 397, 398, 421, 422, 454, 465, 469
low economic policy uncertainty channel 385, 387
low economic policy uncertainty environment 29, 387, 471, 477
low economic policy uncertainty regime xi, xii, 28, 29, 389, 439, 446
lower unemployment 217, 257, 283
low inflation regime xi, 14–18, 27, 28, 54, 126, 127, 142–144, 147, 157, 183, 184, 233, 303, 307–313, 315–317, 320, 324, 326–328, 330, 337, 338, 343, 346, 348, 351, 352, 355, 357–365, 367, 372, 375, 382, 385–387, 391–398, 420, 453, 464–467, 469, 475, 477
Low interest rate pass-through 409
LTV ratio 10, 208, 209, 211, 212, 220
LTV shocks 27, 205, 207, 209, 211, 213
Lucas, R. 307, 335

M

macroprudential policies v, x, 10, 27, 190–192, 205–208, 220, 223
macroprudential regulators, macroprudential regulatory policies x, 26, 161, 223

magnify the transmission of expansionary monetary policy shocks 472
Mankiw, N.G. 14, 17, 305–307, 312, 319, 335, 336, 344, 346, 349, 369, 390, 395
Manufacturing employment responses 288
manufacturing employment share 137–139, 145, 147
manufacturing sector vi, 135–141, 144–148, 150, 288, 289
marginal propensity to consume (MPC) 6, 24, 75, 79, 80, 83, 84
Mathur, A. 176
Mayer, C. 264, 272, 283
Menna, L. 52
Meyer, B. 176
Milanovich, B. 163
mining sector employment share 135, 137–139, 142–144, 148
Mojon, B. 401
monetary policy viii, ix, 2, 3, 6–8, 17, 24, 25, 28, 29, 45, 51, 53, 71, 75–81, 83, 84, 87–93, 95, 96, 99–101, 105–108, 112–115, 117–121, 128–130, 136–138, 142–151, 154, 156, 157, 176, 178, 190, 208, 295, 297, 301, 318, 330, 343, 344, 354, 355, 358–360, 362, 363, 365, 367, 369, 375, 380, 382, 383, 385, 386, 390, 391, 393, 397–400, 404, 405, 409, 410, 415, 427, 434, 439, 440, 442, 449–451, 454, 472–477, 482, 491
monetary policy cycles 406, 454, 465

502 Index

monetary policy indicator 142, 145
monetary policy multiplier effects
17, 390
Monnin, P. 6, 7, 25, 75, 77, 84,
88–90, 101
Monte Carlo Draws 40, 45–47, 56,
57, 62, 69, 79, 98, 109, 111,
113, 123–125, 128, 129, 138,
142, 152, 157, 167, 169, 170,
179, 181, 193, 194, 196, 210,
211, 213, 224–226, 244, 247,
248, 259, 261, 272–277, 279,
287, 314, 325, 328, 336, 338,
353, 354, 360, 362, 382, 391,
393, 395, 417, 420, 421, 428,
444, 446, 447, 460, 462, 463,
465, 473, 476, 483, 486
Morse, A. 163
multiplier effects 17, 18, 28, 358,
389, 390, 393–398, 471
multiplier mechanism 23, 471, 477
multipliers effects of expansionary
monetary policy 394
Mumtaz, H. 90, 120

N

National Credit Act (NCA) vii, x,
10, 26, 190, 221–223, 238
Natvik, G.J. 382, 385
NCA shock scenarios 227
NCA standards 10, 222, 227, 229,
230, 232, 233, 235, 238
Ncube, M. 19, 385
Ndou, E. 19, 38, 55, 79, 91, 138,
190, 193, 207, 209, 222, 223,
230, 232, 243, 293–296, 298,
320, 385, 409, 440
NEER channel 155

negative deviations from 4.5 percent
inflation rate 59
negative economic policy uncertainty
channel 362, 431, 435
negative economic policy uncertainty
dummy 362, 475, 476
negative economic policy uncertainty
shock(s) 23, 382, 422, 428,
429, 432, 443, 445, 453, 456,
460–464, 466, 469, 473, 475,
476, 487
negative effect of loose LTV shock
211
negative GDP growth dummy 67,
228
negative GDP growth episodes 67
negative inflation shock scenarios 59
negative uncertainty dummy 428,
431, 448, 459
negative uncertainty shock scenarios
429
net capital inflow channel 25, 117,
118, 127–130
Neumark, D. 401
new classical economics 3, 14, 305,
319, 334
new Classical theories 13, 304, 335
new Keynesian hypothesis xi, 14, 27,
303, 315–317, 320, 333, 340
new Keynesian sticky price model
17, 390
Niggle, C.J. 403
Nini, G. 416
nominal demand shock viii, 12–14,
304–306, 308, 310, 313–322,
324–330, 335, 337, 367, 368,
370, 371
nominal demand volatility shock
335, 337–339

Index 503

the nominal effective exchange rate (NEER) 140, 152, 154–156, 483
nominal GDP growth 312, 313, 315, 327, 336, 338, 367, 368, 370, 372–375
non-durable goods consumption 171
non-gold mining component 140
non-persistent positive inflation shocks 58
nonresidential fixed capital formation 47
non-residential investment growth 10, 213, 215, 217
Nugent, Jeffrey 242

O

Odedokun, O. 307
OECD 242
Oege, D. 163
O'Farrell, R. 90, 120
Okun, A.M. 282
Okun's law 282
Olivera, J. 191, 192, 208, 222
Olson 295
option to "wait and see" 21, 455
Output-inflation trade-off v, vii, viii, 3, 12, 14, 15, 293–299, 301, 303–309, 314–316, 318, 333–340, 346
output persistence viii, xi, 15, 16, 27, 28, 343–355, 357–365
Output targeting 296
Ozkan, N. 23, 456

P

Paredes, E. 36

Park, H. 21, 455, 456
pass-through of the repo rate to bank lending rates viii
Pastor, L. 416, 427
Pentecôte, J. 459
Pereira, M. 242
persistence of output growth viii, 343, 347
persistence of the economic policy uncertainty shock 425, 428, 434, 485, 486
persistent decline 484, 485
persistently declining uncertainty shock 430
persistently rising economic policy uncertainty shocks 428
personal income tax cuts 242
Perugini, C. x, 26, 162, 189, 192, 203, 206
Philips curve 3, 14, 305–307, 319, 334
Piloiu, A. 481, 482, 491
Pindyck, R.S. 380
Pistaferri, L. 176
policy and political uncertainty 358, 416, 426, 427, 454
policy effectiveness 192, 303, 304, 324, 330, 333, 339, 370
policy efficiency frontier 294
policy ineffectiveness proposition 12–14, 17, 304, 305, 367, 368
policy rate loosening 405, 427
policy tightening phase 426
portfolio inflow 124
positive bank concentration shocks 11, 26, 255, 258–266, 269, 270, 272, 275–279, 281, 288, 289

504 Index

positive economic policy uncertainty 362, 422, 435, 459

positive economic policy uncertainty shock(s) xii, 23, 29, 382, 415–417, 419, 422, 428, 443, 445, 453, 456, 460–465, 469

positive excess capital adequacy ratio shocks, positive excess CAR shock vii, 9, 191–194, 196, 197, 199, 200, 202, 203, 206

positive GDP growth dummy 67, 228

positive GDP growth shocks 41

positive income inequality shocks x, 4, 8, 24, 26, 35–37, 39–47, 49, 50, 52, 161–168, 170–173, 175, 178, 180–183, 185

Positive income inequality shock scenarios 165

positive inflation shocks vi, ix, 5, 24, 51–58, 61–69, 71, 353, 354, 395, 396

positive manufacturing employment share shock 141, 142

positive net capital inflow shocks 122–127

positive nominal demand shock 12–16, 28, 305, 307–312, 315, 316, 318–320, 324–330, 375

positive nominal volatility shocks viii, 12, 333

positive uncertainty dummy 428, 431, 448, 459

positive wage shocks 359, 363–365

precautionary motive 21, 454

price flexibility 15, 16, 27, 320, 321, 343–346, 350, 352–355

price rigidities 318, 320, 321, 324

prices are less rigid 12, 14, 305, 315–317, 320, 346, 349

price stability 2, 4, 6, 8, 14–16, 23, 24, 26–29, 52, 53, 77, 84, 90, 144, 148, 151, 156, 157, 175, 176, 178, 181, 182, 184, 208, 242, 248, 249, 251, 293, 301, 303, 305, 316, 333, 355, 358, 367, 375, 391, 398, 417, 421, 453, 454, 456, 465, 467, 469, 474, 480

price stability mandate 78, 316, 318, 334, 340, 380, 390, 427

propagation of shocks 15, 346

public good 6, 77, 84, 90

Punzi, M.T. 208, 222

R

Rabitsch, K. 208, 222

Rajan, R. 4

Rancière, R. 163

Rawdanowicz, L. 90, 121

real option channel 21, 380, 381, 454, 455, 457, 463, 468

real option theory 21, 23, 379, 382, 383, 385, 386, 455, 463, 472

reduction in personal income tax 53

reduction of the income inequality 48

regime-dependent counterfactual VAR 314, 335, 446

regime-dependent counterfactual VAR models 338, 420, 447, 473, 474

regime-dependent regression equation(s) 310, 370

repo rate tightening 425, 427, 432, 433, 435

residential fixed capital formation 47

residential investment 4, 35, 47, 207, 213–216, 218
residential investment growth 10, 26, 27, 48, 205, 207, 213, 215, 219–223, 234, 237, 238
Richter, A.W. 163
risk premium 399, 404, 410, 442, 484
Robert, S.S. 380
the role of business cycles 94
Romer, C. 5, 53
Romer, D. 5, 14, 17, 53, 305–307, 312, 319, 335, 336, 344, 346, 349, 369, 390, 395
Rondeau, F. 459
Rosen, S. 36
Rush, M. 17, 390

S

Sahu, S. 481, 482
Samarina, A. 90
Sander, H. 401
Sarlo, C. 176
Saxegaard, M. 41, 360, 396, 417, 442, 456, 473
Saxena, S. 459
scenarios of both positive and negative economic policy uncertainty shocks 460
Scharler, J. 401
Scholnick 401
Schüller, M. 401
shares of manufacturing employment 135, 137
Sharpe, S.A. 401
Shrestha, K. 402

shut off 7, 45, 67, 69, 77, 79, 87, 98, 100, 101, 105, 114, 115, 125, 128, 129, 142, 145, 147, 153–155, 157, 170, 173, 178, 181–184, 192, 197, 213, 217, 229–231, 233, 235, 238, 248, 249, 263, 265, 277, 287, 289, 314, 328, 338, 354, 362, 363, 393, 419, 421, 422, 430, 431, 435, 446–448, 473, 474, 479, 488, 490, 491
shutting off the growth of companies' deposits channel 47, 98, 192, 466
Sims, E.R. 442
six percent viii, xi, 8, 17, 28, 29, 126, 127, 151, 171, 178, 183–185, 241, 248, 251
size of policy rate adjustments 80, 380, 381, 440, 450
Smith, D.C. 416
Smith, R.T. 257, 282, 285
Sola, S. 382, 385
South African Reserve Bank (SARB) 2, 5, 38, 52, 79, 91, 136, 150, 190, 193, 207, 243, 256, 270, 296, 307, 321, 347, 360, 370, 382, 391, 402, 403, 416, 417, 428, 442, 456, 473, 483
speculative motive 21, 454
Stein 381
Stephen, B. 21, 416, 427, 455
Stiglitz, J.E. 4, 36, 191, 400
Stone 381
Stopler-Samuelson theorem 106
structure-conduct-performance hypothesis 257, 282, 283, 285

506 **Index**

Sullivan, J. 176
Sun 313, 320
symmetric pass-through 400

T

Taylor, J.B. 295
Taylor rule 482
Terasvirta 349, 372
Theophilopoulou, A. 90, 120
three motives for holding cash 21,
 454
three-variable VAR model 286, 288,
 309, 313, 327, 393
threshold autoregression approaches
 368
Throckmorton, N.A. 163
tightening and loosening phases 405
time-varying approach 406
time-varying interest rate pass-
 through 407–410
time-varying pass-through of the
 repo rate changes to lending
 rates viii, 406, 408, 409, 426
Tirelli, P. 52
Topalova, P. 137, 151
total non-agricultural employment
 136, 138, 139, 142, 150, 151,
 284
trade openness vi, 25, 105–115, 118
transaction motive 21, 454
Transition graphs 372, 375
transitory decline 59, 430, 485, 486
transitory shock 48, 213, 486
transmission of monetary shocks 79

U

unemployment rate 54, 56, 66–68,
 80, 81, 241, 245, 247, 251,
 271, 272, 278, 282
unexpected loosening in labour
 market reforms 241–243, 245,
 247, 248, 251
unexpected reduction in economic
 policy uncertainty ix, 23,
 24, 29, 479, 480, 483, 485,
 487–490
United States of America (US) 7, 88,
 90, 118, 121, 164, 177, 191,
 444
U-shaped relationship 54

V

Vander Vennet, R. 401
van Kerm, P. 191, 192, 208, 222
Van Reenen, J. 21, 416, 427, 455
van Stralen, R. 206, 208, 222
van Vlokhoven, H. 222
vector autoregression (VAR) models
 38
vector error correction (VECM)
 approach 322
Veronesi, P. 416, 427
Vigfusson, R. 59, 97
Voinea, L. 7, 77, 78, 84, 88–90, 101

W

wage growth channels 231
wait and see approach 472

"*wait and see*" behaviour 380
Walso, D. 17, 390
Wang, X. 9, 191
Weiss, A. 400
when inflation exceeds 6 percent 63,
    68, 69, 147, 233, 330
Wilson, M.K. 401
within the 4.5-6 percent band 44,
    232, 233
Wi, W. 19, 441
World Bank (2018) 1, 36, 118

World Economic Outlook (WEO)
    106, 108, 112, 121, 136, 137,
    150, 151, 158

Z

Zhang 280
Zhao, G. 21, 455, 456
Zhu, Y. 416, 417
Zochowski, H. 222

Printed in the United States
By Bookmasters